YOUR COMPLETE 2023 PERSONAL HOROSCOPE

Monthly Astrological Prediction Forecast Readings of Every Zodiac Astrology Sun Star Signs- Love, Romance, Money, Finances, Career, Health, Spirituality.

Iris Quinn

Alpha Zuriel Publishing

Your Complete 2023 Personal Horoscope/ Iris Quinn. -- 1st ed.

We are born at a specific time and place, and, like vintage years of wine, we have the characteristics of the year and season in which we are born. Astrology claims nothing more.
— CARL JUNG

CONTENTS

CHAPTER ONE

INTRODUCTION

If you're familiar with astrology, you'll know that horoscopes serve an important purpose. They assist us in connecting with our genuine selves, our inner selves, and nature.

Astrology is the study and comprehension of the stars, of the constellations that make up the Star Signs, which are decided by something called the Natal chart.

A Natal chart is a person's birth chart; it depicts planetary placements, major aspects, traits, and the houses in which each planet and subsequent sign falls. Many individuals, especially those who are new to astrology, believe that your star (Sun) sign is the only one that -matters. However, the Moon sign and Rising/Ascendant are as essential as Venus, Mars, Mercury, Jupiter, Saturn, Uranus, Neptune, and Pluto.

The 12 signs of Western astrology are Aries, Taurus, Gemini, Cancer, Leo, Virgo, Libra, Scorpio, Sagittarius, Capricorn, Aquarius, and Pisces. Deep learning and self-analysis can take place wherever the planets are located, for example, 'Moon in Cancer,' 'Venus in Pisces,' and so on.

Astrological transits, also known as planetary placements within a Natal/Birth chart, shed light on our desires, strengths, weaknesses, likes and dislikes, attitudes toward love and relationships, and nearly every other element of life and self. The planets, elements, aspects, houses, characteristics, and star signs are the fundamentals of astrology. Let's take a quick glance at these before diving into your 2023 Horoscope.

The Planets

Planets symbolize basic impulses and drives in the human psyche. Planetary influences shape our personalities and character; each planet, along with the house and sign in which it is located, serves as a framework for our inner workings. In astrology, planets are sometimes known as celestial entities. Every living body produces an electromagnetic energy field, which includes delicate vibrations that interact with the vibrations and energy of other living species. Planets are no exception. Each planet has its own aura (energetic frequency), which includes a variety of attributes and characteristics unique to that planet. Furthermore, there is a reason why we term people's energy "vibes" in the modern world! We emit vibrations through our ideas, subtle impressions, beliefs, feelings, and acts; planets emit vibrations as well, and this is an astral blueprint.

Planets are not just astral entities with distinct vibrations, but they also represent an archetype. Universal archetypes pervade human consciousness, the universe, our own selves and psyches, and dreams. We see imagery and symbolism appearing as archetypes in dreams, for example. Carl Jung, the famed psychologist and psychotherapist, proposed a set of "universal archetypes" inherent inside the human psyche, which he believed all individuals shared regardless of where or when they were born. Humankind has universal archetypes such as age, gender, culture, skin color, race, and sexuality. In terms of planets and astrology, we tune into the astral energy of each planetary archetype in waking life (everyday reality) as well as in dreams and sleep, when we are most linked to our subconscious selves. Planetary symbology facilitates comprehension, insight, and self-awareness. Because themes, life cycles, and teachings frequently manifest themselves at crucial times or intervals throughout life, understanding planetary symbolism is an immensely effective approach to reconnect to your actual self.

A final word... A star sign's ruler might be both ancient and modern. In other words, as shown in Pisces and Scorpio, more than one planet might be associated with any one-star sign. This can be perplexing, but the best way to look at it is that your ancient ruler represents a "old" version of you, a part of your soul or mind from a former existence, if you believe in such things, or simply something you outgrew and progressed beyond. Your current self is your ruling planet. For example, Pluto, the planet of rebirth and alchemical transformation, currently rules Scorpio. Pluto represents constructive transformation and progressive development, whereas Mars, Scorpio's ancient (old) ruler, represents fury, violence, lust, and war. We can understand how beneficial this "shift" is when we look at the modern (current) star sign connected with Mars, Aries. Scorpio has left or is actively evolving away from Mars' impetuous, violent, lusty, and warlike qualities. And this is reflected in Aries' dominating characteristics, which include being impatient, competitive, temperamental, and angry to the point of aggression; regardless of how affectionate, caring, kind, or loving an Aries can be, these traits will always remain. This component of self cannot be avoided because it is a basic part of their psyche and genuine essence, hence being dominated by Mars. Furthermore, Scorpio is one of the Zodiac's most soulful and compassionate signs, demonstrating how this powerful water sign has 'leveled-up,' for lack of a better term.

Pisces is another example. Neptune, the planet of illusions, mysticism, spirituality, and the arts, currently rules Pisces. The term "arts" embraces a wide range of concepts, including imagination, creativity, and artistic self-expression. Neptune, on the other hand, is associated with the subconscious mind; compassion, mercy, faith, hope, spiritual enlightenment, and unconditional (universal) love. It represents the divine and is the most spiritually evolved and esoteric planet. And Pisces is the most spiritually advanced star sign, with exceptional compassion, empathy, intuition, and wisdom for their age. Pisces is the twelfth and final zodiac sign, and the only sign that embodies the positive characteristics and characteristics of all 12 zodiac signs. They are the last sign on the Zodiac wheel; you can plainly observe their voyage around the circle; psychic receptivity, intuition, imagination, and dreams all fall within Neptune's domain, and these are attributes Pisces embody and excel at. Thus, the Pisces sign is working on a new octave, a step up from their previous/ancient ruling. Jupiter is the planet of luck and expansion, and it is currently ruling Sagittarius. There is nothing wrong with Jupiter; it does not have the negative stigma that Mars does, and it is not a war-like planet. Sagittarius, on the other hand, lacks the depth and emotional wisdom that Pisces possesses. Jupiter's current governing sign, Sagittarius, represents Jupiter's expansive and "light" nature perfectly. As a result, Pisces may have developed to a higher frequency.

The ancients referred to the astrological planets as the "seven heavenly bodies." Because of their relationship to astronomy and astrology, the Sun and Moon were regarded as 'lights' rather than planets. Mercury, Venus, and Mars were dubbed "personal planets" because they symbolize our most intimate, immediate, and personal desires.

Sun

The Sun represents one's life force, masculine energy, willpower, and ego. Ego can be either positive or negative. The Ego manifests itself through the Sun's qualities and hence pertains to individuality—the "I' and individual consciousness. The Sun dominates the sign Leo and is essentially a masculine planet, also regulating the 5th house. Depending on how weak or strong the Sun is in your natal chart, you will either shine and connect to your strengths in a spectacular way, or you will go through certain periods of growth and personal transformation before you can become whole within. Sun energy is associated with integration and wisdom. Finally, the Sun represents fire, passion, desire, perseverance, and life energy. People with a strong Sun placement are passionate and dedicated in life, to themselves and others, ideas and causes. They also have an abundance of zes! The Sun is the source of all primary and conscious forces, hence this planet represents everything in the light, including your conscious mind.

The glyph (Symbol) of the Sun is a circle with a dot or smaller circle in the center. The larger circle represents Spirit, while the smaller circle represents the fundamental element of self and psyche; completeness. Ego/individual consciousness and consciousness (main circle) (smaller middle circle).

Moon

The Moon is a feminine planet that represents emotions and the subconscious, as well as subtle inner forces and currents. The Moon governs all aspects of family, home, and roots, and it also has a connection to dreams. The Moon represents femininity, nurturance, empathy, the mother, the subconscious, emotions, passivity, tenderness, receptivity, and intuition. People with a strong Lunar (Moon) placement have strong instincts that are well-developed. The Moon is associated with all elements of inner sentiments and wants, and wisdom is down-to-earth, mature, and grounded; humility and grace combined with a powerful feminine energy are the essence of the Moon. This planet's ruling sign is Cancer, and the Moon also rules the 4th house.

Everything 'hidden' falls within the domain of the Moon. Not only are views about roots, home, and family, including our foundations, covered here, but so are prior experiences and the emotional memories we keep on to. Memories that affect our attitudes, behaviors, and beliefs about roots, home, and family aid in the healing of our wounds, allowing us to go deeper into the light. Protection, security, sex, primitive instincts, and survival needs are also in its focus.

Mercury

Mercury is regarded as' the Messenger,' and he rules the signs of Gemini and Virgo, as well as the third house. This is the house of communication, and it represents all Mercury represents. Speech, written and verbal communication, music, and self-expression are all examples of mental processes, as are reason, logic, intuition, rationality, the mind, intelligence, and language. A person with a strong Mercury placement values knowledge and the quest for wisdom. If you have a good Mercury influence in your chart, you may deal a lot with emails, letters, or communications. This messenger planet provides practical and grounded energy while also being psychologically stimulating, wit-enhancing, cerebral, and quick-thinking. Mercury is in charge of higher thinking, imagination, original ideas, and the modelling of new knowledge, concepts, and ideas. It is also in charge of writing, journalism, public speaking, radio, media, TV, or film, and all kinds of creative work.

One feels encouraged to speak their truth, be honest with themselves about their sentiments, and express themselves truthfully. Positive outcomes are linked to emotional intelligence, higher cognition, honest and direct communication, intelligence, and both intuitive and analytical thinking.

Venus

Venus rules Taurus and Libra, as well as the second house, representing love, beauty, romance, relationships, finances, luxury, creativity, and sensuality—pleasure and earthly pleasurable pursuits. Venus is sometimes seen as a Goddess, the Goddess of love, beauty, and sexuality, and this demonstrates what we may learn from her. The impact of this planet is feminine, yet in addition to bringing the divine feminine into our lives, Venus also signifies materialism; money, cash, and resources. Pleasure is anchored in the physical and material realms, therefore Venus impacts us in this way; the worth and value you place on belongings fall under Venus's domain.

Self-worth and self-esteem are also mentioned. Venus can help you gain and strengthen unique spiritual gifts and talents, as well as charm and charisma. Scent, odors, pheromones, the energy exchanges you feel and crave, and almost everything associated with love, romance, and platonic closeness, as well as sexual demands, urges, and experiences, are all included. Another significant theme is security.

Venus represents depth, honesty, and transparency—bonds and love feelings that are anchored in rawness and vulnerability rather than superficiality. Venus' lower vibration, Venus' shadow, manifests as a lack or absence of self-love; themes include issues of worthiness, the ability and willingness to produce abundance and money, and the creation of harmonious, loving, mutually respected, and caring connections. Venus also governs our emotions, sensuous impulses, and instincts. How we approach love, our values and goals in relationships, our inner and outer beauty, how we make ourselves look good, and our charm and social grace are all things to think about. Venus governs artistic impulses and what we find aesthetically appealing—the type of music, art, exercise and movement choices, and inspiration you desire.

Mars

Mars is the masculine and fiery counterpart to Venus, another planet associated with love and sexuality. Mars dominates the sign Aries and is the ancient/old ruler of Scorpio, while also ruling the first house. Mars influences action, willpower, passion, self-confidence, physical strength and vigor, masculine sexuality, and themes of violence, lust, and war (negative/shadow tendencies). Mars encourages healthy assertiveness and the ability to stand up for what you believe is right—for example, fighting for justice or speaking your truth. A strong Mars placement might help you achieve inner strength. Mars is more than just a battle planet; he (being masculine) represents a raging inner fire, a drive for initiative and invention, and primality all at the same time. This planet represents our primitive instincts and desires.

Mars teaches self-respect and when to say "no." Boundaries are a significant phrase. Also, anger can be expressed in a healthy and productive way, which can help you let go of bad feelings.

Jupiter

Jupiter, the planet of good fortune, abundance, and expansion, rules Sagittarius and the 9th house. Jupiter's energy is associated with wisdom, higher learning, spiritual and philosophical pursuits, and personal development and growth. Developing spiritual maturity is an indication of a powerful Jupiter placement, as is having very high ethics and morals. Jupiter's impact shapes our personal beliefs. This planet encompasses scholarly pursuits and consciousness, as well as travel. One enjoys meeting people from different walks of life, learning about new cultures, and broadening their perspectives. It is possible to achieve perception and self-mastery. Jupiter also gives people intellectual energy. They may spend a lot of time thinking about themselves or be very interested in learning about the world, consciousness, philosophy, and the mysteries of life.

The crescent of receptivity rising above the cross of matter is Jupiter's sign (glyph). This refers to the physicalization of ideas and opportunities (expansion), as well as material wealth and abundance, and luck, attraction and manifestation. Jupiter is regarded as a "lucky" planet. Other associations include power, confidence, authority, self-empowerment, and the higher self.

Saturn

Saturn is one of the planets that brings structure and discipline. This planet rules Capricorn as well as the tenth house. Saturn's domain includes all matters concerning authority, linear time, foundations, order, structures, and organization. Saturn is also known as 'father time' or 'the lord of karma,' and is associated with patriarchal energy, masculinity, limits, and limitations. A Saturn placement reflects one's approach to all of these things—authority, structure, and so on. Boundaries, self-respect, the respect we show others, power, law, and order all play important roles. The Saturn placement notes everything related to duties and responsibilities, practical obligations, karmic exchanges entered into with friends and various partnerships (business, platonic, romantic), structures and restrictions; Saturn acts as a father figure in our lives- stern, wise, discerning, and sometimes overly-strict. He is a tough-love teacher who is here to teach us what we need to know, change, grow past, and transcend. Before we can completely enter our adult selves, we must learn from and remove outdated or unhelpful behaviors, modes of thinking, beliefs, ideologies, and recurring cycles. Finally, this planet is all about maturity and adulthood.

Saturn's energy is relatively sluggish, which signifies limitations/restrictions. This planet, on the other hand, is a taskmaster, commanding us to work hard, honor our practical obligations, and respect authority and duty. Saturn energy represents inner strength, stability and security, solid boundaries, and dedication to a route or cause, relationship, or goal. This planet teaches that hard effort and dedication pay off. However, learning can also take the form of karmic lessons, which are cyclic exchanges based on psychological, emotional, or spiritual energies. The unconscious can be brought to conscious awareness through the "tough-love" energy of timeless wisdom and the problems of life.

Uranus

Uranus, often known as the 'Great Awakener,' rules Aquarius and the 11th house. Uranus is associated with uniqueness, ingenuity, intelligence, invention, creativity, and change. Internal upheavals and positive transformation lead to exterior manifestation and progress. Uranus rules illumination, and transformation might be quick or unexpected—there is a catalytic energy.

Science and technology, as well as the advancements they offer, are all part of the domain of this planet. Also, anything unusual, strange, wacky, or bizarre! This planet can assist one in connecting with their inner brilliance, as well as their own imagination and artistic ability. This planet stands for chaos and upheaval, sudden movement and forward progress. It also stands for individual and group growth, freedom, collective memory, awakening, real rebellion, and creative inspiration.

Uranus energy is all about community, individual and collective consciousness, humanitarian objectives, futuristic technologies, evolution, and a higher vibration of wisdom and intellect. Finally, Uranus is associated with illumination and new ways of seeing truth, whether universal or personal realities. In its bad form, it could be a sign of immaturity and uncontrolled rebellion. Instead of looking for truth or light, it would lead to destruction for destruction's sake.

Neptune

Neptune oversees the 12th house and Pisces, the final sign. Spirituality, the arts, inspiration, creativity, mysticism, dreams, psychic abilities, and illusions... These are important Neptune themes. Neptune, known as the "God of the Sea,' has a lot of watery and emotional energy, which reflects in the psychic and intuitive abilities that are available. Pisces is the most spiritual, intuitive, psychic, and clairvoyant sign, owing to Neptune's influence. Neptune can help you achieve spiritual ideals and consciousness, receptivity, personal magnetism, persuasive skills, psychic gifts and abilities, supernatural and extrasensory phenomena, and enhanced & evolved creativity and imagination. Neptune's domain includes imaginative and artistic self-expression, and the media is frequently associated with Neptune's influence; entertainment industries, film and media, and all types of creative trade are included—writing, publishing, illustration, poetry, music, art, and handicraft.

Anyone with a strong Neptune placement is intuitive, sensitive, dreamy, and exceptionally skilled in the domains of imagination and artistic self-expression. People with this influence make excellent poets, painters, musicians, philosophers, psychics, clairvoyants, dream travelers, and artists, as well as being extremely sensitive and sympathetic. This planet is defined by soul and spirituality, as well as a great fascination with and understanding of esotericism and metaphysical concepts. Instincts are powerful, and there is a direct and powerful link to the subconscious as well.

Pluto

Pluto rules the 8th house and the zodiac sign of Scorpio. Pluto represents the themes of death and rebirth, cyclic development and transformation, alchemy, and power. There is ferocity and spiritual maturity, as well as empathy and a strong intuition. Individual and group intuitive abilities can have a significant impact and transformation. Pluto represents renewal, endings and beginnings, destruction leading to creation, conscious and intentional activity. When there is a good placement, power and control can show up in a healthy and empowering way. Self-empowerment happens when we are aware of the themes and cycles that show up in our lives, themes and cycles that either need to be strengthened and developed or let go of.

Pluto, however, has a dark side. Pluto's domain includes an overwhelming desire for power, control, dominance (world or personal), and obsessiveness. Possessiveness, jealousy, envy, greed, destruction, resentment, and a desire for vengeance are all shadow features; feelings of betrayal, rejection, or abandonment can lead to some pretty deceptive techniques. Hypersensitivities can develop from sensitivities. Pluto is related to the pursuit of truth and the deeper significance of life. Self-mastery is attainable; mastery of one's intellect, body, emotion, and spirit, or mastery of one's path and chosen skill (s). Pluto's glyph represents a receptivity to super consciousness as a circle (spirit) above a crescent (receptivity) and a cross (matter). A connection to spirit and the "underworld" (the subconscious) is also valued more than the physical, terrestrial, and material worlds.

Chiron

Despite not being a planet, Chiron is a significant symbol and an astronomical body to be aware of. Chiron is essentially a comet with a peculiar and irregular orbit. This celestial body is known as the 'Wounded Healer,' because it reflects one's deepest scars while simultaneously serving as the greatest teacher. Chiron teaches us how to transform our deepest and darkest wounds into magnificent lessons—trials and tribulations exist to serve us and guide us on a path of self-development. Finally, Chiron is about self-evolution, about becoming the finest versions of ourselves.

Chiron is named after the Greek mythological centaur Chiron, who was both a healer and a teacher. Despite being a powerful person with unique talents, Chiron's wound limited him in many ways; yet, instead of suffering and sinking into darkness and despair, Chiron alchemized his wound and pain into a way to serve others. This is Chiron's message and instruction in astrology.

The major associations you should be aware of are service, helpfulness, inner power, and changing suffering and limits into self-mastery. Through our wounds, we can gain wisdom and self-awareness, which helps us help others on their own journeys.

The elements

Elemental astrology acknowledges the power of the elements.

Fire is lively, passionate, upbeat, and expressive. This basic characteristic represents your need for action, inspiration, and motivating influences. The fire element is linked to life energy, vitality, and self-expression, as well as the conveyance of your feelings, emotions, and communication style; fire is linked to the spirit within—spirit pervades all living things, but it can also be spiritual energy, universal energy, and life force, allowing you to perceive everything as interconnected (Source, the divine). Or perhaps your own inner spirit.

Fire energy is passionate and energetic, upbeat and inspiring. Fire is an expanding, energetic, beginning, and activating element. If you let it, each part of your chart that fire energy touches sparkles like gold. This element is also linked to chi. Chi is a universal life energy that governs lifespan, health, well-being, and vitality. Chi levels are linked to your mental, emotional, physical, and spiritual health. When there is a healthy and free flow of chi, your immune system and other bodily systems are strong.

Chi is sometimes referred to as spiritual energy. It moves through the cells of the body, burning poisons as it travels. On a physical level, impurities are purged, and considerable healing can occur. Chi opens one up to heavenly source energy, spiritual insight, subconscious perception, and expanded & evolved psychic, imaginative, intuitive, and empathic abilities. A good quantity of fire provides for confidence, self-assertion, self-worth, and the ability to complete projects and personal goals with vigor and joy. Fire aids in the removal of stagnant or obstructed energy. Strong fire is also associated with a healthy libido and sexual vitality. Excessive fire can cause rage, irrationality, impatience, aggressive tendencies, and the "dryness" associated with fire; burning out from over-expending energy and having too much yang. Too much fire can cause frequent swearing, hypertension, perspiration, and inflammation. (Not solely based on fire placements in one's natal chart, but on how much an individual incorporates and exhibits in daily life.)

Spicy foods, bright red and orange hues, and loud music such as metal, rock, or any form of dance/drum 'n' bass/upbeat music are ideal for increasing fire. Exercise, dance, and movement can also help. Reds and oranges are bold, fiery, and stimulating to both the senses and emotions. When there is no fire, it is difficult to move on and be inspired or motivated to pursue one's dreams and passions. You may feel compelled to emulate others' inventiveness or even steal ideas, therefore becoming a 'copy-cat.' When you lack inspiration and creative fire, you may lack integrity by acting deceitfully or manipulatively. One can become "stuck in a rut,' seldom or rarely leaving the house, or feeling shy, fearful, tense, anxious, or depressed. When there isn't enough fire, confidence and self-esteem suffer. Unconsciously, one may become an "energy vampire," consuming the time, love, energy, resources, abilities, strength, or life force of others.

Water is receptive, passive, "flowy" (referring to surrendering/going with the flow), malleable, and yin in nature. Yin is magnetic, feminine, and dark—the inner and outer darkness with strong ties to the shadow self. Water is the polar opposite of fire, as yin (water) is the polar opposite and counterpart of yang (fire). Understanding this will help you operate more effectively with your own inner fire and water attributes and features. Water denotes emotions, moods, and inner sensations. There is a reason why almost every human on the planet feels at ease and at home while visiting a beach, ocean, or seaside... The huge and gorgeous immensity of the ocean's waves creates a deep and ancestral sense of belonging, comfort, security, and surrender; one feels "at home" and connected to the planet in an incomprehensible, ethereal, and otherworldly way. This is because of the sea's connection to the subconscious. Water is thought to be a holistic representation of the subconscious mind, with links to the unknown, the "infinite waters of creation," and source energy.

A healthy embodiment of water has a variety of advantages and beneficial outcomes. Feelings and inner moods can be expressed effortlessly and eloquently. Emotions are not chaotic, disruptive, or unreasonable, nor are they destructively screamed or shouted at others. When there is either too much or too little water—the latter resulting in investment piling up and occasional eruptions! Or manipulation, projection, and so on. You don't project unhealed or imbalanced feelings onto others, and your personal expressions are generally fairly expressive and gentle. Constant and harmonic (good) emotional releases occur. Water is also related to memory; therefore, when there is enough water, one can remember situations and past experiences in a beneficial and helpful way. The subconscious mind embodies emotions, moods, inner currents, innate and intuitive wants, as well as "vision." Water influences psychic and spiritual gifts and abilities. Those with a lot of water in their horoscopes are usually sensitive, intuitive, clairvoyant, psychic, or spiritually talented in some way. They might pick up on universal archetypes and concepts that others overlook.

When there is a healthy flow of water in one's life, intuition is "activated" and enlarged. In addition to general (and advanced) kinds of psychic awareness, dream states allow you to access your subconscious and intuitive powers. Many people with strong water in their natal charts have unusual dreams. During sleep, one can astral project, lucid dream, and receive direction, profound imagery, symbolism, and wisdom. Life energy is often strong when water is balanced. Compassion and empathy will flow, and you will be spiritually aware, in tune with the divine and higher levels of awareness. Drink plenty of water, spend time near bodies of water (rivers, lakes, streams, oceans, etc.), work with the water element in meditation, engage in psychic and spiritual development exercises, and aim to improve your intuition to increase the water element. Purple, violet, and indigo meditation or visualization are excellent for boosting your intuitive mind and higher self. All blues are excellent for communicating emotions and inner moods/currents. Furthermore, everything that connects you to your empathic, caring, and nurturing side, such as caretaking, elderly or animal companionship, volunteering, or charity work (including environmental and eco help- not just animals and people!), serves to strengthen the water element within.

Earth is a grounded, practical, and security-driven force. The Earth element is associated with attributes such as organization, order, structure, physical roots, and foundations. If one has a strong earth integration, they are said to be devoted, practical, responsible, and grounded; they feel connected to both their body and the earth, to their house and the surroundings around them. The earthy quality brings sentiments of safety, protection, and warmth. Healthy ground energy is gradual and steady, developing and growing—it brings dedication and a sense of longevity to people, places, relationships, and undertakings. A healthy and balanced weight or physique corresponds to 'just enough' earth, neither too little nor too much. Material goods are regarded as necessary and useful, but they are not adhered to in an unhealthy or self-destructive manner. Wealth accumulation and attitudes toward success, material wealth, and money and resources are progressive and beneficial to personal growth. Having material possessions allows you to cultivate a harmonious relationship with your physical world and "roots."

Hoarding, an overemphasis on material stuff and things, weight gain, lethargy, sloth, a lack of forward motion and inspiration (for projects, hobbies, and creativity), and a general lack of desire for life can all arise from having too much earth. With too much earth, the life force may be depleted. There is also a predisposition to struggle with "letting go." One might become overly committed or unduly reliant on people, places, and things. Excessive earth might also result in a lack of creative and inventive creativity. We may become overly grounded, earthy, and fixated on the past—on old beliefs, attachments, and philosophies. Too little earth, on the other hand, frequently leads to instability and difficulty in a variety of practical matters. Home, money, wealth, resources, business, work, and real-life relationships (i.e. commitment and bonds formed) are brought into focus and decreased. The sense of commitment is diminished, and one does not feel at ease or content in their physical surroundings (s). In terms of health and well-being, malnutrition can occur when there is insufficient earth element energy being incorporated. Immunity may diminish, and body functions and systems may deteriorate.

Eating healthy and nutritious foods can help to balance the earth. Exercise and physical activities that you enjoy—whatever brings you joy and pleasure. Martial arts such as tai chi and chi kung/qi gong are excellent for balancing the earth element (and all of the elements), as are swimming, dancing, sports, nature walks, and yoga. Music, art, imaginative self-expression, conscious dreaming, anything that ties you to your body and the physical realm while simultaneously giving a "transcendental" experience. Gardening, working outside on the soil, and connecting with essential oils and floral essence, crystals and gemstones, herbs, and plants are all excellent methods to connect with earth element energy. Walnuts, berries, seeds, coconut milk, pulses, beans, lentils, sprouts, superfoods, and anything plant-based, raw, and organic are among the greatest foods. Wearing fashionable and "appearance-enhancing" clothing that makes you feel good will raise the earth's energy and help you feel more confident and protected in your own skin. Consider more natural jewelry and accessories such as gemstone and crystal pendants, earrings, rings, and bracelets. Natural essential oils are an excellent substitute for perfumes and aftershaves that contain chemicals and preservatives. Finally, getting creative with cooking, such as cooking with rainbow hues and rare and unique plants, is advised.

Air represents the mind, intellect, reasonable and logical cognition, original thought, and problem resolution. The air element encompasses all higher cerebral, cognitive, and imaginative cognition. Communication in all of its forms is also linked to the air element. Writing, talking, poetry, speaking, teaching, and the ability to express oneself are all symbols of air. The breath and air are inextricably linked... A proper flow of air permits chi—your vital life force—to accumulate. The air element is light, airy, free-flowing, and subjective. Its characteristics are mostly related with the intellect and mental processes, although having strong air energy in one's chart has many favorable effects on the other elements. Strong and healthy air energy can assist you in clearly expressing your emotions (water), providing inspiration and creative/imaginative direction for passion projects and life routes (fire), and helping to anchor wisdom, inspiration, ideas, and beliefs/philosophies into a structured basis (earth).

Air signs are intelligent, intellectual, and self-expressive in general. Each of the three air signs has distinct characteristics relating to communication, ideas, information and knowledge exchange, and aesthetic expression. Just enough air correlates to being calm, instinctively and rationally balanced, having a good memory, and being capable of higher and cognitive learning skills. When there is a balanced air within, one may let go freely and sweetly. There is no need to be correct or 'win' when engaged in constructive discussion or debate; arguments are beneficial and harmonic. In terms of creativity, imagination runs wild, and fresh ideas fly like lightning. When there is healthy air energy, one can connect with their inner creative genius. Too much air causes thinking to become fragmented, frenetic, disorganized, or hyperactive. Information, wisdom, and memories are lost or forgotten, and it is difficult to articulate your truth. You may not take things seriously either; you may take a too careless and light-hearted approach to people, situations, and events. As a result, wit and humor will be misused, such as failing to recognize when "enough is enough," when to tone down the funny comments or banter, and when to take a more measured approach. Someone else's comfort and dignity may be jeopardized (due to shame) and you won't even realize it. Lower mental qualities, such as sarcasm, belittlement, gossip, slander, or bad discourse in general, may be displayed. Thoughts, speech, and minds are frequently misplaced and skewed.

Nervousness and mental worry are also possible outcomes. One can become "mentally hyperactive," constantly needing to chat or gossip in excess, which can lead to emotional, spiritual, and physical health problems. As a direct detrimental result of mental hyperactivity, vital chi (life force) levels may decrease. Neurological connections can deteriorate. Indecision, changing your mind or even changing your life course and direction, and a general sense of uncertainty are all common symptoms. Because of this constant ambiguity, one may block themselves off to new chances, relationships, abundance, connections, experiences, and self-development. Breathing problems such as asthma, poor moral and ethical judgement, inability to let go- so holding onto attachments, slow thought processes, disruptions to cognitive mental processes, polluted (impure) mind and thoughts, diminished imagination, and the need to always be right, defend or prove yourself, or push your views and intellectual superiority on others are all direct physical effects of insufficient air.

Seek mental stimulation, such as through mind games, puzzles, Sudoku, crosswords, intellectual board games, reading, learning about new and interesting subjects, acquiring wisdom on a variety of philosophies and topics, and making a conscious effort to engage in mindful and healthy social interaction, to implement, increase, expand, and integrate air energy (the air element). Conversion, conversation, and communication will improve your mental talents and strengthen the air within you. Meditation, awareness, visualization, and conscious breathing are all excellent methods for balancing and harmonizing inner air with the other elements. These approaches work for both a lack of and an excess of air. Vision boards, mind maps, inspirational/motivational messages, and posters can all be extremely beneficial.

The houses

A specific house is occupied by distinct planets (in your Natal chart). The House system allows you to have a better knowledge of what makes you tick. Each house represents the type of lessons, problems, and life lessons you will face. Themes, abilities, talents, and gifts, as well as energetic symbolism and associations associated with each house, can all be learned in order to broaden your understanding of planetary placements. The Zodiac itself is divided into 12 parts, each of which is ruled by a different sign. The first House relates to Aries, the first star sign, and finishes with Pisces, the 12th sign. In astrology, the house system depicts how planets express themselves, the type of energy and traits that are supposed to be linked with that planet. Why and how energy and themes manifest themselves in your life, including your talents, gifts, hidden and subconscious desires, internal motivations, and passions. What do you hope to achieve or not achieve, what types of connections do you expect to attract and secretly wish for, or naturally gravitate toward? Within the houses, every facet of life and self is brought into introspection and review. Houses can be viewed as an additional level to your astrological self-discovery.

First House

Aries is ruled by the first house, which represents the Self. This house governs personal appearance, self-leadership, new beginnings, and fresh starts. The first house governs new projects and chapters, so you can discover not only your personal identity but also the types of experiences you may attract and manifest in terms of creativity.

The planet Mars rules the first house, which corresponds to the Ascendant (rising sign). This house represents how we project ourselves in a particular way. Positively, the image we portray to others becomes conscious. In a negative sense, this house is associated with defense strategies; how can we shield ourselves from others and our local surroundings? The first house governs all one-on-one and personal encounters in social situations or in public, as they relate to our basic personality and self-identity. Also, the kinds of impressions we produce and how we are seen by others. The first house governs physical appearance, the overall view on life, and major beliefs and philosophies. The "self" is the first dwelling, which develops into "society and service" and beyond. Similarly to planetary positions, each sign resided in a specific house at the time of birth. The knowledge of your planetary house is intended to open doors to healing and progress, allowing you to see tendencies within yourself and make predictions and good decisions for the future. With house knowledge, conscious action is possible. The first six dwellings are known as "personal houses," whereas the following six are known as "impersonal houses."

Second House

The second house is concerned with the physical senses and your immediate surroundings. Taste, smells, sounds, sights, and touch, as well as sensory data and experiences in the physical world—material reality and the material realm—This house is related with Taurus and is ruled by Venus. With enough knowledge of the Taurus star sign, this should mirror the energy and symbolism of the 2nd house.

This house governs money, income, and resources, as well as your feelings and attitudes about self-worth. The kinds of self-esteem we have are related to our material and worldly possessions, as well as how we interact with our physical surroundings. Venus is a sensual sign that enjoys luxury, as well as ruling wealth and money; so, the symbolism of the 2nd house is reflected. The placement of the second house determines whether we have good self-esteem and feel comfortable in our own skin. This house governs the type of personal goods we obtain, our attitude toward them, and our ability to attract abundance. The manifestation of money, as well as our underlying attitudes and values regarding material manifestation, are important subjects. Another major relationship is with the senses and the types of sensory experiences one has. The planet and sign that fall into this house reflect the intensity of your sensuality and receptivity to beauty and feminine energy.

Third House

The third house governs communication and is ruled by Gemini and the planet Mercury. This house encompasses all aspects of communication, including verbal, written, self-talk, thinking, communicating with others, social media, and the imagination in relation to internal cognitive processes. Associations include gadgets and technology, siblings and neighbors, local trips, and community links. With the third house, consider the 'near environment' in your neighborhood.

The House of Communication is related with libraries, schools, community groups, and youth organizations such as scouts, clubs, choruses, and theatrical groups. How one chooses to engage with their immediate surroundings reveals important information about one's true personality and character. Early community and environmental influences define a large part of who we are; we learn our likes and dislikes, as well as our hidden abilities and talents, through experiences and interactions in our local areas. The third house also governs the 'lower mind,' which includes linguistic skills, how we create our views and beliefs, media influence, and speaking abilities. Writing your thoughts and reflections in a journal or dream diary, becoming a professional writer, ghost writer, or author, becoming a motivational or expert speaker on a specific topic, and writing essays or educational study material like coursework are all things to consider. Are you able to convey yourself, your philosophy, your perspectives and beliefs, and your emotions in written or spoken form? Do you find it easy to communicate? These are critical questions.

Fourth House

The Moon and the Cancer zodiac sign dominate the 4th house. The Imum Coeli (IC), often known as the nadir, is another planetary aspect related. The fourth house represents your foundations, home, and roots. It is associated with home, privacy, security, and physical foundations and is located at the bottom of the Zodiac wheel. The fourth house is associated with everything related to one's needs and sense of security. What are our fundamental motivations? Do we require a secure and loving home environment, or would we rather travel and leave our "roots" behind in search of new horizons? The location of the various planets in this house will bring important insights into a variety of concerns.

The 4th house is also related with nurturing and feminine energy; your mother, yourself as a mother (inner motherly instincts), and female guardian energy. This is where you decide how much privacy and emotional affection you want. Your approach to parenting, constructing a solid home and dwelling, and all areas of domestic existence are also important. Those with a strong 4th house placement will be exceptionally good mothers. Finally, instinctual behavior, ancestry, ties to the past, and real estate difficulties all regulate this house of security and home. Domestic life is highlighted, as are maternal instincts and early experiences that shape your approach to parenting. Although not expressly representing materialism or practical issues, the connection to foundations and home and family life naturally brings a practical, grounded, and materialistic component. Emotional connection and requirements in a physical setting, particularly the home.

Fifth House

The Sun rules the 5th house, which is related with Leo. Self-expression, playfulness, creativity, drama, romance, joy, and color are all represented by this house. This house has a light and fun-loving aspect, so whichever planet falls in the 5th house (in your natal/birth chart) highlights these attributes. The 5th house also governs the media, pleasure, and entertainment. Hobbies, crafts, gambling, cinemas, movies, plays, and theatre are all examples. Depending on the other positions (star sign and planet), the 5th house energy can be extremely intense. The main themes are creative self-expression and imagination, and the secondary theme is romance/romantic relationships. Your attitude toward platonic and sexual romance and play will be determined here. Do you consider love to be monogamous or polygamous? Do you prefer long-term commitment or wanderlust? Do you consider relationships to be traditional boyfriend/girlfriend pairings or more 'alternative' or spiritual/soulful ties such as lovers and kindred spirits? Do you believe in soulmates and real love? All of these inquiries are related to the 5th house.

Finally, this house emphasizes our ability to express oneself creatively and artistically. Approaches to sexual play and more innocent and child-like play can be explored, as can your proclivity for parties, costume dress-ups, theatre, and unfettered forms of self-expression.

Sixth House

The sixth house governs your employment, service, everyday habits and rituals, as well as your health and well-being. The 6th house's first main theme, or aspect dominated, is the service or services you provide to society; organization, daily schedules, routines, work habits, and actual professional obligations. The second theme/aspect is well-being and health, in all of its facets. This comprises physical, mental, emotional, and spiritual well-being. Mercury rules the sixth house, which is related with the sign of Virgo. The 6th house represents holiness and purity, pursuing perfection in health, well-being, mind, body, and spirit.

This house encompasses fitness, diet, lifestyle choices, exercise regimens, and self-development rituals. Vegetarianism, veganism, or a raw plant-based diet would fall under this category, as would participating in disciplined sports or movement hobbies for health. For example, martial arts, traditional sports, dancing, and yoga... Natural and organic food choices, as well as eating a traditional diet known by your culture, country, or continent, are all related to the 6th house. Work techniques and methods, daily jobs (as opposed to a career or life path/profession with purpose), order & organization, daily life and chores, errand running, self-development, self-mastery in terms of health and work skills, nutrition, diet, exercise & movement, attitude toward coworkers, helpfulness, and pets are some other associations.

Seventh House

The 7th house represents relationships with other individuals, as well as societal alliances such as business connections. Intimate relationships are also regulated in this house, therefore karmic love contracts, marriage, soulmates, and kindred spirit bonds can all be found here (your attitude towards them, what to expect etc.). This house is linked to Libra and is ruled by Venus. This house of relationships and partnerships is likewise tied to the Descendant (Dsc) aspect.

This house governs companionship, marriage, long-term and short-term partnerships, love affairs, lovers, and the shadow self. The 7th house governs how you relate in relationships, such as by embracing more of your shadow and connecting to your inner darkness, or by aligning with your strengths and light self (positive traits). How much of your genuine or shadow self do you want to show, how frequently, and to whom. Having a "alter-ego" falls under the purview of this house. Business, competitors, attorneys, mediators, contracts, counsellors, husband or wife, negotiator, companions, and parenthood are some terms to keep in mind.

Eight House

Birth and death, sex, metamorphosis, emotional relationships, deep connection, and mystery are all ruled by the 8th house. It is connected with the constellation Scorpio and the planet Pluto. This house governs rebirth and metamorphosis, as well as other people's money, shared resources, finances, inheritances, investments, and bonds, including real estate. This house of depth is also related to karmic and soul relationships, as well as soul sharing.

Here we can learn about attitudes around sex, intimacy, and sharing resources. Beliefs about life's mysteries and the universe can also be found here, though they are not yet at the "spiritual illumination" stage (12th house). Pluto's themes can be seen reflected here in the 8th house. Deep bonding provides insight into our basic personality, as demonstrated by this house. The 8th house energy in a person's natal chart can provide insight and guidance on what they want in a relationship. Furthermore, beliefs and needs are represented, making this home particularly helpful for getting to the bottom of one's emotions (emotional needs, wishes, and desires).

The energy of this dwelling can be fairly high depending on its setting. Sexuality is a significant association, and there is much opportunity for development and personal growth here. Other topics covered include human reactions to crises and transformations, regeneration (rebirth), addictions, psychological impulses, divorce, karmic entanglement, soul links, and inheritance.

Ninth House

In astrology, the 9th house represents the higher mind, expansion, long-distance travel, and international issues. The ruling planet is Jupiter, and the corresponding star sign is Sagittarius. The characteristics of the 9th house can be noticed in the Sagittarius personality and in Jupiter's primary qualities (when in the strongest placement). This house encompasses inspiration, motivation, learning, philosophy, higher education, and study trips. Other significant associations include publishing, authorship, speaking, foreign languages, lecturing/teaching, and many educational endeavors. Here we determine our ability to engage in educational endeavors, long distance travel (growing our horizons), and higher learning (philosophy, spirituality). Luck, risk-taking, adventures, and morals and ethics are all major themes.

Because the 9th house reflects our religious, moral, and spiritual goals and views, one can look to the corresponding planets (seen in the natal chart) for self-reflection and self-evaluation. People who have a strong 9th house or a lot of planets in the 9th house are more likely to seek universal truths and knowledge. They are often free-spirited individuals with strong passions and interests in adventure, travel, and philosophy.

Tenth House

The 10th house is located at the apex (top) of the natal chart. This pertains to your social standing, your public identity. Structures, foundations, accolades, achievements, awards, public image, and personal success are all governed by the 10th house. What are your professional and personal achievements? Also, what is your social role?

Tradition, discipline, fatherly energy, patriarchal institutions, norms, boundaries, and fatherhood are also associated. Capricorn is the sign linked to this house, while the Midheaven is the celestial correlative (MC). Although this is an Aspect rather than a planet, Saturn is the traditional ruler of the 11th house. Career and vocation, societal contribution, public/social standing, recognition, and everything linked to accomplishment and personal achievements are all governed here. People with a strong 10th house are more likely to build a name for themselves, attain fame or success, or become experts in their skill, career, or trade. The 10th house represents self-mastery in terms of career, service, and trade. Finally, secondary connotations include one's attitude toward responsibility, obligation, and "the father" (either an actual father or male guardian, or society as a masculine institution), including paternal figures and employers. The 10th house determines whether you choose to obey the law and respect authority. Also, how great your drive for achievement and success is.

Eleventh House

Friendships, group organizations, teamwork, social harmony, technology, invention, and science are all ruled by the 11th house. This house also includes networking, social media, themes of revolt and social justice, and humanitarian interests and concerns. Uranus rules the 11th house, which corresponds to the Aquarius star sign. The 11th house reflects all of Aquarius' primary characteristics, including creativity, eccentricity, and intelligence, as well as their interest in astronomy, astrology, science, futuristic technology, and evolution.

The 11th house represents one's hopes and wishes for society and the world at large. You most likely have a strong 11th house placement if you have goals to aid others, a group, animals, or the environment. You may also opt to become engaged in your local community in some way (or travel further afield for humanitarian and welfare causes on a global level). In addition to the social organizations and circles you participate in, the friendships and acquaintances you make along the way are important associations. Do you feel connected to your legacy or destiny in the world? Do you have a mission or a sense of service? Are you in touch with your genuine self in regard to society, and do you participate in groups that benefit others? Do you want to make a difference and follow your dreams? These are all questions related to the 11th house. This house represents one's dreams, wishes for humanity, aspirations, and deep inner purpose.

Twelfth House

The 12th house governs endings, as its position at the end of the cycle suggests. This house governs project completions, karmic contracts, old age, surrender, flowing with the flow, spirituality, and all types of completions. The planet Neptune rules this house, which oversees the zodiac sign Pisces. The arts, creativity, movies, dancing, poetry, and the subconscious mind are all important associations here. The 12th house governs everything beneath the surface, including subconscious (behind the scenes) desires, needs, wants, motivations, internal sentiments and currents, emotions, and beliefs. Soul-development, personal and collective karma, private matters, dreams, and spiritual and/or metaphysical studies are paramount.

This house includes, in addition to the primary associations, institutions, hospitals, jails, secret agendas, and enemies; especially one's isolation from them. The 12th house is about spiritual illumination and enlightenment. It denotes the disconnection from societal structures and foundations that limit human evolution and the shift to a more comprehensive and integrated world. karmic completion and karmically clear status, with no soul obligations. As a result, there is a natural disengagement from historical structures and contractual constraints. When there is a strong 12th house planetary placement, one may be in control of their own health (for example, by moving away from hospitals and traditional forms of medicine), or they may have reached a level of spiritual maturity and self-mastery such that jail, fines, or societal punishments are not even an option. There is no need for covert foes or hidden goals when one attains a degree of spiritual consciousness, embodying a higher vibration. Completion is physically integrating the highest level of integrity and self-awareness, thus transcending lesser vibratory methods, thoughts, behavioral patterns, and life cycles.

The aspects

Rising/Ascendant

In astrology, you must be familiar with the Rising or Ascendant sign. The ascendant represents your social or public personality, much as your sun sign is your core personality and your moon sign is your subconscious and emotional needs and triggers. It is how others and the outside world perceive you. It reflects your physical body as well as your outer appearance, or how you show yourself to the world. The Ascendant governs your personal appearance, including how you dress, how you style your hair, and the jewelry and accessories you wear. The Rising/Ascendant adds another layer to your personality and genuine character. For example, say you are a Cancer Sun with Moon in Pisces (double water!), and a lot of earth and water energy in your natal chart (earth and water are both feminine), a Leo rising would give you a whole new identity to your seemingly emotional/watery character. The Rising sign represents your outward self.

North Node and South Node

The North and South Nodes are also referred to as the lunar nodes. They are related to the Moon and are immediately opposite each other, forming the 'Nodal Axis.' The north and south nodes are not planetary bodies, but rather precise points defined by angles that take into account the relationship between the Sun, Moon, and Earth at the moment of our birth, as shown in our natal chart. Lunar nodes are essentially the spots where the Moon's orbit intersects the plane of the "ecliptic." Finally, they represent karma—personal one's karmic balance. The north node reflects the experiences we have and are likely to have in this lifetime that lead to our self-development. The north node promotes spiritual, emotional, psychological, and physical development by laying the groundwork for learning and chances for growth anchored in the material world. It can be viewed as one's destiny, as well as one's legacy and sense of service. The position of the lunar north node decides what you may be destined to do and achieve in this lifetime, what skills and qualities you will acquire and develop, and how, if and when, you will ground these talents into a career, calling, or profession.

The south node represents our sense of belonging and comfort, or what we rely on. The south node represents our inherent strength, talents, abilities, and slightly "overdeveloped" tendencies; the behaviors, gifts, and patterns we are accustomed to. Gifts and skills connected with the south node come naturally to us, yet they might lead to an imbalanced and "extreme" personality. The south node's message is to transcend and progress beyond familiarity and comfort. We're expected to gravitate more toward the north node, striving to embody the traits and opportunities of the north node's symbolism/energy, and becoming less reliant on the familiar south node's energy. We must let go of attachment if we are to come into our genuine strength, path, and mature body. Attachment to people, places, experiences, belongings, beliefs, ideas, or ideologies may be involved; the important thing is that we commit to transcendence. The south node can be compared to a soiled and damaged childhood toy that we can never manage to let go of, despite the fact that it has outlived its usefulness. The north node would be a masterpiece of a book that you've been working on since you were a teenager. It would be a reflection of your legacy and the pearls of wisdom, insights, and life lessons you want future generations to learn from.

The qualities

The qualities in astrology are used to describe the 12 signs of the Zodiac. These are Mutable, Fixed and Cardinal.

Mutable: Gemini, Virgo, Sagittarius and Pisces

Mutable signs can adapt and alter. They are all about adapting self transformation and progress to external circumstances, people, and situations. Gemini, Virgo, Sagittarius, and Pisces are all signs that require movement. Nonetheless, they each have unique ways of exhibiting their mutability. Mutable signs appear at the end of each season and are associated with learning, integration, inner balance, and harmony. These signs are the most adaptable and balanced because they are at the end of each season, which naturally heralds the beginning of a new one. They are powerful and have the potential to bring about significant change. Their role differs from that of the cardinal signs, who are also change and transformation initiators. Mutable signs are older and wiser. They are generally at ease playing the roles of sage, teacher, pupil, advisor, counsel giver, listener, or silent support system. They're like chameleons, versatile and changing.

People having a lot of changeable energy can be compared to a manuscript's top editor. Everything is nearly perfect; the editor adds the finishing touches and makes the final adjustments. Mutable signs offer a golden touch! They can make anything they put their heart and mind to shine, glitter, or have an outstanding quality. With a winning touch, mutable signs or those with a lot of mutable energy 'finish the package.'

Fixed: Taurus, Scorpio, Leo and Aquarius

Fixed signs are 'rooted,' stable, and commitment-driven. They exude an aura that demonstrates a passion and respect for practical matters and foundations. Their approaches and innovations differ, but one thing they all have in common is the capacity to obsess over something they adore. Relationships, monetary goods, beliefs and ideologies, passions, a specific path or course of action, and any attachment are examples. Fixed signs have a strong will. Nothing can rip them away or disrupt their dedication once they set an objective and commit to something. Staying strength and dedication are enormous. On the negative side, it can be difficult to accomplish change when these symptoms are present. You may be stubborn and resistant to change if you are a fixed sign or have a lot of fixed energy in your natal (birth) chart. You can become fixated on ideas, beliefs, philosophies, and opinions, and you might become devoted to a cause. The last feature is, of course, a plus; the fixed quality has numerous advantages.

Every season, the fixed signs appear in the middle. People with a lot of fixed energy are adept at laying the groundwork for goals and foundations. They are natural enthusiasts, cheerful and upbeat about tasks and aspirations to which they are committed. With a spark, an idea may be grounded into something substantial, and they can run the course without swaying or getting sidetracked. There is little manipulation or deception, and everyone is trustworthy, dutiful, and delightfully sincere. Whatever they put their mind, heart, and soul into, they do with honesty and authenticity.

Cardinal: Libra, Aries, Capricorn and Cancer

Cardinal signs are wonderful transformation agents. They usually express motion and forward progress in a creative and artistic way. Productivity is vital to these signs at the beginning of each season. Aries is the first sign of the Zodiac, Cancer ushers in Summer, Libra ushers in Autumn, and Capricorn ushers in Winter. Cardinal signs are self-starters, self-leaders, and self-willed individuals. Positive shifts, change, and transformation can occur; their energy and qualities set things in motion. Each sign contains an element of idealism. They each have their unique style of expressing their sincere desire for transformation and self-evolution.

Cardinal signs like to take the initiative in some manner, shape, or form. They are rarely seen slacking off or melting into the background. Regardless of their individuality, they are all capable of being team players. The disadvantage is that they might be excessively controlling and demanding. Cardinal signs, at some point in their lives, or frequently for some, attempt to control everyone and everything around them. However, if they utilize their innate skills intentionally and productively, they can be inspiring speakers, motivators, and leaders.

CHAPTER TWO

THE SIGNS

ARIES

Constellation: Aries

Zodiac symbol: Ram

Date: March 20 – April 19

Zodiac element: Fire

Zodiac quality: Cardinal

Greatest Compatibility: Leo and Libra

Sign ruler: Mars

Day: Tuesday

Color: Red

Birthstone: Diamond

ARIES TRAITS

- There is no filter.
- Become enraged, then forgets why they are enraged
- They believe that everything is a game that they can win.
- On a dare, they'll do anything.
- Bored easily

WHAT IS THE PERSONALITY OF ARIES?

Aries, at their core, do what they want and do things their way. They are unafraid of controversy, fiercely competitive, truthful, and forthright. An Aries is not burdened by the freedom of choice, and they are arguably the least torn about what they want. They leap into the world with zeal and without reservation. It is one of their most admirable characteristics, but it also costs them a tremendous amount of suffering and grief.

Aries are driven by a need to establish their worth and strength. They take command naturally and are competitive and ambitious. Aries are impulsive and bold.

They are adventurous and enjoy exploring. They are determined and courageous, and they excel at starting new endeavors. They have a lot of enthusiasm and can take action quickly. They can also be impatient, but they have a lot of energy and don't like to waste time.

While Aries enjoy competition, they do not enjoy playing games. They are self-aware, have strong beliefs, and are constantly prepared to defend them.

WHAT ARE THE WEAKNESSES OF ARIES?

Aries people are impetuous, impatient, and fiery. They make no apologies for their rage. They truly mean, "I don't care." They don't always have the best self-control; therefore, therefore they need to practice being patient.

Aries, who are addicted to action and excitement, are frequently the source of their own problems. All Aries desire to feel everything deeply, which is why they can be prone to irresponsible risk-taking. It also indicates that they frequently react emotionally rather than rationally.

RELATIONSHIP COMPATIBILITY WITH ARIES

Based only on their Sun signs, this is how Aries interacts with others. These are the compatibility interpretations for all 12 potential Aries combinations. This is a limited and insufficient method of determining compatibility. However, Sun-sign compatibility remains the foundation for overall harmony in a relationship.

The general rule is that yin and yang do not get along. Yin complements yin, and yang complements yang. While yin and yang partnerships can be successful, they require more effort. Earth and water zodiac signs are both Yin. Yang is represented by the fire and air zodiac signs.

Aries and Aries

A love affair between two Aries people is a total explosion. To make this relationship work, one of them must give up first. Aries is a competitive sign. These two will not only compete with one another, but will also debate in order to make their points. Despite the fact that they are both yang energy, there may be too much combustion and energy for a happy union. This isn't a good match unless both of them have other planet placements that make them nicer people.

Taurus and Aries

Aries and Taurus are a yin-yang couple. Taurus' sexuality can unite with Aries' life energy if they both work together to make it happen. In a good relationship, they can complement each other, but they must learn to respect one another's natural differences: Aries is an impetuous, fighter, and action-oriented sign. Taurus is focused and walks slowly but steadily. This is something that can be accomplished with hard work.

Gemini and Aries

There are numerous opportunities for Aries and Gemini to create a stable partnership. They can, however, thrive together with greater security if they both mature. They both place high importance on freedom, independence, and the satisfaction of gratifying their curiosity. The major difference: Aries' faithfulness against Gemini's infidelity. Overall, this is yang energy that is compatible.

Cancer and Aries

Aries and Cancer have a challenging yin-yang relationship. They might be able to fit together with Aries' patience, a lot of patience. However, if they wish to pursue their connection, they must both put forth significant effort. Cancer will think Aries is too self-centered. Every time the unpredictable Aries decides to go out where the action is, Cancer will feel quite apprehensive. Aries, on the other hand, will become frustrated by Cancer's insecurity. This partnership needs a lot of effort.

Leo and Aries

Aries and Leo are like fire and ice, but that doesn't make their partnership impossible. Because both Aries and Leo have strong personalities, there will be moments of huge outburst. Leo must relinquish some control over the relationship. In exchange for relinquishing some control, Leo can enjoy everything Aries does to express love. Aries has no issues as long as it boosts Leo's self-esteem. Aries values the freedom that Leo provides, which grows stronger the more Aries promotes Leo's self-esteem.

Virgo and Aries

This is a difficult relationship to maintain. Both Aries and Virgo have strong personalities, yet their ambitions are totally different. Aries is an action-oriented mindset, whereas Virgo is always analyzing and shredding any situation that happens. Aries has to progress, but Virgo is impeding him with judgments and reprimands. Maybe, with a lot of effort, they'll discover a way.

Libra and Aries

Because they are compatible signs, Aries and Libra can form a strong partnership. The most difficult aspect will be Libra constantly reminding Aries that there is a better way to carry out this or that action. And Aries will always behave without regard for Libra's point of view. To avoid a breakup over this issue, Aries and Libra will need to appeal to their tolerance for each other's ways. Aries and Libra are on opposite sides of the same axis and must meet in the middle.

Scorpio and Aries

A partnership between Aries and Scorpio will quickly become difficult. Physical intimacy is the best common ground for these two to understand each other. They are, nonetheless, profoundly different in their ways of thinking and feeling. Scorpio desires complete control over the relationship and its partner, but Aries is unwilling to give it up. They are best suited to an occasional relationship.

Sagittarius and Aries

Aries and Sagittarius can have a wonderful partnership. Sagittarius will assist Aries in learning how to let go of the continual obligations and responsibilities that drag it down. In turn, Aries will assist Sagittarius in channeling its life with increased responsibility. They will have a long-lasting connection if they proceed slowly.

Capricorn and Aries

Aries and Capricorn have an extremely difficult relationship. Their personalities are too dissimilar to complement one another harmoniously. Aries acts on impulse without forethought, whereas Capricorn meticulously plans before taking action. Capricorn's continual criticism will not be tolerated by Aries. Capricorn's tone is too authoritative for Aries. Capricorn, on the other hand, will have a tough time supporting Aries' style of life, which Capricorn regards as silly.

Aquarius and Aries

A connection between Aries and Aquarius might be fruitful. Both members must be patient. Both Aries and Aquarius crave freedom and independence. They will understand each other better as a result of this. The troubles will stem from Aries' hasty and sudden actions, whereas Aquarius requires more time and security before moving on anything.

Pisces and Aries

Pisces is too introspective and ethereal for Aries, who is a fire sign that meets life head on. Aries represents a risk that Pisces does not believe they are willing to take. Pisces requires security and tranquility to develop and prosper. These are characteristics that Aries rarely exhibits. Aries must control their impulses in order for this relationship to work.

Love and Passion

When it comes to conquering someone, Aries is primitive. Aries men and women enjoy taking the initiative. Men to demonstrate their masculinity, and women to demonstrate their attractiveness. Because of this, some of their adventures don't go past the initial excitement and mystery of the conquest and end quickly.

When an Aries fully falls in love, there is no room for compromise. They are romantic idealists at heart, and they will do anything to keep the love alive.

Some people are overly optimistic, while others are unable to look past their own ambitions and demands.

Aries need to express themselves physically. They understand how to truly enjoy sexuality. In this area, both men and women born under the sign of Aries are very active and quick to act, but they can also be too demanding at times.

Marriage

To keep an Aries happy in a relationship, their partner must keep the connection from becoming routine and predictable. Aries require activity, variety, and stimulation, but they are usually faithful to their relationship.

Because Aries men are prone to being Macho, they often find it difficult to get along with strong, independent women. But many Aries men are confident enough to know that a partner with character is important, and they give her the freedom and support she needs.

Aries women are known for being difficult to deal with. They are quite dictatorial, and many prefer a passive partner who lets them make the decisions. However, such relationships rarely continue since Aries women desire a powerful and confident mate who is on their level without overpowering them.

It's nothing! Those who break through the barrier will get a loyal, loving companion and partner whose joy in life will keep them going.

TAURUS

Constellation: Taurus
Zodiac symbol: Bull
Date: April 19 – May 20
Zodiac element: Earth
Zodiac quality: Fixed
Greatest Compatibility: Cancer and Scorpio
Sign ruler: Venus
Day: Monday and Friday
Color: Pink and Green
Birthstone: Emerald

TAURUS TRAITS

- Homebody, just wants to cuddle
- There is no middle ground.
- Can dress in the same clothing every day.
- despises major changes.

WHAT IS THE PERSONALITY OF TAURUS?

Taureans are the moss of humanity. A chair made of wood. They are usually content with the way things are. They represent stability. Sitting in the grass, enjoying the air.

Taureans are an oasis of peace, a rock of dependability when everything else seems to be crumbling apart. Their method of operation is based on practical knowledge and experience.

Taureans are preoccupied with the physical world. They are typically grounded and logical. They enjoy routine and are dedicated to their own comfort. They prefer to be in command. They're patient and consistent, and their materialism is an outgrowth of their desire for security.

It's difficult for them to break out of a rut once they've established one. An object in motion remains in motion. The object at rest remains at rest. Beauty is something they appreciate as well as Physical pleasure. They prefer things to remain consistent. They are quite content eating the same meal every day or wearing the same dress for a week. They'd rather have things be constant than chaotically good. They like to figure out what they enjoy doing the most and then take it to the next level.

Tauruses are regal in appearance. They are graceful and hard-working workers. They might be stubborn, headstrong, and set in their ways, but they are also excellent listeners and dependable.

Taurus can go on indefinitely. They are never tired. They resemble machines. And no matter what they throw at them, they will always conquer their challenges because they have planned for every eventuality. They are the hand-crafted trucks that will never fail. They are the bulletproof vests that never wears out.

WHAT ARE THE WEAKNESSES OF TAURUS?

Taureans' negative attributes stem from their materialistic tendencies. They can be extremely determined to seek material success at times. They are not impervious to greed. If they are only interested in their own goals, they may not care about the needs of others.

Taureans are unresponsive to criticism. They don't even respond adversely to it, but it's almost as if they're built of cement, and any response just bounces right off. They refuse to budge.

Tauruses are obstinate. They will not do anything they do not want to do. They are hesitant to change their beliefs since it undermines their sense of security. They can become so accustomed to their routine that they lose sight of what is truly important. Taurus has a tendency to become emotionally and physically lethargic.

They can become stubborn and obstinate and have difficulty listening to others. They can be trapped in the mud, unable to perceive the big picture, like a bull. They are slow to act and may be too focused on the present to perceive the possibility of something bigger. They can also be irresponsible, particularly when young. Struggles with excessive vice consumption. Doesn't understand moderation. When they find something they enjoy, they go all in.

RELATIONSHIP COMPATIBILITY WITH TAURUS

Based only on their Sun signs, this is how Taurus interacts with others. These are the compatibility interpretations for all 12 potential Taurus combinations. This is a limited and insufficient method of determining compatibility.

However, Sun-sign compatibility remains the foundation for overall harmony in a relationship.

The general rule is that yin and yang do not get along. Yin complements yin, and yang complements yang. While yin and yang partnerships can be successful, they require more effort. Earth and water zodiac signs are both Yin. Yang is represented by the fire and air zodiac signs.

Aries and Taurus

Taurus and Aries are a yin-yang couple. Taurus' sexuality can unite with Aries' life energy if they both work together to make it happen. In a good relationship, they can complement each other, but they must learn to respect one another's natural differences: Aries is an impetuous, fighter, and action-oriented sign. Taurus is focused and walks slowly but steadily. This is something that can be accomplished with hard work.

Taurus, and Taurus

Taurus and Taurus is a relationship that can succeed as long as they both remember that neither of them is action-oriented. As a result, the risk in this relationship is that they become too comfortable sitting at home and become isolated from social life. They could even feel bored if their preferred routine becomes a rut. This relationship will require motion.

Gemini and Taurus

Taurus and Gemini have a tough time comprehending each other's basic requirements while they are together. They have extremely different personalities. Gemini represents growth, movement, inconstancy, and infidelity. Taurus is the polar opposite. They will collide repeatedly, but if love is truly what unites them, they will be able to smooth things out and develop a stable relationship.

Cancer and Taurus

Taurus and Cancer can have a great connection since they will assist each other in important ways. Taurus will be in charge of materially supporting Cancer. Cancer gives Taurus emotional support and motivates them to keep working for their home. Cancer will also feel emotionally safe because Taurus provides material security.

Leo and Taurus

Taurus and Leo relationships will be difficult to maintain. Their personalities are diametrically opposing. They can, however, come to complement each other if the relationship is given time and space to mature. They will have difficulty communicating with one another. For example, Leo has social wants, but Taurus has introspective needs. Taurus is agreeable, while Leo is opinionated and commanding.

Virgo and Taurus

Taurus and Virgo have a wonderful relationship that has enormous potential to become steady and dependable. Taurus and Virgo are two earth signs with numerous similarities. They have similar tastes: they both enjoy planning initiatives, bettering themselves, cultivating their minds, analyzing expenses and household demands, and so on. Of course, they must be careful not to get stuck in a rut.

Libra and Taurus

Taurus and Libra relationships are not recommended since both members will feel destabilized by the other's contrasting features. Taurus represents stability, security, and solid ground; Libra represents change, mobility, and perpetual doubt. When Taurus requires confidence, Libra will cast doubt. Even so, if love is present, it is worth a shot.

Scorpio and Taurus

When Taurus and Scorpio unite, the passion, sensuality, and eroticism will be spectacular. However, certain occurrences in ordinary life can generate speed bumps in this relationship. Scorpio is far too domineering. Taurus will not be able to withstand the emotional stings that Scorpio will undoubtedly deliver. Scorpio must accept Taurus as they are for this partnership to work.

Sagittarius and Taurus

Taurus and Sagittarius' relationship can be summed up in five words. Difficult, difficult, and harder. Taurus and Sagittarius have extremely distinct requirements. Perhaps they will understand each other as they grow older and develop in life. However, Taurus and Sagittarius will struggle to figure out how to move the relationship forward while remaining comfortable with each other and their individual lives during their younger years. Sagittarius does not comprehend Taurus' philosophy, "Slowly but steadily."

Capricorn and Taurus

Taurus and Capricorn are two earth signs that work really well together. They will enjoy this relationship because they will do it their way: step by step, planning each movement, perfecting what works, celebrating with a movie at home, and triumphantly reaching the peak. Everything is in their favor for a long-term partnership.

Aquarius and Taurus

Taurus and Aquarius relationships can bear fruit with a lot of hard effort and a lot of patience. Their personalities clash because Aquarius values freedom and independence, while Taurus values home and relationships. But if they each give a little, they might realize that there are moments when each of them needs to be alone, without meaning that they have ceased loving one another.

Pisces and Taurus

Despite the fact that Taurus and Pisces are both yin, this is a difficult partnership to establish. They must give a lot of themselves in order to comprehend their various personalities. Taurus is basically a material being, and its life revolves around material things. In contrast, Pisces is a spiritual being. Although Pisces requires the material, it is more concerned with transcending it. They will both feel comfortable and protected if they learn to complement each other.

LOVE AND PASSION

After overcoming the problems that come with any emotional relationship, Taurus can let down their guard and enjoy their sensuality.

Sexual activity, like eating and drinking, is regarded as a basic requirement. As lovers, they are spontaneous and generous, and their passion is often startling. Sexual dissatisfaction impacts them the most and puts them in a foul mood more than any other symptom.

They enjoy dressing up and dining in upscale restaurants. They make no compromises when it comes to having pleasure and only accept the best. A Taurus companion should expect a life of flair.

They are faithful and trustworthy, and they do not usually seek a paramour since they want to keep a solid relationship above all. They are insecure if their lover does not devote themselves fully, both physically and spiritually.

MARRIAGE

Marriage is a big commitment for Taurus. They desire a secure and long-lasting connection. Because of their pragmatism, they plan everything ahead of time. They frequently choose to get married in a church with a large ceremony.

Some Taurus men become a touch possessive over time. They believe their spouse is theirs, and some go so far as to control all of their behaviors. When this happens, it's preferable to put a stop to it.

Otherwise, the wife of a Taurean has nothing to be concerned about. Her wishes are his command, and he is her devoted husband.

Taurus women are constantly and unconditionally supportive of their partners. They eventually start a family, but that doesn't stop them from cultivating their numerous hobbies, some of which may become more than simply a pastime. Those who marry a Taurus woman will be blessed with a kind and diligent woman.

GEMINI

Constellation: Gemini
Zodiac symbol: Twins
Date: May 20 – June 20
Zodiac element: Air
Zodiac quality: Mutable
Greatest Compatibility: Aquarius and Sagittarius
Sign ruler: Mercury
Day: Wednesday
Color: Yellow/Gold and Light Green
Birthstone: Pearl

GEMINI TRAITS

- Charismatic
- Humor is used as a crutch.
- Could converse with a brick wall
- Uses Arguments to flirt
- Knows a little bit about everything.

WHAT IS THE PERSONALITY OF GEMINI?

Geminis are extremely intelligent and learn quickly. They are astute, analytical, and frequently amusing. They have a childish curiosity and are continually asking new questions.

Geminis have an incredible capacity to judge a person's personality in a couple of seconds, even if they have only met them. They'll be the first to recognize whether someone is bluffing. They are excellent speakers, as well as attentive and sensitive listeners.

Geminis are adaptable, at ease as introverts and extroverts. They respond quickly to the energy of a room. They might be the life of the party or a total bore. They understand how to bring disparate people together and make them get along.

WHAT ARE THE WEAKNESSES OF GEMINI?

Geminis dislike being alone. This is why they have wide social circles and are always accompanied. They are terrified of becoming entrapped in their own ideas. It's not that Gemini aren't creative or brilliant; it's just that they're terrified of their own imagination's power. They're terrified of what they'll discover once they've found themselves.

They aren't frightened of their emotions, but they are always concerned about how they express them, about their words being misunderstood, and about unintentionally hurting someone's feelings. This is a common mistake made by Geminis as a result of how they externalize their fears. They are terrified of becoming engulfed in an emotion over which they have no control. Rather than feeling their feelings, they merely respond to them.

Their mind is a never-ending racetrack. They are continuously searching beneath the surface of their existing reality for something new. They aren't in a hurry to get someplace; they are simply looking for something fresh.

Perhaps the most crucial realization for a Gemini is that there is no final destination at the end of the road. They can't keep running forever. They'll have to take a break and glance around at some time. To accept responsibility for the environment in which they find themselves. They'll have to examine the environment they've created for themselves and decide if it's truly what they want.

RELATIONSHIP COMPATIBILITY WITH GEMINI

Based only on their Sun signs, this is how Gemini interacts with others. These are the compatibility interpretations for all 12 potential Gemini combinations. This is a limited and insufficient method of determining compatibility.

However, Sun-sign compatibility remains the foundation for overall harmony in a relationship.

The general rule is that yin and yang do not get along. Yin complements yin, and yang complements yang. While yin and yang partnerships can be successful, they require more effort. Earth and water zodiac signs are both Yin. Yang is represented by the fire and air zodiac signs.

Aries and Gemini

A steady connection between Gemini and Aries has numerous potential. They can, however, thrive together with greater security if they both mature. They both place a high importance on freedom, independence, and the satisfaction of gratifying their curiosity. The major difference: Aries' faithfulness against Gemini's infidelity. Overall, this is yang energy that is compatible.

Taurus and Gemini

When it comes to understanding each other's basic requirements, Gemini and Taurus have a challenging relationship. They have extremely different personalities. Gemini represents growth, movement, inconstancy, and infidelity. Taurus is the polar opposite. They will collide repeatedly, but if love is truly what unites them, they will be able to smooth things out and develop a stable relationship.

Gemini, and Gemini

A Gemini-Gemini partnership can work if both members focus on their complementary characteristics. They will have a lot of freedom. They will appreciate endless social gatherings where they can chat till they are weary. They will have a seductive and charismatic feeling. However, when problems emerge, no one wants to take care of their responsibilities and commitments.

Cancer and Gemini

If Gemini and Cancer want to be together, they must be patient. Cancer is demanding because it is fearful. When asked for a lot of things, Gemini tends to flee. And Gemini isn't really interested in Cancer's excuses for its insecurity. A Gemini cannot be happy until they have independence. Cancer drowns in a glass of water if not protected.

Leo and Gemini

After smoothing out their inherent rough places, a Gemini and Leo partnership can be one of tremendous understanding. Gemini is a natural seducer. Leo, who is likewise a seducer, will not back its partner's efforts to conquer others. This may cause complications, as Gemini may feel suffocated by Leo's absolute exclusivity.

Virgo and Gemini

A partnership between Gemini and Virgo would be too hard to sustain and become steady because of the diverse ways they exhibit their natures. Both Gemini and Virgo are mutable signs ruled by Mercury, yet they work on separate wavelengths. Virgo is an earth sign, and Gemini is an air sign. Gemini personifies dispersion and unpredictability. Virgo, on the other hand, does not leave anything to chance: it examines its steps indefinitely. This attribute is a hefty load for Gemini to bear on a daily basis.

Libra and Gemini

Gemini and Libra are two seducers that can get along without getting in each other's way. It is a connection that can blossom if they learn to compliment one another's strengths. Gemini has what Libra requires: the flow of energy required to move in the pursuit of greater pleasure. Libra has what Gemini needs: a more ordered existence with a better mix of feeling, thinking, and acting.

Scorpio and Gemini

If Gemini and Scorpio meet together just for the purpose of mutual intimate pleasure, it can be a beautiful experience for both of you. However, if you want to progress and create a relationship, you will have to walk a hard route together if you want it to succeed. Scorpio's jealousy and eruptions will destroy Gemini's chances of remaining by its side.

Sagittarius and Gemini

A partnership between Gemini and Sagittarius might be exciting if they are conscious that developing a lasting union requires certain sacrifices. Gemini and Sagittarius are both very gregarious, mobile, restless, and unstable signs. One of them should lead by example by becoming more solid. If they wish to avoid envy and friction, they must focus on their tendency to entice and dominate.

Capricorn and Gemini

Gemini and Capricorn are not meant to be together. Capricorns will spend their lives criticizing Gemini for its lack of concentration and for changing its mind so frequently. Capricorn's mental rigidity, on the other hand, will swiftly bore Gemini. Gemini will become impatient with the fact that it finds no way to really enjoy life with such a mate. It may work with hard work and a lot of love.

Aquarius and Gemini

Gemini and Aquarius make an excellent couple. They will understand each other almost completely. They are both gregarious and like spending time with their pals. When Aquarius pays attention to others, Gemini may feel forgotten at times, but this will not jeopardize the connection. The emphasis will be on creativity.

Pisces and Gemini

Gemini and Pisces are more likely to split up than get married. Pisces will not feel comfortable in the company of someone as turbulent and unpredictable as Gemini. Pisces requires security and containment, which Gemini cannot supply even if it tried to. Pisces will be irritated by Gemini's lack of focus and propensity of running away from home. It is best to remain mute when it comes to integrity.

LOVE AND PASSION

Geminis are naturally gregarious and like meeting new people. They are romantics who like the start of new partnerships.

Of course, they know how to flaunt their attractions, as evidenced by the fact that many people regard them as wonderful company. They are very sexually active and enjoy trying out new experiences. Sex is enjoyable for them.

Those who fall in love with a Gemini must become used to their mood swings. They can be aloof and unavailable at times, which perplexes their companions, who wonder why. Fortunately, these feelings are fleeting. The Gemini quickly returns their attention and displays their characteristic sense of humor.

Geminis like variety, which is why many of them struggle with monogamy. Some people are involved in two or more relationships at the same time. They normally mature and change over time, while others are unable to suppress their desire to be unfaithful.

MARRIAGE

Geminis are adaptable and cheerful by nature, and they make excellent partners, especially if their partner shares their desire for variety in all areas. Those seeking stability and routine, on the other hand, may find it difficult to keep up with them.

Geminis should think twice about marrying because it can take years for them to settle down and establish a commitment. When they meet the love of their lives, they should live with them for a while to see if they are truly compatible.

Those who marry a Gemini lady will be in the company of a creative and adaptable woman who wants to raise a family without sacrificing her job or her many interests.

When Gemini men decide to end their long years of bachelorhood, they make excellent spouses. Because they are thoughtful, happy, and smart, they are always happy and get along well with children.

CANCER

Constellation: Cancer

Zodiac symbol: Crab

Date: June 20 – July 22

Zodiac element: Water

Zodiac quality: Cardinal

Greatest Compatibility: Taurus and Capricorn

Sign ruler: Moon

Day: Monday and Thursday

Color: White

Birthstone: Ruby

CANCER TRAITS

- Extremely sensitive
- Seeks solace
- Never forgets but always forgives
- There is only one boundary, but it is very firm.
- Takes on the problems of others.

WHAT IS THE PERSONALITY OF CANCER?

The personality of a Cancer is like plunging chest deep into a warm lake. It seems dazzling and cool against your skin, but you know that if you dive in, it will feel heated.

Cancer's self-awareness is cyclical. They're in and out of focus all the time. Their personality is multifaceted. They have a wide range of emotions, some of which are conflicting, but they also have a deep, fundamental self that is constant.

Cancers are burdened by their own tragedies as well as the grief of others around them. They are often tormented by grief. It is difficult for them to communicate their sorrow with others, and they are often scared to be open because they are frightened that others would use their flaws against them. Cancers have learned to conceal their suffering in order not to bother others. They act as if everything is fine when it isn't.

Their emotions are like an open wound. They are sensitive to everything. They quiver like a tuning fork at the slightest provocation. Because they can't forget the emotional sting of a slight, they tend to harbor deep grudges.

WHAT ARE THE WEAKNESSES OF CANCER?

Cancers are introverts. They prefer the security of the known. They dislike change. They are drawn to routine and stability. They want to know what to expect. They are less adventurous than other signs. They have a strong desire to return to the past. They enjoy preserving traditions. They enjoy art that transports them to another era. They enjoy antique stories and art forms. They feel more at ease in predictable situations. They want to know what will happen next. They want to feel like they're part of something bigger. They are not fond of surprises.

RELATIONSHIP COMPATIBILITY WITH CANCER

Based only on their Sun signs, this is how Cancer interacts with others. These are the compatibility interpretations for all 12 potential Cancer combinations. This is a limited and insufficient method of determining compatibility.

However, Sun-sign compatibility remains the foundation for overall harmony in a relationship.

The general rule is that yin and yang do not get along. Yin complements yin, and yang complements yang. While yin and yang partnerships can be successful, they require more effort. Earth and water zodiac signs are both Yin. Yang is represented by the fire and air zodiac signs.

Aries and Cancer

Cancer and Aries have a challenging yin-yang relationship. They might be able to fit together with Aries' patience, a lot of patience. However, if they wish to pursue their connection, they must both put forth significant effort. Cancer will think Aries is too self-centered. Every time the unpredictable Aries decides to go out where the action is, Cancer will feel quite apprehensive. Aries, on the other hand, will become frustrated by Cancer's insecurity. This partnership needs a lot of effort.

Taurus and Cancer

Cancer and Taurus might have a great connection since they will assist each other in important ways. Taurus will be in charge of materially supporting Cancer. Cancer gives Taurus emotional support and motivates them to keep working for their home. Cancer will also feel emotionally safe because Taurus provides material security.

Gemini and Cancer

If Cancer and Gemini want to be together, they must be patient. Cancer is demanding because it is fearful. When asked for a lot of things, Gemini tends to flee. And Gemini isn't really interested in Cancer's excuses for its insecurity. Gemini cannot be happy until they have independence. Cancer drowns in a glass of water if not protected.

Cancer and Cancer

Who will contain who when two Cancers collide? This is the crucial question. Both are insecure beings in need of someone to provide a framework of protection and security. But, being Cancers, one will ask the other to assume that role, and conflict is unavoidable. They will receive plenty of snuggling and pampering, but they will be unable to put their problems aside. It is a challenging, but not impossible, connection.

Leo and Cancer

The prognosis for a Cancer-Leo partnership is bleak. Cancer is too much for Leo to bear. Leo would initially be pleased to have a spouse that demands affection and protection. However, as soon as Cancer begins to silence Leo and blame Leo for not being home, Leo will want to quit the partnership as soon as possible.

Virgo and Cancer

A partnership between Cancer and Virgo might blossom if both parties manage to carve out space for each other without suffocating each other. Cancer and Virgo share many needs: they will seek affection, assist one another in difficult times, feel safe, and share lots of hugs and pampering. Virgo must be careful not to slip into the habit of continual criticism.

Libra and Cancer

Cancer and Libra might have a harmonious partnership if they are both willing to open their up their emotions. Cancer and Libra both have a tendency to close down and hide their genuine sentiments. It is critical that they learn to converse openly about love and their relationship. They can only complement each other in this way. Otherwise, they will become increasingly apart.

Scorpio and Cancer

A partnership between Cancer and Scorpio can be extremely gratifying if Cancer can relinquish control to Scorpio. Cancer should not be concerned about its safety because Scorpio will provide them with whatever they require. In turn, Cancer will shower Scorpio with boundless affection and pleasure. Scorpio is less aggressive than usual in such a partnership.

Sagittarius and Cancer

A connection between Cancer and Sagittarius is not advised, especially for Cancer, who will feel more uneasy than ever. Sagittarius is not a sign that can always provide emotional or material assistance to a relationship. On the contrary, Sagittarius' life is frequently marked by instability, if not carelessness. This partnership can be tried, but Cancer must learn to be more self-sufficient.

Capricorn and Cancer

Cancer and Capricorn can have a wonderful partnership. In terms of safety and material well-being, Capricorn has a lot to give Cancer. Cancer will show Capricorn that life is more than just labor and mental fields: Cancer will teach Capricorn to appreciate life in ways Capricorn has never dreamed. There are no major issues in this connection.

Aquarius and Cancer

A link between Cancer and Aquarius is unlikely. Cancer's incessant requests for love will not be tolerated by Aquarius' free and independent attitude. Aquarius will be unable to reassure the partner, nor will he or she be able to provide safety and security in the relationship. Cancer's eruptions will be immediately noted. Aquarius will seek refuge with its closest companions.

Pisces and Cancer

Cancer and Pisces can have a very strong emotional bond. Their dilemma is who will handle their financial and practical issues. Both are willing to run the house, but neither is willing to accept full financial responsibility or obligations. The success of this partnership will be determined by how they handle this situation.

LOVE AND PASSION

Cancers find it difficult to take the initiative, and they frequently check to see if their feelings are reciprocated before asking for a date. They are typically relatively passive at the start of a relationship.

In the end, though, they display their friendly and warm side, which perplexes individuals who are only familiar with their more reserved and protective side. Sex is a crucial experience for Cancerians. They are innovative and intuitive lovers.

Furthermore, they lavish their spouse with attention and ensure that they always feel appreciated. They enjoy taking them out to dinner or enjoying their company in the privacy of their own home. They avoid those who have an active social life.

They might be too dependent or possessive at times, and even inadvertently, they can be suffocating to the point of breaking the relationship. Some are deeply affected by failed relationships, and can never fall in love again.

MARRIAGE

Cancers are folks who want to settle down and start a family. Both men and women take their roles as spouses very seriously, and they rarely cheat on each other.

They respect family above everything else, and are always eager to offer affection and protection. If their marriage is in trouble, they will attempt to do everything they can to save it.

Cancers feel at ease as housewives and househusbands, and many prefer to care for children while their spouse works. They are incredibly creative and put a lot of thought into the upkeep of their home.

Male Cancers, on the other hand, enjoy taking care of their partners and providing them with the stability they require. They are quite sensitive, in contrast to most males, and they are not afraid to show it. They want their spouse to always feel loved and respected.

LEO

Constellation: Leo

Zodiac symbol: Lion

Date: July 22 – August 22

Zodiac element: Fire

Zodiac quality: Fixed

Greatest Compatibility: Gemini and Aquarius

Sign ruler: Sun

Day: Sunday

Color: Gold, Yellow and Orange

Birthstone: The Peridot

LEO TRAITS

*   Exudes warmth and ingenuity.
*   A little conceited
*   A huge personality
*   Aspires to be noticed.
*   Loves Luxury

WHAT IS THE PERSONALITY OF LEO?

Leos are courageous, warm, and loving. They are also the ideal entertainers. They have the dramatic flair of a Broadway star as well as the charisma of a politician. They have enthralling personalities. They have a way with words and can speak eloquently about almost any subject, regardless of how recently they've been introduced to it.

Leos put their heart and soul into all they undertake. The heart governs them. They are bold and self-assured, and they trust their intuition. Their acts are effortless and natural.

Leos have an insatiable need for advancement that is easily satisfied by the admiration of others. When they are in pain, it is obvious. They will use their rage as a shield to protect themselves from their vulnerabilities. They desire to be viewed as strong because they are afraid of exposing vulnerability, relying on others, and feeling incomplete.

WHAT ARE THE WEAKNESSES OF LEO?

The negative aspects of a Leo emerge when their favorable and outstanding personality traits become excessive. They may appear to be domineering, yet this is due to their hyper-presence and warmth.

Leos have a reputation for being conceited. This isn't bragging to them; it's sharing. Sharing their triumphs with others makes them feel connected, and they want their friends to reciprocate. They want to be celebrated, but they're also delighted to celebrate you.

Leos prefer to feel powerful. They don't necessarily want to be adored or regarded with awe. They simply want to be recognized for being themselves. The distinction between admiration and worship is subtle, but it is the difference between a Leo being consumed with themselves and being concerned with the well-being of those they care about.

They desire to be the focal point of the universe. They want to be recognized as the best and brightest. They desire to be treated exceptionally, but they also believe they are deserving of it.

Leos despise being told what to do. They have complete control over their own worlds and their own fate. Betrayal and abandonment inflict permanent wounds on Leos. Their pride is a sword they use to defend their sovereignty.

Their sense of honor is profound; they hold themselves and others to a very high standard, and they are terribly hurt when that code is broken. Everyone has an innate desire to be acknowledged and validated for their existence. This can result in egotistical or absolutist behavior that borders on the ridiculous.

They despise being told what to do, but if you can get them to listen, they can generally be persuaded—especially if you make it seem like it was their idea all along. But they'll always be resentful that they didn't come to this conclusion on their own. Leos dislike being told what to do, and they especially dislike being coerced. They demand respect and do not tolerate anyone who does not respect them.

RELATIONSHIP COMPATIBILITY WITH LEO

Based only on their Sun signs, this is how Leo interacts with others. These are the compatibility interpretations for all 12 potential Leo combinations. This is a limited and insufficient method of determining compatibility.

However, Sun-sign compatibility remains the foundation for overall harmony in a relationship.

The general rule is that yin and yang do not get along. Yin complements yin, and yang complements yang. While yin and yang partnerships can be successful, they require more effort. Earth and water zodiac signs are both Yin. Yang is represented by the fire and air zodiac signs.

Aries and Leo

Leo and Aries are like fire and ice, but that doesn't make their partnership impossible. Because both Aries and Leo have strong personalities, there will be moments of outrage. Leo must relinquish some control over the relationship. In exchange for relinquishing some control, Leo can enjoy everything Aries does to express love. Aries has no issues as long as it boosts Leo's self-esteem. Aries values the freedom that Leo provides, which grows stronger the more Aries promotes Leo's self-esteem.

Taurus and Leo

It will be difficult to maintain a relationship between Leo and Taurus. Their personalities are diametrically opposing. They can, however, come to complement each other if the relationship is given time and space to mature. They will have difficulty communicating with one another. For example, Leo has social wants, but Taurus has introspective needs. Taurus is agreeable, while Leo is opinionated and commanding.

Gemini and Leo

After smoothing out its inherent rough points, a partnership between Leo and Gemini can have remarkable understanding. Gemini is a natural seducer. Leo, who is likewise a seducer, will not back its partner's efforts to conquer others. This may cause complications, as Gemini may feel suffocated by Leo's absolute exclusivity.

Cancer and Leo

The prognosis for a Leo-Cancer partnership is bleak. Cancer is too much for Leo to bear. Leo would initially be pleased to have a spouse that demands affection and protection. However, as soon as Cancer begins to silence Leo and blame Leo for not being home, Leo will want to quit the partnership as soon as possible.

Leo and Leo

Two Leos can only have a healthy and stable relationship if one of them is a little less Leo than the other. They will understand each other magnificently if one is willing to give up first place in the relationship. If neither is prepared to give up first place, they will continually battle and try to outdo each other in love rather than complete each other.

Virgo and Leo

A partnership between Leo and Virgo will require a lot of effort. Virgo is an overly fastidious and critical sign, and Leo will be reluctant to allow their partner point out their flaws. On the other side, Leo requires regular flattery, and providing such flattery is not a quality present in the area of Virgo. If this partnership is to succeed, Leo and Virgo must get to know each other thoroughly and offer a few inches.

Libra and Leo

Leo and Libra will get along great since they both contribute what the other needs to create balance in the union. Libra, who is an expert in the art of seduction, will constantly flatter Leo. Libra will have a trustworthy reference in Leo to help Libra acquire assurance in decision-making. Take this friendship seriously.

Scorpio and Leo

It is quite tough for Leo and Scorpio to remain in a love relationship. They may be fine for the odd connection, but they are not so good for long-term stability. To complement Scorpio, Leo must set aside its most prominent characteristics: forceful voice, decisiveness, independence, and control. Scorpio will never tolerate such traits in its companion.

Sagittarius and Leo

Leo and Sagittarius will get along great when it comes to having fun and socializing. The issue may develop when Leo accuses Sagittarius of being unstable in life, of constantly changing paths without forethought, and of their desire for unending adventures. When confronted with such assertions, Sagittarius tends to flee. The remedy would be to get down and discuss things out so that a good relationship is not ruined.

Capricorn and Leo

In a partnership between Leo and Capricorn, each person's selfishness will be highlighted. They each seek complete control over everything around them. They are both determined to be the first in the relationship. They each believe they have the finest solutions to various problems. Finally, Leo and Capricorn will simply compete and argue about who has the upper hand in the relationship.

Aquarius and Leo

A partnership between Leo and Aquarius can be tough to establish if Aquarius does not learn how to manage Leo with flattery from the start. Aquarius is not prone to such a technique. Instead of wasting time persuading their Leo partner that they are the best in the universe, Aquarius is engaged in producing and innovating. Aquarius' emotional indifference will be difficult for Leo to tolerate.

Pisces and Leo

Leo and Pisces can have a wonderful relationship that should not be underestimated. This is a yin-yang connection, and they will need to work on the areas that appear to be at odds (such as that Leo focuses on the self while Pisces focuses on others). But they have everything they need to meet both of their requirements. Leo possesses enormous power and will provide Pisces with the security and safety it requires. Pisces will lavish compliments, praise, tenderness, and thanks on Leo.

LOVE AND PASSION

Leos have an undeniable allure and frequently stand out. In love, they prefer to take the initiative and lead. Given the fervor with which they express their desire for someone, it is difficult not to fall into their net.

They are charming and engaging, and they know how to make others feel special. They have a strong sexual allure. Making love is their most natural way of expressing their strong emotions.

Their company boosts morale and positivity because they only see the best in everyone. They are loyal, reliable, and truthful, and they are morally averse to cheating in their relationship.

They want to keep themselves occupied and expect the person they love to share their many interests. Because Leos need to be the focus of attention, they are prone to envy. Their companion will frequently be forced to play a supporting role and let Leo take the lead.

MARRIAGE

Leos need to be in charge of their lives and do things their own way. They are the ideal spouse for some. Others see them as overly autonomous and authoritarian, causing frequent conflict.

Many Leos, paradoxically, expect their partner to live up to them in every aspect. In any event, life is never boring when you're married to a Leo, who will go to any length to keep the passion alive.

Leo women need to be admired and will react violently if they are ignored. They elevate their spouse and provide the necessary support for them to achieve success and professional prominence. They are dedicated and proud wives and mothers. They normally do not give up their occupations to start a family.

Some Leo men are macho, favoring meek, traditional women who are content to stay at home and find it difficult to live with a domineering individual. Leo guys are often affectionate and treat their wives like queens.

VIRGO

Constellation: Virgo

Zodiac symbol: Maiden

Date: August 22 – September 22

Zodiac element: Earth

Zodiac quality: Mutable

Greatest Compatibility: Cancer and Pisces

Sign ruler: Mercury

Day: Wednesday

Color: Beige and Grey

Birthstone: Sapphire

VIRGO TRAITS

- Must feel useful.
- Has a quick solution for everything
- Judgmental but well-intended.
- Superior spatial awareness
- A million thoughts per second

WHAT IS THE PERSONALITY OF VIRGO?

Virgos are often modest individuals. They want to be recognized for their achievements, but they don't require spectacular displays of gratitude to feel worthwhile. They're like little geniuses. They pay attention to the subtleties. When Virgo's toothbrush is moved even a centimeter, they notice.

Virgos are self-conscious about their imperfections. They understand that their actions have repercussions and that they can be accountable for their own misery at times. This is why they frequently say things like "It's my fault" and "I did this to myself."

Virgos are the exact incarnation of the mediaeval philosopher who dwells in a sterile cell, never opening the door for fear of exposing the shambles within. "In order to save myself from myself, I must first destroy myself," their motto says. They desire a pristine, clean existence.

They must be the best in order to feel worthy of their existence. They can become so preoccupied with their own ideal of perfection that they lose touch with their actual desires. They suppress their emotions by locking them up in order to achieve impassivity.

They can appear lot more sensible than they actually are. Their emotions are typically a mystery to them. They have a lot of feelings, but they don't know how to express them. They can only express the ineffable through dry sarcasm.

WHAT ARE THE WEAKNESSES OF VIRGO?

Virgos are perfectionists by nature. Cleaning freaks, they are well-known for their meticulousness. They can see patterns where none exist. They can be picky and too critical.

True, Virgos are particular, but that doesn't always imply that they preserve neat spaces. Their peculiarities and behaviors may not often correspond to traditional notions of cleanliness. They may live in a Tasmanian devil-style dust storm ruin while enforcing a "no shoes in the house" or "no outside clothing on the bed" restriction. Their home may appear cluttered, but they know where everything is. Everything has a purpose. Virgos prefer to be in order, but they prioritize their service orientation over their own comfort. This can indicate that a Virgo is too preoccupied with improving the lives of those around them to devote much time and effort to meeting their own needs. They are rarely driven by self-interest.

Virgos are brilliant as well, but because of their reclusive nature, they sometimes have difficulty expressing themselves. Talking to them may feel like you're hovering on the surface of life, with no idea what they're thinking or feeling deep inside. Their emphasis on thinking and ideas may appear to be a mask for a lack of emotional depth. In reality, they are a fortress within a fortress—the epitome of self-containment. Virgos will be open to everything you have to offer, but they may not see the point of impulsively excavating themselves for the sake of others.

RELATIONSHIP COMPATIBILITY WITH VIRGO

Based only on their Sun signs, this is how Virgo interacts with others. These are the compatibility interpretations for all 12 potential Virgo combinations. This is a limited and insufficient method of determining compatibility.

However, Sun-sign compatibility remains the foundation for overall harmony in a relationship.

The general rule is that yin and yang do not get along. Yin complements yin, and yang complements yang. While yin and yang partnerships can be successful, they require more effort. Earth and water zodiac signs are both Yin. Yang is represented by the fire and air zodiac signs.

Aries and Virgo

This is a difficult connection to maintain. Both Virgo and Aries have powerful personalities, yet their ambitions are totally different. Aries is an action-oriented mindset, whereas Virgo is always analyzing and shredding any situation that happens. Aries has to progress, but Virgo is impeding him with judgments and reprimands. Maybe, with a lot of effort, they'll discover a way.

Taurus and Virgo

Virgo and Taurus have a wonderful partnership that has enormous potential to become steady and dependable. Virgo and Taurus are two earth signs with numerous similarities. They have similar tastes: they both enjoy planning initiatives, bettering themselves, cultivating their minds, analyzing expenses and household demands, and so on. Of course, they must be careful not to get stuck in a rut.

Gemini and Virgo

Because of the diverse ways they express their natures, a partnership between Virgo and Gemini would be too hard to sustain and become solid. Both Virgo and Gemini are mutable signs ruled by Mercury, yet they work on separate wavelengths. Virgo is an earth sign, and Gemini is an air sign. Gemini personifies dispersion and unpredictability. Virgo, on the other hand, does not leave anything to chance: it examines its steps indefinitely. This attribute is a hefty load for Gemini to bear on a daily basis.

Cancer and Virgo

A partnership between Virgo and Cancer can be quite rewarding if both members manage to provide room for each other without suffocating each other. Many of their requirements are shared by Virgo and Cancer: they will seek affection, assist each other in difficult times, feel safe, and share lots of hugs and pampering. Virgo must be careful not to slip into the habit of continual criticism.

Leo and Virgo

A Virgo and Leo partnership will require a lot of effort. Virgo is an overly fastidious and critical sign, and Leo will be reluctant to allow their partner point out their flaws. On the other hand, Leo requires regular flattery, and providing such flattery is not a quality present in the area of Virgo. If this partnership is to succeed, Virgo and Leo must get to know each other thoroughly and offer a few inches.

Virgo and Virgo

A relationship between two Virgos will be difficult since each will strive to dominate the other. Because Virgos are precise and detail-oriented, they will critique one another's activities in order to keep control of the relationship. Neither has the ability to relax and minimize their mental stiffness. It's quite difficult.

Libra and Virgo

A Virgo and Libra relationship is difficult but not impossible. To ensure the success of their partnership, Virgo and Libra should try to reach a compromise. Virgo has to stop being so judgmental. Libra should try to curb its seductive tendencies because Virgo is extremely devoted and will not accept inappropriate behavior in the partnership.

Scorpio and Virgo

A Virgo-Scorpion partnership can be very rewarding. Scorpio will be pleased with its adored Virgo since Virgo will appreciate Scorpio's accomplishments and will not be as critical as other signs. Scorpio's temper tantrums and feelings of jealousy will be handled well by Virgo, who has great analytical skills.

Sagittarius and Virgo

A partnership between Virgo and Sagittarius is nearly impossible to sustain. They are so diametrically opposed that they can barely get to know each other. A volatile, changing, unstable, and reckless individual will not be tolerated by Virgo. Sagittarius will take off rapidly.

Capricorn and Virgo

Virgo and Capricorn will make a terrific couple. Just be careful not to become stuck in a suffocating rut. Both Virgo and Capricorn struggle to actively appreciate life. They should assist one another in this regard. Everything else went swimmingly.

Aquarius and Virgo

A Virgo-Aquarius relationship can work, but only with a lot of effort. Aquarius is overly demanding for Virgo: Virgo limits Aquarius' freedom. Aquarius is too unpredictable and irresponsible for Virgo, who needs organization and control. This will take a lot of perseverance and commitment.

Pisces and Virgo

To make a partnership between Virgo and Pisces succeed, Virgo must learn to manage its criticism. Pisces is so sensitive that it cannot stand being called out for errors. In this situation, Pisces will retreat into their fantasy world, and Virgo will be removed from the connection. This is not a healthy dynamic, and it may be preferable for them to part ways. These concerns can be addressed if they both choose to pursue the relationship. Virgo and Pisces are opposites on the health axis, yet they can find common ground in that they both want to do good.

LOVE AND PASSION

Some Virgos are reserved when it comes to physically showing their affection.
They prefer things to be pure and transparent, and they need to locate the appropriate environment to unwind. If their partners give them the trust they need, they will become open and honest lovers.

They are extremely devoted and expect the same in return. Virgos, who despise deception, try to be honest and direct with everyone.

They are not overly sentimental, and their cynicism often hinders them from forming deep and lasting bonds.

Some people get taken advantage of by people who aren't honest and want to take advantage of their kindness.

Virgos struggle to prioritize their own needs, and it is up to others to ensure that the Virgo's needs are not routinely ignored.

They make an effort to share their interests and live an active and enjoyable life as a couple.

MARRIAGE

They are generally supportive of marriage, but they must first fix their financial position before committing.

They should, on the other hand, temper their predisposition to dispute and criticize if they do not want to weaken their partner's morale and jeopardize the relationship.

In general, they strive like no one else to keep their marriage alive, but if they consider the disagreements are insurmountable, they will not hesitate to end it.

Virgo women, who are extremely adaptable, understand how to balance work and family duties. They want order and efficiency in their marriage, so when they do their married tasks, they do them with the best attitude possible.

Virgo males are also dedicated workers who value their roles as parents and husbands. Furthermore, they are not sexist and would never allow their spouse to perform more than their fair part.

LIBRA

Constellation: Libra

Zodiac symbol: Balance Scales

Date: September 22 – October 22

Zodiac element: Air

Zodiac quality: Cardinal

Greatest Compatibility: Sagittarius and Aries

Sign ruler: Venus

Day: Friday

Color: Green and Pink

Birthstone: Opal

LIBRA TRAITS

- Despises being alone.
- Excellent aesthetics
- Avoids conflict
- Notices everything.
- Prone to fantasizing.
- Unable to make decisions.

WHAT IS THE PERSONALITY OF LIBRA?

Libras are tough to comprehend since they appear to be contradictory on the surface. They are both extroverted and introverted, strategic and impulsive, focused and intuitive. This diversity makes determining their genuine personality challenging. They are a full personality constellation. Libras differ based on who they are with.

Libras place a high priority on empathy. They are open to suggestions. They can act as mirrors for others. As a result, they have strong opinions about other people yet struggle to understand themselves.

They desire to be praised for their appeal rather than their talents. They want to be seen as the responsible figure who can bring order to the chaos around them. When they are unhappy, they experience extreme remorse and shame because they are aware that their sadness affects everyone around them.

WHAT ARE THE WEAKNESSES OF LIBRA?

Libras are people who are sympathetic and empathetic. They are willing to go above and beyond to assist others. They dislike confrontation and avoid it. These characteristics make individuals vulnerable to manipulation by others. Libras are also prone to being indecisive. They are so concerned with other people's emotions that they allow others to make decisions for them.

Libras place a high value on the views of others. Despite their inner fear of negative judgement, they find it difficult to avoid the spotlight. They require attention in order to feel validated.

Libras must realize that positivism is a form of delusion in and of itself. Libras are constrained by the limitations of their bodies and thoughts. They are constrained by the information provided by their five senses. They comprehend the flavor of the world but not its color.

They can't read the underlying micro-signals that others can. For them, the dark pit of the unknown is a terrible place, which is why they must claim to know everything. They have an aura of omniscience about them. However, they have no idea what they're talking about.

RELATIONSHIP COMPATIBILITY WITH LIBRA

Based only on their Sun signs, this is how Libra interacts with others. These are the compatibility interpretations for all 12 potential Libra combinations. This is a limited and insufficient method of determining compatibility.

However, Sun-sign compatibility remains the foundation for overall harmony in a relationship.

The general rule is that yin and yang do not get along. Yin complements yin, and yang complements yang. While yin and yang partnerships can be successful, they require more effort. Earth and water zodiac signs are both Yin. Yang is represented by the fire and air zodiac signs.

Aries and Libra

Libra and Aries can form a strong connection because their signs are complementary. The most difficult aspect will be Libra constantly reminding Aries that there is a better way to carry out this or that action. And Aries will always behave without regard for Libra's point of view. To avoid a breakup over this issue, Aries and Libra will need to appeal to their tolerance for each other's ways. Aries and Libra are on opposite sides of the same axis and must meet in the middle.

Taurus and Libra

A partnership between Libra and Taurus is not recommended since both members will feel destabilized by the other's contrasting attributes. Taurus represents stability, security, and solid ground; Libra represents change, mobility, and perpetual doubt. When Taurus requires confidence, Libra will cast doubt. Even so, if love is present, it is worth a shot.

Gemini and Libra.

Libra and Gemini are two seducers that can get along without getting in each other's way. It is a connection that can blossom if they learn to compliment one another's strengths. Gemini has what Libra requires: the flow of energy required to move in the pursuit of greater pleasure. Libra has what Gemini needs: a more ordered existence with a better mix of feeling, thinking, and acting.

Cancer and Libra

Libra and Cancer might have a harmonious partnership if they are both willing to open their emotions. Cancer and Libra both have a tendency to close down and hide their genuine sentiments. It is critical that they learn to converse openly about love and their relationship. They can only complement each other in this way. Otherwise, they will become increasingly apart.

Leo and Libra

Libra and Leo will get along great since they both contribute what the other needs to create balance in the union. Libra, who is an expert in the art of seduction, will constantly flatter Leo. Libra will have a trustworthy reference in Leo to help Libra acquire assurance in decision-making. Take this friendship seriously.

Virgo and Libra

It is difficult but not impossible to have a successful connection between Libra and Virgo. To ensure the success of their partnership, Virgo and Libra should try to reach a compromise. Virgo has to stop being so judgmental. Libra should try to curb its seductive tendencies because Virgo is extremely devoted and will not accept inappropriate behavior in the partnership.

Libra and Libra

A partnership between two Libras can be wonderful if they each strive to fulfil the other. That is, they must each relinquish enough control to ensure the connection's success. But if they can't, they'll end up competing with one another to see who is smarter and more intelligent.

Scorpio and Libra

Libra and Scorpio relationships can be happy and stable. Scorpio must control its possessive and jealous outbursts. Scorpio can give Libra a sense of safety that Libra doesn't have because Libra is always questioning things and trying to find a better balance.

Sagittarius and Libra

Libra and Sagittarius can benefit each other if they understand their opposing personalities. Sagittarius will benefit from Libra's tranquilly. Sagittarius will urge Libra to be more active and to complete projects faster. They can operate well together.

Capricorn and Libra

On an intellectual level, Libra and Capricorn get along fantastically. In that regard, they are excellent complements to one another and will make excellent companions. Capricorn, on the other hand, does not accept the ups and downs in Libra's life, which are caused by Libra's persistent hesitation over which action to take.

Aquarius and Libra

Libra and Aquarius will get along because they understand each other's basic needs. They will be able to sit down and discuss how to iron out any kinks. Libra appreciates and welcomes Aquarius' humorous thoughts. Libra's gentleness soothes Aquarius.

Pisces and Libra

It will be challenging to realize a partnership between Libra and Pisces. Pisces is too passionate and sensitive for Libra's analytical abilities. Libra is incredibly enticing, yet this will not suffice to provide Pisces' desire for emotional security. Furthermore, Pisces will feel increasingly insecure as a result of Libra's continual skepticism.

LOVE AND PASSION

Getting to know a Libra in depth can be an enlightening experience. They are excellent companions that strive to make the other feel at ease at all times.

They may gain anyone's affection through candlelit meals and intimate chats since they know how to listen and respect other people's merits, and they're quite alluring when offered to.

They are devoted to their lover and regard them as their soulmate. But they feel like they have to tell everyone everything, and they don't understand why others want to keep some things private.

They look to be quite confident in the sexual arena, but deep down they are shockingly sensitive and insecure, and they frequently wait until the circumstances are just right before taking the next step.

They are generous lovers who always consider their partner's requirements.

Many people have developed both their masculine and feminine sides, which allows them to connect with people of the opposite sex.

MARRIAGE

Making a lasting commitment takes patience for the hesitant Libra. They do, however, need to settle down and typically find contentment in marriage.

Because of their fear, their partner will need to confirm their love on a regular basis. Some even instigate confrontations for the sole purpose of testing the bond's strength. Otherwise, they frequently discover the balance they require in their marriage and work hard to maintain it.

Both men and women desire to start a family and give their best. They are extremely helpful to their partner and share all chores with them.

Libras have a keen sense of what others require. They make excellent travelling companions, regardless of distance.

SCORPIO

Constellation: Scorpio

Zodiac symbol: Scorpion

Date: October 22 – November 21

Zodiac element: Water

Zodiac quality: Fixed

Greatest Compatibility: Cancer and Taurus

Sign ruler: Mars, Pluto

Day: Tuesday

Color: Red

Birthstone: Topaz

SCORPIO TRAITS

- The primary feeling is betrayal.
- Okay with awkward silence.
- I'm not sure whether they're serious or joking.
- Eyes that gaze deep into your soul.

WHAT IS THE PERSONALITY OF SCORPIO?

Scorpio personality is a vast gulf of endless complexities (or at least how they project themselves). They are difficult to understand. They function as psychological trap doors.

They socialize through a double-sided mirror, constantly scanning and reading you while you can only see your own reflection. They would rather be the ones asking the questions. They use their perceptive scalpel to remove your skin and inventory your throbbing viscera. They prod and prod. They are aware of the minor details that make you tick. Your stress spots. The deceptive methods they use to obtain the answer they desire. They are acutely aware of power, its flows, and their place within it.

Scorpios, despite their propensity to be widely popular, have a highly lonely nature. They have a brutal outlook on life. Either eat or be eaten. Every human encounter involves the clash of opposing tremendous forces. A confrontation of wants and needs in which someone wins and someone loses. Their understanding of other people's interior systems offers them an advantage over their competitors. They understand how to pit people against each other. They can be forthcoming and elusive at the same time, depending on the situation. They are direct, but not without tact. They are deliberate in the information they reveal. They're not liars, and they don't spread lies, but they're masters at revealing some truths while hiding others behind heavy curtains.

WHAT ARE THE WEAKNESSES OF SCORPIO?

Scorpios are not terrified of most things that other people are afraid of. Not at all. Not suffering. Not even death. They face these realities head on. They understand that death is unavoidable. Instead of inciting terror, this information sharpens their enthusiasm for life. Scorpios live on the precipice of the unknown. That makes life more fascinating.

Scorpios are afraid of being exposed. The sensation of being recognized. Darkness can be a safe haven. Pain can be used to justify not trusting. When they open themselves, they give others authority over them, and Scorpios require control. In the face of an otherwise unpredictable environment, the illusion of control over themselves and others is the only thing that makes them feel secure.

RELATIONSHIP COMPATIBILITY WITH SCORPIO

Based only on their Sun signs, this is how Scorpio interacts with others. These are the compatibility interpretations for all 12 potential Scorpio combinations. This is a limited and insufficient method of determining compatibility.

However, Sun-sign compatibility remains the foundation for overall harmony in a relationship.

The general rule is that yin and yang do not get along. Yin complements yin, and yang complements yang. While yin and yang partnerships can be successful, they require more effort. Earth and water zodiac signs are both Yin. Yang is represented by the fire and air zodiac signs.

Aries and Scorpio

A partnership between Scorpio and Aries will quickly become difficult. Physical intimacy is the best common ground for these two to understand each other. They are, nonetheless, profoundly different in their ways of thinking and feeling. Scorpio desires complete control over the relationship and its partner, but Aries is unwilling to give it up. They are best suited to an occasional relationship.

Taurus and Scorpio

When Scorpio and Taurus join forces, the passion, sensuality, and eroticism will be spectacular. However, certain occurrences in ordinary life can generate speed bumps in this relationship. Scorpio is far too domineering. Taurus will not be able to withstand the emotional stings that Scorpio will undoubtedly deliver. Scorpio must accept Taurus as they are for this partnership to work.

Gemini and Scorpio

If Scorpio and Gemini meet together just for the purpose of mutual intimate pleasure, it can be a lovely experience for both of you. However, if you want to progress and create a relationship, you will have to walk a hard route together if you want it to succeed. Scorpio's jealousy and eruptions will destroy Gemini's chances of remaining by its side.

Cancer and Scorpio

Scorpio and Cancer relationships can be quite gratifying if Cancer is willing to let Scorpio take the lead. Cancer should not be concerned about its safety because Scorpio will provide them with whatever they require. In turn, Cancer will shower Scorpio with boundless affection and pleasure. Scorpio is less aggressive than usual in such a partnership.

Leo and Scorpio

Scorpio and Leo have an extremely tough time staying together in a love partnership. They may be fine for the odd connection, but they are not so good for long-term stability. To complement Scorpio, Leo must set aside its most prominent characteristics: forceful voice, decisiveness, independence, and control. Scorpio will never tolerate such traits in its companion.

Virgo and Scorpio

Scorpio and Virgo might have a really excellent partnership. Scorpio will be pleased with its adored Virgo since Virgo will appreciate Scorpio's accomplishments and will not be as critical as other signs. Scorpio's temper tantrums and feelings of jealousy will be handled well by Virgo, who has great analytical skills.

Libra and Scorpio

Scorpio and Libra relationships can be happy and stable. Scorpio must control its possessive and jealous outbursts. Scorpio can give Libra a sense of safety that Libra doesn't have because Libra is always questioning things and trying to find a better balance.

Scorpio and Scorpio

To maintain a stable relationship, two Scorpios must put in the effort on a daily basis. Scorpios are fiery, jealous, and domineering. They should learn to regulate those traits so that their relationship does not suffer. On a bodily level, both Scorpios will understand each other completely. They will keep their passionate but volatile romance going.

Sagittarius and Scorpio

Scorpio and Sagittarius will initially enjoy their partnership to the fullest: adventures, sensuality, passion, and pleasure. But if Scorpio and Sagittarius want to live together, they will have to work together to solve the problems that have come up because of their major clash: Scorpio's possessiveness and jealousy will clash with Sagittarius' desire for independence and growth.

Capricorn and Scorpio

Scorpio and Capricorn might be a good fit. Scorpio's intuition combines with Capricorn's depth of analysis, and they will have many wonderful times learning new things about themselves and the world around them. They should be careful not to separate themselves from the rest of the world too much.

Aquarius and Scorpio

A partnership between Scorpio and Aquarius is conceivable, but it will require a great deal of tolerance on both sides. Scorpio is too rigid and regimented to grasp Aquarius' yearning for freedom and movement. Aquarius will close down or decide to leave the partnership if Scorpio does not lessen its demands.

Pisces and Scorpio

Scorpio and Pisces have a great partnership because they both feel understood and emotionally contained. Both Pisces and Scorpio prioritize the emotional and spiritual sides of life, and they understand each other brilliantly in this regard. Scorpio's explosive instincts will be tempered by Pisces' tenderness.

LOVE AND PASSION

A fulfilling love life is quite important to most Scorpios. They must express their most private feelings. Their strong sexual appeal makes it quite easy for them to locate mates.

When they choose someone, they want complete dedication, they refuse to accept "no" for an answer, and when they are rejected, they reveal their most obsessive side.

Making love is Scorpio's deepest form of expression and a crucial component in all relationships. They have a lot of fun with their partner and have a busy social life, but without proper sexual commitment, the relationship is doomed to fail.

They make excellent lovers, frequently removing their partner's inhibitions.

Those around them, on the other hand, must have high psychological resistance to offset their constant mood fluctuations. Those who do well will gain a wealth of experience that few others can match.

MARRIAGE

Scorpios have a difficult time finding love. They want to experience everything and are accustomed to having multiple relationships at the same time. They are unlikely to be unfaithful once married. They become devoted and loving lovers who are always willing to help their mate.

When they are insecure, they experience envy and need time to reestablish trust in the other person.

They are not afraid to put all of their financial, physical, and emotional resources at the disposal of their partner and strive hard to keep their partnership together. The ties they form become increasingly strong over time.

Scorpio wives are ambitious and intellectual, with the energy to balance their family and work responsibilities.

Scorpio men are powerful and devoted, although sometimes they go through long periods of silence.

SAGITTARIUS

Constellation: Sagittarius
Zodiac symbol: Archer
Date: November 21 – December 21
Zodiac element: Fire
Zodiac quality: Mutable
Greatest Compatibility: Aries and Gemini
Sign ruler: Jupiter
Day: Thursday
Color: Blue
Birthstone: Turquoise

SAGITTARIUS TRAITS
- There is no inner voice. Says everything.
- Forms opinions based solely on emotion.
- Obsessed with personal development.
- Their truth is wielded like a blunt weapon.
- The party's friendliest guest.

WHAT IS THE PERSONALITY OF SAGITTARIUS?

Sagittarius is the epitome of an empiricist. They will constantly prioritize ideals over feelings and will frequently doubt their identity. They bounce around from job to job, philosophy to philosophy, and belief to belief. They are human condition explorers who are unafraid of change. Sagittarians consider the world to be their playground. They enjoy venturing into the unknown. They want to know how the world works.

Sagittarians are free of any earthly attachments as they embark on an unending quest to find the entirety of the universe within themselves. They are reckless in their pursuit of their desires, and they frequently end up doing and experiencing things that challenge conventional notions of what is possible.

Sagittarius is an adventurer. They are both daring adventurers and cynical critics. They recognize that information comes in two varieties: shallow, disposable knowledge from outside sources and knowledge that comes from within. Sagittarius understands that while exterior knowledge is easily obtained, inside knowledge is immensely deeper and more powerful. They're on a mission to explore the depths of the universe within the human mind. They do this not to demonstrate that they have all the answers, but because they understand that the journey is the destination.

WHAT ARE THE WEAKNESSES OF SAGITTARIUS?

Sagittarius is a warrior-poet sign. They each have a gun in one hand and a book in the other. They represent a never-ending quest for freedom. They are one of the zodiac's most magnanimous and worldly signs. Their unbridled optimism spreads like wildfire. It can be difficult for them to concentrate, but once they set their sights on anything, they will go to any lengths to attain it. Their capacity to overcome seemingly overwhelming obstacles demonstrates their flexible strength.

Sagittarians are not afraid to take risks. They are continuously seeking the next big breakthrough and rarely look back. This proclivity to abandon projects before they even begin sometimes leaves people feeling as if they will never get anything done. They can become so engrossed in a million different projects that they fail to complete any of them.

RELATIONSHIP COMPATIBILITY WITH SAGITTARIUS

Based only on their Sun signs, this is how Sagittarius interacts with others. These are the compatibility interpretations for all 12 potential Sagittarius combinations. This is a limited and insufficient method of determining compatibility.

However, Sun-sign compatibility remains the foundation for overall harmony in a relationship.

The general rule is that yin and yang do not get along. Yin complements yin, and yang complements yang. While yin and yang partnerships can be successful, they require more effort. Earth and water zodiac signs are both Yin. Yang is represented by the fire and air zodiac signs.

Aries and Sagittarius

Sagittarius and Aries can have a wonderful partnership. Sagittarius will assist Aries in learning how to let go of the continual obligations and responsibilities that drag it down. In turn, Aries will assist Sagittarius in channeling its life with increased responsibility. They will have a long-lasting connection if they proceed slowly.

Taurus and Sagittarius

Sagittarius and Taurus' relationship can be summed up in five words. Difficult, difficult, and way harder. Taurus and Sagittarius have extremely distinct requirements. Perhaps they will understand each other as they grow older and develop in life. However, Taurus and Sagittarius will struggle to figure out how to move the relationship forward while remaining comfortable with each other and their individual lives during their younger years. Sagittarius does not comprehend Taurus' philosophy, "Slowly but steadily."

Gemini and Sagittarius

A partnership between Sagittarius and Gemini might be exciting if they are conscious that developing a lasting union requires certain sacrifices. Gemini and Sagittarius are both very gregarious, mobile, restless, and unstable signs. One of them should lead by example by becoming more solid. If they wish to avoid envy and friction, they must focus on their tendency to entice and dominate.

Cancer and Sagittarius

A relationship between Sagittarius and Cancer is not advised, especially for Cancer, who will feel more uneasy than ever. Sagittarius is not a sign that can always provide emotional or material assistance to a relationship. On the contrary, Sagittarius' life is frequently marked by instability, if not carelessness. This partnership can be tried, but Cancer must learn to be more self-sufficient.

Leo and Sagittarius

Sagittarius and Leo will get along great when it comes to having fun and socializing. The issue may develop when Leo accuses Sagittarius of being unstable in life, of constantly changing paths without forethought, and of their desire for unending adventures. When confronted with such assertions, Sagittarius tends to flee. The remedy would be to get down and discuss things out so that a good relationship is not ruined.

Virgo and Sagittarius

A partnership between Sagittarius and Virgo is nearly impossible to sustain. They are so diametrically opposed that they can barely get to know each other. A volatile, changing, unstable, and reckless individual will not be tolerated by Virgo. Sagittarius will take off rapidly.

Libra and Sagittarius

If Sagittarius and Libra can comprehend their opposing personalities, they will be able to aid each other. Sagittarius will benefit from Libra's tranquilly. Sagittarius will urge Libra to be more active and to complete projects faster. They can operate well together.

Scorpio and Sagittarius

Sagittarius and Scorpio will initially enjoy their partnership to the fullest: adventures, sensuality, passion, and pleasure. But if Scorpio and Sagittarius want to live together, they will have to work together to solve the problems that have come up because of their major clash: Scorpio's possessiveness and jealousy will clash with Sagittarius' desire for independence and growth.

Sagittarius and Sagittarius

A Sagittarius and a Sagittarius will have a wonderful relationship, but who will handle the responsibilities? This partnership will be defined by travel, adventure, constant movement, fun, and expansion. They can have a relationship worth sustaining if they can learn to complete each other, that is, fill the urge to keep their home in order and meet their commitments.

Capricorn and Sagittarius

Capricorn will be captivated by Sagittarius at the start of the relationship because of the free and happy way in which Sagittarius lives their life. Capricorn will assist Sagittarius with everyday planning and material support. However, it will take a lot of effort to keep the relationship going in the long run without harshly condemning each other's differences along the road.

Aquarius and Sagittarius

The basic demands of Sagittarius and Aquarius are freedom, independence, social engagement, and making new acquaintances. Even with their differences, these two will feel understood. Sagittarius and Aquarius will be able to establish a long-lasting and stable relationship.

Pisces and Sagittarius

Sagittarius and Pisces are compatible and can build a committed and enjoyable partnership. Pisces will need to learn not to expect Sagittarius to continually demonstrate their devotion. Sagittarius must learn to prioritize Pisces' demands so that Pisces does not become agitated. In terms of the rest, this is a relationship with a promising future.

LOVE AND PASSION

Sagittarians are enthusiastic and affectionate, and they do not hesitate to take the initiative because flirting is in their nature. Flirting is as natural to them as making others laugh or inviting others to a drink or supper.
Because their pleasure of living is contagious, many people find their company invigorating.

It usually doesn't take long for them to seal their attraction to a person in bed. They are quite open to physical contact, and the majority of them are exciting and unique lovers.
Sometimes, relationships that are too intense suffocate them because they need space to relax and be themselves.
They don't enjoy being tied down, and while they wait for the proper moment to commit, they prefer to stay away.
They get tired of doing the same things over and over, so they try to hang out with passionate people who are both mentally and physically active.

MARRIAGE

Sagittarius desires for marriage to always include an element of discovery and adventure. When it vanishes, complications occur.

They frequently remain faithful to their lover once they have taken their vows. They have entire faith in their partner and encourage them to pursue a passion. Jealousy isn't one of their problems.

Sagittarians are incredibly enterprising, yet they frequently lack the practical sense required to carry out their many initiatives. They eventually vent their rage on their self-sacrificing comrades.

When they mature, they learn to channel their energy and relax, and living with them becomes an entirely new experience.

The Sagittarius woman desires children and travels with them whenever possible. The Sagittarius woman will not give up her independence.

The Sagittarius man offers a lot of energy to the relationship, and as long as they stay true to themselves, their marriage will be happy.

CAPRICORN

Constellation: Capricorn

Zodiac symbol: Sea Goat

Date: December 21 – January 19

Zodiac element: Earth

Zodiac quality: Cardinal

Greatest Compatibility: Cancer and Taurus

Sign ruler: Saturn

Day: Saturday

Color: Black and Brown

Birthstone: Garnet

CAPRICORN TRAITS

- Matures early.
- The responsible buddy.
- Driven by motivation
- It takes time to warm up to someone.
- Any emotion that gets in the way of accomplishment is suppressed.

WHAT IS THE PERSONALITY OF CAPRICORN?

Capricorns are disciplined individuals. The wringing of hands, the continual reminders, the strict framework, the ever-increasing ambitions, the never-ending tide of self-criticism They are the epitome of perfectionists. They can become so engrossed in their own internal monologue that it becomes tough to convince them to turn away. Capricorns are frequently referred to as "workaholics."

They are really practical. They are rule-followers with a strong moral compass. It is instilled in them from an early age that their entire feeling of worth and significance is reliant on their capacity to burrow down and force their way to the finish line. This makes them achievement junkies. Their will to succeed reflects their fear of failing. Capricorns experience the most stress when they challenge their own authority. Capricorns are most steady when they are in positions of power. When they are forced to adhere to someone else's agenda, they can become a little out of control.

Capricorns are collectors of responsibilities. And they always seem to take on everything. Capricorns like to be the ones to solve all problems. Their inherent state is one of responsibility. They have a "can-do" mentality. They are both martyrs and heroes. They serve as both guardians and judges. The captains of the team. The supreme commander. The commander-in-chief. The boss. Even when they lead the charge, Capricorns can feel the most alone in the world. They want to be entirely self-sufficient and are afraid to rely on others.

WHAT ARE THE WEAKNESSES OF CAPRICORN?

Capricorns are not obsessed by the desire for attention, but they are not immune to it either. Simply put, they do not engage in attention-seeking conduct. They don't want to be noticed for their appearance, style, or ingenuity. They do not seek to be admired, but rather to be respected. They do not wish to be the focus of attention. Instead, they appear to be trying to prove their own abilities to themselves.

Capricorns are always competing against themselves. They do, however, seek recognition. Not adoration, but only praise. Praise is simply recognizing a job well done. A compliment is a pat on the back. This serves as validation for their general sense of ineptitude and inferiority. They plough through difficulties while wearing blinders until they achieve victory.

RELATIONSHIP COMPATIBILITY WITH CAPRICORN

Based only on their Sun signs, this is how Capricorn interacts with others. These are the compatibility interpretations for all 12 potential Capricorn combinations. This is a limited and insufficient method of determining compatibility.

However, Sun-sign compatibility remains the foundation for overall harmony in a relationship.

The general rule is that yin and yang do not get along. Yin complements yin, and yang complements yang. While yin and yang partnerships can be successful, they require more effort. Earth and water zodiac signs are both Yin. Yang is represented by the fire and air zodiac signs.

Aries and Capricorn

Capricorn and Aries have an extremely challenging relationship. Their personalities are too dissimilar to complement one another harmoniously. Aries acts on impulse without forethought, whereas Capricorn meticulously plans before taking action. Capricorn's continual criticism will not be tolerated by Aries. Capricorn's tone is too authoritative for Aries. Capricorn, on the other hand, will have a tough time supporting Aries' style of life, which Capricorn regards as silly.

Taurus and Capricorn

Capricorn and Taurus are two earth signs that work really well together. They will enjoy this relationship because they will do it their way: step by step, planning each movement, perfecting what works, celebrating with a movie at home, and triumphantly reaching the peak. Everything is in their favor for a long-term partnership.

Gemini and Capricorn

Capricorn and Gemini were not meant to be together. Capricorns will spend their lives criticizing Gemini for its lack of concentration and for changing its mind so frequently. Capricorn's mental rigidity, on the other hand, will swiftly bore Gemini. Gemini will become impatient with the fact that it finds no way to really enjoy life with such a mate. It may work with hard work and a lot of love.

Cancer and Capricorn

Capricorn and Cancer can have a wonderful partnership. In terms of safety and material well-being, Capricorn has a lot to give Cancer. Cancer will show Capricorn that life is more than just labor and mental fields: Cancer will teach Capricorn to appreciate life in ways Capricorn has never dreamed. There are no major issues with this connection.

Leo and Capricorn

A connection between Capricorn and Leo will expose one another's selfishness. They each seek complete control over everything around them. They are both determined to be the first in the relationship. They each believe they have the finest solutions to various problems. Finally, Leo and Capricorn will simply compete and argue about who has the upper hand in the relationship.

Virgo and Capricorn

Capricorn and Virgo will make a terrific couple. Just be careful not to become stuck in a suffocating rut. Both Virgo and Capricorn struggle to actively appreciate life. They should assist one another in this regard. Everything else went swimmingly.

Libra and Capricorn

On an intellectual level, Capricorn and Libra complement each other beautifully. In that regard, they are excellent complements to one another and will make excellent companions. Capricorn, on the other hand, does not accept the ups and downs in Libra's life, which are caused by Libra's persistent hesitation over which action to take.

Scorpio and Capricorn

Capricorn and Scorpio are compatible signs. Scorpio's intuition combines with Capricorn's depth of analysis, and they will have many wonderful times learning new things about themselves and the world around them. They should be careful not to separate themselves from the rest of the world too much.

Sagittarius and Capricorn

Capricorn will be captivated by Sagittarius at the start of the relationship because of the free and happy way in which Sagittarius lives their life. Capricorn will assist Sagittarius with everyday planning and material support. However, it will take a lot of effort to keep the relationship going in the long run without harshly condemning each other's differences along the road.

Capricorn and Capricorn

Two Capricorns in a relationship will completely understand each other. The dangers are: wanting to compete for first position in the relationship, forming an extremely structured relationship, being highly critical of each other in pursuit of perfectionism, and demonstrating excessive stubbornness.

Aquarius and Capricorn

Capricorn and Aquarius will be fascinated by each other at first, but they will not find a safe refuge in their partnership. Capricorn and Aquarius have quite different personalities. They will clash if one expects the other to act in a way that is antithetical to their nature. Maybe they'll make it with a lot of love.

Pisces and Capricorn

Capricorn will provide an incredible world for Pisces since Capricorn will take care of fixing any difficulties, anticipating potential conflicts, and maintaining the home from the start. Pisces will believe that it has discovered the love of its life and will lavishly pamper and caress Capricorn. Pisces, on the other hand, must learn to bear Capricorn's regular bouts of emotional coldness.

LOVE AND PASSION

When it comes to relationships, some Capricorns are fairly traditional. Before asking someone out, these people prefer to be professionally acquainted. If they really like someone, they will ask them to a nice restaurant for supper to create the best impression.

In general, they don't like to get sexually involved unless they have a relationship that is fairly stable and safe. Some Capricorns are really rigid about this. They can only shed their inhibitions with a gentle and delicate companion and become passionate and impulsive lovers when they trust the other person.

Capricorns are prone to becoming petty and even cruel. Those who enjoy an active social life may struggle to adjust to Capricorn's seriousness. They are, on the other hand, exceedingly devoted and consistent, and are not prone to extramarital affairs. They are highly caring when they feel loved.

MARRIAGE

Capricorns take marriage obligations very seriously. They feel that marriage is sacred. When they commit, they do so fully aware that they intend for it to be permanent.

Because Capricorns are orderly, household tasks should be kept to a minimum. They always have money set aside for emergencies. In general, a Capricorn's spouse will not have to worry about money.

A Capricorn's profession might be a source of contention because they can occasionally prioritize it over their personal life. They are so focused on their work in order to be successful that they sometimes neglect their spouse and children. They must make a sincere attempt to balance work, marriage, and family.

Capricorn women manage to balance the demands of their work, children, and spouse because of their maternal instinct. In their more traditional roles, Capricorn males may tend to compartmentalize work, marriage, and family. They are compassionate and caring at home when the timing is right.

AQUARIUS

Constellation: Aquarius

Zodiac symbol: Water-Bearer

Date: January 20 – February 19

Zodiac element: Air

Zodiac quality: Fixed

Greatest Compatibility: Sagittarius and Leo

Sign ruler: Uranus and Saturn

Day: Saturday

Color: Silver and Light blue

Birthstone: Amethyst

AQUARIUS TRAITS

- Intentionally esoteric.
- Does not 'do' emotions, only concepts.
- Thinks conspiracy theories are true
- Loves humanity more than individuals.
- Feels like a stranger all the time
- Personal liberty is extremely important.

WHAT IS THE PERSONALITY OF AQUARIUS?

Aquarians are the classic outsiders. This doesn't mean they like to be alone. In fact, they do best in big groups, where they can charm you with their strange senses of humor, intrigue you with interesting facts about the history of plastic straws, or persuade you to join their reading group. They often make themselves feel alone because they are so quick to disagree, not because they don't know how to get along with others. They try to act strange. Aquarians hang grapefruit peels on the wall and call it art. They act like they like noise music and use SAT words in their inner monologues.

For them, "intelligence" means being able to come up with the most unpopular opinion possible. If they were white sheep, they would dye their wool black to make a point. They are destined to live in a way that goes against the rest of the world. In fact, they create new worlds. In their heads, there is a whole universe, and this universe has its own logic that doesn't match up with reality. They don't tell lies. They are idealists. They don't feel cold. They make sense. For them, feelings are nothing more than holes in their idealistic bodies. Why give in to being sensitive when there is so much to learn, so many problems to solve, and so many worlds to make up?

WHAT ARE THE WEAKNESSES OF AQUARIUS?

They sometimes ask, "Why can't I be normal?" but the truth is that they find normal to be boring, and their self-worth depends on how interesting they are. They don't want to be known. They want to avoid being pinned down. Definitions are binding little rules that other people use to limit their movement, and they must fight against anything that limits their freedom to drift. Between definitions, between the individual and the common, and between themselves and the rest of humanity. The hardest thing for Aquarians is to find a balance between their need for community and their need to be completely alone.

Aquarians always try out new things. They treat their whole lives as one big science experiment, using the element of surprise to see how people react and build theories about how people work. They are walking pieces of abstract art that shatter traditional ways of thinking because they don't care about rules. They are willing to die for "humanity," and all they want is "freedom."

RELATIONSHIP COMPATIBILITY WITH AQUARIUS

Based only on their Sun signs, this is how Aquarius interacts with others. These are the compatibility interpretations for all 12 potential Aquarius combinations. This is a limited and insufficient method of determining compatibility.

However, Sun-sign compatibility remains the foundation for overall harmony in a relationship.

The general rule is that yin and yang do not get along. Yin complements yin, and yang complements yang. While yin and yang partnerships can be successful, they require more effort. Earth and water zodiac signs are both Yin. Yang is represented by the fire and air zodiac signs.

Aries and Aquarius

A connection between Aquarius and Aries might be fruitful. Both members must be patient. Both Aries and Aquarius crave freedom and independence. They will understand each other better as a result of this. Aries will get into trouble because they act quickly and without thinking. Aquarius, on the other hand, needs more time and security before they do anything.

Taurus and Aquarius

A connection between Aquarius and Taurus can bear fruit with a lot of hard work and a lot of patience. Their personalities clash because Aquarius values freedom and independence, while Taurus values home and relationships. But if they each give a little, they might realize that there are moments when each of them needs to be alone, without meaning that they have ceased loving one another.

Gemini and Aquarius

Aquarius and Gemini have strong compatibility. They will understand each other almost completely. They are both gregarious and like spending time with their pals. When Aquarius pays attention to others, Gemini may feel forgotten at times, but this will not jeopardize the connection. The emphasis will be on creativity.

Cancer and Aquarius

A link between Aquarius and Cancer is unlikely. Cancer's incessant requests for love will not be tolerated by Aquarius' free and independent attitude. Aquarius will be unable to reassure the partner, nor will he or she be able to provide safety and security in the relationship. Cancer's eruptions will be immediately noted. Aquarius will seek refuge with its closest companions.

Leo and Aquarius

A partnership between Aquarius and Leo can be tough to establish if Aquarius does not learn how to manage Leo with flattery from the start. Aquarius is not prone to such a technique. Instead of wasting time persuading their Leo partner that they are the best in the universe, Aquarius is engaged in producing and innovating. Aquarius' emotional indifference will be difficult for Leo to tolerate.

Virgo and Aquarius

Aquarius and Virgo can work, but only with a lot of effort. Aquarius is overly demanding for Virgo: Virgo limits Aquarius' freedom. Aquarius is too unpredictable and irresponsible for Virgo, who needs organization and control. This will take a lot of perseverance and commitment.

Libra and Aquarius

Aquarius and Libra will get along because they understand each other's basic needs. They will be able to sit down and discuss how to iron out any kinks. Libra appreciates and welcomes Aquarius' humorous thoughts. Libra's gentleness soothes Aquarius.

Scorpio and Aquarius

A partnership between Aquarius and Scorpio is conceivable, but it will require a great deal of tolerance on both sides. Scorpio is too rigid and regimented to grasp Aquarius' yearning for freedom and movement. Aquarius will close down or decide to leave the partnership if Scorpio does not lessen its demands.

Sagittarius and Aquarius

Aquarius and Sagittarius share the fundamental demands of freedom, independence, social contact, and making new friends. Even with their differences, these two will feel understood. Sagittarius and Aquarius will be able to establish a long-lasting and stable relationship.

Capricorn and Aquarius

Aquarius and Capricorn will initially intrigue each other, but they will not find a secure refuge in their partnership. Capricorn and Aquarius have quite different personalities. They will clash if one expects the other to act in a way that is antithetical to their nature. Maybe they'll make it with a lot of love.

Aquarius and Aquarius

Aquarius and Aquarius can form a completely strong and long-lasting relationship. Their similar personalities assist them in understanding their own basic wants. They must be careful not to abuse their overwhelming need for independence, lest they grow so distant from one another that they each create their own world.

Pisces and Aquarius

Aquarius and Pisces can enjoy a serious and pleasurable relationship if they respect each other's differences from the start. Tolerance is necessary. While Pisces must appreciate Aquarius' urge to be alone , Aquarius must make an attempt to be more emotionally demonstrative.

LOVE AND PASSION

Seductive Aquarians are drawn to individuals who stand out. Above all, they seek people with whom they get along well. When they are interested in someone, they are able to conceal their feelings and appear remote and unapproachable. They'll only reveal their cards if the other person withdraws in disinterest.

They can be very cold and have trouble showing how they feel, but they are experts at keeping their feelings in check, which many people find attractive.

Aquarians enjoy exchanging ideas and their perspectives on physical connection are as unique as they are unpredictable. However, if the connection gets too engrossing, the physical side loses its appeal.

You can't ask an Aquarius to tell you everything about their life, but if you give them the time they need, they will show you that they are smart, interesting, and fun. Assuming they find the correct mate, they learn to show themselves as they are over time and form profound attachments.

MARRIAGE

When Aquarians get over their fears and get married, they are very loyal and have a lot of different strengths. They require some independence as well as a partner who supports and loves them without putting too much pressure on them.

They bring their varied hobbies, as well as a vast list of friends, to the marriage. They want to keep their social calendar busy because life with just one person is never enough for them. They do not believe in materialism. Aquarians, whatever of gender, expect their spouse to assist them with housework.

In principle, they support doing their share to help out at home, but in practice, spending too much time at home overwhelms them.

PISCES

Constellation: Pisces

Zodiac symbol: Fish

Date: February 19 – March 20

Zodiac element: Water

Zodiac quality: Mutable

Greatest Compatibility: Taurus and Virgo

Sign ruler: Jupiter and Neptune

Day: Thursday

Color: Lilac, Purple, Violet and Sea Green

Birthstone: Aquamarine

PISCES TRAITS

*   Can be young and old at the same time.
*   Considers everything to be a sign.
*   Not sure if they dreamed it or it actually happened.
*   Extremely romantic
*   Prone to fantasizing.
*   Has no limits.

WHAT IS THE PERSONALITY OF PISCES?

It can be hard to describe a Pisces's personality because they tend to avoid standing out. Their conduct varies greatly depending on who they are around. Pisces are basically porous membranes that let things pass through them pensively. They are cognitive sea sponges. They are limitless. They tend to have a lot of different personalities, so it's difficult to figure out who they are.

Most Piscean characteristics (dreaminess, emotionality, imagination) are internal processes that are difficult to detect from the outside. This is because Pisces is an inward-looking sign. They are not self-absorbed, but they are self-absorbed.

A Pisces ultimately wishes to dissolve. To free themselves from their bodies and spread love to everything they touch. To live in the thin layer that's just above the material but not quite there. To live their lives as though they were love poems. To realize that reality and fantasy live next to each other on the same endless plane.

WHAT ARE THE WEAKNESSES OF PISCES?

The real weakness of Pisces is that they often cause their own trouble. They're a little obsessed with sorrow. Pisces want to feel everything deeply, and there is a tragic aspect to grief that Pisces truly enjoy. They would rather stew in a deep pit of despair than not feel anything at all. Pisces sometimes put themselves in self-defeating situations because they are looking for heart-wrenching emotional experiences. They then try to make it look like they were unwittingly hurt.

RELATIONSHIP COMPATIBILITY WITH PISCES

Based only on their Sun signs, this is how Pisces interacts with others. These are the compatibility interpretations for all 12 potential Pisces combinations. This is a limited and insufficient method of determining compatibility.

However, Sun-sign compatibility remains the foundation for overall harmony in a relationship.

The general rule is that yin and yang do not get along. Yin complements yin, and yang complements yang. While yin and yang partnerships can be successful, they require more effort. Earth and water zodiac signs are both Yin. Yang is represented by the fire and air zodiac signs.

Aries and Pisces

Pisces is too introverted and ethereal for Aries, who is a sign of activity and meets life without hesitation. Aries represents a risk that Pisces does not believe they are willing to assume. Pisces requires stability and peace in order to develop and flourish. These are traits that Aries almost never possesses. To ensure the success of this partnership, Aries must control their impulses.

Taurus and Pisces

Although both Pisces and Taurus are yin, this relationship is tough to establish. In order to comprehend their various natures, they must invest a great deal of effort. Taurus is basically a physical being, and its life is centered around the physical. In contrast, Pisces is a spiritual being. Although Pisces requires the tangible, it is mostly concerned with transcending it. If they can learn to complement one another, they will both feel secure.

Gemini and Pisces

Pisces and Gemini are less likely to settle down together than to break up. Gemini's volatility and unpredictability will cause Pisces to feel uncomfortable. Gemini cannot give Pisces the traits of security and containment, even if it wanted to. Pisces will complain about Gemini's inattention and propensity to constantly escape the house. Regarding fidelity, it is preferable to keep quiet.

Cancer and Pisces

Pisces and Cancer might develop a very strong emotional bond. Who will be responsible for their finances and practical matters? Both parties are willing to run the household, but neither will want to assume exclusive financial responsibility or obligations. The success of this connection will rely on how this ground is managed.

Leo and Pisces

Pisces and Leo are capable of forming an exceptional partnership that should not be taken for granted. This is a yin-yang relationship, and they will need to address the seeming contradictions (such as that Leo focuses on the self while Pisces focuses on others). However, they have everything necessary to meet both of their requirements. Leo possesses enormous strength and will provide Pisces with the necessary security and safety. Pisces will shower Leo with accolades, praise, tenderness, and thanks.

Virgo and Pisces

For a partnership between Pisces and Virgo to be successful, Virgo must learn to control its critique nature. Pisces is so sensitive that it cannot tolerate being criticized for errors. In this instance, Pisces will retreat into their fantasy world, and Virgo will be excluded from the connection. This is an unhealthy situation, and it may be simpler for them to split. If both parties choose to continue the relationship, these concerns can be resolved. Virgo and Pisces are at opposite extremes of the health axis, yet they might find common ground in their desire to do good.

Libra and Pisces

A relationship between Pisces and Libra will be challenging to achieve. Pisces is too emotional and sensitive for Libra's analytical abilities. The alluring nature of Libra is insufficient to satisfy Pisces' yearning for emotional security. In addition, Libra's persistent uncertainty will increase Pisces's sense of insecurity.

Scorpio and Pisces

Both Pisces and Scorpio feel emotionally confined and understood in a relationship between them. Both Pisces and Scorpio place a high value on the emotional and spiritual sides of life, which they fully comprehend. Scorpio's explosive urges are subdued by Pisces' gentleness.

Sagittarius and Pisces

Pisces and Sagittarius can build a committed and enjoyable partnership that is mutually beneficial. Pisces will need to learn not to require Sagittarius to always exhibit their devotion excessively. So that Pisces doesn't feel concerned, Sagittarius will have to learn to prioritize Pisces' demands. As for the rest, this connection has a positive outlook.

Capricorn and Pisces

Capricorn will provide Pisces with an incredible world because, from the outset, Capricorn will solve all problems, anticipate potential disputes, and maintain the home. Pisces will believe it has discovered the love of its life and will lavish Capricorn with extravagant gifts and passionate kisses. However, Pisces must learn to endure Capricorn's frequent emotional iciness.

Aquarius and Pisces

Pisces and Aquarius can create a committed and pleasurable relationship if they respect one another's differences from the start. Tolerance is necessary. Pisces needs to understand that Aquarius needs to be alone, and Aquarius needs to try to show more emotion.

Pisces and Pisces

In a relationship, two Pisces will have a mystical knowledge of each other's emotions. Affectionate displays will be commonplace between the two. However, disputes can emerge when each party expects the other to provide protection. One of them must be accountable for their financial responsibilities and material security.

LOVE AND PASSION

Every time a Pisces starts a new relationship, they forget about the ones that didn't work out and give it their all. For them, getting to know their partner on a profound level is a gradual but intriguing process that culminates in total togetherness. They enjoy surrounding themselves with an aura of sensuality and sophistication, and they never stop to impress their significant other with thoughtful gifts and delectable feasts.

Those in a relationship with a Pisces become a part of the Pisces' inner circle. They feel extremely special and are showered with attention.

Pisces creates an emotional bond by fusing their bodies with those of their loved ones. They view sexual activity as a sublime experience. Their love is as gentle and consistent as a gentle drizzle. Physical contact allows for a deepening of their relationship.

They quickly develop dependence on their partner, which can occasionally result in a mismatch. They want the other person to be fully devoted and for both of them to gain emotionally from the exchange. A secure partnership provides them with confidence and contentment.

MARRIAGE

All Pisces desire to share their lives with their ideal partner. Some of them keep their honeymoon going for as long as they can after they get married. Their love and commitment make their marriage a magical experience.

For others, though, marriage is a huge letdown because it doesn't turn out the way they thought it would. Because they can't solve the problems that every couple has, they give up at the first sign of trouble. This puts their relationship in danger. Pisces would be better off if they gave up their dreams and started living in the real world.

Women usually put the needs of their partners ahead of their own. They are loving mothers who put their families before themselves.

Men, on the other hand, are sentimental, yet they are always willing to lend a helping hand and have plenty to offer their spouse and children.

GENERAL ASTROLOGY FOR 2023

Let's now look at the general astrology of 2023. This is significant transits that affect everyone, from a holistic perspective.

THE YEAR OF THE WATER RABBIT 2023.

According to the horoscope for 2023, the Year of the Water Rabbit will be a time of calm and peace. This will come after a time ruled by the Tiger that was full of events and changes. Since it's a calm year with a slow pace, this New Year 2023, which is ruled by the Rabbit, will be about rest, peace, and intellectual challenges. So, it's time for each person and the whole world to heal old wounds, find inner balance again, and make plans for the future. It is critical to exercise caution in the face of potential affronts while being clear and awake in the face of one's own urgent urges. In 2023, people who want to move up in society by having their worth recognized will have to know how to work the gears of rhetoric and human psychology if they want their existential dreams to come true.

In 2023, there is a great danger that repressed difficulties will resurface suddenly, which, despite the anguish, will luckily provide the opportunity to address them once and for all. It is therefore prudent to avoid excessive imagination and to refrain from focusing solely on sorrow. Also, avoid being swayed by inadequate facts or a defeatist personal opinion, which could result in the loss of valuable time in important situations.

Is the year 2023 a lucky one? According to the Zodiac, 2023 is a better year for men and women born in the Year of the Rabbit, Year of the Goat, Year of the Pig (Boar), and Year of the Rat.

The year 2023 is ideal for giving birth. It is the year of the Water Rabbit. In astrology, water is a sign of peace and long life, and the Rabbit represents vigilance, wit, caution, deftness, and self-protection. People born in the Water Rabbit year are expected to have good fortune and a serene mind throughout their life.

2023 ASTROLOGY PREDICTIONS

Mercury goes retrograde in Capricorn from January 1 to January 18, which marks the beginning of the new year. Leadership at the global and national levels will be hesitant to make decisions, will seek clarification, and will generally appear to be unsure of how to proceed.

Midway through February, aggressive action that may be severe and boost national egos is likely to take over. Even while the overall trend is improving, the economy will remain perplexing and uncertain through the second quarter. This is mostly caused by widespread concern about economic and global conditions, which fluctuates with optimism.

From mid-July onward, the trends will be clearer, and people will have more confidence in the future. From mid-June until the end of September, we should avoid initiating attacks or making aggressive movements against another person, corporate organization, or country. During this time, the defendant, not the aggressor, will win any conflict, no matter how large or "correct" the assailant is.

The last three months of 2023 will be a time for physical and emotional healing on a personal and global scale, predicts the horoscope.

The transit of Pluto into Aquarius from March 24th to June 11th is the year's most notable and timely event. This Plutonian stay will erode milestones, accomplishments, and certainty. Aside from that, the departure of Saturn from Aquarius will ease initiatives, relationships, or situations of rigor and waiting. His shift to Pisces will compel him to reestablish order where there is chaos. To reach the pinnacle, projects must be modified and lightened.

Jupiter in Aries will continue to expand its endeavors until May 16. It promotes the movement of heaven and earth via signs of the elements of air and fire. His transition to Taurus will provide ease, opportunity, and possibilities to the water and land signs. To counteract all of this, Mars begins his journey in Gemini and ends it in Sagittarius. He will disperse his vivacity, empathy, ambition, perspicacity, subtlety, strategy, and adventurous spirit.

Every zodiac sign will experience certain changes as a result of the 2023 horoscope, and they will gain new life direction and understanding.

ARIES 2023 HOROSCOPE

Overview Aries 2023

This year, people born under the sign of Aries will be able to finish the projects they put off last year. Good luck will show up in your finances, career, love life, and health, according to your sun sign. Even though things will get better for you, you should be careful not to make mistakes that will make your life worse. You'll be happy because your relationships with other people will improve and you'll see the best in everything you do.

In this year, 2023, Jupiter would be in your sign until May, when it would move to the second house of Taurus, which is your second sign. This means that the focus will shift to family and money as the year goes on. Saturn would be moving through your 11th house of Aquarius, and in March, it will move into your 12th house of Pisces. This Saturn transit could make it hard for you to do spiritual things this year. Uranus goes through your second house of Taurus for the whole year, and Neptune goes through your twelfth house of Pisces.

Pluto would be in your tenth house of Capricorn, and in June, it would move to your eleventh house of Aquarius. These planetary patterns will have an effect on your money, love, family, career, and health in the coming year.

People with Aries birth signs would be able to pick up projects they had put on hold before. During the summer, Venus, the planet of love, would be in your fifth house of love. This would be a very good time. Couples should be careful, though, because there is a good chance that relationships will end. The movement of Jupiter and Uranus through your second house of finances would help you have a lot of money. This year, your health will be fine, and your social life will be at its best.

January 2023

Horoscope

A happy month is coming up, Aries. Jupiter in your sign brings you the good life, including trips to other countries, good food, good wine, and lots of other sensual pleasures. Your life is filled with a lot of hope. But you need to be more careful about your health, especially how much you weigh.

There is nothing seriously wrong with your health. It's just short-term stress caused by the short-term planets, and it will get better after the 20th. Since Mercury is in retrograde until the 17th, you should try to avoid medical tests or procedures if you can. Just hold off until after the 17th.

This month, life will move faster. Individual freedom is strong now and will get even stronger in the coming months. When Mars, the planet that rules your horoscope, moves forward on the 12th, you will know more about your own goals. This is an excellent month to make the changes you need to make to be happy in the future.

Even though love doesn't seem like a big deal anymore, single people can find love through their friends, groups, and professional and trade organizations. Friends can be cupid, or someone you thought of as a friend might want to be more than that. Dating can also happen through social media and online activities.

Overall, finance looks good, and it looks like your knowledge of technology is important. The high-tech and online worlds look like exciting opportunities for investors. You spend more on technology, which also helps you make more money. After Uranus moves forward on the 22nd, it will be easier to buy high-tech items.

Mars, which is in charge of your Horoscope, is "off limits" this month and will stay that way until May 4. So, you're "without boundaries" or outside your usual circle of friends, and it looks like you're having fun.

Love

The Mars-Venus trine is in effect from the 4th until the 27th of January. You have a way with words. Your charm draws others to you, which is amplified if there are affinities between you and them. To create and maintain a pleasant, open atmosphere, you need a feeling of purpose.

Those in a relationship are encouraged to shake things up a bit. While your partner may appreciate your efforts, don't go overboard! If you want your relationship to remain harmonious, you should accept your partner's preferences and aspirations.

Singles, this year is off to a great start. You never know who you'll run across in your social circles. Do not hurry the relationship if you want it to last.

Career

You will achieve your goals if you are patient and persistent. So quit placing so much pressure on yourself to get your brilliant ideas approved. The fact that not everyone is like you is a reminder to keep in mind. Your employer, coworkers, or customers require time to master new skills. So, be considerate and provide them with the space they need.

In terms of your career future, the prophecy from the stars isn't all that encouraging. There is a good chance that you and your superiors may disagree. You must do all in your power to prevent this from happening.

It's also possible that you'll be troubled with a sense of uneasiness that will directly impact your work life. You might try to make things right by making fast career shifts or alterations to your company's operations. This would be a really bad move. Any adjustment should only be made after a thorough examination of the situation. In addition, there would be a lot of travel, although this also wouldn't be very productive.

Finance

A prosperous month in terms of cash gain for you. You might expect a bountiful crop of unexpected rewards. Quite a number of you might also gain by speculating. In addition, there is a considerable chance that an elderly gentleman may do you a favor, which could turn out to be a financial benefit.

Furthermore, you'll develop a way of dealing with your superiors this month that will be quite advantageous to your career. This has the potential to be a significant benefit. Last but not least, a close friendship with a number of intellectually and spiritually outstanding individuals will help you both monetarily and spiritually.

Health

This month, the stars are favoring your well-being, so you may expect to be healthy for most of the month. There would be a dramatic reduction in the frequency and severity of acute illnesses like fevers and inflammation. In most cases, they would not harm you in any way.

This also applies to those experiencing any type of dental issue. Denture problems should be taken seriously, although they have a strong possibility of being resolved. For your health, this is a good time, and those who are currently in good health may anticipate staying that way.

Travel

This is a terrific month to reap the benefits of travel, as the stars' prediction is highly positive on the matter. If you want to study or train in a foreign country, you have a good probability of this working well.

You'd prefer to travel by train, road, and air, with a substantial amount of air travel thrown in for good measure. A journey out of the country is a possibility as well. Only a portion of your travels will be for work.

Whatever the case, you'll find what you're seeking on your journeys. The East direction is the best way to go if traveling.

Insights from the stars

Listen to the advice of someone with expertise and affection for you rather than letting go of the topic when the first difficulty or the least inconvenience emerges.

February 2023

Horoscope

This month, Jupiter in Aries and Mars in Gemini will always be there for you, providing you with a steady supply of energy and inspiration. Your morale is high in this positive environment. Ideas and initiatives are in good hands with you! You're chewing at the bit until the 11th since Mercury's inconsistency makes things difficult! With Mercury's transit to Aquarius, there are no more delays or obstructions. From the 12th, what was difficult becomes easy. Your sphere of influence expands to include fresh points of view and people who are receptive to your thoughts. Getting the funding you need to see your ideas through to completion is entirely within your grasp. From the 21st, you'll discover passion when it comes to love.

Love

It's not going to be a happy day till the 20th of this month. Venus, the planet of reflection, nudges you to do so. Instead of rushing things, take some time to think about what makes you happy and how you may incorporate it into your life. The arrival of Venus in your sign on the 21st brings you more self-confidence.

In a relationship, your actions build a gap. It's possible to get bored. Your words may have outstripped your ideas. Instead of adding fuel to the flames, think about how your spouse feels and what they are trying to say. Plan ahead of time to suit their needs.

If you're single, Venus is slowly undermining your sense of self-worth. It forces you to ponder your sexual prowess or the sentiments of the person you are seducing. There will be no more negative feelings on the 21st when Venus moves into Aries.

Career

You've got your ears to the ground. Many individuals come into your life. Every three seconds, you come up with a new concept, but until the eleventh, no one has agreed on it. Avoid being impatient since this will ensure that your ideas receive all the votes. Why? Why? Because you're at a good place in your life. February has the potential to be a fruitful month for you, but only if you exercise patience when the situation calls for it.

Finance

This month, your financial situation appears to be improving and might lead to long-term financial stability. You should expect to receive a bountiful harvest of unexpected financial rewards. Investing would bring in even more money for others, as would the market as a whole.

Health

Thanks to the blessings of Health Dame's fortune, you may anticipate to continue in good health for the foreseeable future. With regular care, people with long-term conditions like rheumatism and other symptoms like gas and wind in the digestive system will find significant alleviation from their symptoms. When it comes to teeth, this is also the case.

In addition, you should anticipate any predisposition to anxiousness to be alleviated and to cause significantly fewer problems than normal. A few flaws will be apparent, but these are readily remedied via regular exercise and a healthy diet. This is a good month for your health because there aren't any significant health risks.

Travel

The stars are smiling at you this month, so you may expect to make a lot of money while you're away. You'd largely take trains and roads, with some air travel thrown in. It is also possible that you will go outside the country.

Part of your travels would be work-related, while the remainder would be personal. However, regardless of the goal, you should be able to achieve it to the fullest extent possible. In addition to making new acquaintances, traveling is a great way to have a wonderful time. The East direction is the best way to go.

Insights from the stars

You're on a roll now! Nevertheless, keep in mind the emotions and sentiments of individuals in your immediate vicinity. Instead of wasting your time, you should invest it in a timely purpose.

March 2023

Horoscope

Jupiter's energies in Aries and Mars' in Gemini will expand your consciousness this month. You put all of your heart and soul into your endeavors. When you do what you enjoy, you're more likely to succeed. Your leadership qualities are further bolstered by Venus, Mercury, and the Sun, all currently transiting through the sign of Capricorn. This is a lucky month for you since you're experiencing a lot of good fortune.

On the 21st, a new Moon rises in your sign, giving you the motivation you need to take action. You take charge of your projects to ensure their success. On the other hand, events and circumstances will force you to examine all you've done. You'll make more money than you think if you don't hesitate.

Love

You're the drummer in your own band. You and your loved ones are in agreement. Everything is going swimmingly. Your charm has a way of enticing even the most skeptics. But if you don't want to face the music afterward, slow down and be more open.

There's a wall built between you and your significant other without your knowledge. Try to be more accessible. Pay attention to what your significant other has to say. If you do this, you won't have to worry about an impending disaster hanging over your head on the 26th!

Everything is OK if you're single when it comes to meeting new people! For the meetings to last, though, it's a lot more difficult! This conflict can only be solved if a genuine relationship is formed. Spend more time with the individual whose company you enjoy and whose thoughts and feelings you find fascinating.

Career

You're in luck till the 25th, so take advantage of it! You succeed because of your own efforts. Everybody admires you for your brilliant ideas. Then Mars loosens its grip on you since it's occupied with other people. Don't get down on yourself if things don't go according to your plan. You have all of the tools to restart them. How? You may start with simple improvements and work your way up.

Finance

A great month for your financial future. Unexpected gains would be a blessing to your bank account, and you would make a tidy profit from speculation. You would be able to get immediate and beneficial results from your work.

Travel

During this time of year, the stars are in your favor, and you'll reap the benefits of travel. This month, you'll travel for professional and personal reasons, respectively. For the most part, you'd take trains and roads, but you'd also take flights.

A journey out of the country is also a possibility. You'd be a huge success in all of this, and your business goals would be achieved. You'd also be able to have a relaxing vacation. The East direction is the best way to go.

Health

According to the stars, there is a lot of good news for your health this month. Toothaches of any sort should become much less uncomfortable. Be careful not to overwork yourself since this may easily disrupt a good mood; create a new routine that doesn't put too much strain on yourself.

You cannot afford to take any shortcuts or risks with your health. Everything else is OK. Those who are already prone to anxiety would not be bothered by an increase in their risk. When it comes to health, this month is a good one to avoid any significant issues.

Insights from the stars

It's fantastic to see that you're moving forward. Be careful to build relationships with your partners, new acquaintances, and loved ones. You will avoid disappointment if you follow this advice.

April 2023

Horoscope

As Jupiter is in your sign in April, it stimulates and fosters your progress in both personal and financial matters. Improving your life or making yourself better. It boosts your self-esteem and your ability to think creatively. You'll be pushed to take action by Jupiter. It opens up new options for you, which fits well with your multitasking tendencies. A more practical energy is urging you this month to look at the financial viability of your plans and objectives.

The dissonances caused by Mars in Cancer should be taken into consideration by looking at external factors. Instead of going all out to win, try to come to an agreement with these responsibilities. Take a look at your finances before you start and be more frugal than usual.

Love

You'll have less room to move until the 12th. Getting that flame going is hard! Having a "win-at-all-costs" attitude doesn't get you what you want. Since Venus is in Gemini, everything works out in the end. Your relationships are fun to be a part of because they are lighthearted.

It is normal for people in a relationship to have different personalities. Mars makes this effect in Cancer's dissonances even stronger. From the 12th, you'll be able to get back together with your partner, who will be more willing to see the good things about your relationship.

Even though your charm makes people notice you, it's still hard to be single. You can be sure that your sex appeal can't be denied. On the 12th, Venus will be in Gemini, which will help you find your way. The unexpected knows how to do what it does best.

Career

It's a success because you're a really creative person. You know how to take chances when you need to, and it's this that propels you to success. You've been outpacing the rest of the pack for some time now. As a result, your good fortune has been boosted. It is in your best interest, and you are correct. For Aries, luck is a good thing, but if your initiatives are going to last, you need to do the math. For the time being, temper your aspirations a bit.

Finance

According to your sun sign, this is not a good month for your financial future. There's a good chance your relationships with your superiors will deteriorate to the point where you'll be forced to take a hit financially. As a result, you must be on the lookout for such a scenario and prepare ahead of time in order to avoid it.

You may not be able to meet your goals if there is a lack of opportunity. It's also possible to focus too much on making unreported cash. Everything in your life will suffer as a result of this. Avoiding unnecessary investments is also important.

Health

During this month, the stars will bestow upon your health and prosperity. Those prone to clammy hands and feet may notice a marked improvement in their health during this month.

If you're dealing with a long-term dental issue, you'll be less bothered and more likely to get cured if you take it seriously. The fact that anxiousness and related problems would be much reduced is also a source of comfort. You are unlikely to encounter any significant health issues in the foreseeable future.

Travel

This is a great month for reaping the rewards of travel, as the horoscopes are quite promising. It's possible that some of you may take pilgrimages to holy sites that will serve as a lasting reminder of your experiences.

Higher education or training in a foreign country would go as planned for anyone who chooses to do so. Traveling for business would be a huge success. You'd primarily travel by train or car, with some air travel thrown in for good measure. It is also feasible to take a trip overseas. The East direction is the best way to go.

Insights from the stars

Instead of retaliating, take a step back and evaluate what's causing the problems. There's a good chance that you'll benefit from this.

May 2023

Horoscope

Jupiter's good influences have been helping you for a few months now. It gives you the chance to rethink your everyday routine or start over with new ideas. After a few days in Aries, he'll be leaving. The month of May is the best time to make use of the lucky star and evolution's many resources.

Make the most of the chances that come your way by taking advantage of them. But to make them real, it will be necessary for you to work out your commitments imposed by the Cancerian energy that you are born into. It's important to remember that the feeling of being squandered will pass.

Your business will be handled by Leo starting March 20th. Even though it appeared to be jeopardized before, it will be completed under the present ideal circumstances.

Love

Until the 7th, everything will be fine. Then things get complicated! The spark of desire that had been rekindled a few weeks ago has gone out again. How? By putting you in situations where you can't get out of them on your own.

To those in committed relationships: Congratulations! You've been busy for a while. Your relationship needs to calm down this month and return to a regular schedule. Soothe yourself instead of pushing things. That special someone will shower you with love and appreciation.

In the case of those who are single, When Venus is in Gemini, your romantic relationships progress in a laid-back and diverting environment. The 7th brings Venus into Cancer, which causes a flurry of restrictions to arise! To keep a relationship going, you need to be willing to make certain compromises.

Career

Taking advantage of Jupiter in Aries' tremendous opportunities and passion is best done now. Take advantage of each opportunity that comes your way. After that, you'll be able to put your life back together. There's no need to panic if you're having trouble getting started or if you've already begun but are having difficulty moving forward. It's better to compromise and get what you want than waste time.

On the 17th, Jupiter turns its attention to the financial sector. If you're a little more cautious than usual, luck will come your way.

Finance

This month's horoscope predicts that you'll have a good month financially. This month, you're more likely to have arguments with your superiors, which puts you and them at odds, but by the middle of the month, you'll be able to work things out, which will lead to a significant gain.

To avoid substantial losses, stay away from any investment activities that aren't absolutely required. It's best to avoid all forms of gambling altogether. However, the current economic situation is not conducive to making investments or creating new businesses. Such preparations should be put on hold for the foreseeable future.

Health

This month, the gods are on your side when it comes to your health, and it is highly probable that you will avoid any significant health issues this month. A quick spell of acute sickness, such as a fever or inflammation, would be alleviated, and these issues would no longer be a major concern for you. Such a respite is possible this month since it is a good one.

However, there are reasons to be wary about one's oral health. This might lead to dental issues if you're not careful. Bone injuries, which are highly uncommon this month, should also be treated cautiously.

Travel

The stars aren't exactly aligned to make this a great month to travel, so you won't get much out of it. During your travels, there is a chance that you will be hurt or have a physical problem. As a result, you should proceed with caution and only take little chances.

You'd like to travel alone and primarily by rail or road, with some air travel thrown in for good measure. Traveling for work or business purposes may account for a portion of your journeys. It's safe to say that they would be a waste of time. The possibility of a trip abroad is not ruled out. The best way to go is east.

Insights from the stars

Don't dwell on the negative aspects of your life if you want them to go away. Also, don't be too self-reliant.

June 2023

Horoscope

Thanks to the Leo and Gemini energy flowing through you, you'll be able to take advantage of Jupiter's possibilities while he's in Aries this month. Mars encourages you to set lofty goals and reach for the sky this month. Taking action and making choices are emphasized. Natural leadership comes from inside so dissonant energies in Cancer will compel you to fulfill duties you were unaware of between January 1st and April 4th, as well as starting on or after January 22nd. Seeing things as inescapable will not help you organize your responsibilities. If you don't have the same sense of risk, aid people who don't have it.

Be a calming influence on others around you even while feeling frazzled. Considering the long term will also help you financially.

Love

You have a great deal of stamina! You're more concerned about how you look than you were before. Your magnetic personality makes you stand out. You make others want to be jealous. We all face the same challenges regardless of whether dating or not! You retake power over your loved ones so that they may learn about this obsession that captivates you, and you do this so that they can share in your joy.

Your imagination may run wild between the twelfth and the twenty-seventh if you are currently in a love relationship. Your relationship will be free of the routine that makes it tough to sustain. It is advisable to take a short vacation from your relationship.

As long as you're single, there's no need to give in to the demands of your partner. You're in charge here, so do anything you want! This month's gathering is expected to be nice and informal. After then, it's up to you!

Career

In addition to the Gemini energies that inspire you, Mars in Leo has a huge impact on your success! It offers you a certain magnetism that attracts others who will help you in your endeavors. Some people will succumb to your charms, which you will exploit without restraint. Be careful not to overlook these minor things while using your magic. In what way? In terms of your financial well-being!

Finance

What the stars say about your financial situation this month paints a bleak picture. You've been asked to investigate this side of things, which aren't quite as flashy. To combat this, lower your sails and demonstrate that you're taking things seriously. Your desires will be fulfilled by doing so.

There's a good chance you'll have a bad relationship with your bosses if the company faces significant losses. You can avoid this if you plan ahead and take proactive measures.
Gambling should be avoided at all costs.

Health

As a result of the favorable conditions, your health should be improving this month. Those inclined to chronic conditions like rheumatism and digestive abnormalities like gas and excess wind in the digestive tract will see a considerable improvement. As a result, taking even the most basic precautions should keep you safe from such issues.

However, you should use caution if you have a prolonged sore throat. Complications should be thoroughly identified and addressed without delay. This might have a negative impact on a healthy and positive body system if it is not done. You have nothing else to worry about other than this.

Travel

Given the omens' unfavorable outlook, it may be tough to reap the benefits of travel this month. Performing artists, including singers, painters, dancers, and others, may not be as creative while traveling. Some of them may even suffer a setback as a result of this.
For the most part, you'd want to travel by train or car, with a significant amount of air travel.

Foreign travel isn't out of the question. Despite the fact that most of this would be related to your career or business, it is almost probable that the expected outcomes would not be met. The most advantageous direction is South.

Insights from the stars

If you put your mind to it, you can accomplish your goals. If you want the magic to work, you can't be irritated by folks who take their time. The best thing you can do for them is to reassure them.

July 2023

Horoscope

As Venus continues her stay in Leo this July, you're more focused on your own needs and desires than ever before. You're looking forward to a fun time. Because of this, it is out of the question for you to suffer in the blazing summer heat. If you want to alter your mind, then you'll do it. The shift from Mercury to Leo opens up many new ways to have fun, and these energy revives your friendships.

This month will be filled with many fun activities and lovely get-togethers. But there are other less joyous emotions in circulation. However, despite your best efforts, it is possible that you may have to deal with a few minor issues.

Love

In recent weeks, there have been fewer seizures or other difficulties. In any case, it's possible that you've come to some sort of decision. If you're single this month, you've got a lot riding on the quality of the relationships your in. In Leo, you'll be able to accomplish your ambitions.

Avoid the "all or nothing" mindset this month if you're in a relationship, as it might lead to long periods of quiet and a crisis of possessiveness. Keep your cool and reassure your significant other that you care by making passionate declarations of your love.

If you're single, this is a great time to meet someone new! Venus is doing an excellent job introducing you to someone very special this month. If you want the magic to work, you must have faith in your sex appeal and be romantic when appropriate.

Career

Despite the fact that you're working on other, more exciting endeavors, a string of unfortunate occurrences has forced you to focus on your present business. You, Aries, seem to be thinking of something else. As a result, you might end up paying the price for not paying attention to these minor issues! So, if you don't want to find yourself in a predicament, you need to think hard. As a result, the projects you're working on will progress in a way that benefits you.

Moreover, you'll be plagued by anxiety for the duration of the month. Your entire professional behavior would be affected. If you're prone to mood swings and are considering making a career or company move, you should do so only after careful consideration. Chances are that despite your efforts, the accomplishments you had in mind would not be realized.

When it comes to money, this industry pulls you back to reality. Unfortunately, you may not be able to use it. In contrast, if you're practical, you'll swiftly bounce back.

Finance

According to the stars, you'll have a gloomy outlook on your financial future. Writers, poets, and others of their kind should stock up on supplies for the rainy day since they are likely to experience a dry period this month.

Risky behavior may have resulted in significant losses for some of you. Avoid all forms of gambling, big or small. It's also possible that your relationships with your superiors may deteriorate to the point where you suffer significant losses. You may avoid this by taking some proactive measures in advance.

Health

The constellations aligned with you this month are highly beneficial to your health. Those with a sensitive chest or lungs and susceptible to chest and pulmonary diseases would likely benefit significantly from the blessings of this month. Overwork can lead to weariness and subsequent sluggishness.

You can easily avoid this if you don't put in too much effort. Everything will be OK after this is completed. This might also assist you in overcoming the potential of some types of nervous system diseases, however, this is a remote possibility. If you take good care of yourself this month, you may expect to be in peak physical condition. The health of your teeth should be given more attention.

Travel

There isn't much to be gained by travel based on the predictions of the stars. Traveling as a writer, poet, or other creative person isn't always easy. In fact, some might be significantly affected by the ineffectiveness of their stay.

The majority of your journey would be via train or road, with some air travel thrown in. The possibility of a trip abroad is not ruled out. In the real world, these efforts are quite unlikely to even result in a holiday, which is unfortunate. The best way to go is East.

Insights from the stars

This month has been a good one for your loved ones! You should definitely enjoy it! But if you want to go farther, you must respond positively to their sensitive expectations.

August 2023

Horoscope

Venus and the Sun in Leo will always be there to support your growth this month. It's a bit of a bummer when Venus goes retrograde, since you won't be able to get what you want quite as fast. An expectation that your impatience cannot bear will be placed upon you. To take benefit of these disadvantages, you must consent. The retrograde of Venus helps you to discover what you truly desire. This Venusian retrograde will also allow you to get up to speed if you've missed anything or someone. If you ease your renowned desire, the transfer of Mars to Libra, which is expected on the 28th, will be simpler.

Love

Venus is erratic and difficult to please. As you relax, your senses are sharpened at the same time. Despite your best efforts, you have no control over the people you care about. Get it by playing the game! Although it is not clear at the moment, you will not regret it.

Certainties crumble under the pressure of the passage of time. The feeling of excitement is no longer present at all. Do not think of these annoyances as a matter of mortality because they are only passengers in your life. But if you're in a relationship, you can use it to your advantage by finding out about your partner's needs and goals, even if they differ from yours.

However, if you are in a relationship, you have the opportunity to take advantage of it by learning about your partner's wants and objectives, even if they are different from your own. You can do this even if the two of you have very different goals in life.

A narrow, vacant corridor separates the couples from the singles. Do not be startled if you feel overwhelmed by uncertainty this month. Now is a wonderful moment to take a fresh look at your methods. The most effective way to convey your emotions is via reflection.

Career

Even though this month is ideal for vacations and recovery, the stars demand that you maintain a strict watch on your activities. On the worst days, a happy and last-minute event might be delayed! Because inconveniences seldom happen in a vacuum, unforeseen financial circumstances may compel you to accept a compromise by pushing back your deadlines. This solution will assist you in resolving a difficult situation, despite its unappealing nature. This industry's financial health may be in jeopardy.

Finance

In terms of your financial future, the stars' predictions aren't all that encouraging. You may suffer significant losses as a result of investing. As a result, you should avoid all forms of investments. Negative feelings against your supervisors or coworkers will almost certainly result in major financial setbacks. But don't worry; they'll calm down once you figure out where they're coming from.

You may, however, avoid this by putting in the effort and preparing ahead. You may put so much emphasis on not making money that you don't know where it came from or getting into shady deals. This is not in your best interest and might get you into trouble. Investing or starting a new business would likewise be difficult because of the current atmosphere.

Health

Maintaining a healthy lifestyle is easier this month because of the favorable alignment of the stars in your favor. The likelihood of having a stomach or other digestive organs that are easily upset is significantly reduced. Coughs, colds, and asthma, which are all common disorders of the chest, will be eliminated.

With good dental care, you can ensure that nothing bad occurs to your teeth because there is a cause to be concerned about the condition of your teeth. It's possible that you're easily agitated and have a little disturbed state of mind, as well. Maintaining excellent mental and physical health may be as simple as remaining calm and balanced.

Travel

As the stars indicate, this month's horoscope does not bode well for anyone looking to make money on the road. This month, you're more likely to travel alone, mainly by car or train, with some flights tossed in for good measure.

In addition, you may have to go overseas for a job or pleasure. Because of this certainty, these efforts are unlikely to produce the promised earnings or deliver the expected joy and satisfaction. East would be the most ideal direction.

Insights from the stars

If the others withdraw slightly, it's because they feel the need to collect their thoughts first. Do precisely the same. It'll be more beneficial in the long run than taking up arms against the heavens themselves.

September 2023

Horoscope

Your ability to deal with Mars in Libra's onslaught will determine whether or not you have a successful autumn season. Antagonism against your sign might have unexpected and even violent consequences because of the opposition it inspires.

Events and circumstances this month force you to make decisions that might lead you into an undesirable scenario. Avoid making decisions based on your emotions if you want things to go nicely. Avoid using anger as a means of resolving your issues.

Take some cues from Venus in Leo to keep your cool and make the most of Mars's Libra energy. Its retrograde provides the impression that nothing is progressing. Taking a direct stroll from the 16th re-establishes your good energy.

Love

Although there is still a significant amount of work to be done, the situation is becoming more transparent. You have until the 16th of this month to give some thought to your goals and objectives. Because of this, it's a good idea to be on the lookout for indications that there could be friction in your relationship. Mars is one of your ruling planets because it makes you want to make a commitment when you see something beautiful. Make an effort this month to accept a future with your spouse rather than dismissing the possibility of one together.

If you're in a relationship, you must be experiencing an amazing amount of love. You are prepared for everything that may occur between you and your sweetheart, regardless of the circumstances. Then comes the beginning of the unpleasantness. It's almost certain that you and your partner will part ways. Put some restraint on your zeal. Wait a moment before continuing to speak. Why? Because what you're doing is not acceptable in this context.

Singles who are actively looking for a romantic partner and have recently found themselves in a relationship rut should not lose hope; the dry spell will eventually end. You can find joy in the little things that life has to offer. Be careful with your words since they have the potential to get ahead of your ideas and ruin a potentially beautiful romance.

Career

Aries! The more irritated you become about the initial delay, the more likely you will have a breakdown. Your brand's reputation will be tarnished as an added benefit. Slow down, even if it's not your style. Please don't be frustrated with those who require additional time to complete tasks. Do not act on impulse while you are at it. The consequences of a contract breach should be considered carefully.

There's a good chance you'll disagree with your bosses. You should do all in your power to avoid such a situation because the consequences would be terrible for your professional future.

Finance

The stars predict that this month's events will not be favorable for your financial progress. Some of you may lose significant money if you speculate on the stock market. To avoid any kind of investment, then, it is best to avoid it at all costs.

There are also signs that any disagreement or litigation you would be involved in would probably be resolved against you, resulting in significant damages. As a result, you must make every effort to postpone any such choice until a more favorable time. Negative feelings toward superiors or coworkers are also likely to develop; avoid this if at all possible to avoid large financial losses. This month's financial outlook is gloomy. So tune in and get right to the point. In this way, you can avoid making a mistake.

Health

When the stars align in your favor, it's an excellent month to be a health freak this month. This month would alleviate short-lived acute illnesses including fevers and inflammations. In all likelihood, you would not be bothered by any of this. Back pain would be alleviated in the same way.

There are, however, reasons to be concerned about an eye infection. While this may cause some discomfort, it may be avoided by taking the proper precautions, such as cleaning up after yourself and taking preventative medicine. Your health has improved significantly in just one month, which is encouraging news.

Travel

As far as benefits from travels are concerned, the prophecy from the stars is not encouraging. For the most part, you'll be on the road or train this month, with some flights thrown in for good measure.

A trip abroad is also a possibility. No matter how hard you work, you can be confident that none of your efforts will pay off in terms of financial gain or personal fulfillment. Unfortunately, this is a real depiction of the situation. It's possible that most of your trip is pointless and could be done without. The West is the best direction.

Insights from the stars

Having too much energy might cause you to do things you don't intend. As a result, instead of getting caught up in endless arguments, try to identify compromises everyone can agree with.

October 2023

Horoscope

The pressure is on you through the medium of Mars until the 12th and until the 22nd through the Sun and Mercury. The Libran energies force you to take a stride forward and then a step backward. You'll be difficult to follow and grasp as a result of this. On the other hand, if you agree, you may go about it in another way. How? With your family, friends, or coworkers by demonstrating mutual respect for one another. This may seem like a waste of effort, but it will protect you from bad outcomes.

If you are unable to listen to the needs of others, you will not achieve your full potential. Your situational analysis also plays a role in the decision-making process. You'll need to calm your infamous impatience to get the most out of this small gem.

Love

Until the 9th, Venus in Leo will keep things harmonious in your relationships. Mercury, however, takes a backseat when it comes to making commitments or expressing your future plans. Consequently, what you say determines the course of your romantic relationships. Be mindful of what you're about to say before you do.

If you're in a relationship, you're especially concerned about Libra's energy. In a situation like this, it's important to keep your beliefs in check. It's important to discover and respect your partner's strengths in order to restore calm.

Until September 9th, Venus promotes meeting new people through fun activities such as going out or watching a movie for single people. Then, it creates seductive links through your employment or other hobbies. Be patient and on time if you want magic to work for you.

Career

Aries, if you want things to move well this month, you'll have to do it yourself! Slow down your maniacal enthusiasm and impatience. Make sure you take into account what other people have to say. If you must say something, speak in a less direct manner. Don't lay the responsibility at the feet of others. Make sure to focus on their strengths and devotion. If you do this, your popularity will soar rather than sink one more notch.

Health

This month, you have a favorable collection of circumstances promoting excellent health. Chronic diseases like rheumatism and gout, as well as digestive system abnormalities like gas and an excess of wind, would be greatly reduced. It's important to remember that this does not give you the green light to abandon all prudence.

You have good reason to be concerned about the status of your oral health. If you take good care of your teeth, you can assure that nothing bad happens. As a result, you have a month in which you will not have to deal with any severe health threats.

Travel

There would be a lot of traveling, which would be quite advantageous. South would be the most beneficial direction to travel. There is a good chance that you'll have to relocate, whether for professional or personal reasons. Decide carefully before making any changes because a hasty move might erase all of your hard work thus far.

For the most part, you'd like to travel alone, either by car or train, with a decent amount of air travel. The possibility of a journey abroad cannot be ruled out. South is the best direction.

Finances

It's not looking good for you financially this month, according to the stars. Jupiter has your best interests at heart. Listen to his advice, even if you think it's too cautious if you want him to give you the best. Consider the long-term consequences of your actions.

First, your working relationships with your superiors may turn for the worst. As a result, significant losses may likely occur. As a result, you must take preventative measures in the early stages of the situation.

Insights from the stars

You'll be fooled by the Libran vibes. Use common sense, even if it bores you, to stay clear of these hassles.

November 2023

Horoscope

You have been through some tough months, yet you've remained fair. Nothing can shake your resolve. Staying calm is something you have to do for yourself when necessary. However, this does not mean that you won't be able to find the time and feel bored at some point. Movement returns to your life as a result of the Venus transit through Libra on the 9th. Fresh air is sent to you on the 11th as Mercury moves through Sagittarius.

This month's astrological forecast gives you chances to reframe your mindset instead of making dramatic adjustments. For the greatest possible outcome, avoid creating confrontation in order to obtain your independence since this would lead you down the wrong path. Instead, practice polite negotiation skills.

Love

After the 8th, you put out the effort. You project a professional picture of yourself. Control your legendary enthusiasm, and you'll reap the rewards. As Venus moves into Libra, things begin to shift. As a result of the tremendous gift of passion you have in your relationships, you'll always be a struggle to follow.

Because Venus is in Libra, you're worried about it. You should be aware of your reactions if you're in a relationship in this situation. You'll be able to preserve the peace if you and your spouse stay diplomatic and affectionate. In contrast, when you stand up for nothing, things are different.

If you're single, you're able to form bonds with individuals who are kind and positive. If you're in this situation, everything is conceivable. Your search for love can end here. Keep a tight rein on your fabled zeal if you want this miracle to last.

Career

Working in a team is a stressful experience, and taking control of the company's day-to-day operations. Despite the fact that this strategy has been working out well for you, this month, it may pull a trick on you.

Always avoid offering directions, Aries, especially if you want to keep your high popularity rating! Think about other people's decisions before trying to overrule them. Instead, share your thoughts with the world because they are awesome.

Finance

Your financial situation is looking up this month thanks to a favorable alignment of the stars in your natal chart. Your business acumen has been on full display this month! Now is the perfect time to trust your instincts and make money. Investors might expect to do well this month if they stick with it. As a result, you may increase business revenues due to improved connections with your superiors.

When it comes to making investments or establishing initiatives, the atmosphere is favorable. As a result, such strategies should be implemented.

Health

The constellations aligned with you this month are particularly supportive of good health. We merely need to provide a word of warning about going too hard too soon. By preventing this and spreading energy smartly, normal operations can keep going without putting too much stress on the system.

The easiest way to do this is to make a whole new schedule of things to do. Maintaining optimum oral health and taking all necessary precautions is also a good idea. From a health standpoint, this month is quite positive.

Travel

This month, you should be able to make a lot of money by traveling, since the stars favor this. Traveling can be energizing and inspiring for artists of all kinds, whether they're painters, musicians, or writers. The amount of time spent on the road would also be highly useful.

Traveling alone is more common this month, with most of your trips taking place by car, train, and plane. You can't rule out a vacation overseas. Whatever your purpose, whether to do business or simply have a relaxing vacation, you'd have a great time doing it. The West is the best direction.

Insights from the stars

The vastness of the universe invites you to revise your preconceptions and assumptions. Keep your accomplishments instead of destroying them in the name of your beloved freedom.

December 2023

Horoscope

This month, Mars in Sagittarius is your best bet for reinvigorating yourself. And Mercury and the Sun, which are both in this sign, add to the effect. With the help of these energies, you're able to achieve your goals with confidence and good fortune. By knowing who you are, you can take back control of the wheel of life.

Dissonances emanating from Capricorn will bring you bad luck despite your fierce will. Do not take them as a personal attack because they are not meant to make you miserable. These risks are designed to keep you from making judgments that might trap you in a deadlock that would be difficult to break out of.

Love

There are excellent moments and periods of doubt until the 4th of this month, when Venus is in Libra. Finally, the tone shifts to Scorpio. Keep your relationships out of the abyss by not taking risks with them that might lead to irreparable harm. Why? Their chances of getting out unhurt would be slim.

For those in a partnership, even if Venus in Libra causes problems, she does not jeopardize your relationship. From the fifth day of her stay in Scorpio, you may find yourself in an impossible scenario. Play it safe this month.

In the case of those who are single, Venus in Libra may have helped you come to terms with the idea of committing to someone. For those who aren't interested in getting married on their vacation, there is a whole other level of excitement awaiting you.

Career

Victory and accomplishments provide you with wings. You're right to want to go further since having a can-do attitude is conducive to pushing the envelope of what is achievable. You have the audacity to do so. You aren't afraid to try new things. Why? Because you want to fight and to do it better than the others. If you don't want to be broken by your desires, be careful not to go overboard.

Finance

Your financial future is in jeopardy this month due to a slew of bad luck stars. There are positive and encouraging influxes to this region from Jupiter's Taurus position. Some of you will suffer losses due to your speculative activities; that is clear. As a result, it's best to avoid all forms of gambling, including online ones.

Furthermore, there are reasons to believe that you'll be prone to conflict with your coworkers or your employees if you are a business owner, which might lead to severe consequences regarding profit. The good news is that you can strive to avoid this. Taking the necessary steps in advance might help you avoid this situation.

It's not a good time to start new initiatives or make investments. As a result, be cautious not to put yourself in unnecessary danger.

Health

As a result of excellent conditions, you should not be concerned about your health during this period. This month would greatly alleviate predispositions to persistent colds and mucus overflow. With the right treatment and care, people with a condition called hemorrhoids can expect a better quality of life.

Despite this, it's important to remember to take care of your teeth as well as your body as a whole! When it comes to this, any lapses in your physical health might have serious consequences. You may expect to be healthy this month, which is a nice one overall.

Travel

This is not a good month for travel: this is a month where you may lose a lot of money since the stars are not in your favor. If you're going on a trip, there's a chance that something may go wrong. Avoid unnecessary risks by being cautious.

You'd primarily travel by road and train, with a small amount of air travel thrown in for good measure. The possibility of overseas travel is not ruled out. These vacations might be a waste of time in every aspect. You would not be satisfied with it. It's best to head East if you can.

Insights from the stars

Be as flexible as you like with your ideas. You shouldn't second-guess your accomplishments, either. Why? This is because the choices that are presented to you are only available for a limited amount of time.

TAURUS 2023 HOROSCOPE

Overview Taurus 2023

Jupiter will be in your 12th house of Aries at the start of the year 2023. Then, in May 2023, it moves to your rising sign. This would be good news for people born under the sign of Taurus. Saturn goes through Aquarius, your 10th house, and then moves to Pisces, your 11th house, in March. This is a sign that the first three months of the year will be good for your career. Then the natives might not be able to get as much out of life.

Uranus will stay in your sign for the whole year of 2023. Since Neptune is in your 11th house of Pisces and Pluto is in your 10th house of Capricorn, the focus would be on your career between May and July of 2023 when your 9th house will move to your 10th house of Aquarius.

When Venus is in Aquarius in January 2023, it can cause problems in your love life. However, when Venus moves to Pisces, a water sign and Jupiter's home, it will restore your confidence in love. You'd be able to get along better with other people.

According to your Taurus Horoscope for 2023, you will spend more time thinking about the future and less time thinking about the present. This year, your career will grow about as much as usual, and there may be some bumps in the road with your money. The love life of a Taurus will be stable, and their health will be good for most of the year.

Whether married or in serious relationships, Taurus couples will have a rough start to the year. It will get so bad that you might even break up with your partner, but as the year goes on, you will figure out how to make things work. According to Taurus zodiac sign predictions, the end of the year will be a time when you and your partner commit to each other.

Keep your pride in check if you want your marriage or relationship to work. You won't get anywhere if you think you're better than your partner. If you are humble, things will get better in your love life.

The year will be good for business people. This year, you will grow your business and make new business deals. This is also the best time for Taureans to switch jobs, ask for a transfer, or get a promotion.

According to your 2023 horoscope, your bosses will be happy with your efforts and hard work and will reward you for it. You will also get along well with the people you work with.

Most Taureans will want to buy land or a house as soon as they have enough money. Putting money into assets is a good idea because it keeps your finances stable. But don't make rash choices that will cost you in the long run. Be careful with your money and don't spend more than you can afford.

Since the financial stars are in your favor right now, now is the best time to put money into something you know will make you a lot of money. Spend your money wisely and pay off your debts as soon as possible.

This year, you will be in good health overall. Unless you make yourself sick, you won't have anything to complain about. To stay in great shape, you should eat well, drink lots of water, get enough sleep, and work out often. The 2023 Health Horoscope shows that you should be ready to deal with minor illnesses that may come up from time to time.

January 2023

Horoscope

You start the year feeling stuck. Dissonant energies put pressure on your career and success, which can be very annoying. Be careful about what you do on January 21 because of the new moon. Try to adjust as best you can to its influences. Don't get annoyed by things you didn't plan.

In January, it's either one or the other. Either you lose your cool and get into a fight, or you keep your cool and turn the situation to your advantage. If you let your worries about work get in the way of spending time with the people you care about, your mood will suffer, and you will be sorry.

Love

Try not to bring your work problems home between January 4 and 27. In the meantime, use the patient energy of Mercury in Capricorn. With Venus on your side on the 28th, you'll be able to get back on track if, unfortunately, your love life takes some damage.

Everything is fine until the fourth, but it gets more complicated afterward if you're in a relationship. If you let your work worries seep into your personal life, they will hurt your partner's feelings. But from the 28th on, you can rest assured that Venus in Pisces makes it easy to get things done.

If you're single, Mercury can help you meet new people. This gives you time to learn more. From the 28th, you enter a perfect time so that a new meeting/date can be planned in a concrete way.

Career

This month isn't so great. You feel your activity is worsening, and everything is going downhill. When you're in a bad mood, you think that some people ruin everything with their new ideas. Taurus, take off your sunglasses! By doing this, you will see that these ideas that scare you have some benefits and can save you time.

During this month, you won't be able to move up in your job, and if you're not careful, you could fall a few steps below where you are now. There is a good chance that some of you would be tempted to break the law to make quick money. Should this be allowed to happen, the results can only be destructive. You must, therefore, make a firm decision not to give in to such temptations.

Finance

On the money side, this sector is subject to unexpected changes. If you have to use your savings, don't make a big deal because it will only be for a short time.

The way the stars are aligned this month is not suitable for your finances. Some of you will almost certainly lose money if you bet on things. So, it would be a good idea to stay away from gambling of any kind.

There are also reasons to think that you would tend to fight with your bosses so much that your relationship with them would go downhill, causing you to lose a lot. This is something you can try to avoid. By taking the proper steps ahead of time, you can stop something like this from happening. This month, the climate would not be suitable for making investments or starting new projects.

Also, a feeling of insecurity would make you more likely to change jobs or business partners quickly. Only make a change after careful thought.

Health

This month, there are no good signs for your health in the stars. So, you need to be more cautious and careful. Those prone to piles should be very careful about what they eat and how they are treated. Carelessness would add to your problems.

Any tendency to get colds or cough up a lot of mucus may get worse. Again, quick action and fixes might be needed to make things right. If you have a tendency to get fistulas, it would require more attention, as would your teeth. Take good care of your teeth during this time, as this could also bother you.

Travel

A month in which you can expect to make a lot of money from travel because the stars are on your side. This month, you will have a lot of self-confidence and guts to make travel decisions. You would carefully plan a trip that would bring in a lot of money.

You would probably travel alone, mostly by train and road, with a fair amount of air travel. A trip abroad is also not ruled out. Not all of your stays will be for business. Whatever the goal, you will reach it. East is the best direction.

Insight from the Stars

Instead of shouting against what's happening, try to see past what you see. After that, you will see all the good things that some bad things can bring you. Good luck will find its way into your life, and most parts of it will do well.

February 2023

Horoscope

Your growth is still being held back by the dissonances that come from Aquarius. This makes it hard for you to stay calm. You are frustrated. Around the 5th, this effect is made worse by the full moon in Leo. Before making a quick decision, take a moment to think about the question.

Don't listen to subconscious dissonances this month. Instead, listen to the ideas that come from friendly planets. They help you see things from other people's points of view. They tell you that even the impossible is possible. Around the 20th, when there is a new moon, your group will try harder to persuade you. If you agree to push the limits of what is possible, she promises you her full support and friendship.

Love

Venus flirts with you until the 20th. She gives you the feelings and pleasures that you love so much. In this almost perfect setting, you will feel good about yourself and the future. On the 21st, it will be stormy if you don't stop being so famously possessive.

Until the 20th, you will make the perfect lover if you're in a relationship. Your partner is there for you. You feel cared for and are happy all the time. It would be wise to accept and understand that your lover has a schedule or other obligations starting on the 21st.

Venus does well for single people. She makes it possible for good things to happen to the people around you. If you want this idyllic scene to last, don't get in the way too much.

Career

Taurus, Saturn is still slowing down your career. So, you think you're having bad luck at the moment. Even though it's not completely wrong, you can do nothing about it. Even though it's not your usual way of doing things, Taurus, try to think of new ways to do things. If you do this, you'll find that progress is good and that things can move quickly and easily forward.

The horoscope has nothing particularly good to say about your professional future. There is a good chance that you will have a major disagreement with your bosses. This should not be allowed to happen, and you should try to stop it from happening.

You might also have a feeling of insecurity that would affect almost everything you do at work. You could try to fix the problem by switching jobs quickly or changing how your business works. This would be a terrible situation to be in. Any change should only be made after being thought about carefully. There would also be a lot of travel, but this wouldn't lead to much either.

Finance

On the money side, a deficit can make your budget unstable. If you don't take sides, you will find a solution that works for everyone.

A good month from a financial point of view. You can look forward to making a lot of money quickly and benefit from investing. There is also a good chance that someone will do you a favor that could be very helpful financially.

Also, this month you'll find a way to deal with your bosses that will make the relationship very good for you. This could be a huge plus. Lastly, hanging out with many smart, spiritually-minded people with gifts would help you in both material and spiritual ways.

Health

This month, the stars are in a good mood to help your health, so you should feel great for most of the month. Any tendency to get sick quickly and severely, like fevers or inflammation, would be greatly reduced. Most likely, they would not bother you at all.

This would also be true for people with any kind of tooth pain. In fact, any problem with your false teeth should be taken seriously, and there's a good chance you can fix it. This is a good time for your health, and people who are already healthy can expect to stay that way.

Travel

Since the stars aren't in a good place this month, you won't get what you want out of travel, nor will you have as much fun as you thought. If you want to go on a pilgrimage to a holy place, you might have to put the trip off or run into problems along the way. It's a different story that your devotion might get you through.

Most of the time, you would travel alone by train or car, with a fair amount of air travel. Even a trip abroad is not out of the question. But none of these efforts would get anywhere. The best way to go is toward the East.

Insight from the stars

You do not like change. It's common knowledge. But don't fight transformation because you need to find your happiness somewhere. In everything you do, stay true to who you are. Stop comparing your life to other people's and do the things that are good for you.

March 2023

Horoscope

The discords that come from Aquarius are getting smaller and smaller. The stress that has been killing you for months is gone. When Saturn moves to Pisces on the 8th, you feel much better. The hard times give way to ease and convenience.

This month, you'll meet new people and make new friends. Your friends won't let you deal with the problems of everyday life on your own; they will show you how to work hard. On the 17th, Venus moves into your sign. This makes you feel good about yourself.

On March 26, March in Cancer tightens the ties that had become loose. Projects that were put on hold are back. You get back in charge of what's going on slowly and gently. Your life becomes more peaceful, which helps you achieve your goals and be successful as a person.

Love

Things start to get better on the 8th, but everything is back to normal on the 17th. The clouds that keep your love from being bright are moving away. There is a feeling of tenderness and understanding. All the lights are green, so you can find the right person to love.

For those in a relationship, your relationship finds its footing. Misunderstandings from the past are improving as people positively talk to each other. You and your partner have more time for each other. Take advantage of this excellent opportunity to resume work on a project you were working on together but had put on hold.

For people who don't have a partner, Open your eyes around the 7th! Someone is interested in you. You still need some time to get things going, but you can start talking. You can create something good beginning on the 17th.

Career

When Saturn moves into Pisces, it improves your relationship and expertise. Because of this and its good luck, you find people you had lost touch with. You feel better, and most importantly, you get back to being able to work.

This month, what you thought was a compromise shines in a brighter light. It stops feeling like everything is ruined. There is a good chance you will want to invest in what you do again under these conditions.

This month, you should get some exciting chances to move up in your career. Your manner of doing work would help you do well. You get things done quickly and like a business. You would probably work very hard and get a lot in return.

If you've been successful, you may want to take advantage of this by changing where you work or running your business. All of this would lead to better opportunities for you. There would also be a lot of traveling, which would be very helpful. This month, you can look forward to doing something important.

Finance

On the money side, everything is fine because you do what needs to be done in an incredibly smart way.

This month, your financial prospects look pretty good and could put you on a solid financial footing for the long term. You can look forward to getting a lot of money quickly. Some people would make money through investments, which would also make them a lot of money.

You would learn how to deal with your subordinates or employees in a way that lets you get the most out of their work. This would be a big plus for you and help you make a lot of money. Also, there is a good chance you would get a favor or a service that would be very helpful. And lastly, your relationships with your bosses would become so pleasant that you would benefit greatly from them.

Health

Since Lady Luck is in the mood to bless your health, you can expect to stay healthy during this time. People with chronic illnesses like rheumatism and similar problems like flatulence and too much gas in the digestive tract can expect to feel better if they normally take care of themselves. This is also true for any kind of tooth pain.

Also, if you tend to be nervous, you can expect that to go away and cause much less trouble than usual. You may notice a certain weakness, but this is easy to fix with a little exercise and good food. This is a good month in which you probably won't face serious health problems.

Travel

A month when it doesn't look like you'll make much money from traveling. You would probably travel by train, car, and air by yourself. Also, a trip abroad is not out of the question.

All these trips might be related to work and other things in equal measure. But no matter why you're doing these things, it's almost certain that you won't achieve even a fraction of your travel goals. As a result, it's a good idea to go over your travel plans ahead of time to see if they'll get you anywhere. The best direction to go would be West.

Insight from the stars

You're going in the right direction! Keep trying to make up for the agony of the past. In return, it revives those feelings, friendships, and tenderness that make good times. It's important to work on how you get along with others. Don't let your emotions dictate your relationship with other people.

April 2023

Horoscope

Even though Pluto's move to Aquarius puts you at odds with modern society, your life is finding its way. Venus, Mercury, and the Sun move through your sign this month.

The sun signs assist you get back on track because they are connected to the energies of Pisces and Cancer. When Mercury goes into retrograde on the 22nd, it's a good time to get involved in an unfinished project. It encourages you to think more deeply so you can reach your goals.

This month, the universe works for you and supports your beliefs. The talks start up again with those who had moved away. People who respect you keep coming back into your social circle.

Love

When Saturn is close to you, you want a stable relationship. Your lover must give your life meaning. You know what you want and what you don't want anymore. You have higher standards. In exchange, you're willing to give your best.

If you're in a relationship, Venus will make you smile. With Mercury, you can talk to people. Mars wants you to make decisions that will make your relationships stronger. If you promised to do something, now is the time to do it.

For singles, the past is becoming less important. You're getting more and more likely to meet someone nice. This will happen this month thanks to the people you know. Now is the time to say yes to outing invites and occasions.

Career

Things are starting to look up in your career. You feel more at ease, and feel like you are at home. Your professional circle agrees with the decisions you make. But you might have to deal with the problem you had trouble in the past with again.

Taurus, you keep doing things the way you've always done them, and it works. But this time, you have to accept some changes if you want to grow.

This month isn't good for advancement in your career and so would be a sign to be careful. There is a good chance that you will have serious disagreements with your bosses. Try as much as possible for this not to happen. Try to be patient and stay away from places that might cause trouble.

Finance

Even if you say the opposite, this sector is doing just as well as before from a financial point of view. A very promising month from a financial point of view. You would make a lot of money quickly, which is likely to happen from trading activities.

You would be able to see quick, useful results from your efforts. You would learn how to deal with your juniors or subordinates to help you get the most out of their work. This could be the most important thing you get out of a month that has been pretty good to you.

Health

This month, the stars don't say much good about your health. A tendency to be nervous could be a problem, and any kind of tooth trouble is likely to need more care and attention. This should be taken seriously. There are more reasons to think that you may be in a state of general weakness and nervousness due to overwork and exhaustion.

You can avoid this by redesigning your schedule and then sticking to it. This would help you a lot and solve a lot of your problems. It's pretty clear that the period ahead of you isn't very good, so you should be very careful with your health.

Travel

A month when the stars are in a good place and it could be an excellent time to go on a trip. Part of your travel this month would be for business, and the rest would be for other reasons. You would probably travel by rail, road, and the air a fair amount by yourself.

A trip abroad is also a possibility. You would be very successful at all of this, and your business goals would be met. You would also have a lovely time traveling. The best way to go is toward the West.

Insight from the stars

There are good signs for a part of your life to start over. It's time to stop thinking about the past and move on. It will not be hard to get money this month, so you will find a way to support yourself and your family.

May 2023

Horoscope

Your life has meaning because of the energy that comes from Pisces and Cancer. People who share your values are getting closer to you. But it's missing that little something that makes the whole thing great!

Jupiter, who moves into your sign on the 17th, gives it life. The lucky star and evolution will help your personal growth. It will give you chances to help you get back on track or restore the balance that has been upset.

This month's alignment with Mercury will make you more kind, respectful, and easygoing. But starting on the 21st, work with Mars in Leo because you'll get more than you think.

Love

With Venus in Cancer starting on the 8th, things look good. When Mercury is around, conversations and feelings are full of kindness and understanding. Your loved ones are set up in an atmosphere of warmth and care. From the 17th on, you'll have good luck. You can jump aboard!

For those in relationships, your relationship is put back together to make you feel safe and look to the future. You are a rock that your partner can rely on. To keep the peace at the end of the month, don't hurt their feelings.

For single people, the energies in friendly signs make it easier to meet someone. A happy life could begin this month! On the other hand, if you want it to go further, you should make peace with what shines at the end of the month.

Career

Things are getting better and better. From the 17th on, you'll have good luck. People who have known you for a long time bring you the opportunities you've been waiting for. So, if any of them brings forward an interesting offer, you should look at it closely because it has every chance of living up to your expectations. Also, starting on the 21st, don't turn someone off by saying you find them shallow.

The stars' alignment this month gives you much hope for your career. There is a good chance that you will have good relationships with your bosses or subordinates. However, don't make any changes without thinking about them carefully first. Traveling won't bring any benefits, though a short stay in the north might be worth it.

Finance

Even if you live a simple life focused on the essentials, this sector is still doing well in terms of money. The stars look good for your finances this month, according to astrology. There is a good chance that your relationship with your bosses would be so good that you might gain money because of it. So, you must be prepared for this possibility and accept all the blessings that come with it.

Health

This month, the stars aren't aligned favorably in terms of health, so they won't bless you with good health. People who tend to get cold hands and feet would have a terrible time. Any tendency to get nervous would also likely get worse, so If you have this problem, a qualified yoga instructor with regular practice could help you a lot and get rid of your problems.

There is also a chance that you will have problems because of your teeth. This means that your dental health needs more care and attention. This period is not very good for your health, so you must pay more attention to it.

Travel

This is a great month to travel and make a lot of money because the stars point in the right direction. You might go on pilgrimages to holy places, which would be a significant moment in your life.

Those who wanted to go to school or get training abroad or somewhere far away would be able to do so easily. Traveling for business would go very well. You would mostly travel by train or car, but you would also fly a fair amount. It is also possible to go abroad. The best way to go is toward the North.

Insight from the stars

This month of May looks like it will be productive and helpful. For magic to work, you need to think about the past. By doing this, you won't make the same mistakes again. Your career might have some little hiccups, but you'll get through them because you're optimistic about the future.

June 2023

Horoscope

Now that Jupiter is in your sign. The lucky star and evolution is linked to Saturn in Pisces. It gives you chances to make your life more comfortable and stable. These chances fit with your goals and with who you are as a person. So, what you have started will only get bigger. Mars and Venus in Leo show a problem if there is one.

Use these tools to help you solve the problem instead of turning them down for the wrong reasons. Think before you say "no" to everything because a charismatic person will help you reach your goals faster if you link your own potential to theirs.

Love

Since last month, the people you love have given you what you want. They don't want to settle for love alone this month. You can expect them to ask for more. You will have to play the big game if you don't want to let criticism and complaints get to you.

Simplicity has a lot of good points for people in a relationship, but it can also be frustrating. Please your partner this month! How? Giving them something they've wanted for weeks will make them happy!

For people who don't have a partner, Venus brings you together with a wonderful person this month. Your charm won't be enough to get their attention, but don't worry, there is a way! Fill them with cool and well-known things to attract this beautiful creature.

Career

Both your growth and your daily work are certain. Nothing is wrong. You're going to have to deal with someone's decisions even though you disagree with them. Taurus, if you fight with someone, it won't help your business. Think of this person as a friend instead. Doing this will save time instead of wasting it by making your opinions stronger and starting fights.

This month, your professional prospects don't look very good. You will probably feel pretty safe, and you may very well change jobs or significantly change how you run your business or service. There is also a high chance of problems with your bosses or people above you.

This should not happen because it will only make your problems worse. There would also be a lot of hard work, which, given the circumstances, would not only not get the results you wanted but also leave you feeling unhappy. Try to act in a stable way and stay away from things that change quickly.

Finance

On a financial level, this is not your main concern, but it can become one if someone close to you starts spending a lot of money on unnecessary things. Stay calm.

This month, the stars don't have anything outstanding to say about your financial future. You would probably fight with your bosses, making it hard for you to communicate with them. This could cause you to lose a lot of money. So, do what you can to stop this from happening by taking whatever precautions you can think of.

You will almost certainly lose money if you take any risk. So, avoiding all kinds of gambling would be a good idea. The climate would also be bad for making investments or starting new businesses. Plans like these should be put on hold for now.

Health

The way the stars are aligned this month doesn't give you much hope for your health. Even though they only last a short time, sudden bouts of acute illness can be troublesome for people prone to them. These should be taken care of right away.

Dental care should be a lot more important, and every precaution should be taken to keep teeth and gums healthy. This month, there could also be problems with the way you think and feel, such as nervous tension and other similar disorders. Calm and balance should be kept, and a special effort should be made to stay upbeat and happy.

Travel

A great month in which you can expect to travel a lot and make a lot of money from travel because the stars are in a good mood. This month, you might feel very sure of yourself and have the guts to do something brave. You would travel alone mostly by train or car, but you would also fly a fair amount.

A trip abroad is also not impossible. Some of these would be for your business or job, and the rest for fun or other reasons. You would do very well with all of this. If you are happy with your trip, you could also have a good time. The best direction to go would be north.

Insight from the stars

The energies of Leo make you question your beliefs, but it's for the best. People will like you more if you add a touch of sophistication here and there. This month, love will grow in your life. All the fights you and your partner or spouse have been having will end.

July 2023

Horoscope

Things are getting better now that Jupiter is in your sign. But you might not be able to see it or think the time is too long. When Mars moves into Virgo on the 11th, the opportunities that are waiting will become clear.

Your loved ones, relationships, and the things you work on continue to make sense. Your life returns to where it was before it got out of balance. But if you want things to really change, you'll have to look beyond what bothers you.

This month is an excellent time to start living a little fancier than usual. You won't become vain because of this, so don't worry. On the other hand, it will make people respect you.

Love

People you care about need your attention, words of love, kindness, and gifts. You can fight it right away and say that simplicity is your trademark. It's summer, and everything is great! If you let go, your love will return to you a hundred times over.

If you're in a relationship, the stars are on your side and want you to feel good about yourself. But don't make it a habit in your relationship to do things that lead to fights. Listen to your gut and try to make your lover happy to avoid this.

For people who don't have a partner, You are getting dates and seducing people in a good way. However, do not rest on your feats! To make magic happen, you have to play well with what shines. How? By taking your new friend to a party or fun place.

Career

You can always count on your daily life and your career growth. Still, people are making you upset by putting sticks in your wheels. When things are bad, you say what you really think. Your popularity rating drops all of a sudden. Bull! You're correct. So, be more careful with what you say. By doing this, you can stop these fights that ruin the mood and make your daily life more pleasant.

This month, the signs are good for you to move up in your career. Even though you would have to work hard, you would get more than enough in return. Your hard work will help you achieve your goals. This would be supported even more by how you do your job, which is to be energetic and strong.

There is also a lot of travel in the cards, which would be very helpful. In fact, this plan of yours would sometimes have some risks built in. You shouldn't do anything too dangerous, which might lead to problems. There's also a chance that a female friend could do you a big favor that would make you a lot of money.

Finance

On the money side, if you see this area melting like snow in the sun, calmly explain what you want to do. People will hear and understand you.
From what the stars say, your financial situation this month doesn't look too good.

There is a good chance that your relationship with your bosses would get so bad that you would lose their trust, especially if you see that big losses are coming. You should be able to stop this from happening with some planning and foresight.

Investing would also almost certainly cause you to lose a lot of money. So, you shouldn't play any kind of game of chance. Also, the climate would not be perfect for investing or starting new businesses. These should be put on hold for now.

Health

This month, your health is likely to be in good shape. People prone to long-term illnesses like rheumatism and digestive problems like flatulence and too much gas would feel a lot better. This means you wouldn't have to worry about these problems if you took normal precautions.

But if you have a sore throat that doesn't go away, you should be careful. This should be looked into carefully to see if there are any complications, and then it should be treated with care. If you don't do this, it could mess up a good health situation that is going well. Aside from this, you don't have any real reason to worry.

Travel

This should be a good month for travel, and you should make good money from it. Most of the time, you would travel alone by train or car, with some flights thrown in. A trip overseas is also not out of the question.

Since not all of your trips would be related to your job or business, you would have a lot of success in getting what you set out to do. You would meet a lot of new people and have a lot of new opportunities. The best direction to go would be east.

Insight from the stars

Leo's energies still give you challenges that you can handle with ease. How? By taming what comes to the fore instead of ruthlessly rejecting it. Avoid spending money you don't have. Spend your money only on things you need and stay within your budget.

August 2023

Horoscope

Despite the fact that the planets are in retrograde, this is not a major problem for you. On the contrary, it may be advantageous to you because no one will hold it against you if you take your time. Before making a choice or studying a proposal, take some time to reflect.

On the other hand, Mars and Jupiter continue to promote your situation's development by providing you with the ease you greatly appreciate. On the other hand, Venus and the Sun in Leo are incarnating conflicts.

Be on the lookout for the negative effects of your possessiveness. Why? Venus retrograde puts you at risk of being caught up in a scenario you don't desire. While you wait for Venus to improve, be calm.

Love

With dissonances and Venus in retrograde, things are likely to get complicated. But if you wish, you can get rid of all these problems. This month, you should stop being so stubborn. Soothe your famous possessiveness and let go when things get complicated.

Being stubborn about what you believe will make things very hard if you are in a relationship. You can avoid that, though. How? By agreeing to follow certain rules or just by giving in to what your partner wants.

Singles, there's nothing really bad to say, but you can expect a period of uncertainty. Take the time to think about the kind of people who would be good for you. Once you've done that, you'll be free of the setbacks that bring you down.

Career

Planets in friendly signs help you reach your goals. So there's nothing for you to worry about. Planets that are in retrograde give you more time to do things. You're happy and feel like you're getting complete peace! Unfortunately, someone who doesn't see this month the same way you do could ruin your good intentions.

This month, the signs are good for your professional advancement. If you get to know a lot of smart people, there's a good chance that you'll be able to make a lot of progress in your career. You would also get a lot out of your bosses, even though you might have serious disagreements with some of them.

There would also be a lot of travel. All of that would be pretty helpful. In fact, there is a good chance that you will get a new job or make significant changes to how your business works, which would require you to move. The best direction is to go west. There's a good chance that your efforts will help you reach the goals you set.

Finance

You are determined to be careful with your money, and you want to reach your goals. If someone says you are cheap, you don't need to bother about it.

The stars don't paint a good picture of your financial future based on what they tell you. Writers, poets, and people like them would do well to save money for a rainy day because this month is likely to be very hard for them.

There are signs that you will lose a lot of money because of wrong business investments, so you shouldn't gamble. There is also a chance that your relationship with your boss will worsen to the point where serious losses become likely. You should take some steps in advance to avoid this.

Health

This month, the stars on your right side are good for your health. People with sensitive chests or lungs prone to problems in these areas are likely to feel a lot better. If you push yourself too hard, you might get tired and feel weak.

You could easily avoid this by not pushing yourself too hard. Once this is done, things will go well. This will also help you deal with the possibility, albeit small, if you have a nervous disorder. If you take care of yourself, you can stay healthy for the whole month. Pay a little more attention to how your teeth are doing.

Travel

This is a good month to make a lot of money from traveling, as this is what the stars say. Travel would give writers, poets, and others like them new ideas and meanings.

You should mostly travel alone by train, car, and road, with a fair amount of air travel. Also, a trip abroad can't be ruled out. Part of this trip would be for work or business, and the other parts would be for other reasons. No matter what your goal is, you will probably be able to reach it through your travels. The best way to go is toward the West.

Insight from the stars

A part of your life is about to get better. Take care of the people you love because they need your attention and a few questions. Be willing to try new things in your life. Don't stay in the same place for too long. To do well in life, you need to make changes.

September 2023

Horoscope

Planets are in retrograde. On the 5th, it's Jupiter's turn to move back. Instead of irritating yourself because things are moving slowly, use the time to see how far you've come. Perfect your projects and what's already going on. Set up what needs to be done and, if necessary, strengthen the bonds with the people you've met. Work hard as you do, and you will get the desired results.

On the other hand, it is still complicated because Venus in Leo is causing dissonance. What is beautiful continues to make you think by giving you new problems to solve. Instead of getting into fights that harm the atmosphere and could put you in danger, smooth out your personal beliefs.

Love

Usually, you reach your goals and often have the last word. Unfortunately, it's hard to get ahead when Venus is in Leo. What is beautiful is holding you up, but it puts you under pressure until you give up. This month, if you want peace, tone down your famous toughness.

If you're in a relationship, forcing your beliefs on the other person will get you nowhere. On the other hand, settling the arguments will be easier if compromises are found. This month, try to find common ground on things that bother you. By doing this, your partner will smile when they see you.

Even when problems go away, singles still have to deal with some issues. If you aren't happy, you might be attracted to people you like but aren't good for you. It will be better to think about it than try to control what happens.

Career

This sector moves slowly, and so do you, but that's no reason to stop doing anything. Taurus, don't put off making decisions for too long. Think about the people waiting for your reply and keep it to a reasonable time. Don't wait forever to ask for information. In conclusion, don't put off until tomorrow what you can do today.

A month full of great chances to advance in your career. You'd work very hard and pursue your goals with a hunter's instinct. This would guarantee success. There would also be a lot of travel, which would help both with achieving planned goals and finding new opportunities.

There is a good chance that something good will happen at work, or your business will have to change significantly. But any change should only be made after a lot of thought. This is even more important because you would probably feel a little bit worried even though things are going well for you.

Finance

On the financial side, an expense that you think isn't necessary can cause a fight with someone. So either you stay stubborn and feel alone, or you give in.

The horoscope has nothing especially good to say about your financial future. Some of you could lose a lot of money if you buy stocks. So, you shouldn't participate in any kind of investment. Relationships with your bosses or coworkers are also likely to worsen to the point where a loss is almost inevitable.

But you can stop this from happening with some focused action and planning ahead. You might also focus too much on making money that can't be accounted for. This wouldn't be in your best interests and could cause you trouble. The climate would also discourage investment or starting new businesses.

Health

Maintaining a healthy lifestyle is easier this month because of the favorable alignment of the stars in your favor. The likelihood of having a stomach or other digestive organs that are easily upset is greatly reduced. Chronic chest illnesses, such as coughs, colds, and asthma, will also be affected positively.

With good dental care, you can ensure that nothing bad occurs to your teeth. There is a cause to be concerned about the condition of your teeth. It's possible that you're easily agitated and have a little disturbed state of mind. With a bit of work, you can keep your mental and physical health in excellent shape.

Travel

This month's horoscope is good for anyone looking to make money on the road, as the stars indicate. This month, you'd prefer to travel alone and primarily by road and train, with a good amount of air travel thrown in.

In addition, you may have to go overseas for a job or pleasure. Because of this certainty, these efforts are likely to produce the promised earnings or deliver the expected satisfaction and joy. East would be the best way to go.

Insight from the stars

Shouting at situations or people won't help you get your business done. Examine each situation with care. By doing this, you'll figure out the best way to solve each problem. This month, your main goal will be to stay healthy. You can do anything useful with your life if you are healthy.

October 2023

Horoscope

While Jupiter and Saturn appear to be taking a backseat, they continue to support your growth. However, you are correct in thinking that things take a long time to manifest. Consider what you'll do when things settle back down to a more manageable pace. It's better to keep your cool than lose your cool.

Despite the odds, October is shaping up to be a terrific month. Unfortunately, the advent of Mars, Mercury, and the Sun in Scorpio might overturn this good omen.

As of the 13th, don't consider other people's actions as attacks on your own identity. Don't accept anything at face value at the conclusion of the month. Let people aid you out instead of arguing with each other.

Love

Venus makes your life hard until the 9th. Things work out well because of her time in Virgo. Beautiful things make you want to do more to make other people happy. Mars in Scorpio, on the other hand, is dangerous. Why? Because it makes you angry over small things.

Things get better after the 10th for those who are in a relationship. The agreement is put back into place. Mars in Scorpio, alas, can mess up everything! So, if you don't want to do something terrible that you'll regret, include your partner in your projects or activities.

From the 10th, if you're single, Venus helps you meet people who are right for you. Coming up on the horizon is a date. If you turn down what is given to you for the wrong reasons, everything will turn out for the best.

Career

October looks good, but it can quickly become a nightmare. Taurus, you have trouble with the energy of Scorpio because of who you are. They get on your nerves and drive you crazy for almost nothing. When you do this, you put yourself in a bad situation from which it's hard to get out. So when someone says something to you, take a deep breath before you answer.

There's nothing particularly good about the predictions for your work this month. There is a strong chance of having major disagreements with your bosses. No matter how hard it is, you should do everything you can to avoid this happening because if it does, it can only be bad for your career.

Throughout the month, you would also have a deep sense of insecurity, which could affect how you act at work. You might choose to switch jobs or run your business quickly. Any change you make should only be made after careful thought and planning. The best direction would be to go West.

Finance

On the money side, you don't like to spend money on things that aren't necessary but are fun. So don't be surprised if people say bad things about you.

The stars say that this month's turn of events won't help you get ahead financially. Yes, there are clear signs that you would lose a lot of money if you took a risk. So, it would be wise to stay away from any kind of investment.

There are also signs that any dispute or court case you might get into would almost certainly go against you, causing you to lose a lot of money. So, you should try to make sure that any decision about this kind of thing is put off until a better time. Relations with bosses or employees are also likely to go downhill. If you can't stop this from happening, you could lose a lot of money.

Health

There isn't much in the stars this month that's good news for your health. If you tend to get sudden, severe illnesses like fevers or inflammations, this could be a problem for you. Obviously, you would need to pay more attention and get treatment right away. This is something you must do quickly.

There is another reason to be aware of the chance of a bothersome eye infection that could cause problems. To keep this from happening, you must take the proper precautions, like keeping things clean and taking the right prescribed medication. This period won't be good for your health, so you should take better care of yourself.

Travel

This is a great month for travel; you could make a lot of money from it because Lady Luck is in a good mood. This month, you'd have a lot of confidence in yourself and the courage to take the lead. You would make work-related travel plans that would be very successful.

You would travel alone mostly by train and road, but you would also fly a fair amount. A trip overseas would also be very likely. Aside from business trips, you would also take vacations, which would give you a break and something to look forward to. The best way to go is to the West.

Insight from the stars

This October could be a great month for you. Be careful of your personal beliefs because they could cause you to miss opportunities or meet the right people. Don't give up on your family and friends just because you don't get along. Even if they drive you up the wall, make room for them.

November 2023

Horoscope

This week, Saturn's retrograde will come to an end. The biggest blockages break up. Things start to get back to where they were before. What had to wait is now happening. Your projects are going in the right direction.

Mercury's exit from Scorpio on the 10th makes you more interested in talking about things. Mars and the Sun are both stuck in this sign until the 22nd and 24th, respectively. In this state of mind, which makes people more likely to say no, watch how you respond. Please think before you make a decision based on what you think you know.

This month, the success of your projects will depend on how well you can work with others.

Love

Mars makes you mad, but Venus in Virgo makes things better until the 8th. Then, beauty won't be as important to you. But you can get ideas from it so that your love stays a little bit in tune. This month, you should be more careful about how you talk to your loved ones.

For people dating, With the planets moving through Scorpio, your relationship has both happy and difficult times. If you want things to be easier, stop being so possessive and let your partner breathe on their own.

Up until the 8th, your love looks good for people who don't have a partner. Then, don't be stuffy if you want things to keep going in the same direction. Don't worry about what will happen tomorrow. Live and date in the here and now.

Career

Everything is fine, but Mars in Scorpio will drive you crazy. Your reactions change all of a sudden. And as a bonus, you see the suspicious looks on other people's faces. With this, everything you've been doing lately will come to an end. So, to avoid this kind of disaster, take a step back and loosen up your beliefs.

This is a good month to get ahead in your career. People who like art and people who work in the fine arts can look forward to a time when their creative work will be very satisfying. Some of you may even go on to make a name for yourselves with what you bring to the table.

There would also be a lot of travel, which would be helpful as well. The best direction would be to go south. Besides traveling, you might also change where you work or do business. But think carefully before making any changes because a hasty move could easily undo a lot of your hard work.

Finance

From a financial point of view, this area is doing great. But don't make any decision on the 27th, because if you do, you'll make a mistake that will cost you a lot.

This month, the way the stars are aligned in front of you promises good luck for your money. First of all, there is a good chance that your relationship with your boss will get better. So much so that it is very likely that you will receive rewards.

You would also almost certainly gain a return on investments, so this is the right month for buying stocks or opening new businesses.

Health

The way the stars are aligned this month doesn't make it likely that your health will get better. Suppose you tend to get chronic diseases like rheumatism and digestive system problems like flatulence and too much diarrhea. In that case, you will have a lot of trouble and have to pay a lot more attention to get the proper medical treatment.

Also, try not to get too angry or nervous, and keep an eye on your teeth to ensure they don't get worse. This is a good month, and you can make sure nothing terrible happens by being extra careful. Overall, you would have to be careful with your health this month.

Travel

This is a great month in which traveling would bring in a lot of money. Writers, poets, and other people like them may have a stretch of financially and creatively productive travel.

You would usually travel by yourself, mostly by car or train, with some air travel. A trip abroad is not impossible, and these efforts will likely achieve some of the goals envisaged. The best way to go is South.

Insight from the stars

You are a lovely person. Your little flaws ruin the mood, though. This month, try to stay calm, even if it takes some work. You will be glad you did it. This is the best time to let go of people and things that aren't helping you anymore.

December 2023

Horoscope

You begin the month with a sense of lightness after being savaged by the planets in Scorpio. You're more open to sharing your thoughts now. When you're at your best, you're on the right side of life. Nearly overconfident, there!

On the 5th, Venus enters Scorpio, bringing with it a brief period of enjoyment. To avoid falling into his manipulations, you must be aware of what he does and how it affects you.

If you want to be a success with this young prodigy, take risks and be light-hearted about it. Embrace the unexpected. Accept the fact that your family and friends may disrupt your daily routines. If you're experiencing discomfort, know that this phase will not last. After a while, everything will go back to normal.

Love

From the 5th to the 31st, you will have to deal with Venus in Scorpio's dissonances. If you don't want to end up alone, tone down your convictions! Do not scream "high treason" over small things.

Venus brings good times and, unfortunately, hard times to people who are in a relationship. All of these ups and downs will seem like too much. Some people will make you believe your relationship is about to end. Don't worry; things won't get that bad.

For people who don't have a partner, This month, it's easy to go on dates. But if you want to take it further, it might be hard. So, if you don't want to be disappointed, don't try to change fate and stay Zen no matter what.

Career

When Jupiter is in your sign and moving backward, the time can seem long. It takes time for your plans to come to life. You have to make the worst days better. But these little setbacks aren't meant to make you feel bad; quite the opposite. They help you plan and organize everything so that you are ready when an opportunity comes. Don't look for bad news everywhere. Keep smiling.

In terms of your professional prospects, it's a good month. People who work in the arts and other similar fields would have a wonderful time. Some of you may even make a name for yourselves with what you bring to the table.

There are signs that you are likely to work hard and go after your goals smartly. And you will be able to do this.

There may even be a change in where your business or service is done. Though changing might be a good idea, you should only do so after careful thought. There would also be a lot of travel, which would be very helpful in the long run.

Finance

On the money side, check all the details if you have to make a decision that will cost a lot. You can be even pickier than usual.

This month, there is nothing particularly good about your financial outlook since the stars aren't in your favor. There are clear signs that some of you would lose a lot of money if you invested. Also, you do not gamble, no matter what kind.

Furthermore, there is a chance that your relationships with your bosses will deteriorate to the point where losses become a real possibility. Take steps to fix the problem early on to stop this from happening.

The environment wouldn't be great for making investments or starting new projects. Plans like these should be put on hold for now.

Health

How the stars are aligned this month is good news for your health in many ways. However, you are warned not to work too hard. This should be avoided at all costs, and energies should be spread out wisely so normal activities can go on without putting too much stress on the system.

This can be done quickly and easily by making a new schedule of things to do. You should also take all the usual precautions for your teeth. Aside from this, you should have a pretty good month regarding your health.

Travel

This is a month when you should make a lot of money from traveling because the stars are in a good place. All kinds of artists should find travel exciting and helpful for getting their creative juices flowing again.

This month, you would probably travel alone, primarily by car and train, with some flights thrown in. A trip abroad is also possible. You would travel for business and other reasons, but no matter what your goal was, you would be able to reach it or just have a pleasant trip. The best way to go is to the West.

Insight from the stars

You still have to work with Scorpio's energy. Don't play his game if you want everything to go well. Stay back and act like you're not interested. Your business will do well, and you'll meet people who can help you do well in the business environment

'

GEMINI 2023 HOROSCOPE

Overview Gemini 2023

Jupiter will travel through your 11th house of Aries until May this year. After that, it will move into your 12th house of Taurus. This is not a very good transit because your opportunities will be limited. And in March 2023, Saturn will move from the 9th house of Aquarius to the 10th house of Pisces. This is a sign that Geminis will do well in their careers. Uranus spends the whole year in your 12th house of Taurus, and Neptune would be in your 10th house of Pisces.

Pluto would reside in your 9th house of Capricorn, however, in May - June of 2023, it will move to your 10th house of Aquarius. Gemini people would be affected by these planetary movements all through this year.

Those born under the sign of Gemini would have a lot of luck with love and marriage this year. There would be a lot of anger and other strong feelings. Like never before, people would want to be with you. You win them over with your charm, especially your wit and sweet tongue. Mars and Venus, the love planets, are moving in your favor this year.

This year, big changes could happen when Saturn moves into your 10th house of career in March. You'd have a lot of energy, and you'd have a lot of work to do. But Saturn would make it hard for you to do well at work and hold up any professional goals you had for the year. Getting along with bosses, business partners, and coworkers may be problematic. There would be problems along the way, so not everything would go as planned. Face problems and stick to your position.

This year would be good for the health of Geminis. You would have good mental and physical health all year long. When Jupiter moves through the 11th house, there is no sickness. Saturn is also good for your health, but it will limit your energy. Be careful not to get diseases that are contagious. If you ate well and worked out, your health would be better for the year. Keep your immune system strong throughout this time. Because Mars is in the wrong place, there may be times when people feel tired. Stay upbeat and be positive.

As 2023 begins, Geminis will be doing well financially. There would be a lot of money coming in. But you might also have to pay for things you don't want to, which could strain your finances. Geminis are told not to spend too much money during the year. Spend on what you need, but not on what you want. Jupiter's good effects on the fourth house would help you make money through land deals.

Geminis would have good travel prospects in 2023. As Saturn is in the 9th house of long-distance travel, natives can expect to take some trips abroad this year. If you live far away from your home country, the first half of the year is an excellent time to return. After the first quarter of the year, Geminis will be able to take many short trips that are both profitable and fun after the first quarter of the year. Be ready to go on unexpected trips as well. The cost might burn your fingers, so be prepared.

Geminis would do well in their spiritual pursuits in 2023. You would learn more about spiritual things as Saturn moves through your 9th house, and Jupiter gives you a year of faith, devotion, and piety. Worship your Creator every day and look for ways to make him happy. If you can, try to fast every once in a while. This will give you both mental and physical energy.

Geminis should reshape or remold their ideas if they hit a dead end this year. You're about to have a time of success, so use it to strengthen your personal and professional connections. If you want to be successful in your career, you need to take advantage of all the opportunities that come your way. Be patient and accept whatever the situation or environment offers without getting angry.

January 2023

Horoscope

You evolve in a pleasant climate. Mars is in your sign, and on the 13th, he will start moving straight again. He helps your wishes come true because he has a good connection to Jupiter. As for the energies that come from Aquarius, they help make everything almost perfect by bringing just the right amount of change. Neptune in Pisces and Venus, who joins him at the end of the month, are the only shadows on the board. These energies want to give you false ideas, but you should stay in touch with reality so your brilliant ideas can come to life.

Venus in Aquarius frees you from feelings that stop you from being yourself when it comes to matters of the heart. Your loved ones feel better all of a sudden.

Love

Venus is in Aquarius from the 4th to the 27th, allowing you to be liberated from emotional shackles that dampen your spirits. Avoiding the unknown and learning how to be romantic are two of its many benefits. You'll be amazed at what you can do in this oppressive atmosphere.

You're available and generous to those already in a relationship with you. You're pleased to fulfill the wishes of your better half.

Every light is lit up so that a new beginning might take place under ideal circumstances for singles. Make a little effort to keep it going at the end of the month if you want it to last. Be more romantic and talk about love more often.

Career

In the following weeks, you'll receive job offers from friends and acquaintances that align with your talents and experience. In addition, you will be able to surpass and exceed yourself as a result. There is no reason for you to lose out on these opportunities when the climate is conducive to your growth. Make sure you know what you're listening to if you want things to change.

You could see a bump in your professional possibilities if you're lucky this month. Get ready for a great future! You'll have a lot to cope with, but you're up to the task.

Your bosses will be aware of your hard work. However, you'll have to watch out for your coworkers, as this could be seen as a form of competition.

It's time for job seekers to step up their game. You'll be able to demonstrate your cerebral prowess thanks to the stars. Maintain your enthusiasm and drive.

Avoid being overly competitive or egotistic about your worth. You may suffer from anxiety and despair if you overestimate your abilities, leading to a lack of confidence. There would be a great deal of time spent traveling, but it would be for nothing.

Finance

On a financial level, the way is clear. You can sleep easily. At the end of the month, if you continue to manage your budget carefully, everything will be fine.

This month, your financial prospects are pretty good because the stars are in your favor. There are clear signs that investments will make huge profits, so it's best to take advantage of any investment opportunity after doing a lot of research. The climate is good for business people to start new projects. So, you should get going on such plans.

Health

This month, the stars are in a way that is good for your health. We need only sound a note of warning against excessive workload. This should be strictly avoided, and energies should be spread out smartly to keep all normal activity going but not put too much stress on the system.

This can be done easily by making a new schedule of activities. There are some good reasons to take care of your teeth and ensure all normal precautions are taken. Aside from this, it's a pretty good month for your health.

Travel

This month, your chances of making money from travel are low because the stars are not in your favor. This month, you would probably travel alone mostly by train and road, with a fair amount of air travel.

Also, a trip abroad cannot be ruled out. But, certainly, these trips would not accomplish even a fraction of the goals. A good amount of this travel would not be related to your business or job. The most helpful direction would be East.

Insights from the stars

The last restraint goes on the 13th, and the horizon is open. You can complete your projects. On the other hand, take off your rose-colored glasses. This will keep you from making strategic mistakes. This month, you need to learn how to connect with people personally and professionally.

February 2023

Horoscope

You keep going in the same direction as last month! You have a lot of bright and ambitious energies that push you to make your plans come true. Happy opportunities come, and you meet people whose ideas you find interesting. You like to try new things and are working on several projects.

But if you want all of this to last, you must be realistic. Some ideas can be done this month, while others can't. Also, don't let the ideas of others fool you around the 5th, or you might have trouble around the 20th. The full moon and the new moon make you more generous but make you more likely to be let down.

Love

Venus in Pisces makes your life hard until the 20th. You feel like your loved ones are getting away from you. Your ability to attract people drops down! Don't despair! When Venus moves into Aries on the 21st, you find your way and the people who are right for you.

Those in relationships have a hard time until the 20th. Your partner wants you to be there more. People say that you don't give as much love as you get. From the 21st, offer a nice thing to do together as a distraction.

For single people, Venus makes life hard until the 20th if you don't get to the point. If it's too hard to be romantic, you should wait. From the 21st, she puts you in touch with people who like you.

Career

Still, everything looks good. You get lucky, and you do everything right. When the situation calls for it, you use it to your advantage. If you happen to meet very strict people, you can make the situation more relaxed by being yourself. Don't listen to your imagination if you want everything to work out for the best of all worlds. Why? Because it would make you more likely to make mistakes that would ruin everything.

During this month, you have a good chance of moving up in your career, but if you're not careful, you could easily fall back a few steps from where you are now.

Finance

On the money side, this doesn't look good, but it's best to get back to the basics. You won't have to deal with embarrassing financial situations that put you on the spot.

If you have a lot of energy and things are going well, you could do very well financially this month. You would have the courage to stand up for what you believe in and the drive to go after what you want and succeed. You would get a lot of help from a good combination of events.

This month, you can expect to get a lot of money quickly. An investment would be a good idea. There is also a chance that your relationships with your bosses will improve to the point where you can expect to gain a lot from this. This month's environment would be suitable for making investments and starting new businesses.

Health

A fortunate set of circumstances favors your excellent health this month, so you have nothing to be concerned about. Those susceptible to chronic colds and mucus discharge would be much alleviated. As long as treatment is handled seriously, those with piles can look forward to a period of alleviation and possibly full recovery.

On the other hand, all of this comes with a warning about the need for proper dental hygiene in everyday life. On this point, any lapse could lead to severe consequences. You should expect to be healthy this month, which is excellent.

Travel

A month when you can expect to make a lot of money because the stars are in your favor. This month, you will have a lot of confidence in yourself and the guts to make decisions. You would put a lot of thought into a travel plan that would make you a lot of money.

You would probably travel by train, car, and air a fair amount when you were on your own. A trip abroad is also not out of the question. Your trips wouldn't always be for business. You would achieve your goal, whatever it is. The North is the best direction.

Insight from the stars

You draw individuals from various backgrounds because of your excellent company. Keep your attention on those you truly connect with if you don't want to disgrace yourself. You will grow spiritually if you work hard to improve your life and find your divine life purpose.

March 2023

Horoscope

You continue to grow in a favorable environment, but Aquarius's radiant energy eventually fades away. For luck to continue to be on your side, you must make wise decisions. This month, your goal is not to change your mind when your projects are experiencing challenges. The best strategy is to work through the problems rather than avoid them.

How? by focusing on projects that have a direct impact. In addition, pay attention to the guidance you'll receive starting on the 8th. No matter how hard it may be, always choose knowledge over expediency. Accept criticism around the 7th since it will help you grow. A close friend saves the day on the 21st of this month!

Love

The energies that come from Aries help your relationships. They start them off with many activities, trips, and projects. It's a beautiful world! Starting on the 17th, pay attention to how you feel and try to calm down. This will keep you from being alone when you don't want to be.

Your partner can count on you to keep things from getting boring in your relationship. You are happy, but only as long as you don't only talk about your plans and goals. This would cause disagreements.

For singles, love can come out of the blue and lead to a passionate and exciting relationship. Don't quit because of a few minor problems. Instead, work hard, and everything will be okay.

Career

The move of Saturn into Pisces shows that there will be some small obstacles in this sector. But if you accept the challenge from the planet of wisdom, you can lessen its effects. Gemini, you have some good fortune in a lot of ways. If you want it to last longer, you must take it more seriously. Pay attention to detail. After that, you'll be happy to see that you indeed are a genius.

The horoscope has nothing particularly good to say about your career. There is a good chance that you will have a major disagreement with your bosses or partners. This should not be allowed to happen, and you should try to stop it from happening.

You might also be filled with a feeling of insecurity that would affect almost everything you do at work. You could try to fix the problem by switching jobs quickly or changing how your business works. This would be an awful situation to be. Any change should only be made after being thought about carefully. There would also be a lot of travel, which would be very useful.

Finance

Everything is fine from a financial point of view. Don't let how you felt on the 26th fool you if you want to keep this little miracle going.

A good month from a financial point of view. You can look forward to making lots of money quickly. Quite a few of you would also benefit from making investments. There's also a good chance that an old friend will do you a favor that could easily help you out financially.

Also, this month you'll find a way to deal with your bosses that will make the relationship very good for you. This could be a significant gain. Last but not least, associating with some smart, spiritually-inclined, and gifted people would be good for you both materially and spiritually.

Health

This month, the stars are in a good mood to help your health, so you should be in great shape for most of this time. Any tendency to get sudden, severe illnesses like fevers and inflammation would be greatly reduced. They would most likely not bother you at all.

This would also apply to people with any kind of tooth trouble. In fact, any problem with your dentures should be taken seriously and has a good chance of getting fixed. This is a good time for your health, and those who are already in the best of health can expect to stay that way.

Travel

This is an excellent month to make a lot of money from travel, as the signs from the stars are very good on this score. Those who want to study or train abroad or in a faraway place have a great chance of success.

You would usually travel alone by rail, road, and the air a fair amount. A trip abroad also can't be ruled out. Only a part of your travels would be for business. No matter your reason, your trips will get you what you're looking for. The best direction is south.

Insight from the stars

Even though this is not your thing, show some emotion in what you do and say. It is not much, but it will bring you a lot. Foreign gains will appear in your life. Keep taking calculated risks; your life will move forward more than you expected.

April 2023

Horoscope

For your part, your work and personal relationships benefit from the Aries energy. When it comes to novelty and change, your mind is open to it. Attracting people to yourself is a natural part of who you are. As soon as someone sees you, they feel drawn to you. You're in excellent spirits in this frantic environment.

All of your firepower is being utilized! Because of this, you are always thinking of new ideas. But if you want these advantages to work for you, you'll need to be realistic. You also need to put some restrictions in place. By being a little more moderate in your expectations, you will be able to avoid disappointment.

Love

This sector is maintained by your ability to divert attention when problems arise. Your charm begins to work wonders on the 12th. Your company is attractive and in high demand. However, even though you are in a whirlwind of seduction that satisfies you, you may feel lonely.

For those in a relationship, your projects or friendships may take precedence over reason. In turn, your other half may feel lonely and let you know. How? By isolating you in silence to draw your attention.

This month, singles, you multiply the meetings! However, if you want one of them to move towards stability, you must take the initiative. How? Don't forget to send out small messages from time to time!

Career

You crave variety because routine bores you. Unfortunately, you must deal with Saturn, who significantly slows your progress. On your worst days, you may feel as if you are on the bench. Gemini, luck continues to smile on you, so take advantage of it rather than trying to avoid what doesn't suit you.

There are very few promising signs for career advancement in the astrological alignment you face this month. You would work very hard, but your goals would elude you. There is also the possibility of serious disagreements with your partners or superiors.

This should be avoided at all costs, as the consequences can only be disastrous. Try to anticipate difficult spots and work your way around them. There would also be significant travel, resulting in no gains, though a trip to the south might yield some progress for you.

Finance

On the financial side, there is a soft heart behind the rough exterior that wants to please. If you don't want to get in over your head with your finances, set a limit and don't go over it no matter what.

This month, your financial prospects look pretty good and could put you on a solid financial footing for the long term. You can look forward to getting a lot of money quickly. Some people would make money through stock trading, which would also make them a lot of money.

You would learn how to deal with your subordinates or employees in a way that lets you get the most out of their work. This would be a big plus for you and help you make a lot of money. And lastly, your relationships with your bosses would become so pleasant that you would benefit greatly from them.

Health

Lady Luck is in the mood to bless your health, so you can expect to stay healthy this month. People with chronic illnesses like rheumatism and similar problems like flatulence and too much gas in the digestive tract can expect to feel better if they take care of themselves. This is also true for any kind of tooth pain.

You can also expect any nervous tendencies to improve and cause less trouble than usual. You might feel weak, but this is easy to fix with a bit of exercise and good food. A good month in which you probably won't face any serious health problems.

Travel

A month when it doesn't look like you'll get much out of traveling because the stars aren't in a good mood. You would probably travel by train, car, and air a fair amount when you were by yourself. Also, a trip abroad is not out of the question.

All these trips might be related to work and other things in equal measure. But no matter why you're doing these things, it's almost certain that you won't achieve even a fraction of your goals. As a result, it's a good idea to go over your travel plans ahead of time to see if they'll get you anywhere. The best direction to go would be South.

Insight from the stars

You get along well with other people and your group. But you sometimes have to take the lead if you want to keep good relationships. This month, you will make progress in your career. Everything is going in the right direction, so you should be happy with yourself.

May 2023

Horoscope

This month, Jupiter's time in Aries is over and you have until the 16th to fill your address book and your schedule with opportunities. Then you will be able to take advantage of all these benefits with the help of Sun in Gemini and Mars in Leo.

Even though you have a lot of energy and drive, take some time to think. Sort through everything you have collected to keep only what is realistic and doable.

Don't forget that Saturn's dissonances are keeping a close eye on you. They're not there to make you unhappy; in fact, that's not why they're there. They put roadblocks in your way to stop you from doing things that wouldn't be in your best interests.

Love

Until the 7th, you decide what happens. Your loved ones meet your expectations. Then the atmosphere could become less lively and lose its charm. If you want to avoid these problems, try to find magic or romance at candlelit dinners as much as possible.

This month is a little chilly for Geminis who are in a relationship. Even though you have enough money to keep going, this might not be enough. To break the ice, tell your partner what you want and how you feel.

Singles, this month, some meetings are canceled, and others are set up. This process can make you feel uncertain or alone. Use this time to consider whether you want to be in a long-term relationship.

Career

It looks like May will be a good month. You experience ease every day. You are doing a great job reaching your goals. But, starting on the 17th, you can feel a sudden stop. Don't move on when this happens. Use this time to review everything you've done in the past few months. After that, you can focus on what's most important, and your plans won't fall apart.

A month isn't good for advancing your career and would also be a sign to be careful as there is a good chance that you will have serious disagreements with your partners or bosses. As much as possible, this should not happen. Try to be patient and stay away from situations that might cause trouble.

There would also be a lot of travel, which seems like a waste of time and money, though there is a small chance of getting something out of going to the west. It would also seem pointless if a lot of hard work didn't lead to any results. You might be tempted to break the law to make money quickly in such a situation. Stop doing these things firmly if you don't want to invite trouble.

Finance

Your romantic relationships can cost you a lot of money. So, don't be stingy with your money, but try to control how much you give and how happy you feel.

A beneficial month from a financial point of view. You would make a lot of money quickly, which is likely to happen. Others would make a lot of money from trading activities, and you would be able to see quick, valuable results from your efforts.

Health

This month, the stars on your right side have a lot of good news for your health. Any tendency to have one tooth trouble or another should become much less bothersome. Be careful not to overdo it, though, because that could easily ruin a good situation. Make a new schedule that doesn't stress your body much.

If you don't take care of this, it could be terrible for your health. The rest is fine. People who are already like this wouldn't be bothered by a tendency to get nervous. A pretty good month in which you probably won't face any serious health problems.

Travel

The horoscope from the stars says nothing particularly good about the benefits of travel. This month, almost half of your trips would be for work or business, and the other half would be for other reasons.

You would probably travel alone most of the time, primarily by car or train. A trip abroad is also not out of the question. No matter why or how you travel, you likely won't get even a fraction of what you planned to get out of it. Thinking carefully about your travel plans before you make them would be wise. The best way to go would be to the west.

Insight from the stars

Your favorite planet, Mercury, wants you to think about everything that has happened in the past few months. Do this even though it is boring. It will be worthwhile. This is an excellent month to invest because your money is set, and you can only pay for what you need during the Mercury retrograde dates in 2023.

June 2023

Horoscope

This month of June is very private, but it's more boring regarding your job. Saturn in Pisces causes dissonances that make it hard to stay on track. Unfortunately, you're not very motivated because you're bored. Even though this isn't the best answer, change your mind as soon as possible. Venus and Mars in Leo work together with Mercury and the Sun in Gemini to make this little trick work. Your life is made more interesting by these sparkling energies. They like it when you talk with your group. They add movement to your life by taking you on vacations or other trips. Also, they tell you to make the most of the relationship that Jupiter gave you a few weeks ago.

Love

It's still a bit boring until the 12th, but don't worry, you'll be able to make up for lost time! Mars and Venus in Leo give your loves lively energy that makes you feel good. Your family and friends make you want to go out, date, and hang out with friends.

Even if you're in a relationship, you can't do much until the 12th, no matter how good your intentions or care. You're bothered by something. Then things improve. You do a great job of putting people at ease and making the atmosphere happy and pleasant.

If you're single, you're feeling a little sad. You're not sure if you want to travel or meet new people. Lucky for you, your friends help you find your way out and learn how to seduce.

Career

Saturn has taken over the wheel of this sector, which is not a good thing. You find the time passing slowly because your promises have yet to be fulfilled. Do not believe you've been cursed! Instead, go through everything that has been presented to you. There is always an opportunity in all of this. You can make it come to life if you want.

This month's star alignment does not bode well for your career prospects. There is a good chance that you will have serious disagreements with your superiors. This would be a disastrous development. As a result, you should work hard to avoid such an occurrence.

Furthermore, you may be burdened by a futile sense of insecurity. This may prompt you to seek redress by changing jobs or business operations. Travel will also yield no benefits, though a trip north may yield some.

Finance

You have until the 11th to update your financial accounts. Do it! Even if you find it annoying, you will not be sorry.

Your financial prospects are excellent this month, as the stars appear to be on your side. You could be a stone's throw away from a sudden gain and not realize it. You will reap a bountiful harvest of unexpected gains this month and will also be able to reap immediate benefits from your efforts.

There is a chance that investments will also be profitable. Most importantly, circumstances will emerge that will allow you to treat your superiors in a way that will be highly beneficial to you. Association with some wise learned people would be equally helpful.

Health

This month, the stars are on your side and will shower you with good health. People who often get cold hands and feet would notice a significant change, as their hands and feet would become noticeably less clammy.

Any persistent tooth trouble would also cause far less bother and, if treated diligently, would have a good chance of being cured.

There is also some solace that predisposition to nervousness and related disorders would be significantly alleviated. Overall, a favorable month in which you are unlikely to face any serious health risks.

Travel

This is not a good month for travel, according to astrology. Any pilgrimage to a holy place would be delayed or stopped by problems. Unfortunately, your dedication would not get you through.

Those who wanted to get a higher education or training abroad or somewhere far away would also have to deal with tough problems. You would travel alone mostly by car and train, with a fair amount of time spent flying. A trip overseas is also a possibility. But these trips would be utterly useless. The most favorable direction is Northwards.

Insight from the stars

It's time to get to know the new people you've met. One of them might be able to help your career move forward. Make your family happy by taking care of things. Always know that your friends and family will have your back.

July 2023

Horoscope

Your primary focus should be on achieving your goals. But the dissonances caused by Pisces and Virgo prevent it from succeeding. When you're feeling these energies, it's hard to know whether or not to have faith. They trick you into thinking you want greater independence, just to change your mind when you ask for it.

You don't want to feel like you're tethered to the ground! The temptation to make a dramatic decision is understandable, but it's not the best option. Waiting while using your relationships to attain your goal will save you a lot of headaches. The best way to deal with stress is to get out and meet new people. Reconnect with the people you've known for a long time. So, by doing so, your thoughts will become more lucid, and the answer will come to you at the perfect time.

Love

Your ability to stay within the boundaries Mars in Virgo places on you starting on the 11th will be critical to the success of your romantic relationship. The planets in Leo promise a month filled with intense feelings and heartfelt vows of love if you abide by their terms.

Bored? Use your imagination to keep yourself entertained. Having a relationship with you is a piece of cake. Don't allow yourself to become enamored with grandeur to the point that you begin to doubt your own happiness. Stay calm and collected, and everything will work out just fine.

When it comes to those looking for a partner, you will meet an attractive individual if you accept an invitation or go on a trip. Creating a connection is the only way for things to progress.

Career

This month, there is little to cheer about. You're more bored than ever by the same old thing. You get the impression that each day is the same. The moment you decide to make any headway; you'll find yourself right back where you started. Gemini! If you don't like it, don't let it stop you from achieving your goals. As long as you're at it, don't drift away.

This month's horoscope does not bode well for your professional aspirations. If you're feeling good about yourself, you might consider changing jobs or making other significant alterations to your business or service. Additionally, you may likely have disagreements with those in positions of authority.

This should be avoided since it will only worsen your current predicament. To make matters worse, you'd have to put in a lot of effort, leaving you frustrated and unsatisfied in the end.

Stability is preferred over erratic behavior, so strive to maintain it. People in your life may not be pleased to watch you grow. Be wary of their words of wisdom since they may want to bring you down or wish for your destruction.

Finance

The money is slipping through your fingers in the financial department. Unless you intend to become broke, set up a budget for each aspect of your life and try to stick to it.

You'll have a fantastic month ahead of you when the stars align, thanks to your positive outlook and boundless energy. As long as you have the confidence to stand up for what you believe in, you will be able to pursue your dreams and make them look effortless.

In this case, you would benefit much from a series of fortunate circumstances, and you can look forward to a bountiful crop of unexpected riches. Profits from investments would be substantial as well. Even more likely, you will be able to benefit much from the good connections you have built up with your superiors. This is a great moment to invest and start new businesses.

Health

This month, the gods are on your side regarding your health, and you will likely avoid any major health issues this month. You would no longer be susceptible to spells of sudden acute sickness, such as fever or inflammation, and these issues would no longer be a problem for you.

There are, however, reasons to be wary of your oral hygiene. Any lapse on your part here could lead to dental issues. Bone injuries, which are highly unlikely this month, should also be treated cautiously.

Travel

The stars aren't exactly aligned to make this a great month to travel, so you won't get much out of it. While traveling, you risk suffering an injury or experiencing some other form of bodily discomfort. Because of this, you should exercise caution and take only the smallest possible risks.

You'd prefer to travel alone and primarily by rail or road, with some air travel thrown in for good measure. Traveling for work or business may account for a portion of your journeys. A sizable chunk of the population isn't very closely linked. It's safe to say that they would be a waste of time. The possibility of a journey abroad is not ruled out, and the most advantageous direction is East.

Insight from the stars

Stop thinking about what's bothering you for a while. Your daily life is greatly improved by the stars in Leo. Be ready because the unexpected can happen and change how things are going. You and your partner will grow closer and eventually get the hang of it and enjoy each other's company.

August 2023

Horoscope

Saturn's dissonances make your life harder, and Mars in Virgo makes this even worse. You are really stuck this month. Your goals are hard to reach right now, but that doesn't mean they're impossible.

Mars wants you to act in a methodical way if you want to reach your goals. Mercury is also in Virgo, so you must pay attention to the little things. Saturn tells you that you will reach your goal in time. Use the energies that come from Leo instead of trying to control fate or events. Get in touch with your coworkers, friends, and people you care about. Put your ideas out there and listen to what others have to say. When Mars moves from Aries to Libra on the 28th, things calm down.

Love

Your actions are nice, but it's not enough. Things are still having trouble getting better. This month, you should go out and meet new people. Go see your friends. Accept invitations and go on trips over the weekend or on vacations. The blockages go away at the end of the month.

If you're in a relationship, you should stay reasonable even if you don't like how things are. Venus likes the way you feel about your partner. She wants you to spend time together in a place where you can talk about how much you love each other and have fun.

Venus promotes and encourages dating and flirting for single people. Where? by yourself or with friends. Wait until the end of the month for things to move forward. Show yourself off in the best way you can for now.

Career

Even though it's a good time to relax and do nothing, this sector worries you. It seems like nothing is going in the right direction. On the worst days, you feel like nothing is moving forward. Problems never happen by themselves, so some people help you figure out what to do. Sad to say, you don't agree with what they say. Don't be afraid. A friend will offer you something exciting.

The way the stars are lining up this month doesn't give you much hope about your career. You would constantly worry about your job, which would drive you crazy. This would change everything you do for your business or job.

It's possible that you could work very hard to reach your goals, but they would still elude you. You would look for a new job or make significant changes to how your business works. All of this, though, wouldn't make you happy. There is also the chance of getting into a big fight with your bosses. As much as possible, you should try to avoid this. Try to think ahead and take care of problems before they get too bad.

Finance

When it comes to money, daily life is secure, but if you want to make a significant investment, you should take the time to research the business you are about to partake in.

This month, you have great opportunities to make more money because the stars are in your favor. Musicians, actors, painters, playwrights, and other artists will likely have a very good month financially and creatively.

In fact, things would be going very well, and you can expect to make a lot of money quickly. Investments would also be helpful and make a lot of money. There is also a chance that a female friend will help you out, which could be a good thing for your finances.

Health

This month, your health will likely be in good shape because of good circumstances. People prone to long-term illnesses like rheumatism and digestive problems like flatulence and too much gas would feel much better. This means you wouldn't have to worry about these problems if you take standard precautions.

But if you have a sore throat that doesn't go away, you should be careful. This should be looked into carefully to see if there are any health issues, and then it should be treated with care. If you don't do this, it could mess up a good health situation that is going well. Aside from this, you don't have any real reason to worry.

Travel

This should be a good month for travel, and you should make good money from it. Most of the time, you would travel alone by train or car, with some flights thrown in. A trip overseas is also not out of the question.

Since not all of your trips would be related to your job or business, you would have a lot of success in getting what you set out to do. You would meet a lot of new people and have a lot of new opportunities. The best direction to go would be Northwards.

Insight from the stars

As of now, the stars in Leo are beneficial to your everyday life. As a result, making attempts to alter the situation is unwarranted. While you're rethinking your ideas, wait. When it comes to pursuing your aspirations, it's never too late. Put your faith in your abilities to make things happen.

September 2023

Horoscope

Pisces and Virgo clash, making it difficult to make progress. Several impediments stand in the way of your success. Discouragement can come out of nowhere. Do not be deceived by these dangers; they are not there to make your life unpleasant. It is best to let go of your hopes and dreams to avoid repeated disappointments. Wait for things to work out rather than trying to rush them.

With the help of Leo and Libra's energies, you'll be able to better connect with others. You should put your efforts here if you want things to get better. Why? Meetings and talks can lead to the development of a project.

Love

It is a good month for you and those you care about the most. You're a success in all you do. That smile of yours is magical. Your followers are desperate to get your attention, and they'll go to any lengths to get it. Listening to the thoughts and feelings of others opens up a world of possibilities.

Even though Mars and Venus favor your relationship, Mercury in Virgo is a thorn in your side. The promise of the Moon this month will not alleviate your other half's resentment. Showing that you are reasonable can help relieve tensions.

Singles can keep meeting new individuals as long as they want! You flirt with a ferocity that reflects your personality. If you want a meeting to develop into anything more, you need to give more attention to the person you like rather than treating them the same as everyone else.

Career

Your progress depends on how often you can take stock and not let things get out of hand. Even though it's not in your nature, Gemini, you should think before you act. Before you send a file, make sure you haven't forgotten anything. Write down everything you need to do in a notebook. When it seems stuck, don't keep going because you think it will work out on its own. Find the answer.

According to the horoscope, there isn't much good news about your career this month. There is a good chance that you will have major disagreements with your bosses. You can avoid this by trying to find trouble spots ahead of time and finding ways around them.

Also, this month would be filled with a feeling of insecurity. This would change the way you work as a whole. You would be unstable if you tried to change your job or how your business works. Any change you make should be done after careful thought. You would also work very hard, but even so, it's likely that you wouldn't reach the goals you set out for yourself.

Finance

On the financial side, it's the same fight, but with more details. Don't buy anything too expensive, because that will put you in the red.

According to your horoscope, this month should be financially good for you. Writers, poets, and other people like them would have a particularly good time financially and creatively.

You would literally make a lot of money quickly. Business and trading would also bring in a lot of money. Also, your relationships with your bosses and partners will likely improve to the point where you can expect to gain a lot from them. Also, the climate could be very good for making investments and starting new businesses.

Health

This month, the stars in front of you are good for your health. People with sensitive chests or lungs prone to health problems in these areas are likely to feel a lot better. There is a chance that overworking yourself will make you tired and weak.

You could easily avoid this if you didn't push yourself too hard. Once this is done, everything will be fine. This would also help you deal with the slight chance that you have a nervous disorder, though it's not likely. If you take care of yourself, you can stay healthy for the whole month. Pay a little more attention to how well your teeth are doing.

Travel

The horoscope from the stars doesn't tell us anything particularly good about what you can gain from travel. Writers, poets, and other people like them might not have the best trips. In fact, some of them could be seriously hurt because their stays aren't productive.

You would travel alone mostly by train or car, but you would also fly a fair amount. A trip abroad is also not impossible. But it's very unlikely that even a holiday, which might not be all that fun, would come out of these efforts. The best way to go is to the East.

Insight from the stars

Don't run away at the first problem. Instead, you should stop and think about it. When that is done, fix what needs to be fixed. You will have to learn to be patient with yourself this month. Do not be in a hurry. Let things work out the way they should.

October 2023

Horoscope

You have the impression that your room for maneuver is shrinking by the day. As a result, it might make you resentful and drive you to make judgments based on the wrong motivations.

A negative attitude toward others or bothersome events will not get you anywhere. Instead, remain a safe distance from the situation. You'll be able to see things in a new light if you do this. As a result, you will act in a different manner. Mars, Mercury, and the Sun in Libra will assist you in this endeavor by fostering friendships and promoting new knowledge while highlighting your strengths. This month, put your lightness to one side and focus on strategy.

Love

Your charm never fails to work. You always get what you want. You can be harsh for the wrong reasons, which is a shame. If you want your love life to look its best this month, show your friends or spouse how much you care. Instead of criticizing them, do what they want you to do.

Your relationship is affected by the needs of your family. Things won't get better if you run away, though. This month, the balance of your relationship will depend on how well you can put up with things that bother you.

For single people, it's easy to meet people, but if you want things to go further, you have to accept some limits. This month, you will meet someone with a future if you enjoy the charm of family life.

Career

This month is not a happy time. You think it takes too long. When things go wrong, you think you're just unlucky. Gemini, don't let fate hit you! For now, you need to use what you have and make it work. How? What? By thinking about what has happened in the past. Tell yourself that this time, which you believe to be so long, is actually your best friend, despite what you might think.

Your professional prospects are not looking too good this month because of the stars. There is a good chance that you will have serious disagreements with your bosses. You must not let this happen and work to stop it from happening. Try to guess where problems might occur and go around them.

During the month, you might feel insecure, which could cloud your judgment. You could choose to switch jobs or business operations quickly without a good reason. Any change should only be made after careful thought. Traveling won't help you in any helpful way, but a trip north could bring you some small benefits.

Finance

On the money side, living from day to day works out pretty well. This month, think about your expenses more often and save money.

This month, your financial prospects look pretty good because the stars are in a good place. There is a chance that your female friend will do you a good turn, which could be a big help.

The month looks pretty good, and you could expect to make a lot of money quickly. Even trading and gambling would be profitable. Also, there are signs that your relationships with your bosses would improve, which would be very good for you. The environment would also be suitable for new businesses and investments.

Health

This month, the combination of stars in front of you is good for your health. If you have a stomach and digestive organs that are easily upset, this will help a lot. So will long-term chest problems like asthma, coughs, and colds.

You should be careful about the health of your teeth because this would bother you, but if you take good care of your teeth, nothing terrible will happen. Also, there are some reasons to think that you might be irritable and a little bit upset most of the time. Stay calm and balanced. You can keep your mind and body in excellent shape with a little exercise.

Travel

The stars don't look suitable for travel this month, so there aren't many chances of making money. This month, you would probably travel alone, mostly by car or train, with a few flights thrown in.

Also, there is a chance that you might work or travel abroad. But it is almost certain that these efforts would not bring the expected profits, pleasure, and satisfaction. The best direction would be to go North.

Insight from the stars

You like to live at your own pace and without problems. Sad to say, it tricks you. This month, you should be happy to be limited in ways that make you want to run away for the wrong reasons. No matter how small an accomplishment is, you should be proud of yourself.

November 2023

Horoscope

Even though you are stuck, a way out is slowly becoming available. How? By getting help from people you know that like you. Sadly, if you mess up, you won't get anything out of it.

This month is an excellent time to take advantage of your relationship without being sneaky. To do well in this little trick, don't give in to the urge to make everyone your friend. Instead, think things through. Find the people who can help you or who have interesting ideas. Make real relationships with them. To help you, think about Venus in Libra and how she deals with people and subtleties.

Love

Your relationships grow in a romantic environment. Your partner or your fans would do anything to make you happy. When Mercury moves into Sagittarius on the 11th, things get more complicated. Changing what is being said won't solve the problem. On the other hand, it will be wiser to show that you are confident about the future.

For people in relationships, even though you try hard and have good intentions, conversations take a more spiteful turn. Anything can be a source of disagreement. To avoid this, you should occasionally feel romantic. Your significant other will be happy.

Singles, When Venus is in Libra, dating is easy as early as the 9th. Your charm works wonders. On the other hand, don't say what you think about relationships because it could turn off people looking for a serious relationship.

Career

If you only think about what's wrong, you will make the wrong choice. So, instead of going over all the mistakes in your work, look at all the good things about it. Have a look around. As you know how to do so well, make happy connections with other people. And if you have brilliant ideas, make them happen. By doing this, you'll get rid of this habit that makes you want to go as far as you can.

There's nothing particularly good about the signs for your career this month. There is a good chance that you would have major disagreements with your bosses. No matter how hard it is, you should do everything you can to avoid this happening because if it does, it can only hurt your career.

Throughout the month, you would also have a deep-seated feeling of insecurity, which could affect how you act professionally. You might choose to switch jobs or business operations quickly. You should only make a change after carefully thinking about it.

Finance

On the money side, being balanced depends on the choices you make. So, weigh the pros and cons before you make a decision.

The stars say that this month's turn of events would not be suitable for your financial growth. Yes, there are clear signs that some of you would lose a lot of money if you invested. So, it would also be wise to avoid all kinds of gambling.

There are also signs that any dispute or lawsuit you might be involved in would almost certainly go against you, causing you to lose a lot of money. So, it would help if you tried to ensure that the decision in any such matter is put off until a better time. Relationships with business partners are also likely to go downhill. If you can't stop this from happening, you could lose a lot of money.

Health

This month, the stars are in a way that is good for your health. People prone to sudden, severe illnesses like fevers or inflammations would feel a lot better, even if they only last a short time. Most likely, this kind of trouble wouldn't bother you at all. The same thing would be true for back pain.

But there are reasons to worry about the chance of an eye infection. This might bother you for a short time, but you could avoid even this by staying clean and taking a right preventive medicine. Overall, for your health, that's excellent news for this month.

Travel

Nothing particularly good about what the stars say about what you'll get out of traveling. This month, you would travel alone mostly by car and train, but you would also fly a fair amount.

There is also a chance that you will travel abroad, but these efforts won't bring the profits or pleasures hoped for. This is a pretty dark picture, but it's true. A lot of your travel may not be necessary, and you could do just fine without it. The best direction to go is West.

Insight from the stars

Novelty solves your problems. This month, you will get out of a rut or get what you want by making real connections with other people. Be willing to make changes that will improve your life and the lives of those you care about.

December 2023

Horoscope

This month, the dissonances from Pisces are made worse by the ones from Sagittarius. They make you feel like you've come to a dead end. This feeling, which should make you unhappy, makes you want to get rid of it at any cost. To do this, you will think that any means are good! Some of them will actually be good. Others won't have the same luck, though. It's a good idea to find your freedom to act. But try not to use plans that will work against you. Instead, it would be best if you focused on opportunities that will lead somewhere. Things will take longer to set up if you take the serious route. But in exchange, you'll avoid avoidable disappointments.

Love

Venus in Libra keeps things calm and peaceful. With the dissonances of Sagittarius on the 5th, the weather could become more unstable. This month, don't make your loves more exciting by making them compete with each other. Why? Because it will lead to arguments and never-ending requests.

For people dating, things can change quickly when Mars is in the picture. This might make you laugh at the time, but this little game could also lead to unpredictable reactions. Don't go too far this month, and everything will be fine.

For people who don't have a partner, Venus moves into Scorpio on the 5th. Even though it doesn't change much about you, it makes you harder to seduce. Your way of doing things could work, but only if you don't take advantage of it.

Career

Before making a decision or starting a project this month, you should consider it. Why? Because you can be led to false ideas that keep you stuck and make it hard to get out. Gemini, for once, don't believe everything you hear. And if you say you'll do something, make sure you do it. By doing this, you'll save yourself the trouble that would have saved you time instead.

This is a good month to get ahead in your career. People who like art and people who work in the fine arts can look forward to a time when their creative work will be very satisfying. Some of you may even make a name for yourselves with your profession.

There would also be a lot of travel, which would be helpful. The best direction would be to go south. Besides traveling, you might also change where you work or do business. But think carefully before making any changes because a hasty move could easily undo a lot of your hard work.

Finance

Check how much money you have before you use your credit card!

This month, your financial goals should be easy to reach, according to what the stars tell you. You would literally make a lot of money quickly. Investments and trading business would also be a great way to make money.

Writers, poets, and other creative types can look forward to an inspiration that will be both financially and creatively helpful. Having friends who are wise and smart would be just as beneficial. Also, there is a good chance that your bosses, business partners, or employees will help you out in a big way. Your relationship with them would change for the better and grow into something good.

Health

This month, you have a number of good things going for you that are good for your health. Chronic diseases like rheumatism and gout, as well as problems with the digestive system like flatulence and too much wind, would get a lot better. This shouldn't be taken as a free pass to stop being careful, though. With regular care, there would be a relief.

There are some reasons to be a little worried about the state of your teeth. If you take care of your teeth, nothing terrible will happen to them. In fact, you have a good month ahead of you in which you won't have to worry about any significant health risks.

Travel

According to the horoscope, this is a good month to travel because the stars are in a good place. Travel can be good for writers, poets, and others like them, both in making money and getting ideas for their work.

You would usually travel by yourself, mostly by car or train, with some air travel. A trip abroad is not impossible. You can be sure that these efforts will help you reach the goals you set out to reach. The best direction is to go South.

Insight from the stars

Don't take the emergency exit if you feel like your freedom is being threatened. Instead, try something new and go through the main door! Single people will finally find their true love. After looking for a long time, you will find that one person who makes your heart full.

CANCER 2023 HOROSCOPE

Overview Cancer 2023

This year, Jupiter moves through your 10th house of Aries until May, when it moves to your 11th house of Taurus. This would put your professional life in the spotlight until May. After that, your attention would shift to money and rewards. Saturn transits your 8th house of Aquarius before moving to your 9th house of Pisces, limiting your opportunities for prosperity and higher education.

Uranus will spend the whole year in your 8th house of Aquarius. Neptune would be in your 9th house of Pisces, and Pluto would be in your 8th house of Aquarius. Pluto stays in Capricorn until May or June, when it moves to your 8th house of Aquarius. The positions of the planets from now until 2023 will affect your life in general all through this year.

Cancerians would have a slow start to the year 2023. Things will get back on track as the year goes on, though. This year, you will be able to deal with problems and crises and get your life back under control.

During this year's transit of Venus and Mars, the planets that govern love and marriage, love will be abundant. Having Jupiter and Saturn in your chart also ensures a more peaceful and harmonious relationship with your significant other. A long-term commitment like marriage is on the horizon for individuals who want to get married. As the year progresses, you will experience a sense of security and stability in your relationship or marriage. Your companion would be able to calm your nerves and alleviate your stress. Family relationships must be maintained throughout the year. For single Cancerians, this is the time of year when you are most attractive to a romantic partner.

In 2023, the professional lives of those born in Cancer will be affected in many ways. You'll need to put in more work if you want to succeed or advance in your career; luck isn't on your side these days. It is possible that Saturn's transit into your 8th house will cause delays and stumbling blocks in your professional endeavors. Maintain a regular schedule and avoid making enemies. This year, you can count on the support of your bosses or superiors in the workplace. A good year awaits those who are involved in business.

In March, Saturn will be transiting your 9th house of Pisces, which means you'll have a healthy year ahead of you. During the first quarter, though, with Saturn transiting your Aquarius 8th house, you may experience health troubles of some form. During this time, be sure to keep a close eye on your health. Keep an eye out for infectious diseases that are making the rounds, and watch your diet. Jupiter's influence on the 9th house ensures that your health will not deteriorate significantly. On the other hand, stress and tension are likely to cause health problems among Cancerians.

This year should be moderately productive in terms of the economy. There will be an inflow of wealth, but savings will not be guaranteed due to overspending. Avoid squandering your money. Gains are possible in May when Jupiter transits to your 11th house. Furthermore, Jupiter's aspect on your second and fourth houses will bring you a lot of land and luxury vehicles. However, there would be spending because of significant events at home. If you've been considering making high-value investments, this year is the time to do it. This year, property disputes will end in your favor.

As 2023 begins, Jupiter will be in your third house of Virgo, making it possible for you to take many short, profitable trips. Jupiter also makes it likely that many long-distance trips will happen during the year. You could learn from their travels and make money from them. Along the way, you would make new connections that would change your life in the long run. Some Cancerians are likely to travel because of job transfers, moving, and other similar reasons. You are asked to be careful when travelling because accidents can happen. You could also lose money or valuables while travelling, so watch out for scams.

Jupiter will be in your 9th house at the beginning of the year, which will help you do some spiritual exercises. This year, you will be more committed to your religious work than ever. Cancerians would be more interested in the occult sciences in the year's second half. Donate food and clothes to people who need them when you can. Those who believe in God are also told to worship their creator passionately all year.

This year, you are encouraged to follow your dreams wholeheartedly. Don't let outside things slow you down or stop you from moving forward in life. Big changes are coming, so welcome them with all your heart. Trust your family and friends, and don't keep judging people. You always have their backs. Put everything you have into your job and get out of your comfort zone. You shouldn't feel down because you'll soon meet some good people. Enjoy the good things that life gives you, and don't be sad about it.

January 2023

Horoscope

You're taking on the new year with the feeling that you're surrounded by others! You feel the strain of Aries and Capricorn's clashing energies. They give you the sensation that you're not doing enough and that your boss or spouse is always dissatisfied with you.

On the 6th, watch out when the full moon is in your sign! The big bad blues could hit you! But if you want to keep going, Neptune and Uranus will always help you as friendly signs. They want you to put things in perspective, so they don't get to you. When it comes to matters of the heart, the atmosphere is not suitable for candlelight dinners and romance. On the other hand, it helps people talk about ideas.

Love

Between February 4 and 27, Venus in Aquarius doesn't care about your feelings. On the other hand, intellectual complicity is very attractive. You will feel alone in this place where there is no love. From the 28th, Venus in Pisces returns to being kind and giving.

This month, Mercury is the main force in zone seven of your solar theme if you are in a relationship. Sometimes the conversations are happy and helpful. Sometimes, they come close to breaking up. But you can be sure it takes more than that for the ship to sink.

This month, Venus is entertaining singles. It forces you to meet someone who makes you want to learn more. Before you get too excited, wait until the 28th to see how things proceed. Venus ties everything together, both in a good way and a bad way.

Career

To achieve your goals, you must work hard every day. Going to work every day means putting in your best effort. Capricorn's dissonances can make it challenging to deal with others, especially on the 6th, when the full moon is in your sign. So, if you're tired of fighting, don't. Take some time off.

In your professional life, this is a wonderful month to make progress. Creative endeavors will be tremendously rewarding for artists and fine art practitioners in the month. You may go on to achieve fame and fortune because of your creativity.

There would also be a lot of travel involved, which would be quite advantageous. In terms of location, heading south is the way to go. You may likely have to relocate your business or work location if you are going on a business trip or taking a new job. However, you should take your time before making any changes since any quick move could potentially erase all of your hard work.

Finance

Purchasing items in multiples of two, three, or four and in various colors satisfies your desire for variety while also saving you money. Make sure this anti-stress therapy doesn't end up costing you money.

This month's astrological predictions for your financial prospects portend smooth sailing toward your goals. This might mean a windfall of cash. It would also be lucrative to invest in the stock market.

For writers, poets, and others of their kind, the coming months promise to be fruitful monetarily and creatively. In the same way, a friendship with wise and knowledgeable people would be beneficial. It's also possible that your supervisors or coworkers will reap substantial rewards from your efforts. Having a better relationship with them would lead to more positive outcomes.

Health

This month, you have a favorable set of circumstances promoting your health. Any predisposition to chronic disorders such as rheumatism and gout, as well as digestive system irregularities such as flatulence and excess wind, would be significantly relieved. This should not, however, be interpreted as a license to disregard all caution. Normal caution would result in masked relief.

There are valid reasons to be concerned about your dental health. If you take care of your teeth, you can avoid any problems. In fact, you have a beneficial month ahead of you in which you will not face any serious health risks.

Travel

This month's travel is unlikely to yield significant returns, as the astrological forecasts aren't very optimistic. Poets and writers who travel may have a very unproductive time financially and in terms of getting ideas for their work.

You'd prefer to travel alone, primarily by road or rail, with some air travel thrown in. An international excursion is not ruled out. There is no doubt that your efforts will fall far short of their intended results. South is the best direction.

Insight from the stars

You can use your irritations and mood swings to your advantage if you really want to. How? By focusing on how your opponents feel. The beginning of the month will be slow, giving you time to align your goals with your divine purpose and make practical plans.

February 2023

Horoscope

You will still have to deal with the conflicting energies from Capricorn and Aries this month. In this cold and demanding environment, you will feel like luck is not on your side. Your professional entourage puts you under pressure. You have to work hard to reach your goals. You might feel like you don't belong or that someone wants to take it from you.

You can count on the Pisces energies to help you hold on. They help you get away when things are getting too bad. They give you little things that make you feel better. The new moon that forms in Pisces around the 20th provides you with inspiration.

Love

With Venus in Pisces until the 20th, you're swimming in happiness. It makes or strengthens bonds of love that make you feel like everything is fine. On the other hand, if you want this utopian climate to last past the 21st, you should try to control how much you depend on other people emotionally.

If you're in a relationship, your partner takes care of you and shows you love. You feel safe and protected. But starting on the 21st, don't blame your partner if they have less time to spend with you.

For single people, Venus brings them together with the right person. All the lights are green until the 20th so that a relationship can start on the best possible note. But starting on the 21st, don't act based on how you feel. Instead, use your head.

Career

It is presently not easy in this industry. Compromises and concessions are a necessary part of achieving your goals. You'll also have to deal with those who aren't afraid to put themselves out there to achieve what they desire. Don't give up, even if these challenges appear insurmountable. Because, despite your fears, you will rise to the challenge and be rightfully proud of what you have done.

This is a good month for your professional career. Fine artists and those who follow in their footsteps would be in their element. You may even become well-known as a result of your efforts. You are working hard and achieving your goals in a timely manner. You'll be successful in this endeavor.

A movement in location may even be necessary, whether a business or service move. Even so, it's probably best to make a change only after giving it some serious thought first. Additionally, there would be a good amount of travel involved, which would be highly useful in the grand scheme of things.

Finance

On the financial front, you can rest assured that your everyday needs will be met. A major buy, on the other hand, is more challenging. Please be patient.

Financially speaking, you're in for a rough ride this month, thanks to a bad mix of stars in your favor. You could lose a lot of money if you were to gamble on the market. The lesson is clear: avoid all forms of gaming, even online ones.

There's a good chance you'll lose your job because of a breakdown in your relationship with your bosses. By taking action early on, you can prevent this from happening. Due to the sluggish economy, investing or establishing new initiatives will be difficult. To put it another way, such plans should be put on hold for the time being.

Health

How the stars are aligned this month is good news for your health in many ways. All you have to do is not to work too hard. This should be avoided at all costs, and energies should be spread out wisely so normal activities can go on without putting too much stress on the system.

This can be done quickly and easily by making a new schedule of things to do. You should take care of your teeth and take all the usual precautions. Aside from that, you should have a fairly good month in terms of health.

Travel

During this month, your chances of making money from travel are not very good because the stars are not in your favor on this front. This month, you will probably travel alone most of the time by train, car, and air.

Also, a trip abroad is not impossible. But one thing is sure: these trips would not accomplish even a fraction of the goals. The majority of this travel would be unrelated to your business or job. The best direction would be to go West.

Insight from the stars

Don't try to solve other people's problems if you want a good February. If you stay away, everything will be okay. Don't make hasty, rash choices that will cost you a lot in a short amount of time.

March 2023

Horoscope

Tensions between Aries and Capricorn start to go away. You should feel much better thanks to Saturn's move into Pisces on the 8th. These energies dispel doubts. They help you avoid dangers that could cause you to lose your money. This month, you start to change in a way that's much better for you.

Planets that move quickly and change into friendly signs make for happy, productive times that make you forget the little things that bother you. They tell you to choose a hobby that calms you down and makes you feel better. The full moon on the 7th gives you great inspiration. On the other hand, try to keep your cool around the 21st, as the new moon in Aries causes arguments.

Love

Things get better after the 3rd, but you have to give in to keep the peace. From the 21st, Venus helps you get back in touch with people who care about you. When Mars moves into your sign on the 26th, you can finally start what you've been putting off since the beginning of the year.

As time passes, you two get along better for people who are dating. It is all about understanding each other so your relationship gets back on track and you feel better now. Don't think about what bothers you if you want this peace to last.

For people who don't have a partner, the planets in friendly signs, on the other hand, kick start what was broken. They make you feel confident that a person or a relationship is real. At the end of the month, Mars wants you to do something that will make you happy.

Career

The arrival of Saturn is good for your business because it reduces the destructive effects of Jupiter in Aries, which frustrates this sector. Even though something better is expected to happen, the tensions don't go away. So, you will still have to work with a stressed-out boss or customers who are in a hurry. Do things at your own pace. Don't put yourself under pressure. If you do this, you'll reach your goals faster than you think.

During this month, you won't be able to advance in your job, and if you're not careful, you could fall a few rungs below where you are now. There is a good chance that you might be tempted to break the law to make money quickly. If this is allowed, it can only lead to dire consequences. So, you must make a firm decision not to give in to such temptations.

There is also a chance that you will have major disagreements with your bosses. Again, this is something you should do everything you can to avoid. Also, insecurity would make you more likely to change jobs or business partners quickly. Only make a change after carefully thinking about it.

Finance

There are no problems with money this month. Happiness never comes by itself. If you need money to pay for a big purchase, you can get it.

If you were full of energy and in a good situation, you would do very well financially in the coming month. This month, you will have the courage to stand up for what you believe in and the drive to move forward with your goals and achieve success. You would be helped a lot by a very good set of circumstances.

In fact, you may expect to reap a big harvest of sudden gains literally. Even gambling would be profitable. There's also a chance that your relationships with your bosses will get so good that you'll benefit greatly from this. The climate would also be good for making investments and starting up new businesses.

Health

A favorable set of circumstances favors your well-being this month, so you have no reason to be alarmed. Chronic colds, excessive mucus secretion, and the like would be much reduced. People with piles might also get some relief and maybe even be cured if they get treatment immediately.

Despite all this, there remains a warning about the importance of good dental hygiene. The consequences of any lapse in due diligence could be severe. Overall, it is a beautiful month for your health, and you can expect it to continue.

Travel

The stars aren't exactly on your side regarding travel this month, which means that you could lose a lot of money. While traveling, you risk getting hurt or having a medical issue. Take precautions and try to avoid any dangers.

You'd largely use the road and rail to get about, with a little bit of air thrown in for good measure. A journey out of the country is also a possibility. These excursions would be a complete waste of time in every respect. Only a tiny fraction of the work would be done for profit, so no money would be made. You'd be left wanting more. The most promising direction is East.

Insight from the stars

If you're looking for love, kindness, and respect, this is the month for you. All of this should be welcomed with enthusiasm, and enjoyment should be had without restraint. Challenges will come your way, but don't let them get the best of you.

April 2023

Horoscope

Even though they are less common, Aries' energies are still very much alive. Mars is in your sign, which strengthens everyone's and your emotional reactions. You're overwhelmed, but you don't know why. You can keep up with the help of the energies that flow through Taurus. They help you keep your cool when things get a lot worse. They give you the courage and persistence you need to avoid making decisions for the wrong reasons.

When Mercury goes retrograde on the 22nd, it helps you put things in perspective and figure out what they mean. Not too far away, Saturn in Pisces tells you to use your skills to get out of dangerous situations.

Love

If you wish to maintain a peaceful state of mind, the forces of Taurus and Mars tell you not to play with the devil. Hold your impatience and avoid putting too much pressure on yourself, even if it seems tough. For the time being, don't worry about all the things you don't know.

When it comes to couples, even though this area of your life is under stress, you shouldn't let it cause you to jeopardize your relationship. Take a breather from the stresses of your relationship and appreciate the benefits of your union.

For those who are single, Venus will be in Taurus until the 11th, so your loves will appear to you in the best possible light. Unfortunately, Venus in Gemini puts a stop to all of this. Keep your spirits up, and don't become discouraged! Keep in touch and strengthen your relationship with Mercury.

Career

To combat the Aries energies is difficult for you because of your astrological sign. This month, because Mars is in your sign, it's even more challenging. To your surprise, Cancer, you have the ability to realize your goals. In other words, don't take anything personally. Think about things from a different perspective. This way, you will be able to observe that things are going well and that you have made progress.

This month, you should have a lot of chances to move up in your career because the way the stars are aligned is perfect for this. You can look forward to a lot of travel, but it might not be profitable.

You would probably work hard and go after your goals in a business-like manner. This would go very well. There is also a good chance that the place where a job or business is done will change. This, too, would be a good thing. All in all, this month would be very good for your career, and a lot could be done during this time.

Finance

On the financial front, everyday life is secure. Everything is fine. However, it becomes a little stuck when it comes to the larger expenses. Instead of obscuring reality, consider this.

A profitable month in terms of your financial prospects. You can anticipate a bountiful harvest of unexpected profits and would also benefit from investments. There is also a good chance that an old friend will do you a favor that will be a financial blessing.

Furthermore, you will learn a new way of dealing with your superiors this month that will make the relationship very beneficial to you. This could be a significant gain. Finally, associating with several talented individuals of learning and spiritual nature will benefit you both materially and spiritually.

Health

This month, the stars are in a good mood to bless your health, and you should be in good health for most of the month. Any predisposition for bouts of sudden acute illness, such as fevers and inflammation, would be significantly reduced. They would most likely not bother you at all.

This also applies to people who have tooth problems. In fact, any problem with your dentures should be taken seriously and treated as soon as possible. This is a good time for your health, and those already in good shape can expect to stay that way.

Travel

Travel's expected prospects will simply not come your way this month, nor will the fun and pleasure associated with it, because the stars are not in your favor. If you are planning a pilgrimage to a holy place, it is possible that the trip will be postponed or that difficulties will arise during the planning process. The fact that your devotion may see you through is a different story.

You would most likely travel alone by rail or road, with some air travel thrown in for good measure. A foreign trip is not out of the question. All of these efforts, however, would be completely futile. The most promising direction is to the East.

Insight from the stars

Instead of fearing the worst, seize the opportunity to assess your feelings, wishes, and the significance of the unexpected hazards. See the best in yourself and push yourself beyond your limits. Take risks and constantly seek ways to break free from your comfort zone.

May 2023

Horoscope

The energies emitted by Jupiter in Aries gradually fade until they vanish on the 16th. Because of Jupiter's influence in Taurus, your life will get back on track starting on the 17th.

The positive and constructive aspect connecting one side to Saturn in Pisces and the other to Mars in Cancer indicates that you will feel much better! The feeling that fate has struck you for unknown reasons fades. It is replaced by the sensation of having a lucky star above your head. Your existence takes on a new dimension in this atmosphere of understanding, good humor, and good fortune. It broadens your horizons, allowing you to utilize your talents, skills, and experience better.

Love

You go along with it, but little by little, things start to get better. Things will get better when Venus moves from Gemini to Cancer on the 8th. Jupiter in Taurus ushers in a positive shift! In this atmosphere of trust and understanding, you finally stop holding back.

For couples, your marriage is regaining its meaning slowly but surely. Mercury's calming effects restore the bonds. Venus, starting on the 8th, brings back feelings. Starting on the 16th, you can make suggestions to your partner without getting turned down.

This month, for singles, the impossible becomes possible. The stars in friendly signs help you connect with someone who might surprise you with how kind and available they are. You decide what happens next!

Career

Keep your head up, Career Cancer! You only have a few more days to deal with the stress of Jupiter in Aries, and then you can breathe again! So don't give up, even if you feel like it. You will feel much better after the 17th. Because of a happy set of circumstances, the facilities will replace the problems and tensions. You will remember how nice it is to do your work in a place where there is understanding and peace.

This is an excellent month to get ahead in your work. Those who like art and those who work in the fine arts can look forward to a time when their creative work will be very satisfying. In fact, your contributions could help you make a name for yourselves. Your creativity will be helpful; this is an excellent chance to step up and use your power spontaneously. Your boss will like you more if you are creative and willing to use your skills to help out when time is of the essence.

Finance

On the financial front, this industry is doing well, but only if you keep your expenses reasonable.

The signs from the stars point to smooth sailing about your financial prospects this month and your goals. You will reap a bountiful harvest of unanticipated profits. Investments and businesses would be profitable as well.

Writers, poets, and others of a creative bent can look forward to a particularly beneficial spell financially and creatively. Association with wise and learned people would be equally beneficial. Furthermore, there is a strong possibility of substantial gains from your superiors or employees. Your interactions with them would improve and grow fruitfully.

Health

This month, a favorable set of circumstances is at your disposal to help you maintain a healthy lifestyle. Those prone to rheumatism and gout, as well as digestive issues like gas and an abundance of wind, would see great improvement with this treatment. However, that doesn't give you the green light to forsake all caution. There would be a veiled sense of relief if you acted normally.

You have good reason to be concerned about your oral health. If you take good care of your teeth, you won't have to worry about anything. Your health will be safe for the month ahead of you, so take advantage of it while you can.

Travel

Unfortunately, based on astrology, this isn't a month to go on a trip and make significant gains. Writers, poets, and others like them may find that travelling is a waste of money and a source of little inspiration.

You'd prefer to travel on foot or by train, although you'd also occasionally fly. We cannot rule out the possibility of a journey to another country. However, it is almost certain that these efforts will not reach even a fraction of their targets. The South is the best direction to go.

Insight from the stars

Every step of your journey takes place in a world that works for you. Don't be afraid to take advantage of the possibilities that come your way, much more than you might expect. There will be a slight improvement in your financial situation this month. Everything may not go as planned, but don't worry; things will return to normal soon.

June 2023

Horoscope

Your life is more peaceful now that Jupiter is in Taurus. However, you may believe that its effects are insufficient. The opportunities have been long awaited. Why? Because the evolutionary star is linked to Saturn in Pisces. This indicates that your expansion is underway; rest assured that it will be done gradually but steadily! However, be cautious because small changes can be implemented this month to improve your daily life.

A proposal made to you between January 1st and November 11th may still be relevant. Take as much time as you need to think, but not for eternity! Saturn assists you, but that is no reason to take advantage of his protection!

Love

Because it is in your sign until the 5th, Venus places you in a favorable environment. Then her voice shifts! For the rest of the month, you'll have other cravings. You're in desperate need of something else, and let everyone know about it in a quiet but unusually firm manner.

In relationships, the planets in Taurus positively influence until the 11th. The conversations are pleasant and productive. Your partner is paying attention to you. Unless you choose to be more outgoing than usual, you may begin to feel isolated once more.

Before the 11th, everything is set up properly for singles! Then, like a soufflé, everything collapses to the ground. Changes can be made if everyone agrees. How? Put yourself in even more of a position of prominence!

Career

This area is noticeably more tranquil. So quiet, you might wonder when things will start to change. You seem to be bored with your own company, don't you? So don't worry about that! You can rest assured that everything will be alright in the end. Don't get bogged down in pondering the meaning of life during this period. Take your time before accepting any money-making opportunity that may come your way.

There are a lot of career advancement opportunities this month because the stars look to be on your side. If you're serious about achieving your goals, you'll put in the time and effort necessary to see them through. You may have to relocate your business or work if you go through this process. this would be a good thing.

In addition, there would be a lot of travel. The best route to head in for this would be west, as it would serve both needs well. Anxiety or worry may be pervading your thoughts at the moment. If you want to make quick money, there's a chance you will break the law to do so. Such tendencies need to be severely restrained.

Finance

In terms of your financial future, this is a very positive month. You stand to benefit significantly from the windfall profits that will come your way and would profit handsomely from such investment or gambling activities.

You will get valuable results from your efforts in a short time and get the most out of your subordinates or juniors by employing a more effective approach. It's possible this could be the most significant gain in a month that was otherwise quite profitable. In addition, there is a strong likelihood that an elderly friend will perform a service or favor for you, resulting in substantial financial gain.

Health

This month's stars in your direction have a lot to cheer you on when it comes to staying healthy. It is expected that any predisposition to dental issues will diminish significantly. There is, however, a warning about over-exertion, which could easily ruin a good scene. Plan a new schedule that doesn't stress your body much.

Neglect and carelessness here could have severe consequences for your health. The rest is fine, as well. Nervousness would not bother those who were already predisposed to this. This is a good month for your health because there aren't any major health issues.

Travel

The stars don't have anything particularly enlightening to say about the benefits of travelling. These trips would be roughly split between work and personal travel this month.

If you're planning on doing a lot of traveling by yourself, the most common modes of transportation will be car and train. The possibility of a trip abroad cannot be ruled out. Regardless of the purpose or mode of travel, it is almost certain that only a small percentage of the stated benefits will be realized, so it is important to plan your trip carefully. The West would be the best direction to go.

Insight from the stars

You are endowed with many qualities! Unfortunately, the others have difficulty distinguishing between them. Instead of wasting time, highlight them! Minor illnesses will disrupt your daily life, but you must seek medical attention before things worsen.

July 2023

Horoscope

Jupiter, the lucky star, and Mars in Virgo are all linked up starting on the 11th. Consequently, things are beginning to look up. The chances are growing better and better, and they're also more exciting. This month, you have an abundance of energy that motivates you to take smart chances. Confidence in your talents and attributes is required for this. You're no longer hesitant to declare your goals. Progress is something you seek, and why not? It will release you from the things that are holding you back from fully blossoming.

A smile spreads over your face whenever you are engaged in some form of activity. You feel as if you're a part of the world. Your friends and family will always be there for you, no matter how risky your plans may be.

Love

Your desires shifted, and those around you assumed it was a passing fad. They're in for a surprise this month! Your romantic side starts to get in the way. You want evidence of love and not just any kind. To get you to like them, they have to be intelligent and beautiful.

When you're in a relationship, you both have different wants and needs while also wanting to keep your assets. This kind of prodigy is impossible to do, but this month it is possible. How? By living a five-star life for a few hours or days.

For singles, A charismatic person who is ready to go out and seduce you is drawn to your charm. Listen to your gut for the magic to work. If you need help, ask your friends what you should do. They'll advise you.

Career

This industry is once again calm and confident. You recover the pleasure of working. Happiness never happens by itself, so people who like you are in contact with you. Your everyday routine becomes more laid back suddenly. If you run into a problem by chance, you solve it without fumbling around in different ways. It's now or never when it comes to accomplishing your goals.

It's a good month for your career because of the alignment of the stars in your favor. On the other hand, travelling isn't likely to bring any benefits, but a short trip to the north might.

Finance

According to astrology, the stars don't look good for your finances this month. There is a good chance that your relationship with your business partners or bosses could get so bad that you might have to lose money because of it. So, you must be prepared for this possibility and take steps well in advance to stop it from happening.

There would be many opportunities, but you would have difficulty getting closer to your goals. You might also focus too much on making money that can't be tracked. This can only make things worse for you in the long run. Change this. You should also avoid gambling this month.

Health

During this month, the stars will bestow upon you good health. You'll notice an improvement in the quality of your hands and feet, as they'll be less clammy.

If you seriously handle your tooth pain, it will cause you significantly less discomfort and a better chance of healing. As a bonus, those with a history of anxiety and other mental health issues will see a big improvement. If you have surgery this month, it is sure to be successful. This month it's going to be a good one for your overall health.

Travel

It may be a month in which it may be hard to make money from travelling, since the stars aren't very positive in this area. A pilgrimage to a holy place would have to be put off or get stuck in problems. Your dedication would get you through, of course.

Those who wanted to go to school or get training abroad or somewhere far away would also have to deal with challenging problems. You would mostly travel by car and train, but you would also fly a fair amount. A trip abroad is also not out of the question. On the other hand, these stays would be a total waste of time. The North is the best direction.

Insight from the stars

Right now, you are in an ascension phase. It is because of this that you encounter various individuals. Don't be afraid to ask for help from those you know and trust. This is the finest time of year to invest in assets that you can utilize to boost your fortunes.

August 2023

Horoscope

You gradually become aware of the opportunities that lie before you. Your abilities are on display. Good fortune results from doing the right things at the right moment. You have the means to enhance your quality of life and make it more comfortable and enjoyable if you so desire. For this tiny miracle to happen without you asking, the people you care about take the initiative.

Your ideas are backed by those who can make them come to fruition. You may question where the trouble is in this wonderful atmosphere. Pluto in Capricorn is still retrograde; therefore, he is still personified by them. Consequently, even if everything is going according to plan, you are pushed to become too concerned for no reason. It's safe to say that there will be no unpleasant shocks this month. Basically, everything is going as planned.

Love

Venus illuminates your sex appeal. Your aura gives off a light that gets people's attention. It satisfies your needs, which gets more and more demanding. This month, you don't want to settle for anything. You want only the best. Your spouse or lover may take a long time to understand. Hold on tight!

If you're in a relationship, your partner is determined to take the lead. Make it clear what you want to avoid being let down. To pull off this little miracle, take advantage of the chances that will come up. The message will be received five out of five times.

If you're single, someone you know may attempt to seduce you. Don't talk about everything and nothing if you want that person to meet your expectations or avoid misunderstandings. Carefully choose the topics of conversation.

Career

You can go on vacation without worrying. Even though the atmosphere makes you want to rest, you don't completely relax. You're thinking about the start of the school year because you want to be ready. So, while lying in your favorite deck chair, you are still thinking about your industry and its future.

This month, the stars are in a good place for your career, so the horoscope for you is pretty good. You will tend to dive into your work with enthusiasm and work exceptionally hard. However, this will not seem like a burden because there will be a lot to gain. You would be able to reach your goals, but you probably wouldn't be happy with your work.

There is a good chance that you would either change your job or get a lot of attention from your career or business. This would be to your advantage in a good month like this one. Still, you are likely to miss a sense of security.

Finance

This sector is doing great, from a financial point of view. Money comes in, but you don't look at what you're spending it on. Even if you can afford it, you should wait until Venus is in retrograde.

You have a lot of positive energy, and if things go your way, you will do very well over the next month. If you had the courage of your convictions, you would go after what you wanted and make it look easy to be successful.

You would get help with this from a fortunate set of events. In fact, you can expect to get a lot of money quickly. Also, stock trading or business would be an excellent way to make money. Also, your relationships with your bosses may get so good that you'll be able to gain a lot from them. It is an excellent time to make investments and start new businesses.

Health

This month, the gods are on your side when it comes to your health, and you will probably avoid any major health issues this year. If you've ever been susceptible to sudden spells of severe sickness like fever or inflammation, you'll be freed of this predisposition. There will be much relief to be had this month, which is a good sign.

Despite this, oral health should be taken seriously. If you're not careful, it might lead to dental issues down the road. Bone injuries are exceedingly rare during this time of year, although extra care should be given.

Travel

Unfortunately, the stars do not favor traveling this month, so it will not be a fruitful endeavor. During your travels, there is a chance that you will be hurt or have a medical emergency. Taking chances is dangerous, therefore, you should exercise caution.

Most of your travels would be by rail or road, with some air travel thrown in for good measure. The purpose of some of your trips may be tied to your employment or business. A good number of them would not be so related. What's pretty sure is that these wouldn't be very useful. A trip abroad is also not ruled out. East is the best direction.

Insights from the stars

The key to getting what you want is clearly expressing what you want at the right time. Mercury and Jupiter encourage you, so go for it! The family comes first this month. All you do is for your family because they look to you for guidance, support, and help.

September 2023

Horoscope

Things are going in the right direction because of you and your partner. On the other hand, if you feel a slight slowdown after the 5th, don't worry more than you need to. Planets are moving backwards, and Jupiter is also moving.

Instead of complaining about something that didn't happen, use it to strengthen the bonds that have already been made. Think about what's available and what's going on right now. Above all, don't give up if trouble seems to come out of nowhere. Why? Because Mars' dissonances have placed you in command this month. So don't fall into the trap and wait for things to return to normal.

Love

Venus wants you to show off and not let your feelings get in the way. Unfortunately, Mars' dissonances can have the opposite effect of what you want. To keep this from happening, don't try too hard and be yourself.

For Cancer in relationships, With Mars' dissonances, your actions or decisions lead to criticism and rebuke. There is tension in the air! If you want peace, find the softness and care that are your trademarks.

For Cancer who don't have a partner, If you change your strategy or way of thinking, it will help you in the long run. Your dates are now different and more promising. This month, you will have to make a decision, and the right one! To do this, you need to find your values and, most of all, be realistic.

Career

Mercury in retrograde might fool you when it comes to your career. Therefore, use greater caution up to the 16th. Check to make sure nothing is missing. Pay close attention to your records. Avoid delaying it till later. Make sure everyone can understand you while you're speaking. Be detailed and concise. Do not listen if someone says you are an over-perfectionist. In the end, you shouldn't let a case or a customer escape your notice out of carelessness.

The way the stars are aligned this month doesn't give you much hope for your job. You would be obsessed with a feeling of insecurity about your job. This would affect everything you do with your business or career.

It's possible that you could work very hard to achieve your goals, but they would still get away from you. You would look for a new job or make big changes to your business. All of this would, however, not make you happy. There is also a chance that you will have a serious argument with your business partners or boss. This should be stopped as best you can. Try to foresee challenging situations and take steps to fix them well in advance.

Finance

If you want to make more expensive purchases than usual, wait until after the 16th. This month, there are a lot of good chances for you to get ahead financially because the stars are in your favor. Musicians, actors, painters, playwrights, and other artists will likely have a financially and creatively successful month.

In fact, times will be very good, and some of you can expect to make a lot of money quickly. Investing would also be helpful and bring in good profits. There is also a chance that a female friend will do you a good turn, which could be a huge financial benefit.

Health

Your health is likely to improve this month due to a favorable set of circumstances. Chronic conditions like rheumatism and digestive abnormalities like gas and extra wind in the intestines will be relieved to a large extent. This implies that as long as you take reasonable precautions, you won't have to deal with any of these issues.

Any chronic throat discomfort should, however, be taken seriously. This has to be thoroughly evaluated for any potential consequences and handled accordingly. Failure to do so might have a negative impact on your health. Aside from that, you have no real reason to be concerned.

Travel

This month, it may be hard to make money from travel since the stars don't look good on this score. Singers, painters, dancers, and other artists may not be as inspired by their travels as they usually are. Some of them could have a setback because of this.

You would usually travel alone and do most of your travelling by rail or road, with a fair amount of air travel. A trip abroad also can't be ruled out. Most of this would be related to your business or job, but it is almost certain that you would not reach your goals with these efforts. East is the best direction.

Insights from the stars

Even though your progression is on track, Mars is slowing it down. Don't get mad, and use the time to work on your relationships or projects. Work on your spiritual side. Make sure you have a working relationship with your divine guides.

October 2023

Horoscope

Things seem to be going nowhere faster than they should. People are notoriously sluggish when it comes to following through on the promises they make. For unknown reasons, some may be reluctant. Things begin to calm down on the 13th, due to the beneficial assistance provided by Mars in Scorpio. You will have to deal with Libra's dissonances even though things are moving forward again. The announcement is expected between the 5th and the 22nd, which may cause you to be skeptical. Stay tight!

Even if you believe you've messed everything up, be patient. Starting on Wednesday, the 23rd, Mercury will be in Scorpio, which removes any doubts or concerns. Together with Mars and the Sun, he nudges you and those you care about to be more honest with one another and open up a dialogue about what's going on.

Love

From the 10th, Venus in Virgo fits your personality. Your loves find their charm and their way all of a sudden. Mercury causes misunderstandings between the 5th and the 22nd, which can throw you off. As long as Mercury is in Scorpio, you can be sure that everything is fine.

For people who are in a relationship, your relationship grows and changes in a confusing environment. The feelings are there, but unfortunately, the conflict comes from everywhere. Your significant other can't be everywhere at once. So do not ask them to do too much.

From the 10th, Venus helps single people meet a charming person. Don't listen to jealous spirits if you want everything to go well. Instead, go with your gut feelings, which will be proven right at the end of the month.

Career

Career setbacks, hesitations, and disappointments continue until the 12th. Please be patient. Then, owing to Mars's valuable competition in Scorpio, the horizon becomes apparent. You no longer waste time waiting for other people's decisions. You take the initiative. You are making up for the time that has passed. There is a slight chance that if someone mistakenly speaks about you, it will cause you to voice your thoughts in an unconventional manner.

There is a positive outlook for your professional development this month. If you're lucky enough to meet a few smart people, your career might benefit greatly from your affiliation with them. The influence of your superiors, with whom you may or may not have considerable differences, would also be quite beneficial to you.

There would also be a lot of travelling involved. There is a lot of value in all of it. However, there is a good chance that your employment may change or that major changes will be made to your business operations, requiring a new location. The west is the best direction. Your efforts have a strong chance of succeeding in achieving your goals.

Finance

When it comes to money, you don't look at what you spend. You are drawn to things that shine. From the 10th, you're more reasonable, which is good.

The stars say that this month will be a good one for your finances. Writers, poets, and people like them would have a particularly good time, both financially and in terms of their work.

You would literally make a lot of money quickly. Investments would also bring in a lot of money. Also, it's likely that your relationships with your bosses and business partners will improve to the point where you can expect to gain a lot from them. Also, the climate could be very good for making investments and starting new businesses.

Health

This month, the stars that are in front of you are quite good for your health. People with sensitive chests or lungs who are prone to health problems in these areas are likely to feel a lot better. There is a chance that overworking yourself will make you tired and weak.

You could easily avoid this if you didn't push yourself too hard. Once this is done, everything will be fine. This would also help you deal with the small chance that you have a nervous disorder, though it's not likely. If you take care of yourself, you can be sure to stay healthy for the whole month. Pay a little more attention to how well your teeth are doing.

Travel

According to what the stars say, this month will be especially good for travel. Writers, poets, and other people like them will have the best trips. In fact, there will be a lot to gain because of how productive their stays will be.

You would travel alone mostly by train or car, but you would also fly a fair amount. A trip abroad is also possible, and it is likely that these efforts will include a vacation, which may be too nice. The best way to go is to the West.

Insight from the stars

If you want your plans and loves to come true, don't pay attention to the prejudices of people who don't share your values. Even though things might seem hard, you should be proud of how well you handle the problems that keep coming up in your life.

November 2023

Horoscope

This November month has everything you could want. You happen to meet people who can help you by chance. Some people offer to help you make your projects happen. When people give you great ideas, you can use them to your benefit. You change the way things are going slowly but surely. One problem is brought up in this positive environment. Venus gives it life between the 9th and 30th of Libra. The discords that link it to your sign mean bad things will happen.

This month, don't see problems as things that will kill you but as challenges that you can easily overcome. How? By making your shell stronger and making your relationships with other people lighter and less exclusive.

Love

Up until the 8th, everything is fine. Then, on an emotional level, you might feel like you're being misunderstood or rejected. Unfortunately, this impression could cause relationship issues, which would be a shame. This month, people aren't as pleasant. Don't get angry, and wait calmly for better times.

Cancer in relationships will often feel like they put in a lot of effort but don't get much in return. Take a step back before making a decision based on this impression. If you do this, you'll find that your partner loves you.

Singles, Venus makes you have a connection with someone until the 8th. Then, when she's in Libra, she causes distance and confusion. Don't worry more than you should. Keep communicating until the situation gets better.

Career

Even though there are hiccups in your day-to-day life, things are looking up for you. You're not afraid to take the lead. And when the situation calls for it, you make drastic choices because you don't want to be stuck in a dead-end forever. Then, all of a sudden, these reactions work and save you time. Some people may be upset by these successes, which is too bad. Ignore their advice and do what you think is best.

A month full of great chances to move up in your career. You would work very hard and, with a warrior's instinct, go after your goals in a focused way. This would be sure to work. There would also be a lot of travel, which would help achieve planned goals and find new opportunities.

There is a good chance that your job will improve or your business will have to change in significant ways. Any change, though, should only be made after careful thought. This is even more important because you might feel a little insecure even though things are going well for you.

Finance

This month, you are exceptionally sensible with your money. You set up a detailed budget on the best days and stick to it. Nothing is wrong!

This month, your financial prospects look pretty good because the stars are aligned in your favor. There is a chance that a female friend would do you a good turn, which could be a massive benefit for you.

The times ahead look pretty good, and you could expect to make a lot of money quickly. Even gambling would be profitable. Also, there are signs that your relationships with your bosses and business partners will improve, which will be very good for you. The climate would also be good for new businesses and investments.

Health

This month, the constellations that are aligned with you benefit your health and well-being. Predispositions to stomach and digestive issues might be alleviated to some extent. Chronic chest illnesses, such as coughs, colds, and asthma, will also be relieved.

As much as it may grate on your nerves if something terrible happens to your teeth, you can avoid it by getting regular dental checkups and cleanings. As a result, some indications indicate you may be temperamental and a little agitated. You can keep your physical and mental health in good shape if you stay calm and peaceful.

Travel

The stars don't look good for travel this month, so there aren't many chances of making money from it. This month, you would probably travel alone, mostly by car or train, with a few flights thrown in.

There is a chance that you might work or travel abroad. But it is almost certain that these efforts would not bring the profits or happiness that were hoped for. The best direction to go would be East.

Insight from the stars

You like to have unique relationships with people. Unfortunately, it tricks you in harmful ways. This month, your relationship will be good if you calm your emotions. Take care of the relationships you have. Stay on good terms with people and stay away from those who want to hurt you.

December 2023

Horoscope

The transit of Venus to Scorpio on the 5th helps to alleviate any difficulties that may have occurred. You progress with an uncommon tenacity as a result of his energizing influence. You feel compelled to pursue your dreams. You strongly desire to accept an offer that has been made to you. Because of their position of authority, you can rely on their complete support. Because of this, you have all of the resources necessary to succeed, but you'll have to battle with yourself.

Why? This is because Mercury is in Capricorn from the 2nd to the 23rd, and he has the propensity to induce you to mistrust what you have stated.

This month, your success is based on your capacity not to question what you have said or done. From the 14th, Mercury will be in retrograde, making it much more difficult.

Love

Venus's time in Scorpio clears up any questions that were raised by her time in Libra. It gives you the promise of solid relationships based on real feelings. Still, be careful of Mercury. Its natural coldness can make you feel like no one else cares as much as you do. This is just a thought.

Venus is good for your heart if you have a partner. You feel well. Mercury, unfortunately, makes little things stressful. If you want to end the year with peace, don't think about the things that bother you. You will be glad you did it.

For single people, Venus helps them meet the right people. Don't ask for proof of commitment right away if you want everything to go well. Because Mercury is going backwards on the 14th, the news will come later than usual.

Career

This month, you have everything you need to make your dreams come true. Luck smiles on you. People who can help you are happy to do so. You have no reason to back down in this situation. Do not doubt your skills or abilities, Cancer. For once, you should believe in yourself and take the chance that comes along. Once you've done that, you'll have all the time you need to get yourself together and think.

Throughout the month, you would also have a deep sense of satisfaction, which could fuel your positive professional behavior.

Finance

On the money side, a vague fear of running out of cash can make you cut back on everything you buy. Stay calm.

The stars say that this month's turn of events won't help you get ahead financially. Yes, there are clear signs that some of you would lose a lot of money if you gambled. So, it would be wise to avoid any kind of investment.

There are also signs that any dispute or court case you might get into would almost certainly go against you, causing you to lose a lot of money. So, you should try to make sure that any decision about this kind of thing is put off until a better time. Relations with bosses or employees are also likely to go downhill. If you can't stop this from happening, you could lose a lot of money.

Health

The combination of stars that you confront this month has a lot of good news for your health. Any tendency to sudden acute diseases, such as fever or inflammations, would get significant alleviation, even if only for a short time. Such issues would most likely not worry you at all. Back pain would be alleviated too.

However, there are reasons to be concerned about the likelihood of an eye infection. This may irritate you temporarily, but it is preventable with adequate preventative measures such as cleanliness and the use of appropriate preventive medicine. Overall, a month is fairly promising for your health.

Travel

Regarding what you can gain from travelling, there's nothing particularly good about what the stars say. This month, you would travel with family and friends mostly by car and train, with some flights.

A tour of another country is also possible. There is a good chance these efforts won't bring the profits or pleasures hoped. This is a pretty dark picture, but it is true. A lot of your travel may not be necessary, and you could get by just fine without it. The best way to go is to the West.

Insight from the stars

Absolute tranquility does not exist. So don't be concerned about other people's delays, unusual ideas, or mood swings. Take them slowly and wait for them to settle down. Pursue your interests with everything you've got. Nothing should be left to chance.

Even though Mercury will be going backwards in 2023, you will do well if you are the best version of yourself.

LEO 2023 HOROSCOPE

Overview Leo 2023

In 2023, Jupiter moves through the 9th house of Aries at the beginning of the year, and then, around May, it moves into the 10th house of Taurus. So, until about the first quarter, you will be blessed with wealth, the chance to go to college, and long trips. Then, starting in May, the focus will shift to your career, which Jupiter will help you move up in. Saturn will stay in your 7th house of Aquarius until March when it will move to your 8th house of Pisces.

You should expect problems with your business deals and relationships for the first three months. Uranus spends the whole year in your 10th house of career, which is about how your career grows and changes. Around May or June, Neptune moves through your 8th house of Pisces, and Pluto moves from your 6th house of Capricorn to your 7th house of Aquarius. These planetary alignments will affect all of Leo's life throughout the year.

Leo men might have difficulty finding love and getting married at the beginning of 2023. However, by the end of the first quarter, all forms of frustration have vanished. Then your hopes, feelings, and expectations about love would go to a new level. Venus and Mars push you to make big changes in your relationship or marriage. From the middle of the year on, your marriage or relationship will take many pleasant turns that make your life brighter and easier. It would bring you and your partner or spouse together even more. Also, you would meet new people who would shape your love life in the future. You and your partner would go on many fun and exciting trips around the last quarter of the year. Your love life or marriage would be going well, and the year would end happily.

Jupiter, the planet that governs our professional success, will traverse your 9th house of Aries until May 2023. Then it moves to your 10th house of Taurus, shining a light on your career and making it better. It gives you more drive to work hard and do well. You'd feel pretty good about yourself, and you'd be able to find your hidden talents. With Jupiter in your sign, you need to settle your goals and get things done. Don't overdo things or get into unsuitable relationships with colleagues or higher-ups. Accept jobs as they come to you and keep moving forward. You'd be on track for most of the year and getting what you want, so don't try to hurry things along.

The horoscopes for Leos predict healthy health in the year. Saturn would alleviate the health difficulties that have been bothering you for a long time. Illness and depression go, and you may expect a year of happiness and health. And the energy you'd get from Mars would keep you motivated and upbeat. However, Leos are cautioned about overdoing it, especially regarding physical activity. Keep to the health goals you set for yourself last year. Keep your mind at ease by relaxing and unwinding from time to time. You'd be better off engaging in outdoor adventures and activities this year.

Financially speaking, Leos may look forward to a prosperous start to the year 2023. Good money will come into your life because of Jupiter's favorable influence on the 2nd house of finances. Even if you save money throughout the year, you may still encounter unexpected expenses. As the year advances, you'll be able to pay off debt and bad loans by purchasing land and high-end automobiles.

As the year 2023 begins, there will be peace and harmony at home, and good things are on the way. This is because Jupiter and Saturn affect the 4th house, which deals with family and home life. Your family would help you and work with you all year. The parents and children would bring joy to the family. However, some family members might have health problems, and worries about them might bother you. Those worries would go away when Jupiter transitions.

Leos will benefit from leisure and business travel in 2023. Jupiter's conjunction in your 12th house would send you on long-distance international trips. You will likely take short journeys following Jupiter's passage in May 2023. Pilgrimage is also in the cards for Leos, who are more spiritually oriented. Most of your excursions would result in financial and knowledge gains. During these trips, you'll be able to meet new people, both personally and professionally. These connections will help you in the long run.

The beginning of the year is an excellent time to engage in religious activities. Leos would grow even more devout after Jupiter's May passage. Religious leaders would enthrall you, and you'd embark on pilgrimages as a result. This year, you may choose to lead a more solitary existence. Serve the poor and underprivileged with all your heart. Give generously of your time, money, and resources to charity. Observe occasional fasting that will help you grow spiritually. Do not neglect to pray to your deity.

Leos would face a challenging year. You must show great courage and tenacity in the face of this challenge. Don't rest on your laurels; you must preserve your personal and professional reputation. Leos are also cautioned against being overly passionate or sensitive in romantic relationships. Stay away from all kinds of risky deals and invest in solid investment plans that won't drain your capital. Once you've achieved your goal, it's time to stop asking for more and enjoy yourself. While forming a partnership might yield lucrative rewards, be on the lookout for scams. Keep up the good effort; it will allow you to live a decent life.

January 2023

Horoscope

As a result of the Aquarian energy, your flaws are enhanced. As a result, you'll tend to push your beliefs on others without even realizing it. Instead of heeding Mars' advice to speak with a sense of fun and ease, you should run away from him. As a result, you will be able to get the full benefits of Jupiter in Aries' pleasant energy.

This auspicious star encourages you to expand your horizons. It opens doors to new possibilities and a broader view of the world. When it comes to issues of the heart, if you can control your shortcomings, everything will be alright. It's also possible, though, that you may have to go through a moment of crisis. The new moon on the 21st is a good time to smooth things out.

Love

If you want everything to go well, you should accept what other people think. Do not control everything as you please, and try not to feel like you're being attacked consistently. Once you've done that, you'll be pleasantly surprised by where your love will go.

For those in a relationship, zone seven of your solar theme is affected by a group of planets in Aquarius. This is a sign of relationship problems that you must consider. Does your spouse blame you? Don't be so authoritative.

For single people, this month, you have the chance to meet someone who isn't like the other people you usually date. For magic to work, you must keep quiet about your success. To make this miracle happen, show interest in this special someone.

Career

Jupiter and Mars keep this sector going and give it energy. You are always successful, and your ideas are excellent this month, but Saturn in Aquarius, which makes you overdo at the wrong time, can ruin all of this. Leo, if you want this month to go well, don't put pressure on others. Give them the time they need to reply.

According to horoscopes, this month looks good for your career. During the month, you will have a deep sense of security at work, which could positively affect how you act professionally as a whole.

Finance

This month looks good from a financial standpoint, but only if you don't listen to these old demons who want you to spend more than you can afford.

The stars say that things will turn out in your favor this month financially. In fact, there are clear signs that investments would bring you good profits. So, investing in stock trading, businesses, or any other kind of investment opportunity would be wise.

There are also signs that if you get into a dispute or court case, you will probably win, which will be good for you. So, you should try to make sure that any decision about this kind of thing is made during this good time. Relations with bosses or employees are also likely to improve, making any project a success.

Health

This month, the stars that line up in front of you are favorable for your well-being. Those susceptible to sudden acute sicknesses, such as fever or inflammation, would benefit greatly. Such an inconvenience would most likely not disturb you in the least. In a similar way, back pain would be alleviated.

The potential of an eye infection is really cause for concern, though. Even though this bothers you for a short time, it may be avoided by using proper preventative measures such as cleanliness and appropriate preventive medicine. In the grand scheme of things, a month's worth of good health is extremely promising.

Travel

As far as benefits from travel are concerned, the prophecy from the stars is not encouraging. This month, you would primarily travel by road and train, with a good amount of air travel, for this month's journey.

Additionally, a trip abroad is not out of the question. It is almost guaranteed that none of this work will result in the anticipated financial rewards or personal fulfilment. These are depressing facts, but they can't be changed. A lot of your travel may not be necessary, and you could get by just fine without it. The best way to go is to the West.

Insight from the stars

Use the time you have and make the most of the opportunities that come your way. As for what really bothers you, don't give it so much weight. Try to get along well with your coworkers, business partners and people in higher positions at work.

February 2023

Horoscope

You're still in the path of the Aquarian energies right now. So, if you want this February to go well, you'll have to watch how you react.

Your instincts tell you that to get what you want, and you have to get right to the point. You're right. Luck is on your side right now. But think about what people around you think.

This will stop a platoon of critics from attacking you! Instead, use your natural honesty to help others instead of just to help yourself. The full moon forms in your sign around the 5th. If you stay realistic, it will help you in the long run.

Love

If you don't want this area to be probed deeply and unnecessarily, use this time to make some changes. Pay attention to what other people or your partner want. Try to answer them as much as you can instead of trying to change them to your advantage.

Leos in a relationship will find that there are still problems this month. To make things better, don't try to make your partner think like you. Give them room to say what they want. Focus on what they do well instead of what they do wrong.

Single people have every chance to have a passionate romance this month. But if you want everything to be okay, don't talk about things that are annoying. Stay positive instead.

Career

You are in Olympic shape! You're ready for battle, so you use all your power. Your arguments destabilize your competitors. Your success and progress are always guaranteed!

Unfortunately, not everyone will agree with your ideas and how you do things, which is sometimes a cookie-cutter method. But if you run into problems, don't think the spell is going to last. Take a step and don't put individuals before the problem. Be more diplomatic, and everything will be okay.

A good month to get ahead in your career. Those who like to be creative and those who work in the fine arts can look forward to a time when their work will be very satisfying. In fact, you may go on to earn a name for yourself due to your efforts.

You may even go on to make a name for yourself with your contributions.

There would also be a lot of travel, which would also be quite helpful. The most useful direction would be south. Aside from travelling, it's possible that you'll change where you work or do business. But think carefully before making any changes since a hasty step could easily undo a lot of your good work.

Health

This month, you have a favorable collection of circumstances favoring your excellent health. Any susceptibility to chronic ailments such as rheumatism and gout, as well as digestive system abnormalities such as gas and excess wind, would be significantly alleviated. This should not be seen as a license to disregard all prudence.

There are reasons to be concerned about your oral health. If you take care of your teeth, you can avoid problems. In fact, you have a good month ahead of you in which you won't have to worry about any major health problems.

Travel

The stars are in a harmonious mood this month, making it a great time to reap travel rewards. Writers, poets, and people of a similar caliber would discover new, inspiring travel opportunities.

You have a tendency to travel by road, train, and a decent amount of air when you're on your own. Additionally, a trip abroad is definitely in the plans. Not every trip you take will be connected to your work or business. Whatever the goal, all of your travels would undoubtedly succeed in bringing you what you were looking for. The most promising direction is the South.

Insight from the stars

If you don't mind, it's time to peek past the surface. You will be surprised by the qualities and power some people have. Since the stars are not in your favor, this is not the best month to make big investments.

March 2023

Horoscope

Saturn will leave Aquarius at the end of this month. So, Jupiter and luck take on their full meaning by giving you chances that will help you do more. When the yoke of Saturn is broken, you will be able to enjoy it fully and not be affected by your moods.

When Mars is in Gemini, he helps you meet the right people and tells you to take advantage of the opportunities that come your way.

He makes you act and react as quickly as he does. Everything about the atmosphere makes it seem like your life is about to change. But Uranus, which Venus supports from the 17th, needs you to stay grounded if you want everything that comes your way to really work out.

Love

After a hard time, you're not giving in! From now on, your loves should give you this little extra that changes everything. To feel good, you have to respect your partner, and they have to do the same for you. This small miracle can be done this month.

With Saturn gone, a weight has been lifted from your relationship Leo! This month, the planets in Aries want you to branch out and try something new. He guides it toward a way of life that will be better for you both.

Leo singles, you no longer see being single as a problem. Instead, you see it as an opportunity that you will take full advantage of. This month, you won't ask any questions when you seduce. With this attitude, things that seemed impossible become possible.

Career

There is a dramatic shift in this sector's fortunes as Saturnian constraints are lifted, and people finally honor their promises. You think this time around, everything is going well! You're going to show everyone what you're made of! Happiness is not a one-person show, so you compensate for lost time using your famous interpersonal abilities. Everything is working in your favor and for the better right now.

This has been a good month for your career chances. Fine artists and those who follow in their footsteps would have a blast. With your efforts, you may make a name for yourself in the future. There are signs that you will put in a lot of effort and work properly to achieve your goals. And you will succeed in this as well.

Your location may change even if you're running a business or providing a service. It's possible to change but do it only after great consideration. Also, there would be a lot of travel, which would be very helpful in the long run. The best direction to head is West.

Finance

When it comes to finances, the Full Moon on the 7th might cause you to be unsure of your financial decisions. It gives you the impression that you're in a dire crisis. Before you start cursing, double-check yourself.

This month's financial outlook isn't great because of the unfavorable constellations you're dealing with. There are clear signs that you would lose a lot of money if you gamble. The lesson is clear: you should stay away from gambling of any kind.

Furthermore, your working relationship with your bosses may deteriorate to the point where you lose money. Prevent a situation like this by acting quickly to correct any issues. The climate would not be suitable for making investments or starting new projects. Such plans should be put on hold for now.

Health

The constellations aligned with you this month are particularly supportive of good health. Just a word of warning: don't push yourself too hard. This should be avoided at all costs, and energy should be dispersed in a thoughtful manner so that routine operations may continue without being jeopardized.

Making a new schedule of activities is an easy way to do this. You should take appropriate care of your teeth and follow all standard precautions. Aside from that, you've had a good month regarding your health.

Travel

This is a month when you should make a lot of money from traveling since the stars are in a good place for this. Artists of all kinds should find travel exciting and helpful for boosting their creative energy.

This month, you would probably travel alone, mostly by car and train, with a fair amount of air travel. A trip abroad also can't be ruled out. You would travel for business and other reasons, but whatever your goal, you would be able to achieve it or just have an enjoyable trip. The West is the best direction to travel this month.

Insights from the stars

You have the opportunity and the chance to get out of the shackles that stopped you from growing. To pull off this little miracle, ignore the sweet sound and remain grounded. You will have to worry more about the health of your loved ones this month. Make sure you help them keep up with doctors' appointments.

April 2023

Horoscope

Jupiter in Aries keeps giving you more options. It gives you an opportunity to show off your skills or share what you know. If you feel like you're at a standstill, you won't feel that way for long. If you agree, the lucky star offers to change your situation or a part of your life. To do all of this in the best way possible, you will have to deal with the somewhat confusing energies that come from Taurus.

Between 1st and 30th, you will mostly have to deal with Mercury. It retrogrades on the 22nd, which causes delays. Instead of yelling, think about what you want to say. Examine what you've been told with care. If you are polite in your conversations, you will come to an agreement.

Love

From the 12th, when Venus is in Gemini, the people you love have a cheerfulness that makes them pleasant to be around. If you want this perfect situation to last, you should stop being so possessive. It's flattering in small doses, but when it happens for no reason, it's suffocating.

Leos, your relationship finds its balance and its agreement. Venus in Gemini changes the way you think through your friends and socializing. But the conversations can still be tense because there are still problems to be solved.

Leo singles, On the 12th, Venus starts to touch Jupiter. It gives you an opportunity to meet someone who isn't like everyone else. Everything is beautiful, as long as you are willing to be surprised by things you hadn't planned.

Career

Luck is on your side, and beautiful opportunities are coming to you out of nowhere. Leo, the stars grant your wish! So now is not the time to dwell on what's wrong! Instead, look at all the benefits you can get. As for people who bother you with their ideas, try to understand them. If you do this, you will see that they are not wrong and that their point of view is interesting and worth exploring.

Career advancement is possible this month, and you may even be able to move up the ladder from your current position if you're lucky. There is a good chance that you would want to start new businesses or investments. Should you do this, the results can only be good. So, you must look into such profitable options.

Finance

This industry is doing well financially. Even so, it's not out of the question that your expectations aren't met. This is an excellent time to check the tiny print before assuming your partner is being frugal.

Your financial status will benefit significantly from your buoyant spirits and favorable circumstances throughout the next month. This month, you'll have the confidence and determination to press on with your goals and achieve them. An incredibly fortunate set of circumstances would tremendously benefit you.

In fact, you may expect to enjoy a bountiful crop of unexpected profits. Profits might be made even through investment activities. In addition, your relationships with your superiors may take on such a lovely dimension that you may anticipate gaining a lot from them. As a result, it would be a good time to invest and start new businesses.

Health

This month's favorable collection of circumstances will ensure that you remain in excellent health, so there is no need to be concerned. Chronic colds, excessive mucous discharge, and the like would be greatly reduced or eliminated altogether. As long as treatment is handled seriously, those with piles can look forward to a period of alleviation and possibly full recovery.

Despite all of this, there is also a warning on the need for good oral hygiene. The consequences of any lapse in due diligence might be severe. In general, this is an excellent month for your health, and you should be able to enjoy it for the rest of the year.

Travel

Because the stars are aligned in your favor, you may expect a bountiful harvest this month. This month, you'll have a lot of self-confidence and the courage to take charge of your own decisions. In-depth planning of your itinerary would result in a successful journey that will get you a substantial profit.

With a little bit of air travel thrown in for good measure, you'd like to travel alone most of the time. Taking a vacation abroad is also an option. It's unlikely that all of your travels will be related to work. Whatever your goal, you'd accomplish it. The best way to go is East.

Insight from the stars

Pay heed to your stubbornness, Leo. Use it cautiously and take pauses as needed. They will motivate you to expand on your own and others' ideas. You will advance in your profession, making your seniors proud of you, and you could just earn that promotion you've been eyeing.

May 2023

Horoscope

Jupiter in Aries will continue to give you opportunities until the 16th, which will help you do more. Then the lucky star will be in Taurus with Uranus, Mercury, and the Sun. This move might seem cruel to you because it will definitely stop this beautiful urge that pushes you to change what needs to be changed.

Instead of giving up or acting out when things don't go your way, take a step back. Use the delays that keep coming up to improve what has been suggested to you recently. Set things up so the people who rejected your projects will accept them. Give them some time, and don't act like it's already decided.

The more you pay attention to what other people say, the more likely you are to be on the right path.

Love

Everything is good until the 7th. Then the fire of love begins to flicker. A sense of loneliness sets in. Mars in Leo pushes you to take action on the 21st. Unfortunately, you might not get the desired results if you don't change your strategy.

Leos in a relationship are about to go through a less happy time, even though things have been looking up. You can get your partner back. But if you want the magic to work, make sure their wishes come true instead of promising them miracles.

If you are single and a Leo, things can happen that leave you alone. But don't worry, it won't last forever! If you're more emotional, things start to go your way again at the end of the month.

Career

Up until the 16th, everything is fine. Then things get complicated! Leo, the stars don't want you to be unhappy. They give you challenges that you are more than up to. Instead of trying to fight bad luck, use your good energy to find solutions. If a project stops going up, use that time to make some changes. When you do this, you will be amazed by your results and success.

There is a good chance that you will have a major disagreement with your bosses. This should not be allowed to happen, and you should try to stop it from happening. You might also have a constant feeling of insecurity that would affect almost everything you do at work. There would also be a lot of travel, but this wouldn't lead to much either.

Finance

Even though daily life is secure from a financial point of view, this is not a good time to make big investments. Wait a little while and use the time to make your project better.

A month in which your finances don't get better. Unfortunately, there wouldn't be a big windfall of money. If you gambled, you would lose a lot of money, and there is a good chance that you would have a fight with your boss or business partners, which would also cost you money.

Health

This month, the stars are in a good mood to help your health, so you should feel great for most of the month. Any tendency to get sick quickly and severely, like fevers or inflammation, would be greatly reduced. Most likely, they would not bother you at all.

This would also be true for people with any kind of tooth pain. In fact, any problem with your false teeth should be taken seriously, and there's a good chance you can fix it. This is a good time for your health, and people who are already healthy can expect to stay that way.

Travel

This is an excellent month to travel and be successful from it, as this is what the stars say will happen. Those who want to study or train abroad or in some other faraway place have a good chance of success.

You would probably travel alone most of the time by train, road, or air. A trip abroad is also a possibility. Only a tiny portion of your travels would be for business. You'll find what you're looking for no matter why you're travelling. The North is the best direction.

Insight from the stars

Your success depends on how well you can understand other people's points of view. If you accept this challenge, you will be surprised by some people's good qualities. Make choices that will move you forward in life.

June 2023

Horoscope

Due to Mars and Venus being in Leo, you should expect an exciting month this month. Your greatest and worst aspects will be on display at the same moment. Your efforts will come to fruition in the current Gemini energy. Others in positions of authority are more likely to assist you if they see your abilities and charisma. You can only make decisions if you are confident in your abilities.

In Taurus, Mercury amplifies the troubles of Jupiter and Uranus until the 11th. They keep you from achieving your goals and may even expose your weaknesses. However, there is a way to avoid it. How? Instead of placing the wagon before the horse, consider your teammates' viewpoints before making a decision.

Love

Your romantic relationships take on a new level with Mars and Venus in your sign. They cause love at first sight, big declarations of love, and intense desires. The downside is that these passions will run up against reality. In these circumstances, it is either one or the other. Either it works, or it breaks!

For Leos in a relationship, you feel a surge of passion! That's enough to rekindle the flame if it starts to go out. But do not overdo it. Why? Because you become unbearable when you go too far.

Leo singles, whether you use yours or not, the result is the same. Your seductive power has reached new heights! Do not stray from this happy atmosphere. This will keep you from getting into a complicated situation.

Career

Those who seem to have set limits on their own progress are in charge of your daily routine and growth. With that in mind, the least you can say is that you're not placing the odds in your favor! Unfortunately for you, Leo, you will have to work with pragmatists. However, in order to get beyond the hurdles that are in your way, follow their advice.

Career-wise, the stars aligning against you in the month don't bode well for you in many ways. It is likely that despite your best efforts, you will not succeed in reaching your goals. There's a good chance you'll disagree with your bosses.

This must be avoided at all costs since the repercussions are unimaginable. Try to anticipate potential roadblocks and negotiate your way past them. There would also be a lot of travel, but it wouldn't provide any benefits.

Finance

The same battle on the financial front! If you require a large sum of cash, do not push it. Have the correct arguments and plan ahead of time. It will be more secure.

This month, your financial possibilities appear promising and might put you on a long-term path. You might anticipate a bountiful crop of unexpected rewards. You would benefit from stock trading, business, and investments, which would result in a large profit.

In any event, you'd have a method of dealing with your subordinates or staff that allows you to get the most out of their services. This would significantly benefit you and might result in significant earnings. Furthermore, there is a chance that an old buddy may do you a favor or provide you with a service that will be highly valuable. Finally, your relationships with your superiors would take on such pleasant dimensions that you would stand to benefit much from them.

Health

Because Dame Fortune is in a good mood to bless your health, you may count on staying in shape during the ensuring time.

As long as proper treatment is maintained, Leos with chronic conditions like rheumatism and other digestive issues like flatulence and excess wind should anticipate significant relief. This is true for any form of dental problem.

You should also expect any anxiety to be relieved and to cause significantly fewer problems than normal. However, with the right amount of exercise and nutritious eating, you may make up for whatever shortcomings you may have. This is a good month for your health, and you are unlikely to have any significant issues.

Travel

This is a month when you can expect to make a lot of money from travel because the stars are in a good mood. You would travel alone mostly by train and road, with a fair amount of flying. You might also go overseas.

Your travels would be partly for business and partly for other reasons. But whatever the goal is, you should be able to reach it ultimately. You would also make good friends and have a great time travelling. The most favorable direction is South.

Insight from the stars

Everything seems to be going well for you at the moment. Keep your cool in the face of adversity, and your image will shine through. If you believe that you are in charge, everything will fall into place for you. Allow no one else to dictate the course of your life.

July 2023

Horoscope

Even though Mars leaves your sign on the 10th, this month will still be lively. Why? Sun, Mercury, and Venus are all in your sign. These energies help you feel good about yourself and bring out your best qualities. They shine this light on you that makes you stand out. You get people's attention without trying to.

Even though this is a good astral climate for you, you need to keep an eye on your ego because it can take over. Unfortunately, this would lead to bad things. Don't try to defend your ideas at all costs to avoid this. Even if you think someone is too cautious or conservative, listen to what they have to say. When your mind is like this, full of wisdom, you will have the chances to grow that you want.

Love

With Mars gone, your desires are wiser, but there's no sign that your loves will be. Even though you don't do it on purpose, your charisma acts like a magic potion. Your sexual appeal gets people's attention. people see you, notice you, and try to seduce you.

In relationships, You're wiser and more caring. Your desires are less intense. Feelings come before passion but you are not immune to a crisis of possessiveness. Why so? Because your charm gets people's attention.

Leo singles, this month, the situation is different. Even though your ability to seduce is always at the top, you are less likely to make a move. On the other hand, it's you who are approached. For the next step, you decide!

Career

Again this month, your success depends on your ability to overcome obstacles. At this point, you may rest easy. There is no doubt that you will succeed! Leo's! Your charm ensures that you're never overlooked. It works for you, but some individuals find it irritating. So be careful not to anger them. Your efforts will be greatly aided by attracting their goodwill rather than their hostility.

This is a month to be on the lookout. There is a strong likelihood that you and your superiors will disagree. This must be avoided at all costs. Make an effort to remain calm and avoid problematic situations.

Some of the time spent on the road traveling might appear to be a waste of time, yet there is a small proportion of benefit to be gained by travelling to the West.

Finance

Despite the fact that your finances appear to be in order, you have the delusional belief that you are completely broke. Ensure that you don't inflict unnecessary pain on yourself.

Financially, this is a really good month for you. You stand to benefit greatly from the windfall profits that are almost certain to come your way and might earn handsomely from stock market activities.

If you put in the time and effort, most of you will be able to see immediate benefits. When it comes to handling your subordinates, you'll want to go to other members of your team for advice. While the rest of the month is fairly profitable, this might very well be the most significant gain. In addition, there is a strong likelihood that an elderly friend will perform a job or favor for you, resulting in a big financial gain.

Health

The stars say there is a lot of good news for your health this month. It is reasonable to predict that any predisposition to tooth discomfort will diminish significantly. On the other hand, overwork could quickly destabilize a good and hopeful situation. Make a new schedule that doesn't overwork your body.

Neglect and negligence here might have serious consequences for your health. The rest goes without saying. A predisposition toward anxiety would not upset individuals already susceptible to it. In general, this is a healthy month with few major health issues to worry about.

Travel

A month when the stars are aligned in a way that makes travel quite profitable. This month, you would travel partly for business and partly for other reasons. You would probably travel alone mostly by train and road, with a fair amount of air travel.

A trip abroad also can't be ruled out. You would be very successful at all of this, and some business goals would be met. You would also have a very pleasant time travelling. The West is the best direction.

Insights from the stars

You keep riding a wave of success, and that's a good thing. For things to go your way, listen to others and give them room to move. It's important to look at life with a positive attitude. This way, you can clearly see the opportunities you have and how to make the most of them.

August 2023

Horoscope

Even though Taurus's dissonances put you in charge, the Sun in Leo makes you want to reach high and far. Don't disappoint them! You keep doing things with the logic and intelligence that make you who you are. You know how to put yourself forward when the opportunity comes up, but you don't do it on purpose. You can make even the most conservative people feel better. Even though it's harder than usual, you handle challenges with style.

Mars's move into Libra at the end of the month gives you a little help that will be appreciated. Venus in Leo is the only shadow on the board. A retrograde is not a bad thing, but since you are worried, don't push things. Wait until things get back to normal.

Love

The excitement and success of the past few weeks are giving way to doubts. Your love will go through a time of not knowing what will happen. You might want to make things happen quickly. Sadly, this would not have the effect that was wanted. Use the time to think about how you feel and what you want.

If you're a Leo in a relationship, take good care of your partner. But the effects aren't as great as they were in the previous weeks. So, you might feel upset and try to do more. That would make you look stuffy, though, so just let things happen.

Leo singles, you no longer have to show that you've done well. But you move forward one step and go back two. You don't follow up on a date because you can't explain why. When Mars is in Libra at the end of the month, you pull yourself together.

Career

The growth of this industry worries you because you suspect someone is interfering with it. You're suddenly thrown in a foul mood. Please, Leo, refrain from seeing evil in everything! It's not your fault that you're facing difficulties; they're there to help you succeed. So, instead of yelling, take on the challenges brought your way.

This month's astrological alignment does not bode well for your professional aspirations. There is a good chance that you and your superiors will have severe disagreements. This would be a disaster waiting to happen. Because of this, you should work to prevent it from happening.

An empty feeling of insecurity may also weigh you down. If this happens to you, you may decide to look for a new career or start your own business to get some relief. It's a bad situation to be in. Take your time before making any significant modifications. Traveling will also be fruitless, but a trip northward could be beneficial in some way.

Finance

If you're worried about your financial situation, do some research first before declaring yourself bankrupt. In this way, you'll realize the true state of your affairs.

As far as the stars are concerned, this is not a good month for your financial situation. Because of your poor relationship with your business partners or superiors, you may have to pay the price for this breakdown in communication. Because of this, you need to be aware of the potential and take action to avoid it.

Most of you would find it challenging to achieve your goals due to a lack of available chances. On the other hand, you run the risk of being overly obsessed with earning money that you can't account for. This will have a negative impact on your current circumstances. Please fix this. It's also a good idea to avoid investments at all costs.

Health

During this month, the stars will bestow upon you health and happiness. You'll notice an improvement in the quality of your hands and feet, as they'll be less clammy than they were previously.

Persistent dental issues would be significantly less problematic and, in fact, would be more likely to be re-solved if they were handled with seriousness. As an added bonus, those with a history of anxiety and other mental health issues will see a big improvement. You should have no major health issues in March. Overall, a good month for your well-being.

Travel

A good month to reap travel benefits, as the stars predict a good harvest. For some of you, making religious pilgrimages will be a life-changing experience.

It will be easy for those who choose to pursue further education or training in a foreign country. You'll also have a great time on business trips! Travel would be primarily by train or road, with some flying thrown in. Traveling outside of the country is another option. The best way to go is North.

Insight from the stars

If your wishes aren't coming true as quickly as you'd like, don't force anything. Use this break that Venus has given you to think about how you feel. Do not let emotions control your life. Don't hurt yourself or the people around you by letting your emotions get the best of you.

September 2023

Horoscope

You're being thwarted by the happenings around you! The unexpected and unexpected obstacles slow down your journey! As a result, you may feel down. In the face of setbacks and disappointments, do not yell.

Mars aids you in coping with risks and finding solutions. Venus, currently in your sign, urges you to give your all no matter the circumstances. It makes you more determined to achieve, no matter how hard it is. It forces you to deal with things rationally and realistically.

You may use your renowned charm to your advantage, but you still need to put in some effort. If you want to attain your goals this month, you shouldn't rely on your famous persuasive skills, even if the conditions are favorable. It's safer if you show your worth.

Love

You get along well with your loved ones and with your partner. Your charm makes people interested in you. Because your social life is improving, your loves are returning to their true colors this month. So, the doubts go away, making space for confidence, feelings, and passion.

Doubts go away for Leos in a relationship. Everything gets put back in its place. This month, your relationship gets a better handle on itself. There are feelings and passion, and everyone shares them. But don't get mad more than you need to, because it will make you feel bad.

This month, things are getting better for single Leos. Mars and Venus show that you will get close to someone with everything you want. But if you want this paradise to last and be peaceful, you need to control your happiness and not do too much.

Career

Your progress has stalled significantly. All of a sudden, you begin to exert pressure on the situation. This, unfortunately, will not have the desired outcome. Leo, if you want your initiatives or ideas to come to fruition, you'll have to go to great lengths to make them happen. Don't put people under strain if you're struggling to keep up. Utilize this time to make improvements to your files and workflow. As a general rule, be more descriptive and allow them time to ponder and answer.

This month's professional outlook isn't looking good for you. You will likely leave your current position or implement a substantial shift in your business or service operations. Also, you're likely to get into disagreements with your colleagues, bosses, or seniors.

This should be avoided at all costs, as it will only exacerbate your problems. Additionally, you'd have to put in a lot of effort, which would not only be in vain given the circumstances but also leave you feeling severely dejected. Make an effort to maintain some degree of steadiness and avoid acting erratically.

Finance

Despite the fact that there are no worrisome announcements in the financial industry, you are particularly concerned about this area. Don't worry about running out of cash.

According to the stars, this month's horoscope does not portend well for your financial situation. You'd likely get into a fight with your bosses, which may wind up costing you a great deal of money. In order to avoid this, be sure to take any precautions you can think of in advance.

Some of you will almost certainly lose money if you decide to invest in the stock market. Gambling of any kind, then, should be avoided at all costs. Making investments or starting new businesses would likewise be difficult in the current environment. As such, these ideas should be put on hold for the time being.

Health

Health-wise, you're in luck this month, so you shouldn't have any major health issues arise during this period of good fortune. If you've ever been susceptible to sudden spells of severe disease like fever or inflammation, you'll be freed of that predisposition. This is a good month, so it's possible to expect some respite.

There are, however, reasons to be wary about your oral hygiene. This might lead to dental issues if you're not careful. Also, be aware of any bone injuries that may occur during this period, which are quite rare.

Travel

A fantastic month for travel since the stars are in a favorable mood to bless your travels. Confidence and the courage to take risks are possible this month. The majority of your journey would be via train or car, with a small amount of air travel thrown into the mix.

The possibility of an overseas trip cannot be ruled out. Some of them might be for work, while others would be for personal reasons. You'd be a huge success in this endeavor. You may also have a good time if you are satisfied with your journey. The best course of action would be to head Northward.

Insight from the stars

When it comes to issues regarding the heart, things look good. On the other hand, it's more complicated when it comes to your job. Getting into a fight won't help you; in fact, it will hurt you. Give in a little. It's going to be better. Your love life and relationship will be full of happiness. During the 2023 Mercury retrograde, you should do something if you are not happy in your relationship or marriage.

October 2023

Horoscope

Jupiter and Uranus' dissonances make life difficult. As a result, you grow up in an environment that demands that you put in your best effort in order to succeed. Things are about to become a little more complex when Mars enters Scorpio on the 13th.

Libra's energies are here to assist you in getting through these difficult times. Rather than being adamant, they push you to find a solution that works for all parties. Unfortunately, Mercury and the Sun's entry into Scorpio at the end of the month will intensify the effect.

If you want to avoid a lot of hassles right now, you should tone down your authoritarian tendencies.

Love

You have trouble with how you feel and how others feel. You feel like you're getting caught in a trap. So, your responses are strange, and your loved ones don't know what to think. Maintain your objectivity. This will keep you from making bad decisions.

For Leos in a relationship, even though the conversations are pleasant and full of love, you feel like something is wrong. Try not to give in. Don't get upset over small things because that could lead to the hostility that would hurt your relationship.

Leo singles, as soon as Venus leaves your sign, the happiness goes away. On the other hand, when Libra is strong, you keep in touch with people you've met. If what you want doesn't happen, stay calm. These setbacks won't last long.

Career

You must be able to persevere and be pragmatic in order to move forward. This month, Leo, you must be more forgiving of yourself and others! Don't get into an argument with individuals who can solve a situation for you. As a result, instead of revealing your innermost thoughts, simply follow their lead. On your darkest days, keep your mouth shut and trust your gut instincts. You may prevent disagreements that can damage your reputation if you do this.

There isn't a lot of good news for your job chances this month, thanks to the constellation of stars. You'd be driven to distraction by a crippling fear of failure in your professional life. All of your company or job-related activities would be affected by this.

You may find yourself working really hard towards your goals, yet your efforts may still elude them. Changing careers or drastically altering your business would be on your list of options. Even so, you'd still be left wanting. An even more serious confrontation is possible with your bosses. To the best of your abilities, avoid this at all costs. Be proactive in anticipating and resolving potential crises.

Finance

You have a very high standard when it comes to your finances. Dollars are dollars, no matter how you look at it. You'll ruin your reputation if you do this.

Because of the favorable combination of stars in your favor, this month is a great time for financial success. This month is going to be a great one for artists of all kinds, from musicians to actors to painters to dramatists, both monetarily and creatively.

In reality, the current economic climate is favorable, and some of you can anticipate to enjoy a substantial financial windfall. Investing might also be profitable and useful. There is also the possibility that a female friend will do you a favor, which could prove to be a cash gain.

Health

For your health, this month is a good time for favorable situations. Those who are inclined to chronic conditions like rheumatism and digestive abnormalities like flatulence and extra wind in the digestive tract may benefit greatly. This implies that as long as you take reasonable precautions, you won't have to deal with any of these issues.

There are, however, reasons to be wary of any prolonged throat discomfort. Complications should be thoroughly identified and addressed without delay. Failure to do so might have a negative impact on one's health. There aren't any other significant reasons for concern.

Travel

This should be a good month for travel, and you should make good money from it. Most of the time, you would travel alone by train or car, with some flights thrown in. A trip overseas is also not out of the question.

Since not all of your trips would be related to your job or business, you would have a lot of success in getting what you set out to do. You would meet a lot of new people and have a lot of new opportunities. The best direction to go would be east.

Insight from the stars

You know that Scorpio's energy doesn't work on you. So, be wise this month. Do not light the powder on fire over something minor. People who have ongoing health problems need to be extra careful. Keep up with your medicine and doctor's appointments in order to get better outcomes.

November 2023

Horoscope

You are surrounded by people until the 24th! When Scorpio and Taurus send out their energies, they block things. You might think that life is hard and the entire world dislikes you. You can be sure that this is not the case! November still has several challenges in store for you, but you can handle them. To be successful at this little trick, look to Venus in Libra and the energy that flows through Sagittarius.

When things don't go the way you want, try to look on the bright side. Do not make it a big deal if someone else gets something you want. Be open to other people's ideas, even if they seem crazy.

Love

Between 9th and 30th, Venus in Libra creates a good environment for your love life. The conversations are pleasant. Your loved ones are under your spell. Sadly, nothing else happens. But your wishes can come true if you're willing to give up some things.

For Leos in a relationship, after the 9th, things get better, but tensions still remain. To make them happy, don't worry about what's wrong! Look at all the good things about your relationship and the good things about your partner.

Leo singles, someone is under your spell. Too bad you don't even listen! So if you want to see it, you should be happy and enjoy the present. It will be better than thinking about bad things and wanting things that can't happen.

Career

This month, you spend your time finding the best solutions to problems. This course of obstacles can make you more tired than it should. When things are bad, you may wonder what's wrong. Leo, it's not easy for you, but you have everything you need to deal with the problems that come up. So stop yelling in all directions and take these risks with a good attitude.

The predictions for your professional advancement this month aren't very good. There is a good chance that you will have serious disagreements with your bosses. You can avoid this by trying to spot trouble spots ahead of time and finding ways around them.

Also, you would feel very insecure this whole month. This would change how you work as a whole. You would be a little unstable if you tried to change your job or how your business works. Any change you make should be done after careful thought. You would also work very hard, but even if you did, it's likely that you wouldn't be able to reach your goals.

Finance

If you have to make a major financial commitment, take the time to consider both the positive and negative aspects of the decision.

Financial forecasts from the stars aren't all that positive, at least when it comes to your long-term financial future. Make sure you've got a rainy-day fund in case you run into a lull in your creative endeavors in the following month.

As a result of your investments and gambling activities, some of you might lose a lot of money. Stay away from all forms of gambling is the clear message. Also, your relationship with your bosses might deteriorate to the point where significant losses are possible. This is something you should try to avoid as much as possible.

Health

This month, the combination of stars in front of you is good for your health. Those with sensitive chests or lungs prone to problems in these areas are likely to feel a lot better. There is a chance that overworking will make you tired and weak.

You could easily and surely avoid this by not overworking yourself. After this is done, things will go well. This would also help you get over the possibility, though it's not very likely, that you have some kind of nervous disorder. Take care of yourself, and you'll be sure to stay healthy all month. Take a little more care of the health of your teeth.

Travel

This is a good month to make a lot of money from travel, as this is what the stars tell us will happen. Writers, poets, and others like them would find new inspiration and meaning in travel.

You should tend to travel alone mostly by train and road, with a fair amount of air travel. Also, a trip abroad cannot be ruled out. Part of this travel would be related to your job or business, and the rest would be for other reasons. No matter what your goal is, it is likely that you will be able to reach it through your sojourns. East is the best direction.

Insights from the stars

The energies of Scorpio are still going around! In these situations, a less direct approach will help you more, whether in love or in business. When things are hard in your life, let your friends and family help you.

December 2023

Horoscope

Mars and the Sun are both in Sagittarius, which is good for you. Mercury also moves through this sign, but not often. These energies are good, lucky, and most of all, very hopeful. If things or people made you mad last month, they will help you this month. Most importantly, they tell you to pay attention to what works for you.

Even though things are easier, Uranus and Jupiter in Taurus always slow down the growth you want. Venus in Scorpio from September 5th to September 29th makes this happen more. The planets in Sagittarius give you a break this month. They tell you to stop trying hard to make things go your way.

Love

When Venus is in Scorpio, your relationships can get into all kinds of trouble. You can avoid that, though. How? By collecting all your good energy and putting it to good use. This month, if your relationship gets rough, do something to make it better.

For Leos in a relationship, If you keep complaining about the same things, you won't get out! This month, your relationship will be able to handle the minor problems and risks that will pop up out of nowhere if you are positive, calm, and caring.

Leo singles, this month, live fully and give yourself what you want. Above all, don't let minor setbacks get you down. Do not worry if you think it's too hard! Don't stop and ask yourself what to do next.

Career

Take a break at the end of the year. Let go of the stress that keeps you going. Forget for a while that you want to reach your goals. Doing this will ease the tensions that are hanging over your head. Also, it will push you to do good things that, strangely enough, will clear up a situation that has been stuck for months. Nothing worth having comes easy. Some people will be easier to get along with.

On the other hand, travel won't bring you any valuable benefits either, though a trip North could bring some small benefits.

Finance

On the financial front, daily living is secure, but things get more problematic when it comes to large expenditures. Be patient.

The omen from the stars does not bode well for your financial prospects. There are indicators that your business and investments will result in significant losses for you. As a result, you should avoid making any new investments. Relationships with your bosses or coworkers are also likely to get so bad that a big loss is almost inevitable.

However, you may avoid this by taking focused action and planning ahead. Some of you might likewise be overly focused on making unexplained money. This would not be in your best interests and might cause you problems. The climate would also be unfavorable for investment or new companies.

Health

This month, the combination of stars in your favor will help you keep your health in check. Those with a propensity to stomach and digestive issues would be greatly alleviated. This includes chronic chest illnesses such as a runny nose or a persistent cough.

With good dental care, you can ensure that nothing bad occurs to your teeth. There is a cause to be concerned about the condition of your teeth. As a result, there are some indications that you may be temperamental and a little agitated. Keeping your mind and body in a state of calm and peace won't take much work and will help you stay in good mental and physical health.

Travel

According to the forecasts from the heavenly bodies, this month is an excellent time to travel. Generally speaking, artists might gain a great deal of inspiration from their trips, inspiring them to produce new works.

You'd largely travel by train or car, with a decent amount of flying thrown in for good measure. Taking a vacation abroad is not a certainty, though. Most of these trips would be for personal reasons, but some would be tied to work or business. Whatever your goal is, this would be a great way to achieve it. The best route is up North.

Insight from the stars

You become pessimistic in the face of adversity. You're not going to get very far with this attitude. Reacting positively, on the other hand, will have a favorable impact on the course of events. Isn't it time to think that you can improve your situation? Take control of your life by working on your low self-esteem.

VIRGO 2023 HOROSCOPE

Overview Virgo 2023

Jupiter, the planet of growth, begins the year in your 7th house of Aries and moves to your Eight house of Taurus in May 2023. As a result, your love/marriage will be blessed and happy during the first quarter. Then, with Jupiter's transit to the 8th house, problems arise. Saturn, the limiting planet, will remain in your 5th house of Aquarius until March when it will travel to your 6th house of Pisces. This will reduce your chances of luck, and you may have issues with children in the first quarter. Then Saturn may bring up health troubles and some form of spending, so be cautious.

This year, Uranus will be transiting your Taurus 9th house, ensuring general prosperity, while Neptune will be transiting your Pisces 7th house, impacting your love life. Pluto would be transiting Capricorn's 5th house before moving to Aquarius' 6th house in May/June 2023. These planetary transits would impact the Virgo's life during the year.

The year begins on a positive note for Virgo's love or marriage desires, owing to the influence of the planets of love, Venus and Mars. You would be lucky to keep your beloved or spouse in your net throughout the year. Your independence and sense of freedom may sometimes be tested, but keep going. Keep your cool and avoid situations that aren't suited for your relationship right now. Find out what works best for both of you. Your love life or marriage evolves slowly but steadily as the year progresses. Make plans for a brighter future with your partner. As the year comes to a close, your love or marriage will begin to bear fruit; you will marry if you haven't already, married people will most likely conceive, and if you already have a child, more are on the way.

Mars would begin the year 2023 by obstructing your career progress and development. You would run out of energy and enthusiasm to keep going. The first quarter might appear to have hit a brick wall, and the situation would become more favorable from a professional standpoint. Jupiter will bestow good fortune on you. If you own your firm, you can launch new endeavors. You would form stronger bonds with acquaintances, which would boost your professional status. You would benefit from partnerships and get more attention, respect, and status at work.

This year will be excellent for Virgos in terms of health. Jupiter's favorable aspects would increase your energy levels and make you more productive in your ideas and activities. Your overall health would be good, which would improve your professional performance. The positive influences on your ascendant house also portend excellent health and happiness throughout the year. However, some Virgos may suffer from weather-related ailments, but there will be no severe consequences. Those suffering from chronic illnesses should exercise caution during the middle of the year. That would be an unusual time for you to be especially careful. Regular medical help would help you stop any health problems before they worsen.

The year 2023 begins with Virgos in a fortunate economic situation. Jupiter's presence ensures a steady supply of cash for the people. Continue to work and explore all options for accumulating wealth. The planets assist you in taking any path that leads to financial security.

The planets will guide you to mature more gently in your domestic life this year. Saturn, however, will push you out of your comfort zone this year. During this time, you will be able to discover a lot more about yourself and your family members. Jupiter's transit in May might cause some uncertainty and misunderstandings in the family environment. Mars would provide the vitality you need to function successfully at home. Even if you deviate from your obligations, it will assist you in getting back on track.

The year 2023 would be pretty beneficial to Virgos' travel plans. Jupiter's relationship to your third house indicates that you will take several short trips this year. Those in the service industry would travel far and short distances extensively. You are also destined to go abroad this year due to the conjunction of Jupiter and Saturn in your 12th house of Leo.

All of your journeys have the potential to offer you benefits. The Moon's North node would aspect your 12th house during the latter part of the year, signifying an overseas trip.

In the life of Virgos, 2023 will be an excellent year for religious rituals. There would be far more devotion to your Gods than there has ever been before. This year, you will be able to make some sacrifices to your God. Going on pilgrimages or visiting holy locations will gain you merits. Jupiter's passage would urge you to give to charity and participate in social activities.

For the coming year, Virgos should avoid making hasty judgments. This year, use your energies to improve your relationships and money. Learn life lessons from the difficult challenges you are now facing. Do not be afraid to make amends or repairs when the occasion calls for it. Give your all to your relationships while being spiritually blessed. Saturn may hinder or confine your forward advance; do not lose heart; instead, be quiet and wait for the tide to change in your favor. And Jupiter would open fresh doors of opportunity this year, allowing you to master new talents.

January 2023

Horoscope

You live in an extremely comfortable environment. Capricorn's energies provide a sense of security. This has the effect of virtually boosting your self-esteem to new heights. You believe you can rely on your instincts.

This month, it will be your best guide. However, you will have to cope with Mars' dissonances in Gemini, which are creating havoc on your profession and prosperity. Your famous pragmatism will have a difficult time dealing with broken promises. Your sense of commitment increases tenfold around the 6th.

Take care not to drain yourself by catching up on other people's faults or taking on their obligations.

Love

The Capricorn planetary constellation drives your affections. It provides them with the stability you want. This month looks peaceful because there is no extravagance around. But starting on the 28th, when Venus moves into Pisces, if you listen to its siren song, it can cause trouble.

Virgos in a healthy relationship, your relationship grows in a happy, helpful way that makes you want to plan for the future. But in the long run, your relationship can become tiresome. Listen to your gut when it gives you ideas that are out of the ordinary.

Virgo singles, A good star keeps an eye on the people you love. So, you get attention even when you don't do anything. At the end of the month, someone could be crazy about you and do everything they can to catch you. Believe in yourself.

Career

This is not a good month. On bad days, you feel like letting everything slip through your fingers, going on vacation, or quitting your job. Even though you may think you only have problems to solve, Virgo, you can look at things differently. What? 'Or' How? By seeing them as problems to you need and achieve your goals with unsettling ease.

Being organized will make it easier for you to get things done. Make a detailed list of the things you need to do each day. Strategize because it can make a big difference in how well you do. You tend to work too much, so plan your tasks wisely.

Surround yourself with good friends who think a lot like you. You will learn many life skills from them, and positive life experiences will help you slowly climb the ladder of success.

No one can tell you what will happen in your life, but you might lose if you let hard times get you down. Your career will require a lot of work, so learn if you have to and keep working to get better.

Finance

On the money front, everything is good for you to have fun. You don't have to spend a lot to be happy, and your costs aren't too high to get you in trouble.

The stars say that this month will be good for your money, and there are signs that investments or stock trading will make you a lot of money. So, you can take some calculated risks with your money this month. Relationships with your bosses or coworkers are also likely to get better without any trouble, to the point where big gains are almost certain.

The climate would be good for new investments or business ideas. You have great ideas for running a business or investing money. Find time to tell the people you trust about these things. You will get good advice on planning and carrying out your ideas.

Health

Maintaining a healthy lifestyle is made easier this month by the constellations that are aligned in your favor. Those with a propensity to stomach and digestive issues would be greatly alleviated. Coughs, colds, and asthma, all common disorders of the chest, will be eliminated.

You'll recuperate more quickly when you have someone to look after you. It's time to look for people who can physically and morally help you. As we get older, our bodies deteriorate and require emotional support.

Understandably, you'd want to keep an eye on your oral health because it may cause you pain, but with the proper dental care, you won't have to worry. It's possible that you're easily agitated and have a little disturbed state of mind. Keeping your mind and body in a state of calm and balance won't take much work and will help you stay in.

Travel

There isn't much chance of making money from travel this month, since the stars don't look good on this front. Most of the time this month, you would travel alone, mostly by car or train, with some air travel thrown in.

Also, you might work or travel abroad. But it is almost certain that these efforts would not bring the profits, pleasure, and satisfaction that were hoped for. The best direction would be to go East.

Insight from the stars

You are no longer required to demonstrate your sincerity. Remember, though, that some people are more relaxed than you. It would be a shame if your popularity dwindled. This month, you will have to develop new ways to use your skills, talents, and abilities.

February 2023

Horoscope

The dissonances emanating from Pisces and Gemini disrupt your peace this month. These energies throw you off balance and use all means possible to disrupt your well-organized existence. At first sight, you may believe that the sky and stars intend to cause havoc. If you examine closely, you will notice that some minor modifications will do you a world of good.

You must take a step back before rejecting a confession of love or making a decision to succeed at this little feat. This may involve some work on your part, but it will spare you from having regrets later on. Be extremely cautious around the 20th since the new moon occurs in Pisces.

Love

Pisces' energies are trying to get you to make a commitment. In return, this possibility is likely to make you lose control. Instead of getting defensive, take a deep breath and think. This will help you find a solution that works for both of you.

Virgos, your partner is the one who drives your relationship forward. This approach suggests that there will be some emotional trouble. If you want to get along with your partner, respond to one of their requests.

Virgo singles, Your desire to meet someone and have a beautiful love story is confirmed. But that's no reason to start something that won't work out for you in the long run. Keep time for yourself to keep this from happening.

Career

Although it is not easy, great things are coming this month. Your task appears less complex, but you approach it with greater optimism. However, you will most likely feel the time is too long and wish for a change. Unfortunately, what is provided falls short of your expectations. If you want to see things improve in this industry, Virgo, focus on the positives rather than the flaws.

You would have good prospects for career advancement if your circumstances were suitable because you will put in the effort and succeed in achieving your goals. There is a good possibility that this will open up a whole new world of opportunities for you, leading to a much better career or a shift in business operations. It's all for the better.

You should also anticipate significant travel, which will be really useful. The most advantageous direction would be east. This phase will also be marked by a daring attitude in your professional pursuits. This would result in improved efficiency and leadership skills.

Finance

On the financial front, if a purchase necessitates hefty financing, you're in luck. But that is no excuse for abusing it. Promise?

However, the stars predict that the course of events will not favor your financial progress this month. True, there are obvious signs that your investments may result in significant losses. As a result, it would be prudent to avoid all forms of gambling.

There are also indicators that any disagreement or litigation you may be involved in will probably be resolved against you, resulting in significant losses. As a result, you must work hard to ensure that any such choice is postponed until a later and more suitable time. Relationships with superiors, business partners, or workers are also likely to deteriorate; avoid such a scenario, or you may incur significant losses.

Health

The augury of stars facing you this month has a lot of good news for your health. Any tendency to sudden acute diseases, such as fever or inflammations, would get significant alleviation, even if only for a short time. Such an issue would most likely not worry you at all. Back pain would be alleviated in the same way.

Attempt to be productive without jeopardizing your health. The best thing you can do is start with what you consume. Prepare a menu of all the foods you enjoy and make healthier versions.

However, there are reasons to be concerned about the likelihood of an eye infection. This may irritate you temporarily, but it is preventable with adequate preventative measures such as cleanliness and the use of appropriate preventive medicine. Overall, a month is fairly promising for your health.

Travel

As far as making money from travel is concerned, the horoscope from the stars doesn't say anything particularly good. This month, you would travel alone mostly by car and train, with some flights.

An international trip is also a possibility. There's a good chance that these efforts won't bring the profits or pleasures hoped for. This is a pretty dark picture, but unfortunately, it's true. A lot of your travel may not be necessary, and you could probably do fine without it. The most favorable direction is East.

Insight from the stars

Even if it's tempting, don't go overboard. Find the best compromise for each situation so everyone can get what they want. Approach life with confidence. Don't let anyone make decisions for you. You have everything you need to make the right choices in your life.

March 2023

Horoscope

This month, you'll have to deal with the dissonances caused by Gemini and Pisces. These energies interrupt both your plans and your peace. They give you the impression that you are being bombarded by occurrences. You get the sensation that your spouse, boss, and others do not comprehend your point of view.

You've lost command of the situation. These occurrences are increased and verified around the 7th when the full moon forms in your sign. Instead of fighting in all directions, look at things from a new perspective. Be open to new possibilities. This possibility is provided by Uranus and Venus in Taurus. Certainly surprising, but if you desire serenity, it is important to give it some thought.

Love

Even though you want to help, it's hard unless you agree to look at things differently. You feel pressure from the forces in Pisces, and Venus in Taurus winks at you. Despite what you think, you have a choice this month and can make a choice.

Still, people are angry about commitment. Your partner criticizes you all the time. When Venus is in Taurus and Mars is in Cancer, you can make a distraction. Show off all your good qualities. It will make your partner feel calm and safe.

Virgo singles, From the 17th, Venus in Taurus plays Cupid. From the 26th, Mars in Cancer urges you to take action. Your loves could match your aspirations if you listen to your gut and not your mind.

Career

Saturn might be blamed for making you feel as if your horizon is obstructed. Aside from demoralizing you, it accentuates the obstacles that Mars in Gemini sends your way. Virgo admits that this month hasn't been all that bright. You can, however, have a unique perspective on it. Is there any other way? By putting a stop to the pursuit of excellence. Doing this will save a great deal of time and improve the quality of your life.

This is a great month to take your career to the next level. Those drawn to the arts and those who practice the fine arts should expect a period of creative fulfilment. With your efforts, you may build a name for yourself in the future.

There would also be a lot of travel involved, which would be quite helpful. The south would be the best route to travel. Aside from travel, you may have to relocate your operation's location, whether it's for work or pleasure. Take your time and think things over thoroughly before making any changes. Otherwise, you might undo all of your hard work.

Finance

A sizable amount of overdue money might fill your piggy bank and give you peace of mind. The stars are aligned in your favor regarding your financial situation this month. As you succeed in your commercial endeavors and investments, you will have a stable source of income. The problem is that excessive expenditure might lead to bankruptcy. Save money by spending a little.

You'll be able to put your money to work for you this month. This month, you have a terrific opportunity to make money by investing in stocks or franchising. You'd likely make a tidy profit from your investments and company ventures.

Health

This month, you have a good set of circumstances for your health. Chronic diseases like rheumatism, gout, and problems with the digestive system like flatulence and too much wind would get a lot better. This should not, however, be taken as a pass to stop being careful.

There are reasons to be a little worried about the state of your teeth. Take care of your teeth and Try to improve your health overall. Make an effort to break bad habits and plan outdoor activities that you can do every day. Make it a habit to make time for these activities, even if you have a busy schedule.

You have a good month ahead, during which you won't have to deal with serious health risks.

Travel

Not a good month to go on a trip because the stars don't seem particularly favorable in this regard, especially if you want to make a lot of money from it. Writers, poets, and others like them may have a financially and creatively unproductive travel period.

You would usually travel alone, mostly by car or train, with a fair amount of flying. A trip overseas is not impossible. But it's almost certain that these efforts won't even come close to reaching a fraction of the goals. The best way to go is to the South.

Insight from the stars

Quit trying to meet everyone else's needs! Think about yourself instead. Do yourself a favor, and don't worry if it bothers people who mean well. Take advantage of the chances that keep knocking on your door to move up in your career.

April 2023

Horoscope

With Saturn in your sign, you'll have to deal with its demands and dreams. Taurus and Cancer energies assist you to succeed in this tiny miracle. They encourage you to try out new solutions to your behavior and inspire you to use your abilities and follow your intuition.

This month, events and circumstances inspire you to put the virtues of letting go to the test since difficulties grow with Venus in Gemini between the 12th and 30th. Taking a step back will allow you to have a more hopeful outlook on the future. This can also help you understand that you have a lot more options than you believe.

Love

Saturn makes you feel more responsible, but it can also get you and the people you love into a lot of trouble. To avoid this, pay attention to what Venus and Mercury in Taurus tell you to do. Don't be as shy as you usually are. Accept that you deserve to enjoy life a little bit more.

Virgos in a relationship: The air between you two is a little cold. Mercury helps you figure out why you're here this month. Also, it gives you ideas that you should use if you want to start a conversation.

Single Virgos, up until the 11th, your love looks good. Then the atmosphere becomes colder. Instead of jumping from one idea to the next, be more spontaneous if you want to catch up. Don't try to change the people you love. Instead, accept them as they are.

Career

Investment and trust are two of the most important factors for a person's success. Virgo, this is your chance to show the world what you're made of. Removing these impediments will help you go forward. Because, even though you may believe you don't have enough time to get everything done, you do.

This month has been a good one regarding your career future. Fine artists and others of their type would enjoy themselves much. With your efforts, you may build a name for yourself in the future. There are hints that you are prone to working hard and achieving your goals on time. And you will succeed in this as well.

Your location may change even if you're running a business or providing a service. Change should only be made after much thought and consideration. Additionally, there would be significant travel, which would be highly advantageous in the long run.

Finance

Although your piggy bank is full, you may have to cut some corners financially to maintain your standard of living. The end of the month is approaching, and while it's not something you want to do, you may be forced to utilize your resources to catch up.

Because of the unfavorable constellations in your chart, your financial situation isn't looking well this month. You stand to suffer significant losses as a result of speculation. The lesson is clear: avoid all forms of gambling at all costs.

In addition, it is possible that your relationship with your superiors may deteriorate to the point where losses are a real possibility. Prevent this from happening by acting quickly to correct the situation. Due to the sluggish economy, investing or establishing new initiatives will be difficult. To put it another way, these plans should be put on hold for the time being.

Health

In the constellations that are aligned to face you this month, you have plenty of reasons to be optimistic about your health. The signs warn you not to push yourself too much. This should be avoided at all costs if you want to keep things running normally and not stress the system.

Make it easier on yourself by making a new schedule of activities. Maintaining good oral health is important, and you should take all the necessary precautions to ensure that you do. From a health perspective, you have fairly positive month.

Travel

This month, your chances of making money from travel aren't very good because the stars aren't in your favor on this score. This month, you would probably travel alone by train, car, and air.

Also, a trip abroad is not impossible. But one thing is certain: these trips would not accomplish even a fraction of the objectives. The majority of this travel would be unrelated to your business or job. The best direction would be to go West.

Insights from the stars

Your sense of order and method is indisputable? Just the opposite. Still, try not to control everything. Let things happen naturally. You will have to find a way to balance your work and your personal life. You've been ignoring your loved ones for a while and need to start paying more attention to them.

May 2023

Horoscope

Saturn keeps pushing you back into your comfort zones while also trying to open your eyes to a new way of seeing the world. As a consequence, you may feel terrific at times and depressed at others. Support from Taurus and Cancer is benevolent yet practical and helps you keep going and helps you locate the materials needed to satisfy Saturn's requirements. They provide you with the security you need to avoid making poor choices. However, a little divine guidance wouldn't hurt!

May 17th marks the arrival of Jupiter, the promising star and evolutionary force, in Taurus. It opens up new opportunities that have been wanted for a while.

Love

Saturnian forces direct your attention here. As a result, you have an austere, gloomy, and often critical view of the situation. Fortunately, friendly planetary energies provide a distraction! They force you to encounter people who can influence your opinion.

Virgos in a relationship, the mood is always a little heavy, but don't worry, everything is OK! You have everything you need to make things go more smoothly. Don't be afraid to utilize it; your other half will thank you.

Virgo singles, the stars recommend you have a charming and delicate meeting. Allow things to happen without interrogating them. If you want to do something, do it! Go for it while you're feeling it!

Career

You do a good job of insuring in your industry. It's OK to ask for help, but don't be afraid to ask for it! Jupiter is in Taurus at the time of its arrival. As Virgos, this is the time to pay attention to what's going on in the world. Think about it if someone offers you a great deal. And don't think you can't do it because you can.

This is a month in which you have little chance of moving up in your profession, and if you're not cautious, you may end up lower on the ladder than you started. You may be tempted to break the law for short-term gains. In the event that this is permitted to happen, the repercussions will be catastrophic. To avoid falling prey to such temptations, you must make a clear commitment to yourself.

There is also a chance that you will have severe disagreements with your superiors. This is something else you should work hard to avoid. As a result of your unease, you're more likely to switch jobs or work with other colleagues. Only make alterations after thorough consideration. Only make changes after careful thought.

Finance

When it comes to money and modest presents, they can help ease tensions, but you don't need to go over your budget. Don't overspend, but do it generously.

This month's horoscope isn't in your favor regarding your financial situation. You will lose money when you trade and invest. This means that you should avoid any investments.

In addition, there are reasons to believe that your relationships with your superiors will suffer due to your tendency to dispute, which might result in significant financial losses. You have the power to prevent this if you work hard enough. To avoid such a situation, you should take the necessary precautions in advance. If you were planning on making any investments or starting any new ventures this month, you'd be better off waiting.

Health

This month, the stars don't have any good news for your health. So, you need to be more cautious and watchful. Those who are more likely to get piles should be very careful about what they eat and how they are treated. Carelessness would only make things worse.

Pay attention to your health and get help for the difficult disease you are dealing with. Even if you have to wait to see a doctor or if you get the wrong diagnosis, you will still get the proper treatment you need. Be humble and use the available medical options.

Any tendency to get colds or have a lot of mucus come out may worsen. Again, this could need quick attention and corrective actions to make things right. Stones and a tendency to get fistula would also need more attention, as would your teeth. Take care of your teeth as this might cause you problems as well.

Travel

A month in which you might lose a lot of money while travelling because the stars aren't very favorable. During your travels, you might get hurt or have some other kind of physical problem. Exercise care and minimize risks.

You would travel alone mostly by car and train, but you would also take a fair amount of flights. A journey overseas is also not out of the question. These stays could end up being utterly useless in every way. Since only some of them would be done for business purposes, they wouldn't make the expected money. The rest wouldn't make you happy. North is the best direction to go.

Insight from the stars

Take a step back when things start to make sense. This will help you understand what they are saying and what you need to do to calm down. Don't miss out on anything that could help your career. Now is the time to reach significant goals in your life.

June 2023

Horoscope

Gains, ties, or a way of life become outmoded due to Saturn's dissonances. Despite your excellent intentions, they will not be able to deliver you much more. Jupiter's fortunate presence in Taurus provides you with the opportunity to make changes.

The lucky star urges you to broaden your sphere of activity through events and situations, allowing you to meet individuals who are unlike you. He encourages you to put your talents and skills to good use.

Unfortunately, an opportunity is sometimes accompanied by a problem that must be solved, so you must overcome your reservations. If you want to capitalize on the opportunities that may occur, you must dare to talk about yourself and your abilities. Be a little opportunistic, and know that no one will judge you for it.

Love

You start to doubt your ability to seduce because of things that happen or how other people act. You don't feel like you have anything in common with people you think are more successful. You are probably thinking about something. Luckily, the light starts to come on the 22nd.

If you're in a relationship, it might not be clear, but your relationship could change. You can stop being so bored, which is bad for your morale if you want to. Let go to make this little trick work.

Virgo singles, the stars are being funny this month and putting you in touch with good people. Instead of thinking about yourself all the time, enjoy life and everything it offers.

Career

The little boost that was hoped for is coming, but it won't be enough. Do you want things to change, Virgo? So, instead of focusing on what's wrong, look at everything you do well and do even better! At first, this may seem impossible, but if you give yourself time, you'll get there so easily that it will shock you. You will get the satisfaction you want if you do this.

As far as your professional future goes, the horoscope doesn't tell you anything particularly good. There is a good chance you will have a big disagreement with your bosses or business partner. This shouldn't be allowed to happen, and you should try to stop it from happening.

You might also be filled with a feeling of insecurity that would affect almost everything you do at work. You could try to even things out by switching jobs quickly or making changes to how your business works. This would be a terrible way for things to be. Any change should be made only after a lot of careful thought. There would also be a lot of travel, but this wouldn't lead to much either.

Finance

When it comes to money, you can live a normal life, but the stars put you on a budget when it comes to fancy things. A good month for your finances. You can look forward to getting a lot of money quickly, and you would also be better off if you invested. There is also a good chance that an old friend will do you a favor that could be very helpful financially.

Also, this month you'll learn how to deal with your bosses, which will make the relationship very good for you. This could be a big advantage. Lastly, being friends with many intelligent, spiritually-minded people with gifts would help you in both material and spiritual ways.

Health

This month, the stars are favoring your well-being, and you should enjoy a period of good health. Sudden acute illnesses like fevers and inflammation would be significantly reduced. You would be completely unaffected by them.

People with any kind of dental issue will also benefit from this blessing. In fact, any issue with your dentures should be taken carefully and has a strong probability of being resolved. This is a good time for your health, and those currently in good condition may anticipate continuing in good shape.

Travel

Since the stars aren't in a good place this month, you shouldn't expect to get what you want out of travel, nor will you have as much fun as you thought. If you want to go on a pilgrimage to a holy place, the trip might have to be put off, or you might run into problems along the way.

Most of the time, you travel alone by train or car, with some flights thrown in. Even a trip abroad is not impossible. Still, none of these efforts would get anywhere. The best way to go is to the East.

Insight from the stars

If you want things to progress, you must be brave and agree to meet new people. Talk about yourself, your accomplishments, and your goals. Your career will go well, and you will work with people who are goal-oriented and focused.

July 2023

Horoscope

Even though Jupiter is the "star of evolution" and gives you chances to do more, Saturn and Neptune are bad news. They make you doubt yourself, which stops you from moving forward. You find it hard to see the good things about the opportunities that come your way. They make you feel bad about yourself, which makes you want to be alone, although Mercury makes it easy to see clearly until the 11th. The advice you get from your relationships is wise and insightful.

Mars moves into your sign on the 11th, which makes you more likely to take charge. It forces you to overcome your fears and take what's on offer. You're bursting at the seams this month, but you can change how things go if you want to.

Love

This month, you have serious doubts about your ability to attract a partner. You can stop this torturous process if you want to. How? Realizing that you have good qualities and everything you need to please someone who wants a real relationship based on intelligence.

If you're a Virgo in a relationship, Saturn will slow things down and cause trouble. Even though Mercury brings back the conversations, there is a lot of silence from the 11th to the 28th. Your options are limited but don't worry, providence will make things right again.

The stars tell you to stay put if you're a single Virgo. Another person sets you up with someone interested in you because of your qualities. Don't pay attention to what's wrong. Take the right path in life.

Career

You may think that things are getting worse as the days go by. It's easy to believe that things and people deliberately try to aggravate you during the worst days. In reality, Virgo, that's not what's going on here. You'll be pushed to new heights by these conditions and these individuals! So, rely on your intuition, abilities, and experience to make the best decisions for you. You'll be able to achieve great things if you do this!

This month, your astrological chart shows just a few promising omens for professional growth. You'd likely put in a lot of effort, but you wouldn't be able to achieve your goals. Disputes with your superiors are also a probable possibility.

Because of the potentially devastating outcomes, this must be avoided at all costs. Try to anticipate and work around any challenging areas that may arise. There would also be a lot of travel, which would, unfortunately, provide nothing in the way of rewards, but a short trip to the South may yield a little percentage for you.

Finance

The worry of running out of money causes you to be extremely frugal. But don't deprive yourself of everything!

If things go smoothly for you this month, there is a strong chance that your financial situation will be stable for the foreseeable future. You might be able to expect to get a lot of unexpected benefits and money from your investments.

If you're a manager, you'll have a system for managing your subordinates or employees that maximizes your return on investment. This would be a huge advantage for you and could even lead to massive profits. Another possibility is that an old buddy may do you a favor or provide you with a service that will be highly helpful.

Health

It's not a good month for your health, as Lady Fortune isn't being cooperative this month and is withholding her blessings. Predispositions to chronic conditions like rheumatism and digestive abnormalities such as gas and extra wind in the digestive system would be more bothersome than usual. As with any type of dental issue, more attention and care are required.

In addition, you may be bothered by a predisposition to anxiety. You should take extra precautions to protect your health in the next few months, as the future seems bleak.

Travel

A month in which the chances of profiting from travel look slim, as the stars are not in a good mood. You would most likely travel alone by rail and road, with some air travel thrown in for good measure. International travel is also not out of the question.

All of these trips might be related to work and other things in equal measure. But no matter why you're traveling, it's almost certain that you won't reach even a fraction of your goals. As a result, it's a good idea to go over your travel plans ahead of time to see if they'll get you anywhere. The best direction to go would be South.

Insight from the stars

Despite what you think, you have everything you need to change how things are going. How? By making the most of the opportunities that come your way. If you don't live healthily, it could hurt your health.

August 2023

Horoscope

Saturn has been telling you for a while that your relationships won't help you much. Your conversations have become less interesting. With people you've known for years, a distance grows. Time makes bonds weaken. In exchange, Uranus and Jupiter provide opportunities to meet new people. They want you to grow up in a different universe of relationships, but one that fits you from now on. If you agree, you can get out of this boring situation this month.

Mars in your sign gives you the courage and daring to take what's offered to you, which helps you do this little trick. Mercury, which is also in Virgo, makes you more understanding, enabling you to make social, friendly, and other connections.

Love

Even though your friends or dates show you the opposite, you're starting to doubt your ability to seduce. Try to be less hard on yourself and look on the bright side of things.

Virgos in a relationship, the mood is dark, but you have the power to change it. At the end of the month, Mars, Mercury, and the sun give you the energy and ideas you need to rebuild your relationship.

Single Virgos If you stay stuck in romantic plans from the past, you will be bored. On the other hand, if you don't question the unexpected and just go with it, you give yourself the best chance of meeting someone amazing.

Career

Now is an excellent time to reflect on your goals. Look over the proposed changes while you're at it, too. Consider them thoroughly and without bias. Never, ever, ever assume it's not for you. An inexplicable transformation has begun in Virgo! Even if you think it's bad news, it's actually quite good for your well-being. Why? for the simple reason that it will allow you to see things in a new light.

An unfavorable month for advancing one's career, as well as a time when one should exercise extra caution. There's a good chance that you and your superiors will have some major disagreements. Ideally, you should avoid this at all costs. Keep your cool and steer clear of problem situations by remaining calm and patient this month.

You may be tempted to break the law to make a fast buck. If you don't want to end up in the abyss, you'll need to rein in these impulses.

Finance

When it comes to money, you can keep your focus on the important things if you save. You think futility is a gimmick. Your financial situation has suddenly improved!

This is a month in which you have the potential to make a significant amount of money if you behave wisely.

You'll have a better shot at financial advancement. Leaving your former job or profession might lead to a rich new opportunity. Despite the fact that money isn't your primary goal, your hunt for a superior firm or business opportunity will result in unanticipated financial gains. It will help you and your family save a lot of money.

You may make a lot of money by investing. As a result, you must take advantage of any opportunity. Stock trading, gambling, and creating new ventures would all thrive in this environment.

Health

This month's horoscopes do not bode well for your health. A tendency to be nervous could be a problem, and any kind of tooth trouble is likely to need more care and attention. This should be taken seriously. There are more reasons to think that you may be in a state of general weakness and nervous problems due to overwork and exhaustion.

You can avoid this by redrawing your schedule and then sticking to it. This would help you a lot and solve a lot of your problems. Clearly, the time ahead of you isn't very good, so you should be very careful and watchful.

Travel

There's nothing particularly fortunate about what the stars say about what you'll gain from travelling. This month, you would travel almost equally for work, business, and other reasons.

You would probably travel alone most of the time, mostly by road and train. A trip abroad also can't be ruled out. No matter why or how you travel, it's almost certain that you won't get even a fraction of what you planned to get out of it—thinking carefully about your travel plans before you make them would be wise. West would be the best direction.

Insights from the stars

You begin to notice that a new relationship is creeping into your life. You won't have to worry about being criticized as long as you maintain your composure. Give back to the community by getting involved in charitable endeavors that benefit those less fortunate.

September 2023

Horoscope

Contrary to popular belief, you have everything you need to start living a more peaceful and enjoyable life.

As a result of the influence of Taurus and Virgo, your growth and success are more possible. Mercury makes you more intelligent. As a result, you have a more precise understanding of what you mean. It encourages you to recognize and make use of your natural talents. It's possible to alter the path of events if you agree with this. How? By Taking advantage of the possibilities that will present themselves and not wasting time on self-reflection! If you're worried about everything working smoothly, don't be! Things are going to go smoothly and at a reasonable pace.

Love

Bad memories start to bubble up. Suddenly, you're feeling down! You don't get better. Your relationship will be back on a smooth path soon, free of the hurts and disappointments of the past. Try to smile again and trust yourself until then.

If you're a Virgo in a relationship, you lose your passion and grow apart. Sadness is in the air. Your relationship needs to get back on track as soon as possible. The fights can get heated this month, but they can also bring your relationship back to life.

Virgo singles, situations make you feel like you might stay single forever. Don't worry, this is not the case. This month, agree to meet someone who isn't like the people you usually date.

Career

This month, the stars allow you plenty of time to contemplate making a business proposal. Taking advantage of this window of opportunity is an excellent idea. This will enable you to make a decision free of outside influence. The 16th is a good day to clean up your documents or computer if you suddenly decide to do so.

There isn't much hope for your professional future in the current month's astrological configuration. Serious disagreements with your superiors are very likely. This would be a disaster waiting to happen. That's why avoiding a situation like this is so important.

There's also the possibility that an unnecessary sense of insecurity plagues you. Resolving this issue may require you to look for new employment or change how you do business. A terrible situation to find yourself in. Take your time and think things out before making any adjustments.

Finance

Keeping your financial life balanced relies on your capacity to make rational decisions about your spending and saving. And if your loved ones come to you and beg for your help, don't be unreasonable in your response.

According to the astrological forecast, it will not be a good month for your finances. There's a good chance your relationships with your superiors will deteriorate to the point where you'll be forced to take a hit financially. If you want to avoid such a scenario, you need to plan ahead to ensure you're prepared.

There would be a lack of possibilities, and you would have difficulty reaching your goals. Additionally, you risk being too obsessed with producing money you can't account for. This will have a negative impact on your current circumstances. Correct the situation. This includes avoiding investments and gambling.

Health

It will not be a great month for your health since the stars aren't feeling generous. For susceptible people, having cold hands and feet would be a nightmare. Any tendency to anxiety would just become worse. There's a strong chance that a skilled yoga teacher and regular practice can help you overcome this problem.

There's a greater chance of having an issue with your teeth. This implies that your tooth health will receive further attention. As a result, your health will require more attention and care in the weeks ahead.

Travel

This is a month in which it may be hard to make money from travelling since the prophesy from the stars is not favorable on this front. A pilgrimage to a holy place would have to be postponed or become bogged down in problems.

Anyone hoping to further their education by going to college or training programs in another country or continent may face some unexpectedly challenging obstacles. You'd largely use the road and train to go about on your own, with some flights thrown in. The possibility of an overseas trip is not ruled out. A trip abroad is also not out of the question. On the other hand, these stays would be a total waste of time. North is the best direction to go.

Insight from the stars

You can alter the path of events. It's better to meet people who live in a different reality than yours to stop repeating your own views and ideas to yourself endlessly. With better lines of communication, your romantic life will flourish.

October 2023

Horoscope

Venus takes control on the 10th, and Mercury leaves on the 5th. Mars enters Scorpio on the 13th. Mercury and the Sun will join him at the end of the month. It's a great time to make changes because Saturn is retrograde and Jupiter is slowing down. Because of the planets in Scorpio, you're in an excellent place to move forward. Saturn in Pisces is a symbol of obstacles that you can conquer.

The people you surround yourself with are the most important part of your support system. There are several ways in which it aids you in recognizing and capitalizing on your worth. If you don't know what to think about a possible opportunity or proposal this month, ask people you trust what they think.

Love

After the 10th, you start to feel better. Venus makes it easier to deal with Saturn. She tells you to stop thinking about the past and focus on yourself. This month, you should change your look and say yes to your friends' offers.

Virgos who are dating, even though the mood is sad, you get a second wind. Mars and Venus want you to take charge of the situation to get your relationship moving again. This month, stop talking and start doing something.

Virgo singles, Don't even think about getting married at any costs! Think about yourself and what's happening now. Also, instead of turning down the invitations, accept them. You will meet new people if you do this.

Career

You are on the verge of fulfilling your request for growth or change. You must decide for this tiny miracle to occur. When it comes to work, you're a Virgo who tends to overthink everything. This is a certain way to end yourself right back where you started. If that's not what you're looking for, talk to someone you can rely on. When you hear what they say, you'll be surprised. The more you listen to them, the more you'll be happy.

According to the stars, this is not a great month for your career future. If you're feeling good about yourself, you could consider changing jobs or making a significant adjustment to your business or service. Because of this, there is a good chance that you will disagree with your bosses or those above you.

There would also be a lot of hard effort, which would fail to achieve the intended outcomes and leave you terribly disappointed. Always maintain some kind of consistency and avoid acting erratically.

Finance

You spend a lot of money because you are in love with someone. So, if you don't want to become broke, you might want to slow down.

According to the stars' interpretation, this month's horoscope does not portend well for your financial well-being. As a result of your tendency to engage in conflict with your superiors, you might suffer a significant setback in your career. To avoid this, you should take whatever precautions you can think of to prevent it.

Some of you would almost certainly suffer losses due to your speculative activities. Gambling should thus be avoided in general. The climate would likewise be unsuitable for making investments or establishing new enterprises. Such ideas should be put on hold for the time being.

Health

This month's star alignment does not provide much hope for better health on your part. People prone to sudden acute illness may be bothered by short-lived bouts of illness. These should be dealt with as soon as possible.

Dental care should be given significantly more importance and all possible measures implemented to preserve healthy teeth and gums. In contrast to other months, this one calls for a higher level of focus than usual.

There may be issues with the mind, such as anxiety and other mental health issues. Calmness and balance must be maintained, with a special effort to stay upbeat and pleasant. Maintaining a healthy diet, regular exercise, and adequate sleep are all necessary for good health. Any excess can lead to an unbalanced existence.

Avoid exhaustion by not overworking. Do not overindulge in eating since this will lead to weight gain. Limiting your intake of alcohol might lead to a higher risk of drunkenness, so be careful. By keeping things in moderation, you'll be able to ensure that your body is in good shape.

Travel

This isn't a good month to travel because the stars aren't aligned in a way that makes it easy to get where you want to go. There is a chance that you will get hurt or have some other kind of physical problem while you are travelling. So, you should be careful and take the fewest possible risks.

Most of the time, you would travel by rail or road, but you would also fly a fair amount. Some of your trips might be related to your job or business. A good number of them wouldn't be so similar. It's pretty clear that none of these would be beneficial. A trip abroad is also not impossible. The best way to go is to the east.

Insight from the stars

Let go of the past's influence this month and have faith in your own abilities. You may count on your closest friends to introduce you to new people. Be prepared for significant changes in your life, and be ready to welcome them all.

November 2023

Horoscope

Jupiter in Taurus opens doors for you. As for the planets in Scorpio, they give you the power to get what you want. You may wonder what the problem is in this environment, which is very good for your growth.

Mercury, the Sun, and Mars are all in the sign of Sagittarius, which creates many different problems. But if you want to, you can get past them. Stop being content with the little you have if you want this little miracle to work. Dare to ask for more because you should. For once, try to make friends. And if you're worried about what will happen, don't be. With the energies that flow through Scorpio, you don't have to worry about going too far.

Love

If you don't let go of the past, the people you love will have a hard time. You will keep making mistakes, and you won't get anywhere. On the other hand, things will be a lot better if you can get away from it. You will meet people who are charming and can decide what to do.

For Virgos in a relationship, the planets in Scorpio will help you take charge. Unfortunately, disagreements can get in the way of this happiness. Your relationship isn't easy this month, but don't worry, it's not in danger.

This month, Virgo singles won't fall in love at first sight, but they will find a great match with someone they already know. Stop asking yourself questions if you want this small wonder to come true. Just live in the moment.

Career

You're in a better position than you've ever been. If you accept a given proposal, you might alter your course of action. However, this may only be achieved if you're willing to take on various tasks. Focus on the positive aspects of a shift instead of the negative ones. Make an effort to see the positive side of things for once. You'll be able to break free of this routine by doing so.

There isn't a lot of good news for your job chances this month, thanks to the constellation of stars. A sense of uneasiness about your job might keep you up at night. You'd have to rethink everything you do in connection with your company or work.

Even if you put in a lot of time and effort, your goals may still elude you. As a result, you'd either look for a new career or significantly adjust your business operations. However, you would still be unhappy with all of this. An even more serious confrontation is possible with your bosses. This should be avoided at all costs. Be proactive and try to predict and solve problems before they happen so you can avoid them.

Finance

Due to a favorable alignment of the stars, you should have a good month in terms of earning potential this month. Artists of all types are set to have a particularly fruitful month in terms of creative production and financial success in the coming weeks.

The tides are turning in your favor, and you may be in line for a windfall of unexpected riches. Profits might also be made through investments. Depending on your luck, you could even receive some cash assistance from one of your female friends!

Health

This month, a good set of events would make you feel good about your health. People prone to chronic diseases like rheumatism and digestive problems like flatulence and too much gas would feel a lot better. This means you wouldn't have to worry about these problems if you took normal precautions.

But there are reasons to be careful about throat pain that doesn't go away. This should be carefully looked into to see if there are any complications, and then it should be treated with care. If you don't do this, you could mess up a good health situation. Besides this, you don't have any serious reasons to worry.

Travel

It might be hard to make money from travel this month since the stars don't look good on this front. Musicians, painters, dancers, and other artists may not get as much out of their trips as they usually do. In fact, this could be a setback for some of them.

Most of the time, you would travel by rail or road, with a fair amount of air travel. A trip abroad is also not out of the question. Most of this would be related to your business or job, but these efforts wouldn't get you where you want to go. The best way to go is toward the East.

Insights from the stars

Don't suffer Saturn's effects; instead, use them to your advantage. This month, stay away from people who don't suit you and get closer to those who do. Things in your life seem to be going in the right direction. You will have more happiness and peace than ever before.

December 2023

Horoscope

You feel calm when Taurus, Capricorn, and Scorpio send out their energies. You feel like you're growing up in a world that fits and gets you. Your relationships with the people you care about are built on strong, honest bonds. You think you are going in the right direction, and you are. So, you have to be practical to take advantage of the opportunities that come your way.

Unfortunately, Sagittarius's dissonances and Saturn's position in Pisces create risks and tensions. If you have trouble, your progress will be slowed down. On the other hand, nothing can stop you if you know what they mean. This month, your growth will depend on how well you can act despite problems.

Love

When Venus is in Scorpio, your relationships are stable and pleasant. You feel like you're surrounded by people who really care about you. Unfortunately, tensions from the outside world get in the way of these joys. Use it to make decisions that will set you free instead of making you stuck.

Even though you and your partner are getting along better, tensions from the outside are trying to cause trouble. You have a choice this month. You can relax and talk to them or ignore them until they get bored.

Venus helps Virgo singles find love by bringing them together with someone they already know. If you want this new happiness to grow calmly, don't tell anyone about it. On the other hand, you have to be determined if you want to show it in broad daylight.

Career

You keep doing your best this month, and it works out well for you. You might feel like you're on the right end of the rope! Unfortunately, the dissonances that come from Pisces and Sagittarius can hit you hard and hold you back. Virgo, if you stop at the first problem, you won't get very far. On the other hand, you get around it with the intelligence that defines you. You will do wonders.

According to the stars, there is a lot of good news about your career this month. Your career will also undergo sudden changes, but most of them will be good. You might get a raise or a new job or find other opportunities.

But you'll probably be busier because you'll have to do more tasks and have more responsibilities at work. You are usually a workaholic, but your plate will be too full this month, and you may feel stressed and tired. But don't worry, your coworkers or business partners will come to your aid.

Don't worry about asking for help. Teamwork is the key to getting through challenging situations at work. Give the tasks to the other people on the team.

Finance

Spending money on frivolous items is no longer an option. First things first. As a result, your financial account will benefit greatly.

As you invest in real estate this month, you may expect a steady flow of income. At the same time, you have a solid financial foundation to meet your obligations when they come due. A lot of physical and mental effort may be needed this month to manage your finances properly. It's going to be difficult, but it's going to be worth it.

However, you still need to exercise caution. It is essential to save your money for financial security. You may even be able to help people in need by sharing your blessings. If this is a good month, you might want to invest in making passive income.

Health

This month, the alignment of the stars is in your favor and is beneficial to your health. Those with an acute chest or lungs inclined to chest or lung disorders are likely to find great alleviation from their problems. There is a risk of tiredness and incapacity as a result of over-exertion.

This is something you can easily avoid by not overworking yourself. When this is done, everything will be fine. This would also assist you in overcoming the potential of some nerve problems which might exist. Take care of yourself, and you will be in good health for the rest of the month. Pay more attention to the health of your teeth.

Travel

The horoscope from the stars doesn't tell us anything particularly favorable about travel. Writers, poets, and people like them may not have the best trips. In fact, some of them could be seriously hurt by how unproductive their stays are.

You would travel alone, mostly by train or car, but you would also take a fair amount of flights. A trip abroad is also not out of the question. But it's not likely that these efforts would lead to even a holiday, which might not be all that fun. The best direction to go is South.

Insight from the stars

The energies of Sagittarius tend to make things hard for you. Stay quiet about your success and victory if you want to avoid these problems. Because life is short, make the most of it. During the 2023 Mercury retrograde, be careful not to overindulge so much that you hurt yourself or others.

LIBRA 2023 HOROSCOPE

Overview Libra 2023

In 2023, if you were born under the sign of Libra, Jupiter would be in the 7th house of Aries until May, when it would move into the 8th house of Taurus. This will affect what happens in love and marriage in the year's first three months. Then, when Jupiter moves through your sign, it brings your finances and spiritual healing to the forefront. Saturn, the planet of discouragement, will be in your 5th house of Aquarius until March when it will move to your 6th house of Pisces. This means your children and love life will be good until March. After that, the transit to the 6th house could cause minor health problems, but nothing major.

Uranus, the planet of change, is in the 8th house of Taurus this year for Libra folks. During May and June of 2023, Neptune moves through the 6th house of Pisces, and Pluto moves from the 4th house of Capricorn to the 5th house of Aquarius. How these planets move through the zodiac sky could affect different parts of a Libra's life.

Venus, the planet of love, will be in a good place for Libras in love or marriage at the beginning of 2023. It would create an environment that would help your love and marriage grow. If you take care of your relationships, many good things will happen with your partner. In this area, especially the second half of the year looks promising.

In terms of career opportunities, 2023 would be a pretty average year. Libras may have problems at work that they can't figure out. But then Venus, your year's ruling planet, would give you the courage and resources to stand up to this tough tide. When it goes through a good part of the zodiac, it could have different effects on your career. Look for people who can assist you in furthering your career. This year, you won't be able to see many benefits.

In general, Libra people will be in good health in 2023.

Jupiter's position in the zodiac may cause health issues for Libras. Take care of your health and be careful, keeping an eye out for early signs of illness. Because of where the nodes are this year, people with long-term health problems are likely to feel worse. Your overall health would worsen from time to time throughout the year.

You will be doing well with your money as 2023 begins. Because Jupiter and Saturn affect your second house of money, your financial situation will be very good. You could save a lot of money for hard times. You could make money through real estate deals and smart betting. During this time, you will be able to get rid of losses, loans, and debts.

Until May 2023, you might have some problems and questions at home. But then Mars, the fiery planet, would give you the energy and willpower to take your place in the household. Then you would be more likely to move with your family. You will get along better with your family after the middle of the year, and your parents and siblings will help you with your home life. But the planets might ask you to make some hard choices about your family that might not go over well with the rest of your family. You could get them to agree with you over time, though.

From a travel point of view, Libra people would do well in the year 2023. As the year starts, Jupiter's 5th house aspect from Aries would hit your 12th house of Leo, and this would be the start of foreign travels for Libra born. You might also go on many short trips because of how the nodes work. Most of your journeys will happen quickly, so be ready financially and mentally. You may have to travel for work when Jupiter passes through your sign at the end of the first quarter of 2023. And your travels would give you good knowledge and sometimes money throughout the year.

Libra people should do good religious things in 2023. As Saturn moves through your 5th house, you'll be more interested in spiritual work. The transit of Jupiter in the first quarter of the year also helps your spiritual life. Your spiritual knowledge and understanding are likely to grow throughout the year. This year, you would fix things by performing some religious ceremonies at home. Some Libras are expected to go on pilgrimages to see great saints and get their blessings. Always ask your parents and older people for permission before going anywhere new.

Don't listen to other people's advice for the coming year. Instead, go with your gut. Don't be stubborn about the decisions you make; instead, leave some room for compromise. Even if you have to help with social causes, take time to look after yourself. Find ways to improve both in your personal life and your job. Try creative things that will pay off both financially and emotionally.

January 2023

Horoscope

The sparkly energies coming from Aquarius and Gemini are great for your sign. They give you more options for what to do. They provide you with something new to think about and put you in touch with people who share your interests. They remove the feeling of being alone that Capricorn often brings to Libras.

There is a good chance that you won't notice how much time has passed when you are in this environment. But watch out for things that won't work around the full moon on the 6th. They make it hard for you to see things for what they are, which could put you in a dangerous situation.

When it comes to love, Jupiter likes to play with your Achilles heel, which is commitment. Instead of diving into contradictions, you should think about this sensitive issue.

Love

Between the 4th and January 27th, Venus in Aquarius brings all of its benefits to the area of your love life. She gets rid of sadness with her brilliant ideas. When you're in this creative and inventive mood, the people you love get out of their depression and come together.

Libras who are in love, your love will last as long as Capricorn's energies do. Sad to say, it makes them bored to death. Now is the perfect time to do something different! The energies that come from Aquarius are positive and encourage you to do it.

Libra singles, Mars and Venus, come together so that the people you love can stop being alone. These sparkling energies make you more likely to meet people from different places and in strange situations. Don't listen to negative people if you want magic to work.

Career

Even though your boss, coworkers, or customers seem to be a bit too demanding, you feel better. On your best days, you will surprise and amaze yourself with how clever you are. But some people may try to get you to give in, and others may turn against your plans. In this situation, you should get away. It will give them time to calm down, and you'll be able to say what you want to communicate better.

This month, it looks like your career will go in a good direction. There is a good chance that you could make a lot of progress in your career if you worked with intelligent people. You would also get a lot from your bosses, even though you might have serious disagreements with some of them.

There would also be a lot of traveling around. All of this would be pretty helpful. In fact, there is a good chance that you will get a new job or make significant changes to how your business works, which would require you to move. There is a good chance that your efforts will help you reach the goals you set.

Finance

On the money side, unforeseen expenses can make you want to put off buying things. Don't think this will last forever because it won't.

According to astrology, your financial future doesn't look good based on what the stars say. Writers, poets, and other people like them would do well to save money for a rainy day because the month is likely to be very hard for them.

There are signs that some of you will lose a lot of money because you are investing in the stock market. The lesson is clear: don't gamble of any kind, and be careful when dealing with people you don't know. Don't be greedy. There is also a chance that your relationships with your bosses will worsen to the point where serious losses become likely. You should take some steps ahead of time to avoid this.

Health

This month, the stars aligned in front of you are good for your health. People with sensitive chests or lungs prone to health problems in these areas are likely to feel a lot better. There is a chance that overworking yourself will make you tired and weak.

You could easily avoid this if you didn't push yourself too hard. Once this is done, everything will be fine. This would also help you deal with the slight chance that you have a nervous disorder, though it's not likely. You could also have problems with your mind because of stress, paranoia, and anxiety. Try meditating to get rid of stress. If you take care of yourself, you can be sure to stay healthy for the whole month. Pay a little more attention to how well your teeth are doing.

Travel

This is an excellent month to make a lot of money from travel, as this is what the stars say will happen. Travel would give writers, poets, and people like them new ideas and meanings.

You should travel alone mostly by train and road, with a fair amount of time spent in the air. Also, a trip abroad is not impossible. Part of this trip would be for work or business, and the other parts would be for other things. No matter what your goal is, it is likely that you will be able to reach it through your trips. The best way to go is to the West.

Insight from the stars

Discordant energies put pressure on you. Don't play their game if you want to avoid problems. Take things easy instead. Libra people in business will have a lot of money and success for most of the month.

February 2023

Horoscope

The happy and positive energies that come from Aquarius and Gemini always help you. They lead to new connections, meetings, and lucky chances. They tell you to make small changes in places where you feel bored. This month is the time to take advantage of the opportunities that come your way if you want to loosen some restrictions that can't be changed. Don't be radical, even if you want to, if you want to make this little wonder happen. Instead, try to find a middle ground and give in a little bit.

This month, Capricorn and Aries could still cause problems in your relationships. By staying calm and listening to people's complaints, you can get what you want while keeping the balance you value so much.

Love

The energies that come from Aries and Capricorn cause problems in your relationships that push them to the brink. The good news is that the energies of Aquarius and Gemini bring back emotional balance. They want you to change your routine by making your ideas more concrete.

Libras in a relationship have a hard time, but they can change things if they want to. Don't get into a fight if you're going to pull off this tiny miracle. Instead, listen to what your partner wants because they are the same as yours.

Libra singles, The stars are doing their best to ensure you meet the right person. Don't let your desire to please take over, especially around the 20th, if you want your dream to come true. Instead, pay more attention to how you feel.

Career

Mars in Gemini energizes you. It shows what you can do and how motivated you are. Because these waves are good, you don't have to think as much. You feel more confident in your qualities. You aren't afraid to say what you think. You go ahead. These reasonable rules reduce the effects of Aries that make things less stable. If, unfortunately, you feel the pressure rising, take a deep breath and move up. You will be proud of yourself and your success if you do this.

Your professional prospects don't look too good this month because of the stars. There is a good chance that you will have major disagreements with your bosses. You shouldn't let this happen and should try to stop it from happening. Try to think ahead and find ways to avoid problematic areas.

During the month, you might also feel a little bit scared, making it hard for you to make decisions. You could choose to switch jobs or business operations quickly for no good reason. Any kind of change should only be made after careful thought.

Finance

On the money side, there isn't much to say, other than that some expenses are still being put off.

As far as your money goes, the horoscope from the stars doesn't tell you anything excellent. There are signs that your investments and stock trading will cause you to lose money. So, you shouldn't play any kind of game of chance. Relationships with your bosses or coworkers are also likely to worsen to the point where a big loss is almost inevitable.

But you can stop this from happening if you work hard and plan ahead. Some of you would also put too much effort into making money that can't be tracked. You should not do this, and it could get you into trouble. The climate would also make it hard to invest or start something new.

Health

It is in your best interest to take advantage of the favorable constellations aligned with you this month to keep up your excellent health. Those with a propensity to stomach and digestive issues would be greatly alleviated. Chronic chest illnesses, such as coughs, colds, and asthma, will also be affected.

With good dental care, you can ensure that nothing bad occurs to your teeth. There is a reason to be concerned about the condition of your teeth. According to the stars, you may have a propensity to be irritated and in a slightly disturbed frame of mind. Maintaining a state of calm and equilibrium will allow you to maintain excellent mental and physical health with only a tiny amount of effort.

Travel

There isn't much chance of making money from travel this month, since the stars don't look good on this front. Most of the time this month, you would travel alone, mostly by car or train, with some air travel thrown in.

Also, you might work or travel abroad. But it is almost certain that these efforts would not bring the profits, pleasure, and satisfaction that were hoped for. The best direction would be to the North.

Insight from the stars

This is the time to stand up for yourself by choosing a lifestyle that works best for you and provides you with what you truly desire. You'll need to take advantage of any chances that come your way. The sky's the limit when it comes to your potential. All will be alright if you have faith in yourself.

March 2023

Horoscope

The energies that gave you the sensation of being as light as air has dissipated throughout the galaxy. On the other side, you can retain whatever offers you joy and enjoyment until the 25th.

Mars in Gemini is still your companion this month. It assists you in dealing with Aries' attacks by allowing you to relax. He advises you to pursue an activity that broadens your horizons and fosters interactions with positive individuals.

The new moon on the 21st foreshadows trouble. They will come with Mars in Cancer on the 26th! It intensifies the dissonances that Aries and Capricorn produce. You're still stranded. Instead, consider the benefits of living a peaceful and tranquil life.

Love

Even though misunderstandings make your daily life more interesting, your relationships are going pretty well. Mars in Gemini gives enough chances to go out and have fun. You see life in multicolor. On the other hand, instead of feeling overwhelmed after the 26th, make peace with what brings you down.

Libra, The tumultuous energies of Aries are getting in the way of your relationship. This electric weather keeps it going until the 25th. On the other hand, after the 26th, it goes back and forth between being attached and not being attached. Find a middle ground, as always, and everything will be fine.

Libra singles, People who are charismatic get your attention, but in the long run, they don't work for you. At the end of the month, the sky wants you to meet a different kind of person. This points to a relationship that will be calmer but also more stable.

Career

Even though it's not easy every day, you keep using your skills until the 25th. You don't have much trouble reaching your goals. Things get tough at the end of the month. You could be disappointed. Is it because you don't think your efforts are getting you what you want? Perhaps. If so, don't be surprised if a serious person appears out of the blue. They want to do good things. They just need to know you better.

There's nothing particularly good about the predictions for your work this month. There is a strong chance of having major disagreements with your bosses. No matter how hard it is, you should do everything you can to avoid this happening because if it does, it can only be bad for your career.

Throughout the month, you would also be affected by a deep-seated feeling of insecurity, which could change how you act at work. You might choose to switch jobs or your business operations. Any change you make should only be made after careful thought and planning.

Finance

If you must make a large purchase, focus on the essentials and avoid unnecessary purchases. You won't have any unpleasant surprises if you do this.

Unfortunately, according to the stars, this month's events won't be favorable for your financial advancement. As you may have discovered, investing and stock trading can result in substantial losses for you. Avoiding all forms of gambling, then, would be prudent.

There are also signs that any dispute or court case you might get into would almost certainly go against you, causing you to lose a lot of money. So, you should try to make sure that any decision about this kind of thing is put off until a better time. Relations with bosses or employees are also likely to go downhill. If you can't stop this from happening, you could lose a lot of money.

Health

This month, the way the stars are aligned is good news for your health in many ways. People prone to sudden, severe illnesses like fever or inflammations would feel a lot better, even if they only last a short time. Most likely, such trouble wouldn't bother you at all. Back pain would be helped in the same way.

But there are reasons to worry about getting an eye infection. This might bother you for a short time, but you could avoid this by staying clean and taking the right kind of preventive medicine. Overall, for your health, that's a month of good news.

Travel

There's nothing particularly good about what the stars say about travel in terms of making money. This month, you will travel on your own mostly by car and train, with some flights.

A tour of another country is also possible. There's a good chance that none of these efforts would lead to the profits or happiness that were hoped for. This is a pretty dark picture, but it is true. A lot of your travel may not be necessary, and you could get by just fine without it. The best way to go is to the West.

Insight from the stars

The energies of Aries make you happy and sad at the same time. If you want things to go well, think about what you want from other people. Try to see the good in everything. Do not even for a second doubt your skills. Things will work out in your life when the time is right.

April 2023

Horoscope

The dissonances that radiate from Aries alter their tone according to the relationship that ties them to Mars in Cancer. Your employer, spouse, or coworkers are difficult to follow. Some people are obstinate. Others will rebel at the first chance they get. The discussions are heated, and differences remain. You're stuck between the anvil and the hammer! Unfortunately, there isn't much you can do but wait patiently until it passes.

You may rely on Venus in Gemini's pleasant and optimistic impulses between the 12th and 30th to assist you. It generates events and conditions that are intended to alter your perceptions. It provides periods of calm that allow you to take a breather.

Love

There are times of happiness in this sector, but there are also times that are harder to handle. From the 12th, Venus in Gemini makes it hard to focus your love on what makes the other person happy. It gives you a detached view of your feelings and commitments.

Libra, your relationship is still a mix of questions and answers. The good waves of Venus help you focus on all the good things about your relationship instead of what's wrong.

Libras who are single this month are torn between wanting a stable relationship and wanting a passionate relationship. From the 12th, Venus's creativity helps you find a middle ground so you don't have to make a choice.

Career

This month, your success will come from making deals and giving in. If you don't, you'll end up in situations where you can't do much. So if your boss is mad, wait until they calm down. After that, you'll listen to what they say. If your coworker is making things hard for you, try talking about something they like. These little tips won't make people better, but they will help you reach your goals more quickly.

A good month for getting ahead in your career. Those who like art and those who work in the fine arts can look forward to a time when their creative work will be very satisfying. You may even become well-known as a result of your efforts.

In addition, there would be a lot of traveling, which would be quite advantageous. There is a good chance that you may have to relocate, whether for work or personal reasons. However, you should take your time before making any changes since a quick move might erase all of your hard work.

Finance

If this area of your financial life doesn't provide joy, don't take it as a sign that you're doomed. Your goals will be achieved if you take advantage of any good opportunity that comes your way.

This month's financial outlook is not good because of the constellations of the stars that are aligned in your favor. To begin with, your relationship with your bosses may take a turn for the worse. As a result, significant losses may likely occur. To avoid this, you'll need a little foresight and planning ahead.

On the other hand, gambling is a surefire way to lose money, and you should avoid it at all costs. In addition, some of you may be tempted to focus too much on making unexplained money. It is to your best advantage to avoid these kinds of endeavors.

Health

You're in a terrific health-promoting mood this month, so take advantage of it. Chronic conditions like rheumatism and gout, as well as digestive system anomalies like gas and excess wind, will be alleviated. It's important to remember that this does not give you the green light to disregard all caution. There would be a veiled sense of relief if everyone acted normally.

You have good reason to be concerned about your oral health. If you take good care of your teeth, you won't have to worry about anything. In fact, this month is going to be a good one for you as you won't have to deal with any significant health issues.

Travel

Since the stars are in a good mood, this is a great time to travel and get a lot out of it. Writers, poets, and others like them would find new ways to travel that would be exciting and give them ideas.

You should mostly travel alone by train and road, but you should also use the air a fair amount. A trip to another country is also very likely. Not all of your travels would be for work or business. No matter what you wanted to do, all of your trips would get you exactly what you were looking for. The best direction to go is South.

Insight from the stars

Instead of getting stuck on unnamed problems or hard decisions, look at life in a different way. Allow yourself to see another world. Work on making your life more stable and organized. Make sure that everything you do is organized to get things done when you need to.

May 2023

Horoscope

Things are still challenging but don't worry; they are not hopeless! When Jupiter leaves Aries on the 16th, your mind is no longer filled with doubts and sureties. On the other hand, Cancer's dissonances are still going on. You find it hard to believe in yourself. Your naturally weak attempts to make a choice are made worse.

When you face your first problem, you tend to drown in a glass of water. You can count on the energies of Gemini and Leo to keep your ship from going down. They help you see that you have more resources than you think. How? By putting you in touch with people who can help you.

Love

Jupiter's DNA is good, but while in Aries, he caused some trouble. His leaving brings back peace, and you can think straight again. You can get off to a good start if you don't care about what Cancer has to say. How? By getting to know people who are different from you.

When Jupiter goes away, it makes things easier for Libras in a relationship. On the other hand, Cancer's impulses bring up old hurts. Change your mind if you want to get your relationship out of this hellish circle. How? By getting away together for a short time.

This month, dates are in store for single Libras. On the other hand, things won't move forward until better times come along. You find charm in a calm and romantic love life.

Career

Until the 20th, it's hard for you to make decisions. Sadly, what you've started won't work out if you wait too long. Even though it's not in your nature, Libra, you should be brave and make a choice. Whether it's good or bad, it doesn't matter. If you do this, you will get rid of a thorn in your side and be able to see better.

In terms of your professional prospects, it is a good month. People who work in the fine arts and others like them would have a delightful time. You may even make a name for yourselves with what you bring to the table. There are signs that you are likely to work hard and go after your goals in a smart way. And you will be able to do this.

There may even be a change in the place where your business or service is done. Though changing might be a good idea, you should only do so after careful thought. There would also be a lot of travel, which would be very helpful in the long run.

Finance

On the money side, if you need a little more cash than usual, you can get it at the end of the month, but only if you are practical.

This month, there is nothing particularly good about your financial outlook since the stars aren't in your favor. There are clear signs that some of you would lose a lot of money if you gambled. The lesson is clear: you should not gamble, no matter what kind.

Furthermore, there is a chance that your relationships with your bosses will deteriorate to the point where losses become a real possibility. Take steps to fix the problem early on to stop this from happening. The environment wouldn't be great for making investments or starting new projects. Plans like these should be put on hold for now.

Health

This month's combination of stars in your favor is quite positive for your health. The stars merely need to raise a warning against overexertion. This should be rigorously avoided, and energies should be dispersed intelligently to maintain all regular activities without putting undue load on the system.

This is easily accomplished by creating a new activity schedule. There are numerous reasons why you should maintain good oral health and take all necessary precautions. Aside from that, you will have a great month in terms of health.

Travel

This month, you'd prefer to travel alone, primarily by road and train, with some air travel thrown in for good measure. A journey overseas is also not out of the question. You would travel for business and pleasure, but whatever your goal, you would be highly effective in achieving it or have a delightful voyage. The most promising direction is West.

Insight from the stars

To avoid going through a rough spot, you must put up with this routine that brings down your spirits. How? By staying in touch often, you can keep your relationship going strong. Things will change for the better right away in your life. Because of this, you should work hard at everything you do.

June 2023

Horoscope

You are always traveling with the energies of Gemini and Leo. They put you in situations where you meet people who can put you on the podium's top step. Don't waste time asking questions that don't have answers. Instead, be happy about what comes your way.

Don't be afraid to try out different solutions because that's where you'll find the key to your success. Also, look over every proposal, even those that seem out of reach. Trust yourself and listen to your gut to pull off this little miracle. Even though it seems hard to understand at the time, you will be surprised by the things you have that you don't know.

Love

To feel good, you need to grow in a universe that works for you, and this month, that's what happens. Your love will take the turn you've been hoping for all of a sudden. Don't listen to grumpy people at the end of the month, or the coach will turn into a pumpkin.

Libra, this month, all the lights are green, so you and your partner can enjoy your relationship. It's time to stop asking a million questions and just enjoy the good times that will come.

Mercury takes Libra singles to an unusual place where you'll meet an interesting person. Talk about your travels, your passions, and things you have in common, and most of all, trust yourself.

Career

It's safe to say that a career is certain, but it can easily become a bore in the long term. People who have the ability to help you evolve come into contact with you to overcome this inevitability. Do not splutter or declare that you are uninterested at this moment. Instead, use the moment to share your goals and desires with them. No, this will not turn you into an opportunistic person, but rather an informed one!

Unfortunately, this month's excellent effects don't bode well for your career aspirations. There is a good chance that you and your superiors will disagree. The last thing you want is for this to happen, so do all in your power to prevent it. Try to foresee potential problems and plan your route around them.

As a result, you may have difficulty making decisions because of a lack of confidence. It's possible to make a rash decision about your career or business and then regret it afterwards. Only after thorough consideration should a modification be implemented. On the other hand, travel won't provide you with any useful advantages, but tiny perks may come your way.

Finance

On the money side, things are stable, but if you don't give your credit card a break, things could get more random.

As far as your money goes, the horoscope from the stars doesn't tell you anything particularly good. There are signs that you might lose a lot of money on your investments. So, you shouldn't play any kind of game of chance. Relationships with your bosses or coworkers will likely worsen to the point where a significant loss is almost certain.

But you can stop this from happening if you work hard and plan ahead. Some of you would also put too much effort into making money that can't be tracked. You should not do this, and it could get you into trouble. The climate would also make it hard to invest or start something new.

Health

The constellations that face you this month favor your health and well-being. Discomfort with stomach and digestive organs would be greatly reduced for anyone with this propensity. Chronic chest illnesses, such as coughs, colds, and asthma, will also be affected.

With good dental care, you can ensure that nothing bad occurs to your teeth. There is a cause to be concerned about the condition of your teeth. According to the stars, you may tend to be irritated and in a slightly disturbed frame of mind. You can keep your mental and physical health in excellent shape with a bit of work.

Travel

Profits from travel are unlikely to be realized this month, as the stars indicate that this is not a good time to do so. This month, you're more likely to travel alone, mainly by car or train, with some flights tossed in for good measure.

In addition, you may have to go overseas for work or pleasure. Because of this certainty, these efforts are unlikely to produce the promised earnings or deliver the expected joy and satisfaction. The best option would be to head North.

Insight from the stars

You have the ability to talk about any subject; you just need the courage to do it. This month, be brave, and you'll get the chance you've been hoping for. Appreciate your friends and be there for them whenever they need you.

July 2023

Horoscope

Mars in Leo still helps you grow. When he leaves on the 11th, you may feel like you can't do anything. If you have doubts, you can rest easy knowing that Venus, the Sun, and Mercury will help you stay on track.

This month, good things happen that put you in touch with people who can help you reach your goals. But even though you are in good time, Cancer's dissonances will cause problems you must work through. If you want your projects to go well this month, take the time to make the changes that are needed. This might seem a bummer at the time, but if you do it, you'll make much more money than you think.

Love

You always get what you want because of how graceful you are. Your loves have this dimension that makes you happy and fits you. Even though things are going well, you are not safe from a crisis. If you don't want that to happen, don't abuse your ability to seduce.

Libra, thanks to your sense of refinement, you and your partner are swimming in happiness. You are in a good time between the 12th and the 28th. Your partner can't say no to you about anything. But don't be too crazy. This will keep from having a fight.

This month, Libra singles get what they want from Venus. It sets up the right conditions for you to meet that special someone. For a beautiful romance to start, all the lights must be green. Don't listen to people's bad ideas about it if you want it to change.

Career

The appropriate person will always come along at the right moment, no matter how difficult your daily routine is. It's as though everything suddenly has an answer. This opportunity also meets your growth, giving it a little extra boost. Because of this, you have no excuse to be sad about your lot in life right now. Check-in with yourself to see whether that's the case. You'll be able to recapture the optimism you've lost in the process.

In terms of your professional future, the horoscope offers nothing particularly encouraging. There is a good chance that you and your superiors may disagree. As a matter of urgency, you must endeavor to prevent this from happening.

Having a lack of confidence may have a negative impact on every aspect of your working life. You might try to restore equilibrium by making short career adjustments or adjusting corporate practices. If this were to happen, it would be a terrible situation. Any adjustment should only be made after a thorough examination of the situation. There would be a lot of time spent on the road, but it would be fruitless.

Finance

Financially speaking, you're always up for a good time. This month, use caution because your pastime has the potential to leave you penniless.

In terms of your financial well-being, this is a successful month. You should expect to reap a bountiful crop of unexpected profits. You might also gain from making investments. Another possibility is that an old buddy may do you a favor that will be financially beneficial.

As a result of this month's training, you'll be able to handle your superiors in a way that will benefit you greatly. This might be a significant advantage. As a last point, it would be beneficial for you to associate yourself with several intellectually and spiritually endowed individuals.

Health

As a result, your health should be excellent for most of this month, thanks to the favorable alignment of the stars. Sudden acute illnesses like fevers and inflammation would be greatly reduced. They're not likely to trouble you in the least.

People with any kind of dental issue might also benefit from this advice. Denture problems should be taken seriously, and they have a strong possibility of being resolved. Your health, as well as those who are already in good shape, is in good hands right now.

Travel

This is a terrific month to reap the benefits of travel, as the stars' augury is highly positive on the matter. Those who want to pursue further education or training in a foreign country have a good chance of success.

If you're traveling alone, you'll probably take trains, roads, and some flights. A journey out of the country is a possibility as well. There will be a portion of your travels that are purely for business. Regardless of the purpose of your travels, you'll be able to find what you need. The East is the best way to go.

Insight from the stars

Your projects are on the verge of success. Unfortunately, you may run into a hiccup at the last minute. Don't let yourself become distracted by the things that upset you. Always be on the lookout for pleasant surprises in your life. You're on the correct path as long as you're seeing favorable results in your life.

August 2023

Horoscope

Because of their charisma, Venus and the Sun in Leo bring out the best in people. Even though you don't make the first move, you end up meeting new people and making new friends. The way you do it makes your group of friends bigger. Your sensitivity to subtleties and your friendliness make for happy and promising relationships. This month, your relationships, invitations, and proposals can bring light to a part of your life that Saturn controls.

On the other hand, they can't make it go away. So, you will have to decide what to do. Take this chance to make your point so that when Mars moves into Libra on the 28th, you will be able to stand out more clearly.

Love

You are successful, which is a good thing. But you should sort out the people you meet, how you feel, and what you want. You can do it when Venus is in retrograde. How? By making them feel alone and uncertain from time to time.

Libra, you and this person always get along well. On the other hand, delays or misunderstandings will ruin moments or exits. Don't think of them as deaths, but as breaks, you can take together.

Libras who are single are going on fewer dates, which is good because it's time to make a decision. Take some time alone to think about things. You can start deciding at the end of the month.

Career

In this area, the mood is sour. You feel like every day is the same. You have to work to keep your place. Simply put, you're bored! You might be thinking about how to end this frustrating situation in August. Libra, think carefully before handing in your resignation! Even though your job isn't exciting, it gives you a good deal of security.

This month, you should get some exciting opportunities to move up in your career. Your way of working would help you do well. You take action and do things in a businesslike manner. You would probably work very hard, and your hard work would pay off well.

If you're feeling good about your success, you might decide to move your job or business to a new location. All of this would help you have better opportunities. There would also be a lot of traveling, which would be very helpful as well. Expect to accomplish something important this month.

Finance

If you are waiting for a large sum of money, it can take longer than you expect. So wait, and if you need to, try again so that time doesn't drag on.

This month, your financial outlook is pretty good and could put you on a solid financial footing for good. You can expect a lot of money from sudden gains and investments, which will also bring you a lot of money.

You would learn how to deal with your subordinates or workers in a way that lets you get the most out of their work. This would be a huge benefit for you and could lead to a lot of money. Also, an old friend might perform a favor or help you out in some way that would be very helpful. And finally, your relationships with your bosses would become so pleasant that you would gain a lot from them.

Health

Lady Luck is in the mood to bless your health, so you can expect to be healthy for the month. Libras with chronic diseases like rheumatism and similar problems like flatulence and too much gas in the digestive tract can expect to feel much better if they keep up with normal care. This would also be true for any tooth trouble.

Also, if you tend to be nervous, you can expect that to go away and cause much less trouble than usual. People might notice a certain weakness, but this is easy to fix with a little exercise and good food. A good month in which you probably won't face any serious health risks.

Travel

A month when it doesn't look like you'll make much money from traveling because the stars aren't in a good mood. You would probably travel by rail, road, and the air a fair amount when you were by yourself. A journey overseas is also not out of the question.

All these trips might be related to work and other things in equal amounts. But no matter why you do these things, you can be sure that not even a tiny part of your goals will be met. So, it would be a good idea to look over your travel plans ahead of time and see if they serve any purpose. The best direction to go would be East.

Insight from the stars

The stagnation periods aren't there to make you unhappy. Take them with a good attitude. After that, you'll know why they came into your life. Your career will go well because of luck. Everything you've ever wanted will come to you.

September 2023

Horoscope

All month long, Venus, which is linked to Mars in Libra, keeps helping your relationships and projects get done. You change in a world that you like, and that fits you. Because of this, you feel like you've gotten that much-wanted balance back. Unfortunately, if you don't want these good things to go wrong, you'll have to learn to control your happiness.

Your life is going in a different direction this month, but you'll have to handle it well. Work as hard as you need to succeed at this little miracle. If you need to, improve yourself. In other words, don't rest on your laurels and even less on your relationships. Of course, they can help you, but that doesn't mean you don't have to keep trying when things get hard.

Love

When it comes to charm and getting someone to like you, you're all in. So, the people you love are in their best light. When you feel this good about yourself, anything is possible. But if you want things to change the same way, you must keep your passion in check. How? By not hurting the feelings of other people.

Things are going well with your partner, Libra. Things are going well with your agreement. The problems of the past are becoming less important. But they can be brought back to life at any time! If you want to avoid these problems, try to keep your excitement in check.

Single Libra, A recent meeting can lead to a strong emotional connection. Do not repeat the same mistakes from the past if you want everything to go well. That means you shouldn't try to change the people you love. Instead, you should accept them as they are, flaws and all.

Career

You save time because of your fantastic charm. Unfortunately, you should be aware of the potential dangers of having this resource on your side. Why? Because this month, conservatives believe in the qualities of well-done work and the value of experience. Work as hard as you can, even if it may be challenging. Regardless of the circumstances, maintain a professional demeanor. You'll be able to put a stop to those rumors that irritate you and bog you down.

The stars look to be in a good mood this month, making it a great time for job progress. To achieve your goals, you'll likely put in a lot of effort and do so with businesslike efficiency. You may have to relocate to a new location, whether a new career or a new business. Everything would work out in the end.

There would also be a lot of travel involved. For both purposes, this would be quite advantageous. You may also experience some anxiety due to a nagging sense of unease.

Finance

On the financial side, while this sector does not offer any specific problems, keep an eye on it from time to time to ensure everything is in order.

A month in which you will not be able to attain much financial success and may even bring definite destruction upon yourself if you are not careful. There is a strong risk that you will be motivated by a nasty streak that will drive you to badly exploit your juniors, workers, or even individuals in the social strata below you for personal gain.

Your efforts would be greeted with opposition, resulting in an uncomfortable scenario. Trading would also result in significant losses for you. As a result, you must avoid all forms of gambling. The atmosphere would also be unfavorable for making investments or starting new initiatives, which should be put on hold for the time being.

Health

This month, the stars in your direction have a lot of good news for your health. You can expect any tendency toward tooth trouble of one kind or another will improve. However, the stars caution against excessive workload, as this could easily ruin a good condition. Make a new plan that doesn't put too much stress on your body.

If you ignore this, it could be very bad for your health. Everything else is OK. Having a tendency to be nervous wouldn't bother people who are already like this. A pretty good month in which you probably won't face any serious health risks.

Travel

There's nothing particularly good about what the stars say about travel in terms of making money. This month, about half of your trips would be for work or business, and the other half would be for different reasons.

You would probably travel alone most of the time, mostly by car and train. A trip abroad is also not impossible. No matter why or how you travel, you likely won't get even a fraction of what you planned to get out of it. Thinking carefully about your travel plans before you make them would be wise. The best route to go would be West.

Insight from the stars

A part of your life has the potential to start on the right foot. So let go of old grudges rather than reawakening them for the wrong reasons. Listen to your gut and go with your heart because they will never steer you wrong.

October 2023

Horoscope

Even though Venus leaves Leo on the 9th, the energies that change in Libra will still support you. Up until the 23rd, the Sun wants you to be more assertive. Between the 5th and the 22nd, Mercury wants you to connect with other people and be sure when you talk about your ideas.

Mars makes you want to go further until the 12th. Unfortunately, Pluto's dissonances and the boundaries you've set make this a bad time. You may feel like you're being squeezed between walls. On the other hand, if you step back, you'll see that these limits are helpful.

This month, you have the chance to reach your goals, but only if you are realistic and plan ahead.

Love

After the 10th, your loves lose the excitement that made you happy. Things are different, and so are people. You might feel like you're on the sidelines or in line. Do not complain about your fate. Instead, use it as a chance to think about how you feel.

Libra, you may feel like your partner is leaving you behind this month. Don't try to force things. Do not take offense. On the other hand, you can keep the deal going by being nice and putting your best foot forward.

Libra, if you're single, your charm always works like magic. You make new friends. Things won't get any better this month, though. Keep the bonds the best way you know until the time is better.

Career

Your legendary sense of subtlety works. You get where you want without getting on someone's bad side. If you feel you are being turned down, let your charm take over, and voila! However, if you run into someone who doesn't care about these things, you should try something else. Be businesslike. It will definitely be safer, and as an advantage, will lead to something unexpected.

A good month in which you can do many good things for your career. You would likely work very hard to make your goals come true. You'd have a lot of success with this. There would also be a lot of travel, which would help.

In fact, if you are successful, there is a good chance that you will move to a different job or business. All of this would be good, but you should think hard and carefully before making any changes.

Finance

In terms of money, you've done the best in this area despite all odds, and you've shown it this month. The question is, "How?" By showcasing a unique strategy for asset management.

According to astrology, the stars don't look good for your finances this month. There is a good chance that your relationship with your bosses could get so bad that you might have to lose money because of it. So, you must be prepared for this possibility and take steps well in advance to stop it from happening.

There wouldn't be many opportunities, and you would have a hard time getting anywhere close to your goals. You might also focus too much on making money that can't be tracked. This can only make things worse for you in the long run. Change this. You should also stay away from investments.

Health

The stars are kind to you this month and will shower you with health blessings. If you suffer from cold hands and feet, you'll notice a dramatic improvement in your condition, with hands and feet that are less clammy.

If you're dealing with a long-term dental issue, you'll have a better chance of getting it fixed if you take it seriously. Predispositions to anxiety and related illnesses would be alleviated as a result of treatment. Overall, it's a good month for your health, and you're unlikely to encounter any significant issues.

Travel

Since the signs of the stars are good, this is a great month to travel and make a lot of money from it. Some of you would go on a pilgrimage to holy places and sites, which would be a defining moment in your lives.

Those who wanted to study or train abroad or in a faraway place would be able to do so easily. Business trips would be very successful. You would travel mostly by train or road, with a fair amount of air travel. A trip abroad is also a possibility. The North is the best direction.

Insight from the stars

This month may bring some minor setbacks. Allow people some breathing room. Instead, take a little time to think about yourself; everything will fall into place at the right time. You'll have a lot of chances to improve your standard of living.

November 2023

Horoscope

At the beginning of the month, you feel like things are not easy. Don't worry, and it won't last long! From the 9th, you will feel more energetic because Venus will be in your sign.

Then, Mercury, the Sun, and Mars in Sagittarius give you the energy and drive to keep going forward despite the problems. So, your natural charm works so well because it's mixed with strange confidence. Because of this, you approach people and situations with a very positive attitude! Because of this tiny miracle, sometimes luck will come your way when you least expect it. Suddenly, it will be because of the negative people who brought your mood down at the beginning of the month.

Love

It's still hard until the 8th. When Venus is in Libra, though, the shadows of the past fade away. This month, you want a relationship that is easy and fun and doesn't put you under pressure over small things. This great wish could be granted surprisingly easily.

Libra, after a little sad time, your relationship is back to where it started. Your relationship gets new life from friends, trips, and getaways. Everything is fine between you two at the end of the month.

Single Libra, Do you think it's taking too long? Don't worry, the wait will be over soon, and you'll be able to make up for lost time. The pace picks up after the 11th. A romantic relationship can develop quickly from a meeting or a friendship.

Career

You'll have a great month because of your innate ability to build strong bonds with others. You create a welcoming atmosphere around you, even with strangers, without exerting any effort. They feel like you've known them for a long time and that you're buddies in a matter of minutes. As a result, these folks make your life simpler and are eager to assist you whenever needed.

This month, your professional prospects don't look too good. You are likely to feel pretty safe, and you may change jobs or make a big change in how you run your business or service. There is also a very high chance that you would have a disagreement with your seniors or bosses.

This should be avoided because it will only make your problems worse. You would work hard, which, given the circumstances, would not only not get the results you wanted but also leave you very unhappy. Try to act in a stable way and stay away from erratic actions.

Finance

In terms of money, now is the time to make any necessary plans. Why? For the simple reason that you've mastered your financial situation, everything you do will be flawless.

According to the stars, this month's horoscope doesn't portend well for your financial situation. As a result of your tendency to engage in conflict with your superiors, you might suffer a significant setback in your professional relationships. To avoid this, you should take whatever precautions you can think of to prevent it from happening in the first place.

Trading would also almost certainly make you lose money. So, it would be a good idea to stay away from any kind of gambling. Making investments or starting new businesses would be difficult in the current environment. To put it another way, such initiatives should be put on hold for now.

Health

This month, the Gods are kind to your health; if you're lucky, you won't have any serious health problems. Any tendency to get sudden, severe illnesses like fever or inflammation would go away, and such issues wouldn't bother you as much. This is a good month, so such relief can be looked forward to.

There are reasons, however, to be careful about dental health. If you aren't careful, this could cause issues with your teeth. You should take care to prevent any bone injuries, which are unlikely to happen this month.

Travel

This month is not a good time to travel because the stars are not in a good place for that to happen. There is a chance that you will get hurt or have some other physical problem while you are traveling. So, you should be careful and only take minimal risks.

You would usually travel alone, mostly by train or road, with a fair amount of air travel. Some of your trips could be related to your business or job. A good number of them would not be so related. What's pretty certain is that they wouldn't be beneficial. A trip abroad also can't be ruled out. East is the best direction.

Insight from the stars

As you progress, everything returns to normal. You've figured things out. A new chapter in your life has begun. This month, try to live in the now without worrying about the future. Think beyond the box when it comes to your work. Take what you've learned from others and apply it to your own life.

December 2023

Horoscope

Mars and the Sun, both in Sagittarius, are with you. These energetic, happy, and lucky vibes pull you toward them. They put you right in the middle of the action by making you meet new people and see the ones you already know. Because these waves are good, you don't hesitate as much as you usually do. You're not afraid to choose! When you have projects, friends, and ideas, you feel happy.

When things look so good, you might wonder what's wrong. Mercury is in Capricorn. His dissonances make people talk a lot. They tell people to make you feel better. From the 14th, this effect is made worse by his retrograde. This month, think about people who make you feel good and inspire you.

Love

Venus in Scorpio is in control of your love life. What is beautiful doesn't affect you much, but it can affect your friends or spouse. Feelings are silent. Some people might be clingier than usual. Stay calm while you wait for things to get better.

Libra, Even though the mood is happy and pleasant, your partner could be upset by your success. If so, just take things easy and as they come. Take your partner with you, because it will change how they think.

Single Libra, Different people are drawn to you because of your charm and how you try to seduce them. Check to see if this special someone is right for you before you start. This will keep you from getting involved in a complicated relationship that would be hard to leave.

Career

The planets in Sagittarius stimulate your enthusiasm. They inspire you to push yourself to new heights and take risks. The decisions you make bring you luck, not luck to you. Libra, you'll finish 2023 on top! As a result, don't hesitate to take advantage of every opportunity that presents itself. It's impossible to become an opportunistic person just because you're successful in your field.

You might end up working very hard to reach your goals, which would be good for your organization or business because it would help it succeed and make money. You could look for a new job or make big changes to how your business works. This should be done after a lot of thought about what the best course of action is

Finance

Again this month, you've done an excellent job managing your funds and preparing for the end of the year's expenses.

The omens from the heavens provide a bleak picture of your financial future this month. There is a good chance that your relationship with your bosses would get so bad that you would lose their trust, especially if you see that big losses are coming. With some planning and foresight, you should be able to stop this from happening.

In all likelihood, some of you will lose a lot of money when you trade. As a result, you should abstain from participating in any gambling, and in addition, the climate would not be ideal for new companies or investments. For the time being, these opportunities should be put on hold.

Health

This month, your health will benefit from a good set of circumstances. Those prone to rheumatism and other chronic illnesses, as well as digestive system abnormalities like gas and an excess of wind, would benefit greatly from this treatment. As a result, taking even the most basic precautions should keep you safe from such issues.

If you have a prolonged sore throat, you should take precautions to avoid getting an infection. This has to be thoroughly evaluated for any potential consequences so that you receive the best possible treatment. If you don't do this, your health might be in jeopardy. Aside from that, you have no real reason to be concerned.

Travel

Given the omens' unfavorable outlook, it may be tough to reap the benefits of travel this month. Artists such as musicians, painters, dancers, and others may not have as fruitful a time on the road as usual. On the other hand, some of them may suffer a setback.

You'd probably go by train or road, with some flying thrown in, and you'd probably be traveling alone most of the time. The possibility of a journey abroad is not ruled out. Despite the fact that most of this would be related to your career or business, it is almost probable that the anticipated outcomes would not be reached. The East is the best way to go.

Insight from the stars

You're more likely to progress when you're in a good mood. Your abilities and merits have been noticed and acknowledged. Don't let negative thoughts get in the way of your success in this exciting environment. Your loved ones care about you, and you should be thankful for their existence in your life because they care about you.

SCORPIO 2023 HOROSCOPE

Overview Scorpio 2023

In 2023, Jupiter will transit the 6th house of Aries until May, following which it will transit the 7th house of Taurus. This would cause several financial issues in the year's first quarter. However, its transit to the 7th house will bring excellent fortune to Scorpios in love or marriage. Saturn, the planet of discipline, will be transiting the 4th house of Aquarius until March when it will change to the 5th house of Pisces.

When Saturn transits Aquarius, it impacts your domestic life and well-being. Its transit through Pisces has an impact on your love life as well as your relationships with children if you have any.

Regarding the outer planets, Uranus is transiting into Scorpio's 7th house of Taurus, which governs their relationships. Neptune enters the 5th house of Pisces, while Pluto transits the 3rd house of Capricorn until May/June 2023, when it switches to the 4th house of Aquarius.

With this yearly transit, both the outer and inner planets have the potential to interfere with Scorpios' lives.

Scorpios' love and marriage prospects will benefit from a serene atmosphere in 2023, thanks to Venus, the planet of love. Venus' transit through the zodiac sky will be beneficial to your love life. Things can also become complex at times. It is recommended that Scorpios form long-lasting ties. Accept individuals as they come into your life, let go of your ego, and love and affectionately hug your partner/spouse throughout the year.

Scorpios' professional and business chances would be excellent in 2023. Natives will benefit from services as the year begins. However, if you want long-term rewards, you must put in a lot of effort and dedication. Saturn's transit after the first quarter of the year would result in beneficial improvements in your job field. If you desire to establish your own business, there is plenty of opportunities. In this regard, do not disregard the advice of elders and peers. Scorpios interested in business will find that partnerships yield wonderful results. Workplace problems do arise from time to time. There may be occasions when you have an incompatible relationship with a coworker.

Scorpios could expect to be happy and healthy in the coming year. Since Jupiter is in the 8th house and Saturn is in the 10th house in relation to your Ascendant house, you should be fine. You would have a lot of energy, and your immune system would be strong for the time of year.

Scorpios' financial situation will improve this year. This would be a profitable era since Jupiter would be aspecting your 11th house of profits. The inflow of wealth would be continuous and would not stop. However,

Scorpios are encouraged to limit their spending, which might strain their budgets. They are urged to avoid speculative dealings, gambling, and high-value purchases for the remainder of the year. This cannot be avoided when it comes to medical expenses for family members. Make a plan for the worst-case scenario.

For the Scorpios, the year 2023 begins with a hint of great sadness regarding family. Saturn being in your 4th house of home life and happiness means that there will be a lot of problems and delays. If someone in your family died or got sick, it would weigh you down. Things will improve when it moves into the fifth house of Pisces in March. Family members would notice your actions, and your goals for home life would slowly start to take shape.

Scorpios will have an average year in terms of travel this year. Jupiter's aspect on the 9th house promises long-distance travel for the locals this year. They are also likely to travel abroad due to the Moon's node's aspect on the 12th house. Natives are more inclined to go to distant regions for study, work, or pilgrimage. This year, some Scorpios will be able to return home after a long absence.

Scorpio people interested in spiritual things will have a good year in 2023. You could worship your native god and become more spiritual. Ask for the blessings of older people and religious leaders because you can learn from them and follow their advice during this time. Donate to charity and do social work that will make you feel good about yourself.

Scorpios should try to keep their distance this year, which will help ease tensions. A good year is promised, but Scorpios are told not to be in a hurry and to take things slowly. You would benefit from being patient and persistent in the coming year. Don't be too emotional with your partner, and don't keep anything from them.

January 2023

Horoscope

Capricorn's energies limit your options, which is in your best interest. The Aquarius planets are eager to provoke you, but if you play the game, you may escape their annoying consequences. You may not be swamped with invitations and trips if you focus on the planets in pleasant signs. What you can expect: a routine existence with no shocks. As an alternative, it ensures your complete tranquilly from every angle.

Be prepared for an uncomfortable journey if you venture outside your comfort zone. When it comes to Aquarius, you're in for a treat that's both intriguing and conflictual at the same time.

Love

Your best friend isn't Venus. His being in Aquarius means there will be annoyances, misunderstandings, and other roadblocks. What looks simple is hard to do after the fourth. As of the 28th, when Venus move into Pisces, calm and harmony returns to your life.

Uranus makes the annoying effects of the planets in Aquarius even worse. If you want peace, stay away from the devil. If, despite your best efforts, your partner goes crazy, just wait. On the 28th, everything is in order because Venus is in Pisces.

Single Scorpio, Use the energies of Mercury in Capricorn to avoid being let down. Take the chance to strengthen relationships, and don't get too lazy in case of an unexpected encounter. Be wise enough to wait until the end of the month if you want to get further.

Career

There will be times when you feel overwhelmed by how much is going on. You'll also have times when things are quiet that will worry you. Scorpio, don't think that other people are trying to hurt you. Jupiter is in sector six of your solar chart, and he is the one who makes your career go up and down. So when you have a lot of work to do, don't count the hours, and when things slow down, take a break.

The way the stars are aligned this month doesn't give you much hope for your career. You would be obsessed with how uncertain you feel about your job. This would change how you run your business or do your job.

It's possible that you could work very hard to reach your goals but still not reach them. You would change jobs or make significant changes to how your business works. But none of this would make you happy. There is also the chance of getting into a big fight with your boss or business partner. This should be avoided as much as possible. Try to think ahead and take care of problems before they get worse.

Finance

On the money side, it's the same battle! Slow down on your spending so that your money doesn't run out at the wrong time.

From what the stars say, it looks like this month won't be good for your finances. There is a good chance that your relationship with your bosses would get so bad that you would lose their trust, especially if you see that serious losses are coming. You should be able to avoid this by being prepared and thinking ahead.

Taking business risks would also likely cause some of you to lose a lot of money. So, you shouldn't take part in any kind of gambling. Also, the climate would not be very good for investments or starting new businesses. So, for now, you should put such opportunities on hold.

Health

This month, no favorable collection of circumstances will encourage your excellent health, as the stars are not in a supportive mood. Any tendency to chronic conditions such as rheumatism, gas, and excess wind in the digestive tract would irritate you more than usual. As a result, more care would be required.

Investigate any chronic cough very carefully, as this might be an indication of a rheumatic heart at the moment. There should be no negligence on this score; take adequate precautions. This month, you should also prioritize your dental health. This month, pay extra attention to your teeth since they may be bothering you.

Travel

A great month to make significant gains from travel since the omens from the stars are auspicious. You would most likely travel alone by rail or road, with some air travel thrown in for good measure. A journey overseas is also not out of the question.

You would be highly successful in your journeys since not all of your trips would be linked to your career or business. Travel will expose you to new people and open up new doors of opportunity. The most promising direction would be East.

Insight from the stars

You can cross the boundary if you believe your universe is too tiny. This is possible, but only if you remain calm under all conditions. This month, you must be patient with yourself. You've done your part, and now you must wait patiently for the universe to do its own.

February 2023

Horoscope

The energies that come from Pisces make your field of action more extensive. They make you feel at ease, which brings out the best in you. They understand how you feel and what you want to do. The weeks of routine and being alone are coming to an end.

This month, good things are going to happen. You will still have to deal with the conflicting energies that come from Aquarius, though. They cause misunderstandings in your relationship, which can make you act in extreme ways that don't show who you are. Around the 5th, this effect gets stronger when the Full Moon is in Leo. If you want to keep the peace, don't cross the border of your universe and test the devil.

Love

The energies from Capricorn and Pisces help improve the area of your life you love. But watch out for Uranus in Taurus, which tries to push you into your comfort zones. Don't take everything at face value to avoid these problems.

Scorpio, your peaceful way of life is favored. On the other hand, with your partner, things can get stuck. This month, you should get a list of complaints that you should answer calmly.

Single Scorpio, Planets in friendly signs work together to bring you together with someone who has everything you need to be happy. If you want the magic to work, don't always say you're on your own.

Career

Even though this area is doing pretty well, you might not be happy with it. Around the 5th, you might feel like your progress is being slowed down or that you are in a bad environment. Scorpio, get rid of your bad thoughts because they'll make you make a wrong choice. Instead, try to see the good things about yourself and the people around you. If you do this, you'll find that everything is fine.

This month, it looks like your career will move forward in a good way. There is a good chance that you could make a lot of progress in your career if you worked with several intelligent people. You would also get a lot from your bosses, even though you might have serious disagreements with some of them.

There would also be a lot of moving around. All of this would be pretty helpful. In fact, there is a good chance that you will get a new job or make significant changes to how your business operates, which will necessitate your relocation. There is a good chance that your efforts will help you reach the goals you set.

Finance

On the money side, things are stable as far as the money you need to live each day. On the other hand, if you want to invest, ignore what other people say.

Based on what the stars say, your financial future will be promising this month. Writers, poets, and other artists like them would do well at what they do and be known for it.

You will get enough money to take care of yourself and your family. Taking care of your money with discipline will help you pay for your family's daily needs.

Things point to the fact that you would make money from the investments you make. Many people will advise you on how to make more money, but you have to be very careful to get rid of the ones that don't fit your goals and values.

Health

This month, the stars in front of you are good for your health. People with sensitive chests or lungs prone to health problems in these areas are likely to feel a lot better. There is a chance that overworking yourself will make you tired and weak.

You could easily avoid this if you didn't push yourself too hard. Once this is done, everything will be fine. This would also help you deal with the slight chance that you have a nervous disorder, though it's not likely. If you take care of yourself, you can be sure to stay healthy for the whole month. Pay a little more attention to how well your teeth are doing.

Travel

The horoscope from the stars doesn't tell us anything beneficial about travel. Writers, poets, and people like them may not have the best trips. In fact, some of them could be seriously hurt by how unproductive their trips are.

You would travel alone mostly by train or car, but you would also take a fair amount of flights. A journey overseas is also not out of the question. But it's not likely that these efforts would lead to even a holiday, which might not be all that fun. The best direction to go is West.

Insight from the stars

You can say what you want; there's no problem with that. But don't forget to be nice if you don't want to make yourself more enemies. You are surrounded by the right kind of energy, which will help you have a positive outlook on life.

March 2023

Horoscope

The doors open, and barriers come down. The relationship problems get better. The energies that come from Pisces make these small miracles happen.

When Saturn moves into this sign on the 8th, it repairs the bonds that arguments and criticism have broken. You have more time for yourself and others because of all the good vibes. There are good things about being you. In your case, you feel more comfortable.

As time goes on, you have more room to move. After a hard time, you feel like you're starting over. Venus tries to get back together with someone or an old love starting on the 17th. If you still have doubts, Mars will show you how you really feel as early as March 26.

Love

This area that gives you trouble is taken care of by the energies that come from Pisces. They get rid of the differences by putting you in touch with people who have the same values as you. This month, the stars show you how much they love you. In exchange, don't look for bad things everywhere.

Slowly, exchanges based on mutual understanding are starting up again. Your relationship determines where it stands, what it excels at, and how it can assist you. From the 17th, agree to do what your partner wants for the sake of your relationship.

Single Scorpio, Over time, things fall into place so that you can have a good relationship with someone. Rather than leaving it on the doorstep, if you want it to last, make room for it in your life.

Career

Saturn's move into the sign of Pisces is like a soothing balm. You feel more comfortable putting your many skills to use. The sky is clear. You think no one can stop you from getting where you want. If someone gives you a surprise offer at the month's end, take it immediately. You won't be sorry, because it will help you make more money.

A month with lots of great chances to move up in your career. Like a hunter, you would work very hard and go after your goals with a single-minded focus. This would make sure that it works.

There is a good chance that your job will improve or that your business will have to make significant changes. Any change, though, should be made only after careful thought. This is even more important because you might feel a little bit scared even though things are going well for you.

Finance

On the financial side, this area doesn't cause any particular problems, but it would be nice if they could get better. So, if luck passes and it goes in your direction, do not ask yourself unanswerable questions.

However, the horoscope has nothing good to say about your financial future this month. There are signs that you will lose a lot of money when you trade stocks. So, you should stay away from any kind of risky business. Relationships with your bosses or coworkers are also likely to worsen to the point where a significant loss is almost inevitable.

But you can stop this from happening if you work hard and plan ahead. Some of you would also put too much effort into making money that can't be tracked. You should not do this, and it could get you into trouble. The climate would also make it hard to invest or start something new.

Health

The constellations that face you this month favor your health and well-being. Patients with a history of sensitive gastrointestinal tracts or other gastrointestinal disorders should expect great relief this month. Coughs, colds, and asthma, which are all common disorders of the chest, will be eliminated.

With good dental care, you can ensure that nothing bad occurs to your teeth. There is a reason to be concerned about the condition of your teeth. It's possible that you're easily agitated and have a little disturbed state of mind. You can keep your mental and physical health in excellent shape with extra care and exercise.

Travel

There isn't much chance of making money from travel this month, since the stars don't look good on this front. Most of the time this month, you would travel alone, mostly by car or train, with some air travel thrown in.

Also, you might work or travel abroad. But it is almost certain that these efforts would not bring the profits, pleasure, and satisfaction that were hoped for. The best direction would be to go West.

Insight from the stars

All the lights must be green for your deepest wishes to come true. If you say yes instead of no, this little miracle will happen. Make sure you do something worthwhile every day of your life. Don't waste your time and energy on things that won't help you get ahead.

April 2023

Horoscope

This month, some relationship problems are likely due to the fast-moving planets in Taurus. You can be stubborn about small things. From your point of view, you might seem suspicious for no good reason. But don't worry, nothing too bad is going to happen because Saturn and Mars are sending you their wise and kind energy.

You can't get on the wrong side of the force if you use these energies. Instead, they try to get you to look at things differently. They make you want to be kind, which brings smiles, trust, and mutual respect back. If it is too much, Saturn and Mars gently reframe what is most important. Because of this, fights don't last as long as they used to. They turn into something helpful and rewarding.

Love

This month, don't get into a fight, no matter how intense the urge is. Both you and the person you want to seduce should hold back. Take your time instead. Pay attention to the talks. Deepen the bonds. If you do these things, you'll be able to build a relationship based on real, long-lasting feelings.

Scorpio in a relationship, Saturn and Mars keep things on track, but Taurus' energies try to stir up trouble. Don't listen to words that bother you. Instead, be brave enough to show the tenderness you keep hidden for unknown reasons.

Single Scorpio, Your happiness lies with someone who isn't like the people you usually date. This month, learn to control your instincts and move slowly. This increases the likelihood of your wish coming true.

Career

As difficult as it may be, this industry is thriving. You may put your abilities to use for the second time this month as you have done so brilliantly. It's appreciated that you've taken the time to share your thoughts. Unfortunately, you may run against conservatives who are adamant about sticking to their guns when it comes to beliefs and practices. Your business will suffer if you engage in strife, Scorpio. On the other hand, saying yes to everything and acting on your instincts will have a greater impact.

Opportunities for progress in your job might arise from favorable situations. To achieve your goals, you would have to put in the effort. If this were to open up a whole new world of possibilities for you, you might end up with a better career or an entirely new company model. Fortunately, everything has turned out better than expected.

You should also plan on doing a lot of traveling since this will be quite useful. This time period will be marked by a willingness to take risks in your professional endeavors. This would lead to more efficient operations and better leadership skills.

Finance

Even though there is enough money to cover daily needs, a return of funds could be long overdue. Follow it so that the delays don't get too long.

The stars say that this month, things will go in your favor financially. In fact, there are clear signs that investing would bring you a lot of money. Because of this, it would be wise to start a new business or investment.

This month, you will win the big prize. Your business will do well, and you will put money into another business that needs your knowledge and skills in your field.

With so many ways to make money, it's no surprise that you'll be able to buy the things you need and want to make your life easier. Yes, you will have more money, and you can live well this month. But watch out for the people around you. You probably know how to handle your money well, but not how to deal with your feelings.

There are also signs that you will almost certainly come out on top if you get into a fight or go to court.

Health

This month, there's not much in the stars that's good news for your health. If you tend to get sudden, severe illnesses like fevers or inflammations, this could be a problem for you. You would need to pay more attention and get treatment immediately. This is something you must do quickly.

There is another reason to be aware of the chance of a bothersome eye infection that could cause problems. You must take the proper precautions to keep this from happening, like keeping things clean and taking the right medicine. The next few months won't be good for your health, so you should take even better care of yourself.

Travel

There's nothing particularly good about what the stars say about what you'll get out of travel. This month, you would travel on your own, mostly by car and train, with some flights.

A tour of another country is also possible. There's a good chance that all of these efforts won't lead to the profits or happiness that were hoped for. This is a pretty dark picture, but it is true. A lot of your travel may not be necessary, and you could get by just fine without it. The best way to go is to the East.

Insight from the stars

Despite what it seems like, conflicts are meant to shake up things that are stuck. This month, be open and willing to listen. You will be glad you did it. This month, your finances will improve because your investments will finally start to pay off.

May 2023

Horoscope

Since last month, relationship problems caused by Uranus and Mercury in Taurus have been a sign that something will change. It happens on the 17th when Jupiter moves into Taurus. The fact that the lucky star and evolution are in opposition to your sign means that your peace will be disturbed. How? By chances that come up out of nowhere but are silently hoped for.

This month, you can make changes, but they can't get in the way of your goals. Take the time to learn what is being asked of you if you want to do well in this little trick. Also, stay true to your habits by keeping your projects quiet. With Mars in Leo starting on the 21st, pay close attention to what shines instead of rejecting it.

Love

If you agree, your love can go to a new level. To do this, you will need to smile at luck instead of trying to get rid of it. Ignore outside influences if you want to pull off this little miracle. This will help you look deeper into situations or people.

Scorpio in a relationship, With Taurus's energy, it's not always easy to keep things in balance. The arrival of Jupiter can make things easier or harder. If you have something to say, do it nicely. This will stop the imbalance.

Single Scorpio, Everything looks good. You might meet someone, or a friendship might get stronger. Mars gives you a challenge starting on the 21st! If you agree to do it, your love will take the turn you wanted.

Career

The long-awaited progression is finally starting to look its best. But the choice is up to you. Scorpio, if you want, your current situation can get a lot better, but only if you're willing to work as a team. Take the time to think about it if it bothers you because you have it. Don't say "no" until the other person is done talking. Listen to the whole thing and ask for some time to think about it.

This is a good month to get ahead at work. Those who like art and those who work in the fine arts can look forward to a time when their creative work will be very satisfying. Some of you may even go on to make a name for yourselves with the things you do.

There is a chance that you would move where you do business or work, whether for a job or a business. But think carefully before making any changes since a hasty move could easily undo a lot of your hard work.

Finance

On the money side, be careful not to mix up cash receipts and expenses around the 5th. Be extra clear and make sure you know exactly where you are.

This month, the way the stars are lined up doesn't look good for your finances. First of all, there is a good chance that your relationships with your bosses will get worse, so much that it would become very likely that serious losses would happen. You need to think ahead and plan ahead to stop this from happening.

Spending a lot of money is always a red light. When managing your money, make sure you're making smart choices and that you've followed your plans for figuring out risks. If you invest in a company in distress, you might lose it.

You would almost certainly lose a lot of money if you made investments, so you shouldn't start any new businesses or trade stocks. There is also a chance that some of you might focus too much on making money that can't be tracked. Such activities wouldn't be good for you, so you should try to stay away from them.

Health

The way the stars are aligned for you this month makes it unlikely that your health will improve. Chronic diseases like rheumatism and digestive system problems like flatulence and too much diarrhea would cause you a lot of trouble, and you would have to pay much more attention to getting the proper medical treatment.

Also, you shouldn't let yourself get too irritable or nervous, and you shouldn't let your teeth get worse. This is a good month, and if you pay extra attention, you can make sure nothing bad happens. Overall, it is a month where you have to be careful.

Travel

The stars don't show that this is an excellent time to travel, so this is not a good month to go on a trip. Writers, poets, and people like them may have a stretch of financially and creatively unproductive travel.

You would usually travel alone, mostly by car or train, but you would also fly a fair amount. A trip to another country can't be ruled out. But it is almost certain that these efforts won't reach even a tiny part of the goals. The best way to go is to the South.

Insight from the stars

Jupiter and Mars bring movement back into your life in different ways. Instead of rejecting it, try to get it under control. You won't be sorry. It's never too late to make up with the people you care about. You need them in your life, so you should stop fighting and get along.

June 2023

Horoscope

Since last month, a change has started, and Jupiter is the symbol of it. The lucky star is linked to Saturn and gives you chances to improve your life in a way that makes you feel safe and secure. This might sound good, but since Uranus is still around, we should expect these changes to happen in fits and starts and not always smoothly.

This month, the opportunity that comes is represented by the Leo sign. It will be hard to negotiate, but you will get a nice improvement or win. You'll have to go against your nature for this little miracle to work. How? By telling people what they want to hear and putting their minds at ease about things that worry them.

Love

After a time of peace and quiet, your loves become filled with passion. Even though this sign makes you nervous, don't worry. Everything will be fine. Unless, for unknown reasons, you turn into a tyrant and oppressive version of yourself.

Scorpio in a relationship, When Venus and Mars are in Leo, fights and complaints take on a different tone. You have a choice this month. Either give them some room, and everything will be fine, or add fuel to the fire.

Single Scorpio, By chance, Venus brings you together with a lovely person. Even though this sign is not what you want, don't ignore this charming person. Instead, pay attention to them. You will be surprised by how good they are as people.

Career

You have the power to change your career. All you have to do is make the right choice. Scorpio, if you want to change things up, you'll have to deal with things that make you mad. So stay calm so you can finish the negotiations in your favor. After that, you can do whatever you want, because your skills are in demand.

In terms of your professional prospects, it is a good month. People who work in the fine arts and others like them would have a very good time. Some of you may even make a name for yourselves with what you bring to the table. There are signs that you are likely to work hard and go after your goals intelligently. And you will be able to do this.

There may even be a change in where your business or service is done. Though changing might be a good idea, you should only do so after careful thought. There would also be a lot of travel, which would be very helpful in the long run.

Finance

Your daily life is financially secure, and your piggy bank works like a charm. But don't be fooled by how you feel.

However, there's nothing particularly good about your financial prospects this month because the stars aren't in your favor. Clearly, taking risks in business would cause you to lose a lot of money. The lesson is clear: you shouldn't invest in stocks or do anything else that could go wrong.

Also, there is a chance that your relationships with your bosses will get so bad that losses become a real possibility. Take steps to fix the problem early on to stop this from happening. The environment wouldn't be great for making investments or starting new projects. Plans like these should be put on hold for now.

Health

The way the stars are aligned this month doesn't look good for your health. Overwork and weariness can lead to a general condition of weakness, with nervous disorders making matters even more difficult. If you don't want this to happen, don't put yourself under undue stress.

Another reason to be very careful about your dental health which could give you some trouble. Any bone injury should also be treated immediately since it could lead to trouble. In general, a pretty good month for your health.

Travel

This is a month when you should make a lot of money from travelling because the stars are aligned in a good way. All kinds of artists should find travel exciting and helpful for getting their creative juices flowing.

This month, you would most likely travel alone by car, train, and a fair amount by plane. A trip abroad is also a possibility. You would travel for business and other reasons, but no matter your goal, you would achieve it or just have a pleasant trip. The best direction to go is West.

Insight from the stars

To make the changes you want, you must take steps. This month's changes will require you to be at peace with what stands out by listening to your gut. Do not escape your responsibilities and obligations. Be someone who other people can count on.

July 2023

Horoscope

Again, the energies of Leo stop the evolution that Jupiter represents. Even so, the tensions calm down, and you find your clarity. Mars moves to Virgo on the 11th, and happiness never comes by itself. From that point on, you have all the power you need to negotiate the offers you get in a way that works for you.

Providence brings you together with people who can help you complete your projects. But you will still have to deal with the problems that come from Leo. Don't get too comfortable between the 12th and the 28th. Instead, watch everything and take the time to get the details right. Don't be afraid to say what you want.

Love

Venus in Leo is still making you feel the passion. Everything could go well, or they could fall into the destructive paths of desire. If you want peace, don't add fuel to the fire because you already know what will happen.

Scorpio in a relationship, The situation can be hard to handle until the 10th. Now that Mars is in Virgo, you can make sense of things. Your couple might have some fights until the end of the month, but you'll stick together.

Single Scorpio, You evolve in different worlds. So, you can expect to meet people who are attractive because of how they look and people who are attractive because of how smart they are. Listen to your intuition. She looks out for your best interests.

Career

Discords from Leo make it challenging to move forward. You like the opportunities that come your way, but they have problems that make you decide not to take them. Since problems never happen by themselves, you feel sad. You aren't very friendly, which isn't a good thing. Scorpio, if someone makes you an offer after the 11th, you should take it even if there are things about it that bother you. Why? Because in a few weeks, they will be gone.

This month, you will have good opportunities to advance in your career. This month will almost certainly be marked by hard work. You would be so focused on reaching the goals that you would put in everything you could to get the job done. This month, this will bring a lot of success.

There would be a lot of travel involved, which may or may not be advantageous in the long run. Aside from traveling, you would probably also change the place where you work or run your business. This would also be good for your future plans, which will happen this month. All in all, a really fruitful month.

Finance

Even though nothing bad is said about the economy, this area can worry you. Leave old problems behind.

The way the stars are aligned for you this month is anything but good for your finances. Some of you will almost certainly lose money if you speculate. So, avoiding all kinds of gambling would be a good idea.

There are also reasons to think that you might argue with your bosses so much that your relationship with them worsens, causing you to lose a lot of money. You can avoid this if you make an effort and can stop this from happening by taking the right steps ahead of time. This month, the climate is not good for making investments or starting new projects.

Health

The stars have not bestowed any health blessings on you this month. As a result, additional caution and attention are required. Those who are more likely to get piles should be very careful about what they eat and how they are treated. Carelessness would only make things worse.

Any tendency to get colds or have a lot of mucus come out may worsen. Again, this could need quick attention and corrective actions to make things right. Stones and a tendency to get fistula would also need more attention, as would your teeth. Take care of your teeth during this time since this could also cause you discomfort.

Travel

A month in which severe losses from travel are possible, as the stars are not very helpful in this regard. During your travels, you might get hurt or have some other kind of physical problem. Exercise care and minimize risks.

You would travel largely by road and train, with some air travel thrown in for good measure. A journey overseas is also not out of the question. These journeys could end up being utterly useless in every way. Since only some of them would be done for business purposes, they wouldn't make the expected money. The rest wouldn't make you happy. The North is the best direction.

Insight from the stars

Your success depends on how well you can combine discernment and persistence. After that, you won't be forced to make hard decisions. If you want great things to happen in your life, you need to take the first step.

August 2023

Horoscope

You are being pressured to accept a social or emotional commitment by Jupiter and Uranus. A marriage proposal or a request for professional cooperation can be made to you. Unfortunately, you likely disagree because of the dissonances brought on by Leo. On your darkest days, you consider these viewpoints to be a curse. You exhibit an attitude that shows lack of interest when you are more cheery.

Fortunately, Mars and Mercury in Virgo inspire you to consider offers made to you more thoroughly. Instead of concentrating on those who are less optimistic, they urge you to see the good side. If you don't want to lose an opportunity, go beyond your convictions this month.

Love

Venus is still in Leo and is also retrograde at the moment. Do not view a hesitancy or an accident as a sign of impending treachery if you want to avoid needless devastation that you will later regret. It will be more beneficial to maintain composure and remain impartial.

Scorpio, You must be accessible to your partner to spend time with them and listen to them if you want your relationship to be peaceful. Unfortunately, your relationship will experience unending turmoil if you are distracted.

Single Scorpio, You are placed in challenging circumstances by Venus' dissonances. Its backward motion accentuates this effect. You can choose for simplicity if you like. How? By paying close attention to those with whom you truly connect.

Career

The stars agree on everything this month! An offer of a partnership must be considered, and you must also accept it as a bonus. Because you have already experienced disappointments, Scorpio, do not place too much emphasis on particulars. Use this experience to your advantage instead. How, What, or Both? by resolving the minor issues and developing your abilities. Consider your passions while also finding your smile and business sense.

Given the favorable star alignment confronting you this month, you should have plenty of opportunities to develop your job. Expect to travel frequently and for the best of reasons.

You would typically put forth a lot of effort and pursue your goals with businesslike efficiency. This would do fantastically well. There is also a good chance that the location of activities, such as a job or business, may shift. This would also be a good thing. Overall, this month would be quite helpful for your job aspirations, and a lot may be accomplished during this time.

Finance

If you take advantage of what is being presented to you, this industry's financial performance will improve much more.

A prosperous month in terms of your financial potential. Many of you might anticipate enjoying a bountiful crop of unexpected rewards. Many of you might gain by speculating as well. Another possibility is that an old friend may do you a favor that might easily result in financial gain.

Additionally, you'll have a way of dealing with your superiors this month that will make the relationship very favorable for you. This may represent a significant benefit. Lastly, forming relationships with many intellectually and spiritually brilliant individuals would be advantageous to you on both a monetary and spiritual level.

Health

You should stay in excellent health for most of this month because the stars are in a great mood to bless your health. Any propensity for episodes of abrupt acute illness, such as fevers and inflammation, would be greatly reduced. They most likely wouldn't trouble you at all.

People with any kind of dental issue will also be affected by this. In fact, any problem with your dentures should be taken carefully and has a strong probability of being resolved. Your health is in good hands right now, and those who are currently healthy may anticipate maintaining that health.

Travel

This month's travel prospects just won't materialize, and neither will the fun and pleasure that go along with them since the stars aren't in your favor. Planning a pilgrimage to a sacred location may be delayed, or problems may arise while carrying it out. The possibility that your dedication will carry you through is something entirely else.

You would typically go alone by road or train with some air travel. Even a journey abroad is possible. However, none of these initiatives would be very fruitful. The best direction is east.

Insight from the stars

Be more open to those you love and pay close attention to what others say. You will avoid the inconvenience, which lowers your mood. Most areas of your life will see good fortune. Because of work well done, you should be proud of yourself.

September 2023

Horoscope

You profit from the influence of those who can help you evolve a part of your life thanks to the favorable effects of planets in friendly signs.

You get proposals, and opportunities come up. People are willing to talk with you, and your expertise and background are in high demand, so you might be curious about the issue in this specific advantageous circumstance. You and your convictions, which drive you only to see the negative in opportunities that come your way, are its physical manifestation.

If you agree, do not use the failures of the past as a guide this month since they will only encourage you to reject everything in its entirety. Consider them learning experiences that you can put to good use.

Love

Venus' dissonances cause conflict and uncertainty in your romantic relationships. Your feelings are strong, and suddenly, your relationships are challenging. If you don't want to be alone, consider your options carefully or take a step back.

Venus ignites the fire in your relationship, while Mercury prompts thoughtful and fruitful conversations. By being open and honest this month, you can reduce tension. Avoid talking about specifics of the past, though; it won't be helpful.

Single Scorpio, A wonderful encounter creates distance and closeness with a known person. You may choose between complexity and simplicity this month. So give it some thought before making a choice.

Career

This industry is a delicate topic this month. You examine what is being provided to you with suspicion. On your worse days, you come across as disinterested. Scorpio, don't turn down an offer. Still, have a look. Don't concentrate on the negative. Be optimistic and consider all the options available to you. Avoid alienating those who appear to be excessively superficial while you're doing it.

In the upcoming month, intriguing opportunities for work progress ought to materialize. Your working style would help you succeed. You have a businesslike efficiency and are action-oriented. You would typically put in a lot of effort and receive a lot of credit for it.

Encouraged by your success, you could decide to expand by changing your operation's location, whether a job or a business. All of this would be done to improve your chances of success. Look forward to making a huge accomplishment this month.

Finance

The necessities of daily existence are taken care of in terms of money. However, your leisure money is drastically decreased unless you make the appropriate business choice.

This month's financial outlook is quite promising, and it might put you on a firm financial foundation for the long term. You may enjoy a bountiful crop of unexpected benefits and would profit through speculation, which would result in significant gains.

You already have a style of managing your subordinates or workers to get the most out of them. You'd gain a lot from this, which may lead to a lot of money. In addition, an old buddy may be willing to help you out in some way, which would be a huge help. Finally, your relationships with your superiors will take on such pleasant dimensions that you will gain greatly from them.

Health

Since Lady Luck is in the mood to bless your health, you can expect to stay healthy during this time. People with chronic illnesses like rheumatism and similar problems like flatulence and too much gas in the digestive tract can expect to feel better if they normally take care of themselves. This is also true for any tooth pain.

Also, if you tend to be nervous, you can expect that to go away and cause much less trouble than usual. You might feel physically weak, but this is easy to fix with some exercise and good food. A good month in which you probably won't face any serious health problems.

Travel

A month when it doesn't look like you'll make much money from traveling because the stars aren't in a good mood. You would probably travel by train, car, and air a fair amount when you were by yourself. Also, a trip abroad is not out of the question.

All these trips might be related to work and other things equally. But no matter why you're doing these things, it's almost certain that you won't reach even a fraction of your goals. As a result, it's a good idea to go over your travel plans ahead of time to see if they'll get you anywhere. The best direction to go would be East.

Insight from the stars

You're well aware that crises don't end well. So consider and evaluate the circumstances and happenings. By doing this, you will get success right away. Your home environment will be one of harmony and calm.

October 2023

Horoscope

Your growth is going as planned. The planets that develop in Virgo support it. Despite these thoughtful preparations, you struggle to make a choice. On your worst days, you strongly dislike what is given to you. By discouraging past events, you are motivated to accomplish nothing more until the 12th.

On March 13, Mars enters your sign. It motivates you to take action and make choices. Act calmly and wisely if you want your expansion to be long-lasting. Spend some time reflecting while your head is resting. If you must, wait until the 23rd. Why? Because when Mercury enters your sign, it will sharpen your insight and intuition. You'll have the ability to choose wisely.

Love

When Venus moves into Virgo on the 10th, your loves find peace that makes you want to give your best. Beautiful things make you feel good and happy. It's fun. But bad memories make it hard to bring up your feelings. You find your mind at the end of the month.

Problems from the past have a terrible habit of returning to the surface. Change the subject if you want peace! Also, show your partner that you care about them. Do things that make you happy. By doing this, you will bring harmony back to your relationship.

Single Scorpio, Mars, and Venus bring you together with someone you already know. Don't force anything if you have trouble investing. You should be more at ease by the end of the month.

Career

You have had time to consider what has been suggested since last month. You get to make a choice this month since Mars enters your sign on the 13th. Scorpio, the decision is yours! You may either harness this energy for your benefit or use it against you. Therefore, now is the moment to combine your intuition with your experience if you truly want things to proceed in the correct direction. You'll end up with this tale that overwhelms you if you do this.

A month full of intriguing chances for job progress as the stars seem to be on your side. To achieve your goals, which you will pursue with businesslike efficiency, you tend to work extremely hard. You could change the location of operations during this phase, whether it be a job or a business. All of this would be for the best.

In addition, there would be a lot of traveling. You may feel a bit uneasy, which might bother you a little. In fact, there's a potential that some of you would be tempted to break the law to make quick money. Such tendencies should be stopped firmly.

Finance

Financially, although the end of the month is assured, leisure time is constrained until you decide to alter the situation.

A highly beneficial month in terms of your financial possibilities. You would benefit greatly from any unexpected earnings and profit from the speculation, reaping significant gains.

You would be able to quickly and effectively benefit from your efforts. Others among you would know how to treat your juniors or subordinates in a way that would allow you to get the most value out of their assistance. This may very well be the most significant gain in a month that is otherwise highly profitable. Furthermore, there is a good chance that an old friend may do you a favor or earn you a sizable profit.

Health

This month, the stars in your direction have a lot of good news for your health. You can expect any tendency toward tooth trouble of one kind or another will improve. There is, however, a note of warning against overwork, as this could easily ruin a good situation. Make a new plan that doesn't put too much stress on your body.

If you ignore this, it could be terrible for your health. Everything else is fine. Having a tendency to be nervous wouldn't bother people who are already like this. As a rule, this is a relatively healthy month in which you are unlikely to encounter any significant health issues.

You probably won't face any serious health risks in a pretty good month.

Travel

There's nothing auspicious about what the stars say about what you'll get out of travel. This month, about half of your trips would be for work or business, and the other half would be for other reasons.

You would probably travel alone most of the time, mostly by car and train. A trip abroad is also not impossible. No matter why or how you travel, you likely won't get even a fraction of what you planned to get out of it. Thinking carefully about your travel plans before you make them would be wise. The best direction to go would be West.

Insight from the stars

Don't make a bad decision because you think the past has tricked you. Wait, and if you need to, take a step back to adjust better how you react. This month, you should pay close attention to your overall health. To be useful, you need to be in good health.

November 2023

Horoscope

You can remain objective due to the planets in Virgo. Unfortunately, Venus departs you on the 8th, leaving you alone with Mars, Mercury, and the Sun in Scorpio.

The opposition between Jupiter and Uranus indicates that things will be tricky. Your argument will be illogical. Authoritarianism will result from your innate authority.

Unless you have the foresight to communicate with Saturn in Pisces, things will be different in these circumstances. You will pause to reflect. You will act with the efficiency that you are known for. Your natural skills will be shown to their maximum extent. The expansion of your position is subjugated to your inner understanding this month since it is your finest guide.

Love

Venus in Virgo will keep your affections alive till the 8th. His absence leaves you with these internal torments that drive you to withdraw. This, however, is avoidable. How? By recalling the pleasant moments, you shared with previous romances.

Scorpio, Everything in your relationship should be nice. To accomplish this tiny miracle, you must break your poor habit of sabotaging anything pleasurable. Take a step back this month before making a choice.

Scorpio single, Someone responsible and steady represents your happiness. You might be able to meet them this month. To do this, agree to go out of your sanctuary and, more significantly, pursue those negative memories that want to arise.

Career

You have two options this month. Either you react immediately and make a decision that will ruin your accomplishments, or you take a step back and everything will be alright. Don't take things literally, Scorpio! Take a step back and reflect. You will discover that everything is alright and that you have no need to be sad.

A favorable month in which you can significantly improve your career prospects. You are likely to work hard to achieve your goals. You would be quite successful at this. There would also be a lot of traveling, which would be advantageous.

Indeed, if you are encouraged by your success, there is a good likelihood that you will change the location of your operation, whether it is a job or a business. All of this would be for the better, but you should consider it carefully before making any changes.

Finance

On the financial front, while current expenses are guaranteed, your leisure budget is always kept to a bare minimum. However, as far as the stars are concerned, this is not a good month for your financial prospects. There is a significant risk that your relationships with your superiors may deteriorate to the point where you will have to incur a loss as a result. As a result, you must prepare for such a scenario and take preventive measures well in advance.

Possibilities would be scarce, and most of you would struggle to achieve your goals. There is also the risk that some of you may get overly focused on generating undeclared money. This will almost certainly have a negative impact on your whole position. Please correct this. Investments should be avoided as well.

Health

The stars are not in a good mood this month and will withhold their favor for your excellent health. Those prone to chilly hands and feet would have a difficult time. Any predisposition toward anxiety would be exacerbated. A skilled yoga instructor and consistent practice might do wonders for your ailment, allowing you to be free of your worries.

There is also the possibility that you will experience troubles as a result of tooth decay. This entails paying additional attention to and caring for your dental health. The period ahead is not good for your health and will need more attention and care.

Travel

A good month for reaping a bountiful crop of travel benefits, as the stars' omens are particularly favorable. Some of you would go on pilgrimages to holy locations, which would be a defining moment in your lives.

Those wishing to pursue further education or training in another country or location would have their plans carried out effortlessly. Business travel would be a huge success. You would largely travel by rail or road, with some air travel thrown in for good measure. A trip overseas is also an option. The most favorable direction is North.

Insight from the stars

Your love life and business success are dependent on your wisdom. So, reject outside forces and take a step back. You will make the finest decisions this way. Your social life will improve because you are ready to step outside your comfort zone and meet new people.

December 2023

Horoscope

Venus is in your sign from the 5th to the 29th. This might make you seem hard to deal with, but things will be different this time.

From 2nd to 23rd, Mercury in Capricorn calms you down. Your feelings and thoughts are smooth because of these long-range and quiet waves.

Starting on the 14th, when you downgrade, you go backward. So, it's time to make peace with what couldn't be made peace with before. Mercury can help you change the way you think. It helps you realize that things will happen in the future. It shows you that you don't have to ruin everything to move on in life. Use this state of grace to incorporate your environment into your growth.

Love

Your romantic relationships will resume after a dry spell. The tribulations of the past disappear. You're ready to start loving again. You feel open to experiencing new emotions. Mercury, who makes you a pleasant person with other people, attests to this minor miracle.

Mercury, which is linked to Venus, starts conversations that aim to lay out your cards and talk about your shared future. Take the chance to tell your partner how you feel. This will clear up any questions they have.

Single Scorpio, your sex appeal increases when Venus is in your sign. You will have a lot of luck! For the next step, you decide whether you can live a perfect life or make a lifelong commitment.

Career

Wait till the fifth if you aren't sure what you want. From this day forward, Venus begins to enlighten you. It gives you instructions. Happiness is not a one-person show. Mercury directs your attention to what matters most. Scorpio, your business is about to embark on a long-anticipated growth. Instead of wasting time pondering these concerns, take advantage of this current moment.

You will receive accomplishment awards for your hard work, indicating that you are successful, credible, and dependable in your profession. Regardless of your work achievements, you should always be confident in your abilities and strive to improve yourself.

Office rivalry will bring out the best in each of you. So, try hammering out new ideas and muster the guts to submit them to your superiors. If you are fortunate, you will win.

You'd have to put in a lot of effort to see results, but it would be worth it in the end.

Finance

On the money side, this area is favored, so you will have a lot of room to move. So make the appropriate choice, and you won't be in a panic at the end of the month.

Your progress at work will assist you in meeting your financial commitments. This indicates that you will not have a financial problem. However, you must be honest about your profits and spending. By monitoring your money, you will be able to determine if you will be able to meet your responsibilities on time or whether you will need to seek a loan to meet your obligations.

Health

This month, the Gods are on your side regarding your health. You won't have serious health problems this month if you're lucky. Any tendency to get sick quickly, like a fever or inflammation, would disappear, and these problems wouldn't bother you as much. Since this is a good month, such relief can be expected.

But there are reasons to be careful about your teeth. If you don't do this with care, it could hurt your teeth. You should also be careful if you break a bone, which is very unlikely during this month.

Travel

This isn't a good month for travel since the stars aren't aligned in a way that would make it a good idea. There is a chance that you will get hurt or have some other kind of physical problem while you are traveling. So, you should be careful and take the fewest possible risks.

Most of the time, you would travel by rail or road, but you would also fly a fair amount. Some of your trips might be related to your job or business. A good number of them wouldn't be so similar. It's pretty clear that none of these would be beneficial. A trip abroad is also not impossible. The best way to go is to the East.

Insight from the stars

It's safe to say that everything is in order for your expansion to go off as planned. Do not succumb to the temptation to take the short way; rather, follow the road of knowledge if you do. In order to appreciate your accomplishments, you must take the time to do so. Also, work on your deficiencies so they don't get in the way of your development.

SAGITTARIUS 2023 HOROSCOPE

Overview Sagittarius 2023

As the year starts for Sagittarians, Jupiter is in the 5th house of Aries. In May, it moves to the 6th house of Taurus. So, Sagittarians will have a good love life in the first three months of 2023. They will also have good luck and fortune, and their children will bring them happiness. Then, when Jupiter moves into the sixth house, there could be problems with money and health. In March 2023, Saturn will move from your 3rd house of Aquarius to your 4th house of Pisces.

Saturn is likely to favor many short trips during the first three months of the year, and if you have siblings, it could cause trouble. Then, moving through the 4th house could affect your family life and make it harder for you to do things.

As for the outer planets, Uranus spends the whole year in the sixth house of Taurus, and Neptune moves through your fourth house of Pisces. Pluto will stay in the second house of Capricorn until May or June of 2023 when it will move to the third house of Aquarius. All the planets will be moving quickly through the zodiac sky in 2023, which could be a hectic time for Sagittarians.

The first half of 2023 would be a good time for your love life since there doesn't seem to be much in the way. As the year goes on, you would notice that your feelings and passion for your partner grow. Then, around the middle of the year, there could be signs of dissatisfaction and disappointment with your partner, which could cause tension and make you unhappy.

This year, Saturn could slow down or stop your career plans. Until about the middle of the year, you might run into problems and roadblocks that make it hard for you to move forward. But if you do well, you could move up without doing much. You would keep being positive and willing to try new things, and this would take you places throughout the year. From a career point of view, the second half of the year wouldn't have much going on. But then you would feel like you had to grow all the time. You keep getting ideas from the planets around you.

Sagittarius born can expect to have average health in the year 2023. If your Ascendant house is set to get the aspects of the Moon's node, it could cause health problems. Unwanted medical bills would start to bother you all of a sudden. Worries and stress about your personal life and work would greatly affect your overall health and well-being for the year.

Sagittarians would be doing well financially at the start of the year 2023. Jupiter in the fifth house means that you will have some luck and good fortune. However, moving to the 6th house in May 2023 could lead to losses and money you don't want to spend. Unplanned medical bills for your family could use up your savings. So, use your resources well when you get them.

This year would be good for the family life and well-being of people born under the sign of Sagittarius. With Jupiter's influence, your family life would have a good atmosphere. This year, your parents, siblings, partner, and children, if you have any, would all help you in a good way. You'd feel very lucky to have them in your life. Having good things happen at home would keep you on your toes. When Saturn moves through your 4th house of family in March, it will ensure everyone in your family is happy and healthy. Peace and harmony would rule, and you'd be able to learn from the older people in the family. But Sagittarius natives should be careful about the health of their families.

The year would be good enough for Sagittarians to go on trips. When Saturn moves through the third house, there are many short trips throughout the year. Due to Jupiter's influence on the 12th house, which is about trips abroad, there is also a chance of going abroad. Sages will likely return to their home country after March when Saturn moves through the fourth house of Pisces. You should take long trips with your family because they are fun. Some of you might even be able to go on pilgrimages, something you've wanted to do for a long time.

Your spiritual actions will go very well in the year 2023. As the new year starts, you would be able to worship and hold ceremonies that would benefit your family. After the first quarter, Jupiter and Saturn would move through your sign, making you more devoted to your God. There are chances to learn more about spiritual things this month. Help those who are poor, in need, and deserve it. Assist people who can't pay for their education and career goals.

An excellent year in which all doors seem to open easily. Don't be lazy; go ahead and try everything. Make sure that both your personal and professional lives are peaceful and stable. This year, don't take on any risky projects, or you might lose a lot of money. Since you are lucky, do charity and social work that will make you feel good. If you trust your gut, believe in God, and spend time with good people, this year will be great.

January 2023

Horoscope

The energies that come from Aquarius make things better for you. They make your relationships and conversations with people you care about more fun. Your dear independence is no longer roundly condemned. On the contrary, it's valued and appreciated. You start off this new year full of joy and freedom.

Just a stone's throw away, Jupiter in Aries sends you waves of good fortune. It gives you more drive so that your life aligns with what you want. But for it to happen, you'll have to deal with Mars's opposition. It makes you allergic to any kind of involvement, which would make the changes you're offered less stable. To avoid the problems this opposition will likely cause, just agree to a few small rules, and everything will be fine.

Love

The energy coming from Aquarius and Aries is good for the people you love. They make you feel different in ways that make you want to charm and love. But Mars may try to get you to make a commitment even if it's not what you want right now.

Mars makes your relationship with your partner, who is full of doubts, worse over time. If you don't want these things to keep happening, try to clarify your schedule or attitude.

Single Sagittarius When planets are in friendly signs, it's easier to meet that special someone. Trust, and a delicious feeling of being in on something can happen quickly. If you want this happy life to last, you should deal with your desire for commitment instead of ignoring it.

Career

Your business will be put in place when Jupiter moves to Aries. It gets you going with its energy and ambition. You want to do great things and do well. All of this is possible, but only if you set a goal and don't change your mind along the way. Sagittarius, you can hang out with your friends as much as you like, but don't include them in your plans.

This month, your professional prospects don't look very good. You are probably going to feel pretty secure, and you may very well change jobs or make a big change in how you run your business or service. There is also a high chance of problems with your bosses or people above you.

This should not happen because it will only make your problems worse. There would also be a lot of hard work, which, given the circumstances, would not only not get the results you wanted but also leave you feeling very unhappy. Try to act in a stable way and stay away from things that change quickly.

Finance

On the financial front, you conserve money and are frugal with your spending. Don't go overboard; otherwise, your friends may believe you're being stingy.

This month, the stars don't have anything very good to say about your financial future. You would probably fight with your bosses, which would make it hard for you to communicate with them. This could cause you to lose a lot of money. So, do what you can to stop this from happening by taking whatever precautions you can think of.

You would almost certainly lose money if you speculated. So, it would be a good idea to stay away from all kinds of gambling. The climate would also be bad for making investments or starting new businesses. Plans like these should be put on hold for now.

Health

This month, the gods are on your side when it comes to your health. You won't have serious health problems this month if you're lucky. Any tendency to get sick quickly, like a fever or inflammation, would disappear, and these problems wouldn't bother you as much. Since this is a good month, such relief can be expected.

However, there are reasons to be cautious regarding oral health. Any sloppiness in this area might lead to dental complications. You should also be careful if you break a bone, which is very unlikely during this month.

Travel

This isn't a good month for travel since the stars aren't aligned in a way that would make it a good idea. There is a chance that you will get hurt or have some other kind of physical problem while you are travelling. So, you should be careful and take the fewest possible risks.

Most of the time, you would travel by rail or road, but you would also fly a fair amount. Some of your trips might be related to your job or business. A good number of them wouldn't be so similar. It's pretty clear that none of these would be beneficial. A trip abroad is also not impossible. The best way to go is to the East.

Insight from the stars

You develop in a favorable and innovative environment. However, resist the urge to relax and prepare yourself not to lose touch with reality. This will save you from unwanted hassles. Your life will continue on its current course, and no obstacles will arise to hinder your progress.

February 2023

Horoscope

The luck that comes from Aries gets a boost from the energies that come from Aquarius. Your life takes a happy and welcome turn in this very pleasant setting. You can turn everything you touch into gold. Proposals come to you in a way that seems to be planned. People who like you come into your life. The full moon in Leo on the 5th pushes the limits of what is possible. You're doing great! But you will have to deal with Mars in Gemini if you want all these blessings to come true over time. The fact that it goes against your sign makes you want to avoid any kind of commitment or contract. Think about this point. This will make sure you don't turn down a chance for the wrong reasons.

Love

This month, Mars in Gemini shows all of its depth. It moves you forward one step but backwards two steps. This indecision could hurt your relationship with the person you love. If it's very hard, don't lose hope. After the 20th, Venus in Aries helps you make the right choice.

Your relationship is a mess because Gemini and Pisces are at odds with each other. Doubts seem to come out of nowhere. Your partner could give you a choice between two things. Venus in Aries, which starts on the 21st, helps you get back into balance.

Single Sagittarius, Until the 20th, Venus's dissonance gives you a taste of the charm of fusional love. Before you make a promise or run away, wait until Venus moves into Aries. It will help you decide what's best.

Career

This industry is flourishing. Every day, you are at ease. When it comes to work, your colleagues are drawn to your energy and enthusiasm. Keeping your eye on the prize is the best way to keep things operating smoothly. Don't let yourself get carried away by happiness and achievement. Why? Because doing so might harm your career. Don't succumb to temptation and stick to your guns.

Both heavenly favor and good fortune are on your side. The possibilities of you going back to school or pursuing a higher degree are excellent because you already have a rewarding career or business. You're in for success and prosperity when it comes to your professional endeavors.

Finance

Because you are frugal, this industry is running like a well-oiled machine on the financial front. When it comes to budgeting, you take things very seriously.

Consume wisely and avoid areas where it is easy to get carried away. Even though your financial situation is expected to remain solid in February, it is imperative that you keep track of every dime.

If you do well at work, you may be rewarded with a raise or other significant compensation, which will allow you and your family to make ends meet during times of financial stress.

As you progress in your career, your ability to persevere and dedicate yourself to your work will be a stepping stone. You'll be rewarded for your hard work, and you'll be able to take advantage of new opportunities. Both starting your own business and joining a team with higher income and perks are possibilities.

Health

This month, your health is likely to improve due to favorable circumstances. It would be especially beneficial for those susceptible to long-term health issues, including rheumatism and digestive system disturbances like gas and wind. This implies that as long as you take reasonable precautions, you won't have to deal with any of these issues.

Any chronic throat discomfort should, however, be taken seriously. This has to be thoroughly examined for possible consequences and treated with extreme caution. If you don't, you run the risk of jeopardizing your current good health. You have nothing else to worry about other than this.

Travel

This month, it may be hard to make money from travel since the stars don't look good on this front. Singers, painters, dancers, and other artists might not get as much out of their trips as they usually do. In fact, this could cause some of them to fall behind.

Most of the time, you would travel by rail or road, but you would also fly a fair amount. A trip abroad is also not impossible. Most of this would be related to your business or job, but it's almost certain that it wouldn't get you where you want to go. The best way to go is to the South.

Insight from the stars

Some restrictions can be avoided. As a general rule, accept those things that can't be changed. This will keep you from missing opportunities that may have been lucrative. Your career will improve a lot, and doing what you love will bring you great joy. If you are passionate about something, you should go for it with all your might.

March 2023

Horoscope

Mercury and Saturn move from Aquarius to Pisces. So, things that were easy now start to get hard. Even though these things are uncertain, the energies that come from Aries always help your projects. So they are not in any danger. They are just late because of the things you have to deal with.

Mars in Gemini makes this happen more until the 25th. Focus on projects or ideas that are possible instead of trying to hide or avoid problems. Also, think about what's best for you instead of what's best for others—having goals that help you reach your goals will make things easier to do.

When the full moon in Virgo comes around on the 7th, it forces you to see how good it is to be realistic.

Love

The planets in Aries help and support this sector. They give you the experiences and moments you love so much. But when you're angry, try to be a little less direct than usual. Your energy is too much; you need to get it under control. Think about how people feel and try to reassure them when you need to.

Your relationship goes through ups and downs. When everything is going well, you're sure you're with the right person. If you don't agree, these sureties fall apart. Your relationship needs to make a turn. Instead of fighting it, just accept it.

Single Sagittarius, Good vibes from Aries make it easier for people to meet and fall in love at first sight. Don't say you love them on the second date if you want to keep your living space. Your wish will come true if you can calm your legendary passion.

Career

Saturn's exit from Aquarius leaves you with Jupiter in Aries. The catch is that Mars' dissonances have a tendency to unsettle you. Although the temptation is tremendous, Sagittarius now is not the time to have fun! Try to be as focused on your goals as possible. If you see that your delays are suddenly becoming longer, use the opportunity to improve yourself. Be intelligent and pay attention to what you are told.

This month's prediction for your career's progress is pretty favorable. There is a good chance that you will get considerable professional benefits from your relationships with various intelligent people with whom you may come into contact. Some of your superiors might also be a huge advantage, even though you may disagree with some of them.

There would also be a lot of travelling. Everything would be beneficial. In reality, there is a good chance that you will be changing jobs or making significant changes to your business operations, which would require a change of location. There is a strong chance that your efforts will successfully achieve your intended goals.

Finance

If you don't know how to say no when it comes to money, someone might make you bankrupt! So, as quickly as possible, commit this word to memory.

According to the stars, you'll have a bleak outlook on your financial future. Writers, poets, and others of their kind should stock up on supplies for the rainy days, as you will likely experience a dry period in the month.

You might lose a lot of money if you engage in speculative behavior. The lesson is clear: avoid all forms of gambling. Your relationship with your business partner might potentially deteriorate to the point where you could lose a lot of money. The best way to avoid this is to take some preventative action.

Health

This month, your health will benefit from a favorable alignment of the stars. You will benefit greatly from treatment this month if you're suffering from chest or lung-related issues. If you push yourself too hard, you run the risk of weariness and the subsequent weakness that comes with it.

By not overworking yourself, you may easily avoid this. Once this is done, everything will be fine. In addition, this would enable you to overcome the likelihood of some nervous diseases, but this is a very remote probability. Taking care of yourself during the month will ensure that you remain in peak physical condition. Don't forget to brush and floss your teeth more often.

Travel

This is a good month to make a lot of money from travelling, as this is what the stars say will happen. Travel would give writers, poets, and others like them new ideas and meanings.

You should travel alone, mostly by train and road, with a fair amount of time spent in the air. Also, a trip abroad can't be ruled out. Part of this trip would be for work or business, and the other parts would be for other reasons. No matter your goal, you will probably be able to achieve it through your travels. The best direction to go is West.

Insight from the stars

Don't run away when problems come up. This is a sign that you need to get back in touch with the real world. By going back to the basics, you'll feel better. People in business will face some problems, but they need to stay consistent and dedicated for things to get back to normal.

April 2023

Horoscope

The energies of Aries are getting weaker, but don't worry: Jupiter is still there, and the Sun will keep shining on you until the 20th. They tell you to do what you're good at or what you're passionate about.

On the other hand, Pisces and Gemini create dissonances that slow down the pace. They cause contradictions that, if you're not careful, can make what's being done less effective. This month, you must stay focused and not give up on your goals if you want to achieve them. You may have to work hard at this, but it is possible.

Use the practical energies that come from Mercury in Taurus to make your projects more stable. When it goes into retrograde on the 22nd, it tells you to be practical and put your money where your mouth is.

Love

Jupiter is looking out for you and the people you love. It makes you feel good and helps you understand. But Saturn is not too far away and can put out the flame of love at any time. To avoid this, find a good middle ground between what you love and what you do.

Between the 12th and the 30th, Venus makes it hard for you and your partner to agree on anything. Put more into your story to get rid of these disagreements. Bring a little more stability to your relationship. This may not be important to you, but it will improve things.

Single Sagittarius, People are drawn to you and want to help you. You multiply your conquests. You feel well. But if you want a more honest and satisfying relationship, you will have to give up some of the independence you value so much.

Career

Your luck, which has carried you for several months, may seem to be dwindling now that Saturn is blocking your path. Try to view things in a new light before you succumb to pessimism. For the time being, fortune favors you, but if you want to make the most of it, you must choose knowledge over luck. You'll succeed in your endeavors if you do this.

You'll be praised by your coworkers or business partner for your ability to maintain a work-life balance. Your professional life will provide you with the finest possibilities to improve your sense of self-worth and self-assurance. Throughout the month, you'll be a source of inspiration for everyone around you, and your coworkers will be grateful for your positive attitude.

Finance

YOUR COMPLETE PERSONAL HOROSCOPE 2023· 321

As far as your finances are concerned, everything is good until you decide to incur an enormous cost. Before making a final decision, make sure that this purchase is financially beneficial.

In terms of your financial future, the stars' predictions aren't all that encouraging. You might lose a lot of money if you were to speculate. As a result, you should abstain from participating in any type of gambling. Negative feelings against your supervisors or coworkers will almost certainly result in major financial setbacks.

However, you may avoid this by taking focused action and planning ahead of time. Some of you might put too much emphasis on making money that isn't yours. Taking this course of action would not be in your best interest and might lead to problems for you. Investment and new ventures would not be encouraged by the current atmosphere.

Health

This month, the combination of stars in your favor will help you maintain a healthy lifestyle. Predispositions to stomach and digestive issues would be significantly alleviated. This includes chronic chest illnesses such as a runny nose or a persistent cough.

With good dental care, you can ensure that nothing bad occurs to your teeth. There is a cause to be concerned about the condition of your teeth. As a result, some indications indicate you may be temperamental and a little agitated. It's possible to maintain excellent physical and mental health if you maintain a state of calm and equilibrium.

Travel

The stars don't look good for travel this month, so there aren't many chances of making money from it. This month, you would probably travel alone, mostly by car or train, with a few flights thrown in.

Also, there is a chance that you might work or travel abroad. But it is almost certain that these efforts would not bring the expected profits, pleasure, and satisfaction. The best direction would be to go North.

Insight from the stars

Saturn starts to show you the bad things that come from being independent. So, if you don't want to end up alone, think about all the good things about having a stable life. You can always start working on your plans. As long as you have the right help and tools, you're good to go.

May 2023

Horoscope

When Jupiter is in Aries, you change in a way that you like and works for you. When he moves to Taurus, the pace will slow down, and there will be less excitement. If you want to stay on the same path after the 17th, you'll have to change, even if it's not what you want. Wait because there isn't much else you can do.

When Mars moves into Leo on the 21st, it brings back the optimism and confidence that helped get past the problems. It makes you want to break out of these time-wasting habits. Mars tells you to try something new if you want to keep your health or get it back. So, what was lost because people were too negative is now important again.

Love

Jupiter in Aries makes you forget about the limits that Saturn puts on you. His departure on the 16th makes them come back. A less festive time is coming, but don't worry, it won't last long. Mars in Leo helps you establish an arrangement that maintains your affections and their progression.

The contradictions go away on the 8th, but they can return on the 22nd. To avoid this, Mars in Leo tells you to spice up your relationship and coax your other half. How? by filling them with bright, shining little touches.

Single Sagittarius, Your affections might cross an empty passage following the departure of Jupiter in Aries. Be comforted; it is only a short term! Mars in Leo pushes you to catch what you missed because of a misunderstanding.

Career

Jupiter continues to draw you along in its wake. You are enterprising. You view your professional sector in different colors. Unfortunately, the warning indicators that have been nagging for a few days will become more obvious. If you feel that the situation is not as excellent as expected, do not worry. Adapt to circumstances and grow better with these commitments that horrify you. In doing so, you will find the basic stability you require.

There is nothing particularly encouraging about the augury for your career chances this month. There is a definite probability that you might get into severe conflicts with your superiors. Such an eventuality should be evaded, no matter what the effort needed, since should this happen, it can only be bad for your career aspirations.

You would also be impacted by a deep-seated sensation of uneasiness throughout the month, which might affect your whole professional behavior. You might prefer to choose fast changes of employment or business activities. Whatever adjustment you make should only be done after sufficient thorough thinking.

Finance

On the financial side, this industry is performing well, but it will not last if you support someone in problems. So help if you wish, but don't run dry.

The course of circumstances would not benefit your financial progress this month is what the augury from the stars has to say. True enough, there are significant signals that investments will cause substantial losses to you. Therefore, it would be prudent to avoid any form of stock gambling.

There are also indicators that any disagreement or litigation you would be involved in would probably be resolved against you, resulting in damages of a severe kind. You must therefore attempt to see that the judgement on any such subject is postponed until a later and more beneficial date. Relations with superiors or workers are also likely to nose-dive; prevent such a scenario, failing which you would have to pay significant losses.

Health

This month, plenty is promising for your health in the combination of stars that faces you. Any propensity to sudden acute diseases, such as fever or inflammations, while of brief duration, would gain significant alleviation. Such difficulty would, in all probability, not worry you. Back problems would be similarly alleviated.

There are causes, however, to be cautious about the risk of an eye infection. This might annoy you temporarily, but even this could be averted by sufficient preventative steps like cleanness and using relevant preventive medicine. Overall, a month, it is fairly optimistic for your health.

Travel

There's nothing particularly good about what the stars say about what you'll gain from travelling. This month, you would travel alone mostly by car and train, with a fair amount of air travel.

There is also the possibility of going on a tour outside of the country. There's a good chance that all these efforts won't bring the profits or pleasures that were hoped for. This is a pretty bleak picture, but unfortunately, it's true. A lot of your travel may not be necessary, and you could do very well without it. West is the best direction.

Insights from the stars

This month is starting off well and will end the same way. But you must be able to handle a break that lasts a few days. Watch how things go. Then you can easily pick up where you left off. This month, the planets are aligned in your favor, so everything in your life will get better.

June 2023

Horoscope

With Mars and Venus in Leo this month, you will finish your projects. These energies urge you to conquer the hurdles that come your way. They provide you with their drive to undertake and specially to meet individuals who will be likely to support you. But don't forget some details if you don't want to be held up by problems that can't be solved.

After that, Saturn's dissonances won't cause you to waste time anymore. Instead, they will give you that experience that will change a lot of things. Also, you will still have to deal with Gemini's energies for the rest of this month. Don't spread yourself too thin. The only way to achieve your goal is to focus on one thing at a time.

Love

Even though Saturn puts limits on you that you can't get out of, the energies in Leo push you to get out. This escape can come from meeting a really nice person or just going somewhere for a few days with some nice people.

Keep cuddling your partner and pouring all your love into them. Pay them more attention than you usually do and show it. Take them on a trip for the two of you if you can. All of these benefits will make up for Saturn's annoying effects.

Single Sagittarius, Venus is in Leo this month, which is good for you. This beautiful energy gives you the chance to seduce someone who is different from your usual methods of seduction and who can also make your life better. Does it tempt you?

Career

This month, rest assured, you are on the correct route. Your famed good sense of humor attracts the right individuals. Besides, they are motivated to help you and make your life simpler. Everything must take place in the best conditions possible unless you hide these aspects that you regard lightly. Instead of racing to get everything done as fast as possible, Sagittarius treats some files with great attention.

The career of Sagittarius will be successful in all efforts. You will experience obstacles in your work, but with your knowledge and future studies, you can address the issues effortlessly. You would find it hard to pick in case of confrontations or fights at work. You may feel torn between your buddies, yet the decision will be vital. Sadly, one may continue to be loyal to you while the other could conceive of your decision as a sort of betrayal. Be attentive to issues like these. You might desire to transfer due to the harsh work atmosphere, but you can overcome this by merely having a solid work ethic and understanding.

Finance

On the financial side, again this month, handle your famed generosity cautiously because it might cost you greatly at the end of the month.

This month, the arrangement of stars confronting you does not augur well for your financial prospects. To begin with, there is a significant risk of your ties with your superiors taking a nose-dive. So much so that considerable losses become very likely.

Investments would also very probably end in enormous losses to you. Therefore, you should keep away from stock trading of all sorts. There is also the potential that some of you may be inclined towards concentrating overly on creating undeclared money. Such hobbies would not be in your best interests and should be avoided.

Health

This month, you're in a position to take advantage of a number of favorable health conditions. Chronic diseases like rheumatism and gout, as well as digestive system abnormalities like gas and an excess of wind, might all be significantly alleviated. However, this should not be interpreted as a green light to act recklessly. There would be a veiled sense of relief if you acted normally.

Because of the status of your teeth, you should be concerned. If you take good care of your teeth, you can avoid any unpleasant surprises. Your health will be safe for the month ahead of you, so take advantage of it while you can.

Travel

Not a month in which travelling would bring in a lot of money since the stars don't tell us much about this. Writers, poets, and other people like them may have a stretch of travel that is both financially and creatively unproductive.

You would usually travel by yourself, mostly by car or train, with some air travel. A trip abroad is not impossible. But it is very likely that these efforts won't reach even a tiny part of the goals. The best way to go is to the East.

Insight from the stars

This month, you have the chance to break out of the routine that makes you feel down. However, stay quiet about this opportunity because Saturn could ruin everything without warning. If you want to keep your relationships with other people in good shape, you should try to avoid constant misunderstandings and fights.

July 2023

Horoscope

Leo's energy has been making you want to live better for a while now. This month, you are getting close to your goal! With Mars in Leo, you'll be able to get around any problems that come up.

Mars moving into Virgo on the 11th, though, brings back responsibilities. Don't think of them as inevitable, and don't let them get you down. Keep going forward, and have faith in your luck. Why? Because Venus, Mercury, and the Sun are all in the sign of Leo, which is a sign of luck and enterprise. They give you brilliant ideas that make up for the harshness that comes from Saturn's opposition to Mars. They connect you with people who can help you reach the top.

Love

The constraints of Saturn get worse. If you feel like you're stuck, don't worry because there is a way out! Venus makes you want to try a different way of living.

Your relationship still doesn't feel right. Its growth is limited by some commitments that can't be pushed down. To lessen the bad effects of these restrictions, keep showing your partner acts of kindness and telling them you love them.

Single Sagittarius, Venus, or Mercury, makes you grow and change in a world where you might meet an interesting person. To do well at this little trick, you must smartly go beyond the obligations that limit your life. When you're done, your life will shine again.

Career

It takes longer to get things done now that Mars has moved into Virgo. It's a blow to your reputation as an enthusiastic person. When you're having a bad day, you're especially cruel or critical of certain individuals or circumstances. Don't cling to the past, Sagittarius! It's time to move on to something else and try out some new ideas. Make the most of it if you're presented with a proposal that goes this route.

As long as you put in the time and effort, you can accomplish your objectives and make your dreams come to life. It's possible that you'll advance in your profession if you remain steadfast in your efforts. You must take the initial step. The key to achieving your goal is to keep going.

Inequality at work is on the verge of becoming a reality. It's possible to feel unstable on a daily basis, no matter how hard you work. Change this mindset because it might jeopardize your development. It might also portray a threatening working environment. The best course of action is to restore the proper equilibrium.

Resolve your internal conflict. Changing your perspective and approach to problems might make it easier to cope with stress and have a more optimistic attitude toward life.

Finance

On the financial front, you can be comfortable that your daily needs will be met, but when it comes to major expenditures, carefully analyze the benefits and drawbacks before making a decision.

Financially speaking, you're in for a rough ride this month, thanks to a bad mix of stars in your favor. You might lose a lot of money if you decide to invest in this market. It should go without saying that you should abstain from all forms of gambling.

Also, your working relationship with your bosses could get worse to the point where you lose money. Prevent this from happening by acting quickly to correct the situation. Making fresh investments or starting new enterprises would be difficult in the current environment. As a result, such ideas should be put on hold for the time being.

Health

The combination of stars confronting you this month is favorable for your health. There is nothing more we can do except issuing a warning about over-exertion. In order to maintain regular activity while not putting undue strain on the system, this should be avoided at all costs.

This may be easily accomplished by drawing up a new schedule of activities. There are a few reasons why it's important for you to keep your teeth in good shape and take the necessary precautions. With the exception of this, your health has a good month.

Travel

This is a month when you should make a lot of money from travelling because the stars are in a good place. All kinds of artists should find travel exciting and helpful for getting their creative juices flowing again.

This month, you would probably travel alone, mostly by car and train, with some flights thrown in. A trip abroad is also possible. You would travel for business and other reasons, but no matter what your goal was, you would be able to reach it or just have a very pleasant trip. The best way to go is to the South.

Insight from the stars

Even though you feel like you're in an endless tunnel, the light isn't far away. Go there on your own. You will be glad you did it. Some disappointments in life are hard to get over, but you have to if you want to do great things with your life.

August 2023

Horoscope

Pisces and Virgo's dissonances are preventing you from achieving your goals. You can't live your life the way you want to because they restrict your choices and bind you to old habits. You will not be able to avoid these responsibilities if you engage in a constant state of conflict. In fact, it will make them more prominent. If you don't alter anything, you'll not get anywhere. Only when you recognize your talents and abilities, they may develop. In addition, meeting people who aren't like you will offer you a much-needed lift.

Make the most of what you have to offer the world. Expand your horizons intellectually by learning new things. Why? Because the key to finding answers to your difficulties rests in trying out a variety of approaches.

Love

You change in a place that is strict, tight, and suspicious. So, you're on edge because it's not in your nature to be confined. Venus gives you a chance to make changes. How? Find a goal, or try to find one again. After that, your well-known optimism will take care of the rest.

The influence of Venus lifts your spirits and gives you a new lease on life. It tells you to keep going despite risks in your relationship. As a bonus, it makes your luck better. If you're nice to your partner, everything will be fine.

Venus continues to take her role as a matchmaker very seriously by connecting you with people who could improve your life. This month, she gives you breaks so you can think about how you feel.

Career

The zeal of the preceding months seems to have dwindled to a trickle. As a result, it appears like your job and routine are limited. You're bored to tears on the worst days! You find the decisions made uninteresting. Too much is demanded of you by your professional colleagues. Consider your options, Sagittarius, before you make a sudden shift! Don't let these minor inconveniences derail your plans for the long term. It's okay to change your mind while waiting for things to improve.

This is a month in which you have little chance of moving up in your profession, and if you're not cautious, you may end up lower on the ladder than you started. It's possible that you'd be tempted to break the law to get quick cash. It would have devastating consequences if it happened. As a result, you must make a firm decision not to give in to such pressures.

There is also a good chance that you and your superiors may have severe disagreements. Avoid this as much as possible. In addition, you'd be more likely to switch jobs or hire new employees quickly due to a sense of uneasiness. Only after great consideration should any changes be made.

Finance

Financial stability is guaranteed, but only if you carefully conduct your bookkeeping. If you want to avoid a haphazard approach, be specific and avoid wasting time.

With your positive outlook and abundant vitality this month, you might perform quite well financially. You'd have the guts to stand firm in your beliefs and the motivation to keep pushing forward in order to succeed. An incredibly favorable set of circumstances would tremendously benefit you.

Actually, you might expect to reap a bountiful crop of unexpected profits. Even taking a chance on gambling would pay off. Investing and starting new businesses would be easy in this environment.

Health

This month, a favorable collection of circumstances will help you maintain a healthy lifestyle, so there is no need to be concerned. Those with susceptibility to persistent colds and mucus discharge would be much alleviated. The good news for those suffering from piles is that with proper treatment, they can experience some alleviation and perhaps a full recovery.

Despite all of this, there is also a warning on the need for good oral hygiene. If you're not careful, you might end up in a situation that's difficult to fix. You should expect to be healthy this month, which is generally nice.

Travel

A month in which you can expect to make a lot of money because the stars are in your favor. This month, you will be very sure of yourself and have the guts to make decisions. You would spend a lot of time planning a trip that would make you a lot of money.

You would probably travel by train, car, and air a fair amount when you were by yourself. A trip overseas is also not out of the question. Not every trip you take will be for business. No matter what your goal was, you would achieve it. The best way to go is to the West.

Insight from the stars

Trying to find safety fails miserably! Try hard to make your dreams come true. This will lead you to the well-being you want so much. Due to a lack of communication, your love life may face difficulties.

September 2023

Horoscope

Saturn slows your development, but Uranus and Jupiter push you to work harder than you've ever worked before. Because of this, your mood swings between pessimism and optimism. Make a difference instead of working yourself to exhaustion against an impenetrable barrier. Avoid rehashing the same ideas over and over again. Be confident in yourself!

The friendly planets Mars and Venus inspire you to broaden your horizons. Your natural abilities can be used to achieve a project that is essential to you. These stars connect you to those who can help you realize this tiny marvel. One of them comes into focus at the end of the month when the Sun moves into Libra.

Love

Even though things are bad, the people you love are your best support and a source of motivation that can't be beaten. They make you want to move on. This month, your passion will carry you. It gives you new ideas and goals to work toward. It shows you your talents and any hidden qualities you may have.

Things from the outside can ruin the mood. Venus, on the other hand, helps you make things right. This month, your relationship will stay strong and grow in the best way if you do small things for each other or work on a project together.

Single Sagittarius, This month, a meeting can quickly turn into something more emotional. You may get the impression that you've found your soul mate. As long as you have the knowledge to put your anxieties aside, there are no clouds in the sky.

Career

Don't give up if everyone doesn't share your ideas or wishes. Instead, try presenting things in a different way. Sagittarius, your activity area smells like mothballs. So, you're right to want to give it a little bit of a makeover. To be accepted, you need to explain why your arguments are valid. Pay attention to people with conservative ideas and those who are cheap. Don't be in a rush. You will get what you want, and your activity will be more fun if you do this.

There is a good chance that you will have a major disagreement with your bosses. This should not be allowed to happen, and you should try to stop it from happening.

You might also have a feeling of insecurity that would affect almost everything you do at work. You could try to fix the problem by switching jobs quickly or changing how your business works. This would be a terrible situation to be in. Any change should only be made after being thought about carefully. There would also be a lot of travel, but this wouldn't lead to much.

Finance

On the financial side, if you want to make changes, you can, but only after the 16th and after you've given it some thought.

A good month from a financial point of view. You can look forward to making lots of money quickly. You would also benefit from making investments. There's also a good chance that an old friend will do you a favor that could easily help you out financially.

Also, this month you'll find a way to deal with your bosses that will make the relationship very good for you. This could be a huge plus. Lastly, hanging out with many smart, spiritually-minded people with gifts would help you in both material and spiritual ways.

Health

The stars are in a good mood for your health this month, so you should be in great shape for most of this time. Any tendency to get sick quickly and severely, like fevers or inflammation, would be greatly reduced. Most likely, they would not bother you at all.

This would also be true for people with any kind of tooth pain. In fact, any problem with your false teeth should be taken seriously, and there's a good chance you can fix it. This is a good time for your health, and people who are already healthy can expect to stay that way.

Travel

Since the stars aren't in a good place this month, you won't get what you want out of travel, nor will you have as much fun as you thought you would. If you're going on a pilgrimage to a holy place, you might have to put the trip off or run into problems. The fact that your dedication may carry you through is another story entirely.

Most of the time, you would travel alone by train or car, with a fair amount of air travel. Even a trip abroad is not out of the question. But none of these efforts would get anywhere. The best direction to go is West.

Insight from the stars

Clarify your thoughts and feelings, even if it makes you feel like a downer. Doing this will allow you to express yourself more clearly, and people will be better equipped to assist you. Your life is overflowing with possibilities. Choosing which ones work best for you is entirely up to you.

October 2023

Horoscope

Fast-moving planets in Virgo create dissonances, which cause the vise to tighten. As a result, you may feel that nothing you do is working. In contrast, the planets in Libra are there to lift your spirits. They inspire you to be flexible and optimistic in the face of adversity. This is despite the fact that events and circumstances require that you pay close attention to the specifics.

You can improve your accuracy by reducing your adequacy! It may be tedious, but it's the only way to remedy the problem. Let go of your desire to break through the barriers placed on you. Encourage pessimism instead of ignoring it, as well.

Love

Things get more complicated over time. But you can avoid the things that will bother you when Venus is in Virgo. Be there for the people you love, even if it's just for a little while. It won't change the way your life goes, but it will help you sort out your feelings.

Your life as a couple is not easy. You can, on the other hand, make it easier. Stop at your house. You'll have to work hard to get back on time. If you can, try to care about what is going on in your home.

Single Sagittarius Venus has set up a meeting that might surprise you. But if you want it to go further, you'll have to settle for a quiet, even homey, lifestyle. The scales will tip in the right direction if you use your emotions.

Career

You're not bursting with excitement. Something or someone may have let you down recently. In addition, you think it will take a long time to get your heart's desire. You're bored to tears on the worst days! Sagittarius, while this area is devoid of pleasure, it does provide you with a great deal of security, despite the fact that you view it as a nuisance. When making a decision, it is crucial to consider both the positive and negative aspects.

Your astrological chart shows just a few promising omens for professional growth this month. Even if you put in a lot of effort, reaching your goals remains elusive. There's a good chance you'll disagree with your boss.

To avoid this at all costs is imperative since the consequences might be catastrophic. Make an effort to anticipate and avoid troublesome areas. There would also be a lot of travel, but it wouldn't provide any benefits at all.

Finance

On the financial side, pay more attention to this area, even though it doesn't pose any particular problems. Be more specific in how you run your daily business.

This month, your financial prospects look pretty good and could put you on a solid financial footing for the long term. You can look forward to getting a lot of money quickly. You would make money through investments, which would also bring in a lot of money.

You would also learn how to deal with your subordinates or workers in a way that lets you get the most out of their work. This would be a big plus for you and could help you make a lot of money. Also, there is a good chance that an old friend will do you a favor or provide a service that would be very helpful. And lastly, your relationships with your business partner or new investment company would become so pleasant that you would benefit significantly from them.

Travel

A month when it doesn't look like you'll make much money from travelling because the stars aren't in a good mood. You would probably travel by train, car, and air a fair amount when you were by yourself. Also, a trip abroad is not out of the question.

All these trips might be related to work and other things equally. But no matter why you're doing these things, it's almost certain that you won't achieve even a fraction of your goals. As a result, it's a good idea to go over your travel plans ahead of time to see if they'll get you anywhere. The best direction to go would be South.

Insight from the stars

Your charm often gets you what you want. On the other hand, this month, things will go in the right direction if you take life more seriously. Hold on to the people who mean the most to you and always ask them for advice when life throws you a curveball.

November 2023

Horoscope

The strain eases on the 9th, thanks to Venus' transit through Libra. Inhale and exhale. The worst of Saturn's effects are beginning to fade. That being said, the star of wisdom and insight is keeping a watchful eye on you! It keeps getting in the way of your progress. So you can see how long the time is! Mercury enters your sign on the 11th, so you'll have to put up with it for a while. On the 23rd and 24th of that month, the Sun and Mars will align with it. These forces, which are linked to Venus in Libra, restore your sense of hope.

This month, despite the dangers you face in one area of your life, you have more room to move. You're getting more and more comfortable. You've gained the confidence to attempt the previously unthinkable because of the friendships you've formed.

Love

From the 9th, things get better. It is verified on the 11th. Lovers who have experienced heartbreak eventually rediscover their zeal for life and their joy for life again. When it comes to your romantic life, this month is all about making a fresh start.

Your relationship has been difficult for a while now. Fortunately, this month has seen an improvement. Slowly but surely, you and your partner will discover the joys, happiness, and pleasures that will ensure your union's long-term success. Everything is well towards the end of the month.

Single Sagittarius, Slowly but surely, the past and its disappointments fade away. Your friends and family will soon hear about a new gathering that has been scheduled. Accept that things happen in stages if you want it to turn into something more romantic.

Career

This sector is set up in a way that makes you feel overwhelmed. It looks the same every day. You feel like you're always doing the same thing and that nothing will ever get better. If you keep having the same thoughts, Sagittarius, you will make the wrong choice. To avoid this, you can talk about your ideas, which, despite what you might think, will be met with excitement and real interest.

A month that is not good for getting ahead in your career and would also be a sign to be careful. There is a good chance that you will have major disagreements with your bosses. As much as possible, this shouldn't happen. Try to be patient and stay away from places where trouble might happen.

There would also be a lot of travel, which might seem like a waste of time that wouldn't lead anywhere. A lot of hard work would also seem pointless if it didn't lead to anything. In this kind of situation, some of you might be tempted to break the law to make money quickly. Stop doing these things if you don't want to invite trouble.

Finance

This sector is doing well financially, but you may have to spend money to fix up your home or replace an old appliance.

A beneficial month for your finances. You would make a lot of money quickly, which is likely to happen. You would also make a lot of money from investments.

You'd get quick, valuable results from your work and learn how to manage your juniors or subordinates so that you could get the most out of their work. This could be the most important thing to get out of a pretty good month. Also, if an old friend does you a favor or service, you have a good chance of making a lot of money.

Health

This month, the stars in your direction have a lot of good news for your health. You can expect any tendency toward tooth trouble of one kind or another will improve. However, the stars send a note of warning against overwork, as this could easily ruin a good situation. Make a new plan that doesn't put too much stress on your body.

If you ignore this, it could be terrible for your health. Everything else is OK. Having a tendency to be nervous wouldn't bother people who are already like this. This is a pretty good month in which you probably won't face any serious health risks.

Travel

There's nothing particularly good about what the stars say about what you'll get out of travel. This month, about half of your trips would be for work or business, and the other half would be for other reasons.

You would probably travel alone most of the time, mostly by car and train. A trip abroad is also not impossible. No matter why or how you travel, you likely won't get even a fraction of what you planned to get out of it—thinking carefully about your travel plans before you make them would be wise. The best direction to go would be West.

Insight from the stars

Things begin to improve. To make this tiny miracle happen, Try doing things in order for once. It will be less risky. You'll be happy because you'll finally have what you've always wanted.

December 2023

Horoscope

Your astrological ruler, Mars, is currently in your sign. Between 1st and 22nd, there will be no change in solar position. Mercury enters Sagittarius on the 1st and will remain there until the 24th. These energies provide the tools and opportunities you need to begin over. They encourage you to take back your cherished liberty.

Saturn, alas, remains. Its goal is to keep you from going into rabbit holes that will go nowhere. So, if you find yourself unable to move forward, avoid using force. Why? As a warning indication that what is being presented to you is not what you want or need. When things begin to go the correct way, know that you will achieve your goal in the end.

Love

Feelings have nothing to do with you. You don't want to think about the past when you hear about this. So, you are more flirtatious because you don't really want to be in a relationship. But by the end of the month, things could be different.

You're moving like the wind this month. You live however you want. So, your other half might use tricks to get you back into the fold. Don't get angry, and know your presence at home is wanted.

Single Sagittarius, you're not ready to settle down. But that doesn't mean you should stay at home and think about how bad things were. So, you make a lot of conquests, and love will find you by chance.

Career

Sadly, things aren't getting any easier in this field. The planets are reasonable enough to keep you busy for a while, but they also provide you with a measure of security. Even if you're aware of this, you will nevertheless want to break free of this professional shackle. So it's fine if you come across something different. Make certain that what you're offering is reliable and sturdy before you send anything out.

This month's combination of stars does not bode well for your professional future. Serious disagreements with your superiors are very likely. This would prove to be a disastrous turn of events. Because of this, you should work to prevent it from happening.

An empty feeling of insecurity may also weigh you down. If this happens to you, you may decide to look for a new career or start your own business to get some relief. This is a situation that should never arise. Changes should only be made after considerable thought and consideration. Also, no matter how far one travels, there will be no benefits, albeit a trip to the North could be beneficial.

Finance

Efforts to save money begin on the second day of the month. You'll save even more money on the 14th. However, you should exercise caution and avoid becoming too frugal, as this is not your style.

According to the stars, this is not a good month for your financial well-being. Because of your poor relationship with your superiors, you may have to pay the price in terms of financial losses. You must be on the lookout for such a scenario and take action to prevent it from happening.

Having fewer options would make it difficult to achieve your envisioned goals. Additionally, you run the risk of being too obsessed with producing money you can't account for. This should be avoided. Additionally, you should stay away from making any kind of financial commitments.

Health

The stars are kind to you this month and will shower you with health blessings. There would be considerable improvement in the condition of those with cold hands and feet, with hands and feet that are favorably less clammy.

Anyone who has a long-term problem with their teeth should expect to be less bothered and more likely to get the problem solved if they take it seriously and seek treatment. An added benefit is that people who suffer from anxiety and other related conditions would see great improvement. You should have no major health issues this month. Overall, a good month for your well-being.

Travel

It's a tough month to make money from travel because the stars aren't on your side, according to the astrological forecast. A pilgrimage to a holy place would undoubtedly be either postponed or slowed down by the obstacles that arise. Of course, your dedication would keep you going.

Individuals with aspirations of pursuing education or training in a foreign country may also encounter extremely challenging obstacles. You'd largely use the road and train to get about, with a little bit of air travel thrown in for good measure. Foreign travel isn't out of the question. Although these trips would be a waste of time, they would also be a waste of money. The North is the best direction to go.

Insight from the stars

You can regain your freedom, but only up to a certain point. Don't try to pass it if you don't want to hit a wall. Stay humble despite your success. Don't let your pride make you look down on the people who helped you get to where you are now.

CAPRICORN 2023 HOROSCOPE

Overview Capricorn 2023

Jupiter, the planet of fortune and knowledge, will spend the first quarter of this year in Capricorn's 4th house. Then it moves to the 5th house of Taurus in May. So, at the start of the year, Capricorns will have a happy home life, do well in real estate deals, and gain materially. With the move to the 5th, love, luck, and children become more important. Saturn, the planet of discipline, moves through Aquarius, which is your second house. This affects your finances. Then, in March 2023, it moves to your third house of Pisces, which affects how you get along with your siblings and travel.

Uranus will transit through the 5th house of the horoscope for Capricorns. Neptune moves through your 3rd house of Pisces at the beginning of the year, and Pluto moves through your Ascendant. In May and June 2023, Pluto will move to your 2nd house of Aquarius. Capricorns' lives are definitely affected by these planetary movements throughout the year.

This year, you will take care of your love life and marriage. Capricorns will have a good year in the long run. On your part, you wouldn't have to do much. A partner or spouse would be drawn to you this time and become your loving friend. Venus makes it easier to get along with your partner for the year. Your love life would be peaceful and happy.

This year, Capricorns will have average luck in their careers. As the year starts, you will have good work relationships with your peers and the people in charge. This is because of Jupiter's good qualities. This is a good time for Capricorns to get ahead in their careers. Saturn, however, may provide some challenges to your career.

Capricorns will have a year of good health and happiness in 2023, thanks to the influence of the planets. As a result of achieving both personal and professional success, you'll feel better about yourself, leading to more excellent health. When it comes to health care decisions, trust your intuition. Do not ignore any indications of illness that raise a red flag. The problem may be avoided if you receive prompt medical attention and use effective preventative measures. Also, relax and recharge your batteries from time to time.

In 2023, Capricorns would do well with their money. At the beginning of the year, Jupiter will be in your 11th house of Scorpio, which is a good time. Money would come in well, and you'd be able to pay off loans, debts, and overdue bills. Capricorns, however, may have to make financial sacrifices this year due to financial obligations related to their families. With Jupiter moving through the 4th house of Aries, you would get a lot of real estate and nice cars. Landed property deals could be good for you in the year's first three months. This year, money would also come from a legacy or an inheritance.

With Jupiter in the fourth house of Aries at the beginning of the year, Capricorns may feel pressure from their families. When it passes, things will get better. Both Saturn and Jupiter make sure that your family life is going well. There would be good relationships at home, partners would be loyal, and you would be more devoted to your family than you usually are, which is not like you. Throughout the year, you would have many wonderful times with your family.

Regarding travel, the Capricorns will have a pretty good year. As the new year begins, Jupiter favors some short trips that aren't too far away because of work. After the transit of Jupiter in May 2023, you'll be able to take long trips for fun and pleasure. Some of you may be going home for the first time in a long time. Traveling this year, Capricorns should exercise extreme caution when it comes to their wealth and health since problems and mishaps are almost inevitable for those born under the sign.

The year 2023 would be a good time for you to do religious ceremonies. As Jupiter moves through your 9th house, you will become more interested in religious acts during this time. Your faith and sense of belief would reach a whole new level. Pilgrimages are likely if you want the same thing in recent years. You would also do pujas for the planets and take steps to fix any bad doshas. Do social and charity work that will bring you many blessings throughout the year.

Be realistic about your goals for the year and confident you will achieve them. Keep a positive outlook and trust your intuition even when things look bleak. Use your position to help improve society and discover ways to live that benefit everyone. You'll reach new heights if you're honest, loyal, and disciplined in your job. You would face problems, so be firm and steady and stick to your policies no matter what. Keep dreaming big because you have a lot to do this year.

January 2023

Horoscope

You feel tight at the start of this year. You are burning with the need to reach your goals or to be on your own. You can't wait any longer. So, people don't take you too seriously. You are ready to fight the first challenge from the outside.

The full moon makes you irritable, so watch how you act around the 6th. But this state of being is not a small thing. Do you have a plan or project that you are working on? Even though Jupiter is in a different sign from yours, it is still possible for Jupiter to give you some opportunities. The important thing is whether or not you can trust them. Dare to put your cards on the table to do this. It will definitely make things more complicated, but you'll know if you have to deal with it or not.

Love

You're angry, which doesn't help with things that have to do with your heart. If you aren't careful, you'll have a rough time on all fronts, making things hard for you. You might feel like time is moving slowly. Understanding comes back on the 28th.

When the moon is full, you must say what you think. In return, your partner may feel too much stress from all the negativity. The amount of talking is kept to a strict minimum. Venus helps you be forgiven after the 28th.

Single Capricorns, Things keep coming up until the 4th, making things more complicated. Get to know your loves better to keep them from going in the wrong direction. With Venus in Pisces, all the lights will be green starting on the 28th.

Career

Even though you try hard, you just can't get yourself together until the 13th. When you think you have everything in order, something unexpected comes up. After this challenging time, something better starts to happen. You are all over the place. There are proposals for you. You have to wait and see if they can be trusted or not. Take your time to think about it, even if others want you to hurry up and make a decision.

The way the stars are aligned in front of you doesn't look good for your career. There would be a lot of short trips that wouldn't bring the expected benefits. On the other hand, a trip to the North would be helpful. During this time, it's not likely that people you know will be able to help you much.

So, it would be a good idea to trust in your ability to solve problems. But there are reasons to think that the working conditions and atmosphere would stay pretty good. This would be a big reason to be happy. Overall, it was a month when you had to be careful with several sensitive matters.

Finance

Saturn watches over this area in terms of money. It doesn't make you make sacrifices, but it does keep you from wasting money, which isn't so bad.

Even though you'll be hanging out with many smart and spiritually gifted people this month, it won't improve your finances. There is a good chance that you would have to work hard to reach your goals, and even then, you might not get very far.

The climate would also not be suitable for making investments or starting up new businesses. They might get stuck. Also, banks or other financial institutions would unlikely approve any pending loan applications or requests for new advances. Also, people who do business overseas would probably have to deal with adversity.

Health

A great month when the stars are aligned to give you good health, and you don't have to do much but sit back and enjoy it. Your body would get the most out of what you eat, and your health would shine as a result.

Not only would you be very busy and full of energy during the month, but you would also keep your mind and body in good shape. There are some reasons to be careful about boils that might make you uncomfortable for a short time. With quick medicine, you don't have to worry about anything.

Travel

Since this part of the astrological forecast isn't very good, you wouldn't gain much from travelling this month. But there are some people who have to travel to keep their jobs or businesses going. The answer would be to find a middle ground where you cut your losses and do as much as possible on your travel situation.

Artists, singers, dancers, and others like them wouldn't get the usual benefits from travel. Those who go abroad to study at a college or university may face different problems. Business trips to other countries would not be very productive either. North is the best direction to go.

Insight from the stars

The full moon establishes this month's mood on the 6th. Think about the pros and cons of your thoughts, decisions, and actions before you act quickly. If everyone in your family gets along, you will have a happy home life.

February 2023

Horoscope

The energies of Capricorn, Taurus, and Pisces put you in a comfortable place where you can show off your best qualities. Your mood is less defensive. So, you are easier to reach. You are interested in what other people have to say. You always show empathy in how you say what you think. So, the past few weeks' tensions are starting to disappear.

But the conflicts that come from Aries are still going on. The 21st, when Venus moves into this sign, confirms them. Even though it's less dangerous, it makes you feel uncomfortable. You want to take charge, but something keeps you from doing so. It won't help to yell in every direction. Use this time of peace to think about what you want to accomplish.

Love

The energy of the friendly signs makes you more available to your loved ones and helps them find their way. Use it to fix relationships that have been hurt by conflict until the 20th. Don't make the same mistakes again if you want peace to last after the 21st.

Venus in Pisces brings back communication with your partner. You are willing to do what they want. Between the two of you, things are easy. But watch out for the dissonances that Venus in Aries still gives you.

For single Capricorns, Venus in Pisces makes it easier for you to connect with someone special. Your charm stirs up sincere feelings. At the end of the month, instead of blocking this special person's ideas, accept them.

Career

You are working hard in this sector. To achieve your goals, you don't count the hours. The only problem with this helpful program is that you can get stressed out. In these situations, your mood can change quickly, which can throw off your business partners. To avoid this, be kind to people who don't have as much stamina as you do. Don't rush them. Give them the time they need. If you need to, share what you know.

The combination of stars facing you doesn't look good for your career. There would be a lot of hard work, but the benefits would not match the work done. Also, travel is mentioned, but this too wouldn't live up to expectations in a meaningful way.

Connections won't help you much during this time, but some female coworkers or friends will try to promote your professional achievements. It would be better to rely mostly on your own skills and work—a month in which you would have to work very hard to keep going.

Finance

On the money side, money keeps coming in. But the delays are getting longer. Don't put yourself under pressure. Everything will turn out fine.

The stars don't seem to be in a particularly good mood this month, so you shouldn't expect anything good to happen financially. Even if you worked very hard, your current operations wouldn't give you the expected or planned results. There are also no good signs for starting a new business or expanding an existing one.

If you tried to get a loan from a bank or other financial institution, your project would probably move slowly and get in the way. There is also a chance that people who deal with parties outside your country will have a hard time and even lose money.

Health

A good month in which you will be healthy, grow and get stronger thanks to the food you eat. This means that you are in good health and your body is getting the most out of your food. Any sudden, severe illness should be taken seriously, and treatment should be started right away.

If you treat these symptoms as soon as you notice them, you can be sure that nothing serious will happen. A good month that doesn't require much attention.

Travel

The stars are not aligned in a way that makes this a good month for making money through travel. During your travels, you could get hurt or have other physical problems. You should be careful because of this.

Also, your job or business would require a certain amount of travel this month. This wouldn't work out very well, though. Even trips to the West, which is the best direction, would not help. Some of you might go on a trip abroad, which wouldn't get you anywhere and might not help you achieve your goals.

Insight from the stars

If you want peace to rule your life and your love, give your entourage time, and don't let your ambitions take over. The whole month will be full of love and romance. You and your partner will have a lot of fun. Find ways to make memories with the person you care about most.

March 2023

Horoscope

The Aries energies are still putting you under pressure. A chance or an opportunity needs to be confirmed. As a result, you feel that you need to make a decision as soon as possible. The energy in the friendly signs is there to support you. They keep you from making rash decisions.

Saturn's transfer urges you to focus on what suits you and is convenient for you beginning on the 8th. These energies relieve stress and encourage you to take your time rather than haste. They inspire you to consider your goals. Saturn establishes a buffer zone so the external agitation does not affect you as much as it used to. As a result, you develop this discernment that allows you to make the best judgments for yourself.

Love

You're becoming better and better. You gradually regain command of the situation. But the situation is still tense! Venus in Taurus, which starts on the 17th, brings you back in touch with people who share your values. Your loved ones find their way and get back to basics.

The dissonances that come from Aries spoil your mood. Your level of understanding is low, and you are irritable. Things started to get better on the 17th. From the 26th, you should be happy to go along with what your partner wants to do.

Single Capricorn, The stars make things happen that are good for your love, a chance meeting, or the start of a romance. Leave your pain alone if you want things to go well. Accept what you are given at the end of the month.

Career

Your daily growth hasn't been natural for a while now because it depends on choices that don't always make sense. But you find ways to make things work, thanks to your legendary wisdom and experience. When Saturn comes into your sign, you should feel much more relaxed and less stressed. In this situation, you can breathe and still do your job well.

But even if you worked extremely hard, you probably wouldn't get the desired results.

There would be a lot of travel, but it wouldn't go as planned, though a trip to the South might be helpful. It would be best to rely on your skills and resources as much as possible. Overall, it is a month in which you must be very careful about dealing with difficult situations.

Finance

From a financial point of view, this sector is doing great. But you could treat yourself around the 7th. If so, make a rule for yourself and stick to it.

You should do very well financially this month because the stars are aligned in your favor. People who do business with other countries or across state lines would do very well and gain a lot. You would be able to get the planned gains from your current operations during this time.

Also, this would be a good situation for people who want to grow their businesses or start new ones. Those who have loan requests pending with any bank or financial institution will be able to obtain the loans they require. It's important to remember that working with women in business or the workplace would be beneficial.

Health

A month in which you're almost certain to be in good health. People prone to long-term problems like rheumatism and too much gas in the digestive tract will feel much better. They only need to use the usual amount of care to get relief from their illnesses.

The food you eat will really feed your body and keep you in great shape. You will have above-average reproductive vitality, giving you a healthy mind and body. There are a few reasons to take a sore throat seriously if you have one. The rest should go well.

Travel

The signs from the stars make it clear that there isn't much chance of making money from traveling. People whose jobs or businesses take them around a lot will not get much out of the exercise. You wouldn't be able to make much money from your business trips. Going in the best direction, South, would not change the situation. You could worsen your problems by going on expensive trips abroad that don't accomplish your goals. This could make things much worse for you. Under these circumstances, you should keep your plans as simple as possible.

Insight from the stars

Planets in friendly signs act like a wall that keeps outside pressure away from you. Be open to new ideas, and don't be afraid to try them out. You won't be sorry about it. It's time for you to make changes that will make your life better. Make sure you don't go down a path in life that will bring you down.

April 2023

Horoscope

Pressure from Aries starts to go away, and since happiness never comes on its own, you benefit from the energies moving through Taurus. Your mood is better when Saturn is close by. This month, your ambitions still drive you, but in a calmer and organized way.

This month, Mercury helps you figure out what you really want. From the 22nd, when it goes into retrograde, it's an excellent time to finish up an unfinished project. Use this time to narrow your attention to the things you enjoy or that allow you to make the most of your abilities. Mars in Cancer is the only shadow on the board, and it will try to get you off track. How? By using your emotions as a guide!

Love

Taurus' energies foster a sense of security in your romantic relationships. It's beautiful that they give you a positive outlook on life. This month, try to enjoy the good things about being romantic. This will keep you from being let down by things you don't really need.

Your union gets back to its normal speed. Everything about it is perfect for you. However, it's possible that your partner will become tired of you after a while. Take a few distracting steps every now and then to avoid problems.

Single Capricorn, Although you may be surprised and seduced by an encounter, this should not be an excuse for succumbing to the siren's song. Instead, stick to your habits and meet more people. After that, you can get to work.

Career

You're still having a hard time with your regular tasks. Achieving your goals requires making concessions and finding solutions. As a result, you're starting to feel a little worn out. All of a sudden, you find yourself running out of patience. If you're a Capricorn, take a walk outside around the 6th of the month and breathe some fresh air. By doing this, you can avoid starting a fight that will be difficult to resolve and, as a side effect, make your life even more unpleasant.

This is a good month for your career, with lots of opportunities for advancement. Most importantly, you have a decent possibility of realizing the benefits you desire. And it's all done without a lot of effort or difficulty.

In addition, you may be able to expand your life in a meaningful way by interacting with others who are more knowledgeable than you. This would add a much-needed dimension to your overall work. A little bit of travel is also a good idea. Some female coworkers or associates may be able to offer you a valuable favor.

YOUR COMPLETE PERSONAL HOROSCOPE 2023· 349

Finance

This sector is doing well financially because you are naturally frugal and a great manager.

On the other hand, the augury from the stars doesn't show much good news for your finances this month. You might work hard to reach your goals but not get anywhere because of a series of unfortunate incidences. On top of that, the environment would not be favorable for expanding operations or starting new businesses.

People who work in the arts, like painters, writers, sculptors, and so on, should be prepared for a tough time. Since things are not going well, it would be best to stay out of sight until the bad spell is over.

Health

The way the stars are aligned this month is a clear blessing for your health. In this case, you have nothing to worry about. In fact, your body will get the most out of the food you eat, putting you in the best shape possible. This would mean having a healthy body and mind. You would be able to keep moving and doing things.

Any kind of infection in the chest or lungs must be treated immediately. If this is done, there is no danger or reason to worry. If you didn't do this, your problems would get much worse. The tiniest of details should not be overlooked this month.

Travel

During this month, you should try to travel as little as possible, since doing so won't get you what you want and may even make things worse. There are signs that people whose jobs or businesses require them to travel a lot will be let down.

You wouldn't gain much from traveling, and even trips to the best direction, the West, wouldn't help. People who trade with other countries or have any kind of business with other countries may find, much to their dismay, that their trips abroad turn out to be useless.

Insight from the stars

People play tricks on you by playing on your emotions to get you to give in. Take the lead this time. How? By putting money away at the right time. You will have a lot of opportunities in life, but you should only take the ones that will help you reach your fullest potential.

May 2023

Horoscope

The wild energies of Aries are getting less powerful. On the other hand, those who come from Taurus get their strength back. All of this is proven true on the 17th, when Jupiter moves into Taurus, signaling the return of peace.

Even if you still have to deal with Cancer's energies, the dawning of a new day brightens your day. As a result, you're more likely to participate in the discussion. You've got a lot more patience than you used to! Your decisions are based on what makes sense. The opportunities that present themselves are no longer a source of anxiety and frustration! The risks that were expected to happen don't happen. This month, what Jupiter in Taurus gives you is in line with your values and principles. If you agree, that's fine.

Love

Your affection for your loved ones grows even though you aren't always able to give them your full attention. As a result, you'll feel better when interacting with people or your partner. Concentrate on the positive attributes if you want to make progress.

Things are getting better. As a result, you feel better and better. This month, you will probably spend more time with your partner. If you want the agreement to stay in place, give compliments instead of suggestions.

Single Capricorn, Love returns to a more regular pattern after a period of uncertainty. The meetings and exchanges are becoming increasingly frequent as well. If you want a long-term relationship, you shouldn't focus on the things that irritate you.

Career

Even though this sector is still stressful, it can be dealt with. As stress levels drop, people become less impatient. You find your place. Starting on the 17th, the ideas become concrete proposals. If someone gives you something, Capricorn, tell yourself this is your opportunity. If you do this, you will grow in a universe that is right for you.

A month in which your work is pretty good. There is a good chance that you will achieve the goals you set for yourself, but it would take a lot of hard work. Some of your plans may also involve a certain amount of risk. But since this is a good month, there is almost no chance that something terrible will happen.

Still, it's best not to take chances. The expected gains will not come from travel. There would be a lot of fighting and scheming at work. Also, one of your female coworkers or friends would do you a big favor that would help you greatly.

Finance

When it comes to money, your income could change at the end of the month. You can do what makes you happy all of a sudden.

This month, nothing good will happen to help you financially. This month will be hard for people working with other countries or groups from different states. In fact, they may find themselves working hard to achieve their goals, which may still elude them despite all their hard work.

Also, the climate would not be an excellent place to invest or start a new business. So, if you have plans like this, you should put them off until later. Partnerships and groups of professionals can also cause trouble. Keep your head down until the bad spell is over.

Health

A great month when the stars are aligned to give you good health. You will not only stay healthy, but you will also look great because your body is getting the most out of what you eat. This is the way things should be in a good month.

You are physically, emotionally, and mentally happy all month long. You are always busy and full of energy. The stars want you to be happy throughout this month.

Travel

A month when you won't make much money from traveling because the stars are all against you getting this blessing. Even more so, if you have to travel a lot for business or official work this month, you might not have much to show for your travels at the end of the month.

Even if things were normal, business travel wouldn't be as profitable as it would be in a typical month. Even going in the best direction, the South, wouldn't have the usual effect. Artists, writers, singers, and people like them would find their travels mostly empty and unproductive.

Insight from the stars

This month, be happy and give compliments. This will help your relationships because people will live up to what you expect of them. Work hard to make sure you get what you want. You shouldn't allow yourself to be lazy.

June 2023

Horoscope

The harmonious connection between Jupiter and Saturn shows that your growth is in progress. You can start to work on your goals beginning this month. If you have ideas, now is the time to make sure they come true. The link between Jupiter and Saturn fits with the way you do things. So, take your time, and no one will blame you! Your hard work and willingness to keep going will now be seen and appreciated.

Everything is going well until the 11th. Then, look at what's happening and ask yourself if you're being too hard on others or the situation. If so, you can try to change your strategy by being more friendly and spontaneous.

Love

Venus in Cancer puts you under stress until the 5th. Then you can make up for your absences, unavailability, and mood swings and get back on track. How? Give your loved ones gifts and make big love declarations under the stars.

Between the 5th and the 27th, you have a free field where you can relight the flame. It doesn't really matter what the costs are because the goal has been met; what matters is that it was accomplished!

Single Capricorn Venus doesn't have much of an effect on you this month. So, you will meet a person, but not just anyone. This shows that you can do great things when you're not in a hurry.

Career

Even though you have too much to do, you are like a fish in water. Your patience is awesome, you have great ideas, and you're very good at being everywhere at once. You get right to the point in these situations. Because of this, it can make you a demanding person who expects a lot from other people. Capricorn, ignore what they say if you hear people talking about you behind your back. Your friends and colleagues will be thankful for what you do.

If things go your way, you should do well with your problems over the next month. You would get the expected benefits and wouldn't even have to work hard or do anything out of the ordinary. Also, there wouldn't be any stress at work, making it fun to go to work.

Some female coworker or friend would do you a big favor that would be very helpful. There would also be some travel, which would also be very helpful. Overall, a good month during which you could make a lot of progress.

Finance

From a financial point of view, this is a good time for growth, so grab the ball. You will be glad you did it.

The stars have nothing outstanding to say about your money situation this month. Almost every dispute or lawsuit you might be involved in would go against you. Try to get a decision put off until a later, better time.

People who do business with the government would have to go through a tough phase, as would those who do business with other countries or between states. In short, you would have to work hard and struggle to achieve your planned goals, and even if you did everything right, you wouldn't make much progress. Banks and financial institutions aren't likely to approve loan requests that are still being processed or steps taken to get new loans.

Health

This is a lucky month for your health, as the stars will look out for you. You'd not only feel great, but you'd also look great since your body would be getting the nutrition it needs from your food to the fullest.

A happier emotional and mental state would allow you to live a far more fulfilling and rewarding life. Fortunately, if caught early enough, eye infections can be easily treated, and your month won't be ruined.

Travel

During this month, you won't be able to get the usual benefits from traveling because the stars don't look good. If your job or business requires you to travel a lot, this may not amount to much this month.

Even if you didn't have to work, most travel during this time wouldn't be enjoyable or bring you any significant gains. In some situations, it could even make things worse. This would be true even if you traveled in the best direction, North. If you went on a business trip abroad, you would add a lot to your losses.

Insight from the stars

You need to take a break this month. So, it makes sense that you might want to let go! Do it, and you won't be sorry! To make progress, you must avoid procrastination. Make efficient use of your time. Try new things and push yourself to the limit at the same time.

July 2023

Horoscope

Taurus and Pisces energies allow you to progress at your speed. You take advantage of any opportunity that comes your way, but you do so with the attention to detail that is your trademark. As a result, you are progressing as planned. When Mars moves into Virgo, things take on an entirely new meaning and perspective.

From the 11th on, you have the chance to push the limits of what is possible. You can put your skills and talents to good use if you want to. You will meet people who can push you to grow. Cancer's dissonances will continue to affect you until the 23rd. You may get rid of annoyances by remaining cool in every situation.

Love

Venus wants you to pay attention to the tiniest details, which are actually extremely significant. Get out of your legendary reserve if you want your loves to wake up. Don't be afraid to flaunt your success. Also, don't be surprised if something unexpected happens. Give in gracefully.

Cancer's dissonances are still shaking up your relationship. There are two ways to calm things down. Either you break your piggy bank or do something that will go down in history and give your partner peace of mind for decades.

Single Capricorn, This month, things happen that force you out of your habits and into a new world. You'll meet someone who will put you under their spell. For the next step, believe in yourself. You will be glad you did it.

Career

As of the 11th, your growth is on the right track. The same is true if you wait for a problem to be solved or for ease to come. When Mars is in Virgo, it brings out the best in you. Your plan works out. You know what to do and when to do it. When you need something, you push the limits of what is possible, and it helps you a lot.

This month, your professional prospects are pretty good. You would get the expected benefits, but you might have to do a lot more work. But work would become more enjoyable because the atmosphere would be calm and free of tension.

Some of the women you work with or know would be very helpful and do you a big favor. This would help your chances of getting a job. Expect to do a lot of traveling that pays off. In general, it is a good month.

Finance

On the financial side, unusual circumstances require more resources. You can listen to your heart, but you should also consider what makes sense. If you don't, you might make a choice that costs you more than you thought.

An unlucky month for your finances, according to the stars. Writers, painters, sculptors, and other creative types should prepare for a time of tremendous financial hardship because that might happen.

Even if you were friends with some smart people, you would find it hard to achieve your goals, and even if you did, you wouldn't be very successful. Any pending loan request or plan to get a new loan from banks or other financial institutions is unlikely to be approved. Plans for expansion or starting a new business should be put on hold for now since the time isn't favorable for them.

Health

Thanks to the blessings of the stars, this is a fantastic month for your health. People prone to long-term conditions like rheumatism and complaints like too much gas in the digestive tract will feel much better. The body will be able to fully utilize the nutrients and make effective use of the food eaten for nourishment.

There is a wealth of possibilities for you to live a more fulfilling and rewarding life. Not only in better shape physically but also in a much happier state of mind and heart.

Travel

The stars are not aligned in a way that makes this a good month for travel. Artists, actors, poets, and others in the same line of work would find that their trips to do their jobs don't lead anywhere.

As a result, those who have to travel frequently for work or business may find that their performance falls far short of expectations. This may be especially difficult for sales and marketing professionals. There are also signs that a trip to another country during this time would be just as useless. The best direction would be to go South.

Insight from the stars

The change you've been hoping for is about to happen. To meet it, you should get dressed up and agree to leave your world. Get over the past mistakes. Do not let them define your life.

August 2023

Horoscope

You keep getting better in a world that works for you. Jupiter's Providence provides you with gifts that improve your life. Uranus brings a little bit of the unexpected into your life without making it too unstable. Saturn, on the other hand, gives you plenty of time to get things done.

Everything is fine and getting better. If you'd like to go even further this month, you can do so. Mars and Mercury in Virgo draw attention to how serious you are and how responsible you feel. People who can help you grow will pay attention to you because of who you are. You can talk to them until the 31st. However, if you need to make a decision, you should do it before the 27th because Mars enters Libra on the 28th, making things more complicated.

Love

Venus doesn't have a significant effect on you, but it does have some impact. This month, she makes things worse. Don't take them as signs that love will let you down. Venus makes you aware of something that is meant to push you to make a choice.

There are no conflicts planned. Nothing is wrong. On the other hand, you can get closer to your other half if you want to. How? By spending a few days somewhere else or doing something out of the ordinary.

Single Capricorn, Your dream could come true if you meet that special someone. How? By agreeing to go to a place or area you don't know much about. Or by doing something you like, like a sport or activity.

Career

Capricorn, if you want to go further, you should think about what you suggested a few days or weeks ago. Use this time to carefully read a contract or learn more about something that interests you. Don't forget to think about what you like. You will get what you want if you do this. The expected changes will work out well for you.

Your job prospects are pretty good this month. You might be able to expect to make money, but you would have to work much harder than usual to do so. You could also improve your chances by going on short trips. The workplace atmosphere would also be very friendly, with no sign of trouble. This would make work fun, which would make you happy.

Also, there's a good chance that one of your female friends or coworkers will do you a big favor that will help your career. Overall, this month should be pleasant and helpful, full of accomplishments.

Finance

On the financial side, if a project is delayed, look at it as a good thing and use the time to think about whether you still want to be in this business.

According to the stars, there isn't much good news about your money this month. People who do business between states and other countries would have to deal with challenging conditions. In fact, you would have to work very hard to get the results you want, and even then, you might not get very far.

It wouldn't be a good time to invest or start new businesses. These will probably get stuck. Also, there wouldn't be much chance that banks or other financial institutions would approve any loan applications already in the works. This is not a good time for you, so staying out of the spotlight might be best until the bad time is over.

Health

The stars are shining brightly on your health this month, so take advantage. Your body and mind would benefit significantly from a diet rich in vitamins and minerals, as your system would utilize them to their maximum potential.

There are a few reasons to avoid overworking yourself. As long as it doesn't put too much strain on your body, a reasonable timetable should suffice. A positive outlook and feeling upbeat would keep you physically active and energized throughout the month.

Travel

During this month, the wisest of you can drastically cut back on your travel plans to avoid the adverse effects of the stars, which will keep you from making any significant money through travel. People who have to travel a lot for work or business may be the ones who suffer the most.

But it's comforting to know that these things will lead to better times. Artists, singers, dancers, and others like them may not get the usual benefits from their travels, either. Exporters and others who work with countries outside of the U.S. should also try to avoid going abroad as much as possible since they might not get much out of it.

Insight from the stars

You'd rather do things slowly. But if you want things to change, the time is now. So take your chance and go! Because the future looks promising, you should keep moving forward in your chosen direction.

September 2023

Horoscope

You keep getting better in an environment that helps you grow. When Mercury is in Virgo, you can look at things and plans in great detail. Your thoughts are alive and are working at full speed. You are extremely efficient. As usual, you put your work first. So far, you have not had any particular problems.

Unfortunately, with Mars in Libra, you might have some problems if you don't move on. This month is the time to sync your personal and professional lives. Why? So you don't end up in a bad situation or make a choice you'll later regret. Mars tells you to think about other people if you don't want to be blamed.

Love

Venus still has a tiny effect on the people you care about. Some bad things may happen and catch you by surprise. This month, how your love life goes depends on how well you can find a middle ground. Everything will be fine if you can get your personal life and your work life to work together.

For a while, everything is fine. But the same problems can pop up out of nowhere and cause you and your partner to fight again. But you can avoid it. How? By being there for your partner often and with warmth.

Single Capricorn, You have a good chance of connecting with someone. There is, however, a catch! This month, don't say you're too busy to go out because you have too much work.

Career

This month, a big step will be taken in this field. The bad news is that this good news could be stifled by those who disagree with your goals and ideas. Capricorn, you are a natural star because you are strong and practical. This month, these traits won't help you at all. So, when dealing with specific individuals, use tact and say what they want to hear if you have to. As a result, you'll make rapid progress toward your objectives.

A month with mostly good energy that will help you achieve your professional goals. You may be able to look forward to a lot of travel, which would be very helpful. There is also a good chance that you could make a lot of money from a favor done for you by a female coworker or friend.

A lot of work would be required, but it would be enjoyable due to the positive work environment. But there are reasons to think that some of you might be tempted to break the rules to make quick money. If you gave in to such a temptation, you would never get out of trouble. So, don't do things like that and make the most of a good situation.

Finance

If you're looking to make a big purchase, you'll be able to do it when Venus' retrograde period ends on the 16th.

Your financial future doesn't look very good based on what the stars tell you. Those involved in international trade would be disadvantaged and may have to deal with some difficulties. In fact, you would have to work quite hard to reach your goals, and even then, you probably wouldn't do very well.

In addition, the business climate would remain unfavorable for new businesses and investments. They might get stuck. And finally, any request for a loan or new money from a bank or other financial institution wouldn't have a good chance of being approved.

Health

A great month during which luck is on your side, and you don't have to worry too much about your health. In fact, you can look forward to a period of good luck during which your body will be able to get the most out of the food you eat, absorbing the nutrients and giving your body extra strength and vitality.

You can really look forward to enjoying life and living it more fully and richly. A fun month to look forward to, during which you can stay healthy and have a lot of fun just by not doing anything stupid.

Travel

According to the stars, this month is not a good time to travel. Not only would it not be profitable, but it could even cost you money. On your trips, at least a few of you could get hurt or have some other kind of physical trouble. This is especially true for those of you who like to take risks and try new things.

Even if nothing else went wrong, the trips taken during the month would not have the effect that was hoped for. Even trips to the South, which is the best direction, would be the same. The same thing will happen on trips abroad. In fact, because these things are expensive, they can sometimes make your losses much worse.

Insight from the stars

On the contrary, Mars does not make you miserable. It serves as a reminder of what went wrong in the past so that you don't repeat it. Listen to your intuition and follow your instincts. You can never go wrong if you follow your intuition, no matter what most people think.

October 2023

Horoscope

The dissonances from the planets in Libra force you to live by their rules. When you negotiate, you find a middle ground. You do your best to make yourself more available. Your fans will be sad to find out that this wonderful time will not last.

The transit of Mars into Scorpio on the 13th encourages you to assume leadership responsibilities. It makes you live your life based on your values. This position, which is a bit extreme, may irritate people with soft hearts. So, if you don't want to let criticism get to you, be a little more flexible in dealing with other people, your crew, your fans, or your spouse.

Mercury in Scorpio, which starts on the 23rd, makes you want to lay your cards on the table, but most importantly, do so in a graceful manner.

Love

You may have gone off the rails. Venus in Virgo helps you figure out what you believe in. Despite the pressures and criticism, you continue to pursue your ideals with your loved ones in hand. The mission is done brilliantly by the end of the month.

You prioritize achieving your goals and initiatives above all else. In other words, you're not available to your partner. Unfortunately, this way of life leads to criticism, which you can ease by making a few changes.

Single Capricorn, You have a chance of meeting the right person. Make an effort to be available if you want to build a relationship that will last. Give them time, and don't put them off because you have other things to do.

Career

Libra's dissonances keep pushing you to be more nuanced in your approach. Sometimes you have to work with gullible people who don't know anything about business. On the 13th, the sky starts to clear up. You can make more radical decisions. But be sure to warn the people who need to know and don't put them before the facts. If you don't like this, you should wait until the 23rd.

A pretty good month for your career to get the expected benefits, but you would also have to work very hard. But doing hard work in a great workplace makes it fun, which is what you can expect.

There is a good chance that a female coworker or associate will do you a big favor that will help your career in a big way. This would really help you. Those who work in the pure sciences and medicine may be able to expect to do incredibly well. Traveling, on the other hand, would be highly beneficial.

Finance

From the 9th, you become more reasonable when it comes to money. You have a keen eye for detail when managing your assets. If you're hoping for a positive response at the end of the month, you'll receive one.

A good month for your finances, during which you could make a lot of money, but not without any problems. The success of your projects, no matter what they are, would be boosted by your friendships with smart, spiritually-minded people. In fact, this would add a delightful layer of culture and sophistication to your entire working life.

You'd be able to achieve most of your goals and make the most money from them. Still, you'll likely run into problems along the way. There is also a chance of being late for an important meeting. But success is sure to happen. A good time to not only get a lot done but also to feel a lot of satisfaction.

Health

A month in which your health has been blessed by the stars and you have little to be concerned about. As a result, your system will not only be healthy but also look healthy, and you'll be a lot more energetic and active.

Only one thing could go wrong: an accident or a violent, serious injury, so extreme caution is advised. This, though, is a remote possibility.

Always keep an eye on your health. You may uncover long-term health issues this early in your life. Rest, a good diet, avoiding stressful circumstances, and bottled-up emotions can all help keep things from getting worse. Storing up destructive emotions can lead to the development of a hidden sickness, which can then lead to other problems.

Travel

The stars don't look good for you this month when it comes to travel, so don't count on going anywhere. Artists, singers, dancers, actors, and people like them would not be able to make any money during their stays.

Most of you fit this description. The stars predict sales and marketing workers will be the hardest hit. They may not be able to meet the goals set out in the contract. Traveling also wouldn't be all that enjoyable and there may also not be the usual second chance. People who want to go abroad to get a higher education may face different problems. This month, the best direction to travel is North.

Insight from the stars

You've regained control of your life, which is a good thing. Using firmness, however, will do you no good; instead, use tact and diplomacy. You must be on the lookout for potential threats to your well-being. If you make a single mistake, your overall health could be in jeopardy.

November 2023

Horoscope

You are surrounded by planetary forces that stimulate and support your growth. You're shielded from danger by a force you can't put your finger on. With an approach that is uniquely yours, you suddenly make significant progress toward your goal. You're determined to alter the direction of events with Mars in Scorpio till the 24th. Despite the positive atmosphere, there is a glimmer of doubt on the blackboard.

When Venus is in Libra from the 9th to the 30th, its dissonances tell you that there will be tensions that you will have to ease. Your personal growth has accelerated considerably in the past month. If you want things to go well, be sure to tell your friends and family what you plan to do. Why? for the simple reason that they are terrified of change.

Love

Everything is fine until the 8th. Then there's Venus in Libra, which brings the problems back. Things can grow frustrating if you can't keep the attention of your significant other or your followers. Be soothing in order to avoid criticism. It's small, but it'll spare you a lot of hassle down the road.

Things are back to normal now. Sadly, this happiness won't last long. When Venus moves through Libra, your partner is more likely to be in a mood that irritates you. Keep your cool, and everything will work out.

Single Capricorn, Getting someone to like you is a piece of cake. Sadly, this good fortune might be broken if you don't do what's right. Give someone you've met sometime this month, even if your time is valuable.

Career

You are doing great this month, and the right people come into your life at the right time. Your decisions are sound. Customers and employees are drawn to you because of your charisma. Under these conditions, you are sure to make progress. You seem too good at getting what you want. However, all of this can be stopped by people who aren't as brave as you, Capricorn. Take the time to tell them how you will do it. This will give them peace of mind.

This month, you would have great opportunities to move up in your career, but you would also have more work to do. You may be looking forward to getting what you expect. There would be no stress in the workplace, and everyone would enjoy coming to work.

In addition, a female coworker or associate may be able to help you advance your career. This should have a significant impact. In addition to that, traveling would be a great way to make money. In this situation, you would also get a lot of pleasure from your work, which would give you a sense of accomplishment. Overall, this is a good month for you, and you should do well at work.

Finance

Financially, this industry is booming because, by its very nature, no one throws their money away. As a result, the necessities of daily life are well covered, as is leisure time.

This month, your financial situation looks pretty good. There is a good chance that an old friend could do you a big favor that would help you greatly. You could expect more good luck if you worked with someone of the female sex in a business partnership or partnership. This could also make a lot of money.

It would be an excellent time to start new businesses and invest. And those of you who have similar plans should get them moving. Also, there would be a good chance that banks and other financial institutions would approve any loan requests already in the works or any new proposals for new loans.

Health

This is an excellent month for your health. The stars are aligned in your favor, so you don't have much to worry about. People prone to long-term conditions like rheumatism and digestive tract problems will feel better.

When your body absorbs all the nutrients from the food you eat, you will feel good about your health and look good. Not only will you be very active and full of energy, but your mind will also be in good shape. A nice month that would require you to do very little work.

Travel

According to the stars, this is a good month to travel. Those whose jobs or businesses require a lot of travel may be in an enviable position, with things going as planned and meeting your expectations.

People in sales and marketing would do well if they went in the most favorable direction, which is South, as it would lead to the expected result. Also, there is a good chance that business trips outside the country will live up to expectations.

Insight from the stars

Even though it's not who you are, try to be comforting to other people. This won't change how your life goes, but it will keep you from dealing with things you don't need to. Because business is booming and you're making more money than you expected, you're going to expand your operation.

December 2023

Horoscope

Luck is constantly on your side, and you plan to take advantage of it. However, the pace is less steady than it was last month.

This month, your progress is helped by Mercury in Capricorn from the 2nd to the 23rd and by Venus in Scorpio from the 5th to the 29th. Because of these planetary energies, it's no longer a good idea to make decisions based just on your judgment but rather to persuade your coworkers or partners. Mercury helps you build your personality so that you can do well with this little trick. He is connected to Venus and tells you to strengthen the bonds that link you to the people who can help you.

You finish the year without major issues. However, if you have periods of inaction, do not become alarmed. Seize the moment to do a self-evaluation.

Love

Until the 4th, you have to put in some work. Then, with Venus in Scorpio, you go through a time of ease, which you love. This month, you are back in complete charge of the situation. People know they can count on you and your loyalty without you doing anything special.

It's time for your relationship to get back to cruise speed after a period of ups and downs. As a result, it's time to revisit the projects that were put on hold. Why? Because it'll provide your spouse a lot of comfort for years to come.

Single Capricorns, You could meet your soulmate. You don't have to do anything at all to succeed at this little wonder. And if you want to, you can even talk to them about your latest business plan! This special someone will be enchanted!

Career

Now is not the time to make a decision about anything. Instead, think about the work that has been done in recent times. Capricorn, even though you are very focused, take short breaks. Why? Because some files need to be worked on. People need to know what happened after an event. A project needs your attention to keep going until next year.

According to the horoscope, the stars don't see much hope for your career this month. With much more work to do, you would put in a lot of effort for what would definitely not be enough payoff. The situation would be made better in some ways by a pleasant and stress-free work environment. But only so much and not more.

Travel would likewise fall short of your expectations, yet a trip to the South might provide some benefits. Not enough to make up for the whole thing, it must be said. Contacts won't be very helpful, making a difficult situation even harder. Also, don't do anything illegal, which could worsen your problems.

Finance

You'll go over your budget if you wait until the last minute to make your holiday purchases. So, plan ahead of time instead of dwelling on something that will occur on the 24th.

Because the stars are favorably aligned, this month has good financial prospects. There is a good probability that an old friend could help you out in a big way. Some of you would also be lucky that a partnership or a professional relationship with a woman would be beneficial.

You would also know how to handle your employees or subordinates in a way that lets you get the most out of their work. This would be a big win. The climate would also be good for investing or starting new businesses, so those with such plans should go ahead and implement them.

Health

A month in which the stars are very kind to your health, and you have nothing to worry about. Your body would get the most out of the food you eat, which could show in your glowing health.

Not only will you be very active throughout the month, but you'll also be in such good shape that life will be much richer and fuller in every way. There is a chance of overworking. But you can get past this with a smartly planned schedule that doesn't stress you. Overall, it's a good month that lets you enjoy life.

Travel

The stars are in your favor this month, so you may expect to reap substantial rewards from your travels. Most of you would be able to accomplish your goals with ease if you had to travel frequently for work. Travel options include flying, taking a train, or driving. The South is the most favorable direction.

Some of you may also be able to make a profitable business trip abroad for international travel. You would also have a nice vacation.

Insight from the stars

Everything is going well this month. Be prepared for brief moments of inaction, however. They're designed to get you thinking about how you might improve your plan. Be wary of bargains that seem too good to be true. During the Mercury retrograde period of 2023, avoid making any speculative investments you are unsure about.

AQUARIUS 2023 HOROSCOPE

Overview Aquarius 2023

As the year 2023 begins, Jupiter will travel through Aquarius' third house of Aries. Then, in May, it moves to the 4th house of Taurus, where it will remain for the remainder of the year. As a result, relationships with siblings and short trips will be most beneficial till May. The emphasis would then move to domestic welfare, maternal ties, and property deals. Saturn, positioned in your Ascendant house at the start of the year, will move to your Pisces 2nd house in March 2023. Saturn emphasizes the need for stability and achievement in your first house.

It would be detrimental to your health throughout this time period. After the transit, Saturn would have less of an effect on your finances, and you might feel like your money is tight.

Regarding the outer planets, Uranus spends the entire year in Taurus' 4th house. At the beginning of the year, Neptune would be in your 2nd house of Pisces, while Pluto would be in your 12th house of Capricorn. Then it will transfer to your Ascendant house in May-June 2023. The way these planets move across the zodiac sky would affect your life on Earth.

Because of Venus's influence, love and marriage will be favorable for Aquarians in the coming year. You would be able to make a significant difference in your relationship or marriage. Instead of using traditional approaches, devise creative ways to entice your spouse to join you. These days, you'd have the audacity to persuade your lover. You would have plenty of leisure and adventurous time with your sweetheart. You would also have the required freedom in your personal space.

The coming year will be favorable for Aquarians' job prospects. As the year begins, your Scorpio 10th house will receive aspects from Jupiter and Saturn, ensuring significant success and development in your business or profession. Throughout the year, ensure you acquire good advice and assistance from elders in the sector. Promotions and raises may elude you, but you will be fairly compensated for your efforts at the end of the year.

Aquarius folks will have a year of moderate health. Saturn in your Ascendant house may sometimes cause health concerns for the inhabitants. Chronic Aquarius residents should monitor their health closely throughout the year, as it may deteriorate. Discipline your nutrition, physical activities, and mental problems. Find any and all ways to improve your health favorably.

The beginning of the year brings wonderful financial fortune for Aquarians. The location of Jupiter and its transit in May provides a continual supply of funds for the people of this zodiac sign. Gains from a partner or spouse are also on the cards for some Aquarians this year. However, this is not the time to make high-value investments. Certain auspicious ceremonies at home, such as house renovation, marriage, and childbirth in the family, will need a large portion of your finances throughout the year. Maintain a separate fund to deal with unexpected medical bills.

Aquarius people's domestic life will be routine until May when Jupiter transits the 3rd house. However, family life would take center stage with the transit to the 4th house in May. Your home and family ambitions will now become a reality. However, you must first determine what is possible for the home in the long run. You may need to reconcile with family members throughout the year. In the coming year, strike a nice balance between your personal and professional space. Prepare for any financial or medical emergencies that may arise in your family. Relax, enjoy beautiful times with family and friends, and take the tension and pressure out of household life.

Aquarians would enjoy a good year in terms of travel concerns in 2023. Rahu, the Moon's node, is positioned in the third house of the year, favoring frequent short-distance trips for Aquarius people. They would be favored with long-distance travel after Jupiter and Saturn transit after the first quarter. Aquarius locals are more inclined to travel for professional reasons, and their journeys will bring them good fortune. Saturn in the Ascendant house may cause accidents, so Aquarians are advised to be exceptionally watchful and cautious in their travels.

The year will be highly auspicious for Aquarius people's spiritual endeavors. Your faith and belief in God will be unaffected by the difficulties you face throughout the year. Jupiter's conjunction in your 9th house after May 2023 would bless you with a long-desired pilgrimage. This year, you will do some rites or religious ceremonies to honor the gods as a preventative step. When the destitute and needy approach you, make donations and offerings to them.

Aquarius folks should reconsider their life objectives and goals for the coming year and adjust them following practical themes. Get rid of anything that irritates you, and stay pragmatic this year. Aquarians are asked to put aside their personal goals and work for the greater good of humanity. Sharing and caring for others will give you happiness and a peaceful life. But don't neglect yourself; take some time for yourself and enjoy the beautiful things in life. This is an excellent year to learn a new skill, take a vacation, and get to know your loved ones better.

January 2023

Horoscope

You have an excellent opportunity of getting what you want and accomplishing what you want to do. Saturn, which is in your sign, is then joined by Venus, the Sun, and the new Moon. Your fast energy makes it possible for new projects to start. You stop being so stagnant.

Jupiter and luck will give you opportunities that will make you very happy. But for everything to go well, you will have to deal with people who are not ready to change. In return, try not to act based on your feelings but on what makes sense. Don't be too attached to your independence, but weigh the pros and cons before you make a choice that could affect all of your assets.

Love

Mars keeps making the area where you love come alive. It breaks this pattern that makes you nervous and want to run away. In this setting, you show the best parts of yourself. But you'll have to accept a few small rules if you don't want the coach to turn into a pumpkin.

This month, you have a strong need to change your mind, which is fine. But don't change direction if your projects or ideas fail. If you accept them, everything will work out.

Single Aquarius, This month, love at first sight, is the theme. Someone's original ideas may surprise you and win you over. But for the magic to work, you'll need to plan your time.

Career

Jupiter helps you get back into the swing of things. It inspires you to start something new. You feel like you are waiting less as things seem to come together more quickly. You can develop more creative ideas because your work is less tedious.

This month's horoscope doesn't seem good for your job prospects. You'd have to put in a lot more effort for a lot less money if you increased your workload. A relaxed and stress-free work environment would go a long way toward making up for the bad scenario. But not any more than that.

Travel would likewise fall short of your expectations, albeit a trip to the South might provide some rewards. Not enough to make up for the rest of what happened. A difficult circumstance will become even more challenging if you have no one to turn to for aid. Your problems will only get worse if you engage in illegal activities.

Finance

Take advantage of this time to make good financial resolutions. You should check your accounts and make a budget. It might not be much fun, but it will be helpful this year.

Because the stars are in a good mood, this is a month with good financial prospects. There is a good chance that an older friend could help you in a big way and bring you a lot of money. You'd have much more good fortune if you could form a business relationship or professional alliance with a woman. This would be a huge asset for you.

You would also know how to handle your employees or subordinates to get the most out of their work. In the long run, this is a massive win for the company. Investors and entrepreneurs should take advantage of the favorable conditions to move forward with projects they've been contemplating for some time.

Health

During this month, the stars are in your favor regarding your health, so you have nothing to worry about. Your body would get the most out of the food you eat, which could show in your glowing health. Your ability to reproduce would also be at its best.

Not only will you be very busy all month, but you'll also be in such good shape that your life will be much richer and fuller in every way. There is a chance that you will work too hard. But you can get around this by making a smart plan that doesn't put too much stress on you. Overall, it's a good month that lets you enjoy life.

Travel

A month when you can expect to make a lot of money from your travels because the stars are in your favor. You would travel a lot for work and be quite successful at reaching your goals. You could fly, take the train, or drive.

There is also a chance that some of you will have a successful business trip abroad. The best direction to go would be South. You would also have a nice vacation if you choose.

Insight from the stars

This month, you have everything you need to do well. But don't get too upset when someone says no. Accept what doesn't work for you. At the start of the year, there will be a lot to do. But in the end, you will be able to conquer them because you have the right tools at your disposal.

February 2023

Horoscope

The energies coming from Aquarius, Gemini, and Aries continue to help you grow and change. Jupiter makes things go well so you can meet the right people. You feel bubbly and happy when Mars is in your sign. As for the Sun, Mercury, and Saturn, they put your personality, ideas, and experiences in the spotlight because they are in your sign.

In this lovely climate, you can be sure of everything. You have a lot of work to do! Since all the lights are green, everything seems to be set in stone. On the other hand, you will have to deal with the full Moon in Leo on the 5th. It pushes you to do too much, which would hurt your vision. Keep your head down to avoid these problems.

Love

Mars, which is in your love zone, gives you the best of itself so that you can have a perfect life. He is connected to Jupiter and makes happy things happen that make you forget the usual. Everything is fine, as long as you stay realistic about certain limits.

You make choices so your relationship doesn't get stuck in habits that you find disgusting. But around the 5th, think about what your partner wants and what they believe. This will help you avoid a huge problem.

Single Aquarian, There is a good chance that the person you love will share your values. Pay attention to what you say around the 5th if you want the magic of love to last.

Career

You make your voice heard like a boss! Your well-known enthusiasm inspires people; they won't think twice about going out of their way to help you or do what you ask. In this fresh and active environment, your work seems easier and, most of all, more enjoyable. You see good things in what you do. On your best days, you have plans for what will happen next. Saturn is still in your sign, though. So if you feel things aren't moving quickly enough, don't worry about it.

The way the stars are aligned in front of you doesn't look good for your career. There would be a lot of short trips that wouldn't bring the expected benefits. On the other hand, a trip to the North might be helpful. It is unlikely that any of your contacts will be able to help you during this time.

So, it would be a good idea to trust in your ability to solve problems. But there are reasons to think that the working conditions and atmosphere would stay pretty good. This would be a big reason to be happy. Overall, it was a month when you had to be careful with some sensitive matters.

Finance

On the money side, money comes in and goes out just as quickly. So, if you want to keep your accounts going, you should keep a close eye on them.

Even though you'll be hanging out with many bright and spiritually gifted people this month, it won't be good for your finances. There is a good chance that you would have to work hard to reach your goals, and even then, you might not get very far.

The climate would also not be suitable for making investments or starting up new businesses. They might get stuck. Also, banks or other financial institutions would unlikely approve any pending loan applications or requests for new advances. Also, people who do business overseas would probably have to deal with a fair amount of adversity.

Health

A great month when the stars are aligned to give you good health, and you don't have to do much but sit back and enjoy it. Your body would get the most out of what you eat, and your health would shine as a result.

Not only would you be very busy and full of energy during the month, but you would also keep your mind and body in good shape. There are some reasons to be careful about boils that might make you uncomfortable for a short time. With instant medicine, you don't have to worry about anything.

Travel

Since this part of the astrological forecast isn't very favorable, you wouldn't gain much from travelling this month. But there are some people who have to travel to keep their jobs or businesses going. The answer would be to find a middle ground where you cut your losses and do as much as you can on your winning streaks. The best direction would be North.

Artists, singers, dancers, and others like them wouldn't get the usual benefits from travel. Those who go abroad to study at a college or university may face different problems. Business trips to other countries would not be very productive either.

Insight from the stars

When the full Moon is in the sign of Leo, you tend to lean toward the dark side of the spectrum. To avoid this, think about other people's thoughts and feelings. Your self-confidence will help you do amazing things in your life.

March 2023

Horoscope

You feel energized by the energies that come from Aries and Gemini. Luck continues to smile. You have a lot of ideas and projects you're working on. Saturn leaves the sign of Aquarius on the 8th. During his time in your sign, he helped you organize your ideas, making them hard for them to come true. So, you may have found that time seems to go by slowly.

This month, the limits come off. The field is open to you. Your connections with other people are great. You want to get things moving in the right direction, which drives you. Mars is in Gemini until the 25th. Until then, you bounce ideas around. You act well and quickly. All the lights are green this month so that you can take advantage of any sudden opportunities.

Love

Planets in friendly signs give you the freedom to be yourself without explaining why. You feel good, and this makes your loved one happy. But after the 17th, it gets harder if you don't agree to be home more often.

Uranus sends you a few warning shots, but your zest for life softens their blows. Unexpected things keep your relationship interesting, and there are no problems. But if you feel like things are getting tense after the 17th, try to calm them down.

Single Aquarius, Everything starts so that your love life is what you want it to be. You are content. Your independence may become a problem starting on the 17th. Keep it or calm it down. You get to make the call.

Career

Your business is in good shape now that Saturn has left your sign. You have more room to move. You're no longer trapped. Jupiterian effects also play a role in bringing happiness. All of a sudden, the chances that come up are more appealing. Some might lead you to this long-awaited success. You can take advantage of anything that comes up around the 3rd. You won't be dissatisfied.

However, the combination of stars facing you doesn't look good for your career. There would be a lot of hard work, but the benefits would not come close to matching the work. Also, travel is mentioned, but this too wouldn't live up to expectations in a meaningful way.

Contacts won't help you much either during this time, but some female coworkers or friends will try to promote your professional achievements. It would be better to rely mostly on your skills and work—a month in which you would have to work very hard to keep going.

Finance

This industry's stock price may take a slight dip for no apparent reason. Don't get upset. Look at it as a chance to learn how to handle your money better.

The stars don't seem to be in an excellent mood this month, so you shouldn't expect anything good to happen financially. Even if you worked very hard, your current operations wouldn't give you the expected or planned results. There are also no good signs for starting a new business or expanding an existing one.

If you tried to get a loan from a bank or other financial institution, your project would probably move slowly and get no positive results. Those who engage in business with parties outside their country or of different legal standing are more likely to encounter difficulties and even lose money.

Health

A good month in which you will be healthy and grow and get stronger thanks to the food you eat. This means that you are in good health, and your body is getting the most out of the food you eat. Any sudden, severe illness should be taken seriously, and treatment should be started right away.

If you treat these symptoms as soon as you notice them, you can be sure that nothing serious will happen. A good month that doesn't require much attention.

Travel

The stars are not aligned in a way that makes this a good month for making money through travel. During your travels, you could get hurt or have other physical problems. You should be careful because of this.

Also, your job or business would require a certain amount of travel this month. This wouldn't work out very well, though. Even trips to the West, which is the best direction, would not help. You could go on a trip outside the country, but that might not help you reach your goals either.

Insight from the stars

Uranus sends you a warning sign as soon as you abuse your freedom. This month, Venus is in charge of it. Do not rebel. Listen to her. Your love will pay you back 100 times over. Keep your faith in yourself and your skills, and use them to improve yourself and your life. Do not be afraid to show the world what you can do.

April 2023

Horoscope

The energies that come from Aries are starting to become less intense. Why? Because the ones from Taurus have taken their place. Because of this, the atmosphere is calmer and more realistic. As a result, people will become picky and more difficult to persuade.

This month, things will be a little less easy and a little harder. Mercury in Taurus is very stubborn, so you'll have to deal with it all month. Mercury will be in retrograde on the 22nd, so you will have to deal with his refusal to try anything new. Mars wants you to stick with your cause instead of giving up while you wait for better times. Take this occasion to look at the details you may have missed causing these problems.

Love

The vise is becoming more and more tense. Consider yourself lucky, and don't think the sky is on your tail. It's not what it appears to be. You will have to make minor concessions to keep your loved ones happy. How? By not constantly proclaiming your individuality!

You are moving around a lot and will be held responsible for everything that goes wrong! Arguments are welcome, but they may only serve to aggravate the problem. Put yourself in the other person's shoes instead of trying to persuade them. Show them your affection if you can.

Single Aquarius, Your charm is always great, but you must make some changes if you want the encounters to go further. Think about what the people you meet want. This will keep you from being all by yourself.

Career

This month Jupiter in Aries shows you what he can do for you. So, if you want things to go your way, now is the time to take advantage of the chance. Aquarius, don't try to get conservative people to agree with you. Instead, find people who believe in the same things you do and are willing to give you that much-needed boost.

There's nothing very good about the work outlook for this month. Even if you worked very hard, you probably wouldn't get the gains you wanted.

There would be a lot of travel, but it wouldn't go as planned, though a trip to the South might be helpful. People you know wouldn't be as helpful as usual, either. Because of this, you should rely mostly on your skills and resources. Overall, it is a month in which you must be very careful about dealing with complex situations.

Finance

From a financial point of view, this sector can leak for no good reason. So, instead of looking elsewhere, fill in the holes and get back to your business as soon as you can.

Your financial future doesn't look all that good. You might have to work very hard and struggle to get the results you want from your current operations. There is a good chance you won't be able to do this simple task well. Also, the climate would not be suitable for growth or starting new businesses.

Some of you who have bids for loans pending with banks or financial institutions or would like to submit such proposals are in for a bumpy ride ahead of them. Be prepared for the worst-case scenario because you will be put in a tough spot.

Health

A month in which you are almost sure to be in good health. People prone to long-term problems like rheumatism and too much gas in the digestive tract will feel much better. They only need to use the usual amount of care to get relief from their illnesses.

The food you eat will really feed your body and keep you in great shape. You will be above average in terms of your reproductive abilities, which means you have a healthy body and mind. There are a few reasons to take a sore throat seriously if you have one. The rest should go well.

Travel

You can expect to make a lot of money from your business or official travels during this month. There are signs that some of you will have a good flight and maybe an equal number of good train or road trips. The best direction for your travels would be to the South.

Those interested in the fine arts may have an enjoyable and exciting trip, some of which may be to a new place. This month, going somewhere would be good for you.

Insight from the stars

Uranus is poised to issue an ultimatum to you this month. Temper your sense of self-reliance to avoid it. Consider what others say, even if you think their ideas are outdated. Your family and friends will be happy with how your life is going. They will give you the support you need to move forward.

May 2023

Horoscope

Even though you're making slow progress with Jupiter in Aries, you're making the most of opportunities. It gives you the will to keep going even when things don't go your way. As long as Venus is with you until the 7th, you will feel at home anywhere and with anyone. Luck smiles on you. You feel like you've hit the jackpot! The atmosphere will change with Jupiter moving into Taurus on the 17th.

People are getting tougher on you. Strength will not save you time; it will take you longer. Instead, use these hazards to figure out what is wrong so that you can fix it. From the 21st, when Mars is in Leo, tensions and refusals will go away if you act positively.

Love

Dissonant energies make it harder for you to act, which can be very annoying. Don't be all or nothing if you want your love to last over time. Look at the good things about a calmer life instead of focusing on negative things.

When you have astral dissonances, you become very present and stifled. So, you step back and let your doubts settle. Find the proper middle ground, and your partner's criticisms won't surprise you.

Single Aquarius, Your charm works like magic. People are easy to meet but don't stick around for long. If you want your relationship to last, try to show more of your feelings. And if you can, smile and accept the limits.

Career

It's time to take advantage of the opportunities that present themselves in May, especially between the 1st and 7th. After the 16th, though, things become more difficult. But these problems are not impossible to solve. Everything will be fine if you are practical when you need to be. On the other hand, trying to force your views on others can only lead to frustration.

There's nothing good about your job prospects this month. Even if you worked really hard, you're unlikely to get anywhere near the goals you set out to achieve. The way things are going, this just isn't going to happen.

Travel also wouldn't give you what you were hoping for, but a trip to the West might bring you some luck. There are also grounds to believe that your connections would not help you very much. So, it would be best to rely on your skills and hard work. Not a good time and you should only get through it if you know how to handle difficult situations well.

Finance

On the financial side, this market is still a little loose. So if you can, be a little more thrifty. You'll be back in the game in no time if you do this. So, you can relax a little. What? 'Or' How? By working on one thing at a time.

The signs from the stars don't give you much reason to be optimistic about your money this month. You might find yourself working hard to reach your goals but not getting anywhere because of a series of bad things. On top of that, the environment would not be suitable for expanding operations or starting new businesses.

People who work in the arts, like painters, writers, sculptors, and so on, should be prepared for a tough time. Since things are not going well, it would be best to stay out of sight until the lousy spell is over.

Health

This month, the way the stars are aligned is a clear blessing for your health. In this case, you have nothing to worry about. In fact, your body will get the most out of the food you eat, putting you in the best shape possible. This would mean having a healthy body and mind. You would be able to keep moving and doing things.

Any kind of infection in the chest or lungs must be treated immediately. If this is done, there is no danger or reason to worry. If you didn't do this, your problems would get much worse. Those are little things that you should not ignore.

Travel

The stars say that this is an excellent time to travel and make a lot of money. Most of you could travel a lot for work and business and be very successful at it. Most of these trips would be by train or car, but some would also be by plane.

Some of you may also travel abroad on a successful business trip, while others may also travel for pleasure, perhaps on vacation with your family to an exciting location. This month, the best direction is West.

Insight from the stars

It's not easy to live with the energies of Taurus. But you can ease some of the stress if you want to. How? By working on one thing at a time. Follow your heart, and think about what you're going to do before you do it.

June 2023

Horoscope

This month, Taurus and Leo are causing problems that slow your progress. You might be wondering why this spell is taking so long at first. Don't worry, this is not the case. If you run into problems, it means you aren't making the right decisions or are making them for the wrong reasons.

Instead of attempting to persuade your partners that your ideas are sound, take a break. Think about how you can best use the things you're good at. Also, make sure your ideas are easy for other people to understand. Since the end of last month, the spirits don't like it when things change. On the other hand, they value what makes them feel good and safe.

Love

With Venus and Mars in Leo, the people you love will have both great and rough times. These forces put you in situations that bring out your best and worst traits. However, if you're able to control your desires, you'll be rewarded tenfold by the people you care about.

This month, the things that were wrong last month are even worse. Find the right balance before your partner gets tired of you. Stay away when it's right. To please your lover, put them first.

Venus and Mars in Leo are good for you, Aquarius, but only if you behave yourself. This month, a charming person is interested in how smart and funny you are. If you want to see them again, you must be polite and wait.

Career

brilliant thoughts naturally guide you. As a result, they find themselves at odds with others who hold on to their convictions. Aquarius, you're loud enough to be heard; however, this will have the opposite effect on your business. Instead of raising your voice, lower it and try to get to know them. If at all possible, make your suggestions as easily implementable as possible. Doing this will eliminate the difficulties.

How the stars are aligned isn't very good for your professional success. Despite your efforts, it does not appear that you will achieve your objectives. There would be risks involved in some of your plans and efforts. Under these conditions, avoiding taking any kind of risk would be best.

There is also a good amount of travel shown. But again, you wouldn't get the gains you were hoping for. Even so, you might be able to get something out of a trip to the North. A month that doesn't look good for your career.

Finance

If you have a lot of bills to pay this month, don't think of it as a curse but rather as a chance to get your finances in shape.

This month, nothing good is likely to happen that will help you financially. This month will be hard for people working with other countries or groups from different states. In fact, you may find yourself working hard to achieve your goals, which may still elude you despite all your hard work.

Also, the climate would not be a good place to invest or start a new business. So, if you have plans like this, you should put them off until later. Partnerships and groups of professionals can also cause trouble. Keep your head down until the bad spell is over.

Health

This month, luck won't be on your side when it comes to your health. During the ensuing time, you will have to pay more attention to and care more about your health. You should see a doctor as soon as the first signs of a problem with the digestive organs show up. If this is done, it will solve a lot of possible issues. It's a better way to keep an eye on your health. Most of the time, as we gain weight, we get sicker. Even though being fit is no guarantee of good health, most health problems are caused by being overweight.

Take advantage of therapies and use your energy to do something worthwhile, so you don't always turn to comfort food. Plan your diet and work out. If you like to play sports, you can also get a lot out of swimming and badminton. Keep a healthy way of life to avoid health problems. This month, how the stars are aligned is not good for your health, and the only way to get through this is to be careful and cautious.

Travel

According to the stars, this is a great month in which you can expect to get a lot out of your travels. Artists, poets, writers, playwrights, and other people like them could go to new places and have a great time and learn a lot.

You would have a very successful trip abroad, achieving all of your goals. You would have a good time even if you travelled within the country for business or official reasons. North would be the best direction to go.

Insight from the stars

You will run into many problems if you do too much. On the other hand, everything will be fine if you agree with yourself. This month will have a lot of good things happen. Be happy and mark the important moments in your life with your friends and family.

July 2023

Horoscope

You keep going even though you're experiencing astral dissonances. Uranus and Jupiter in Taurus represent the challenges you must face this month. After that, you'll have to cope with the rejections that Leo's energy will bring about. For these little wonders to succeed, you'll need to use energy sources you've never used before. They have the ability to help you, despite their appearance.

To achieve your goals, you need to do things in order. Before you begin, take some time to clarify your thoughts. Do not be afraid to reassure your group or the people you are talking to. It might not be necessary, but it will improve your relationships.

Love

Most problems get better when Mars leaves Leo. Unfortunately, your relationships change over time when Mercury, Venus, and the Sun are in your love charts. You can avoid this problem if you want to. How? By not getting rid of what seems to stop you.

Even though everything is quiet, you must make peace! Give the emotional side more weight if you want to pull off this little miracle. Be kind and sometimes do nice things for your partner when you can.

Single Aquarius, You get to know someone through your ideas and conversations. To get further, don't get stuck in endless word games. Instead, use your sensitivity and intuition to make a connection.

Career

You are in situations that require you to be practical and keep things simple. Aquarius, if you don't want to end up with many hassles and problems, you should slow down. This prospect can be a massive pain at the time, but it will help your business. Plus, it will save you time rather than waste it. So, pay attention to what's important, and when it's time to rest, it will happen on its own.

A month when the stars in front of you doesn't help you get far in your career. Even if you worked very hard, reaching the goals you set for yourself would be hard. This would make you feel disheartened.

Travel is also an option, whether it's for work or volunteer purposes. However, the anticipated advantages may not materialize in this case either. In general, having contacts would also be very useful. But it would be best to depend mostly on your skills and hard work. Overall, it is a month, which doesn't look good for your job prospects.

Finance

On the money side, this area needs a major upgrade, so now is the time to take a good look at it.

The stars have nothing outstanding to say about your money situation this month. Almost every dispute or lawsuit you might be involved in would go against you. Try to get a decision put off until a later, better time.

People who do business with the government would have to go through a rough patch, as would those who do business with other countries or between states. In short, most of you would have to work hard and struggle to achieve the planned goals, and even if you did your best, you wouldn't have much success. Banks and financial institutions aren't likely to approve loan requests that are still being processed or steps that are being taken to get new loans.

Health

With the help of the stars, you can look forward to being healthy throughout this month. You would be healthy and look healthy because your body would get the most out of what you ate.

This would not only give you a lot of energy and make you very active, but it would also make you happy emotionally and mentally. This would help you live a much fuller and richer life. There are reasons to be careful about eye infections, which would not change the scene if they were treated quickly.

Travel

This is an excellent month to travel since the stars predict you will make a lot of money while you're out and about.

If things go as planned, you'll have to take a lot of trips. These endeavors would be highly effective in helping you achieve your goals. People in the creative industries, such as actors, dancers, and musicians, would have a blast and earn a lot of money travelling. This month, your best bet is to head West.

Insight from the stars

Your success will depend on how well you can appreciate what is there. Closed doors will open if you succeed in this challenge. You must put your faith in the process and surrender your will to the will of the cosmos.

August 2023

Horoscope

This month, the problems are all about the same. Uranus and Jupiter in Taurus make it hard for you to move around. As for the Sun and Venus in Leo, they work against you getting what you want. These risks are meant to make you aware of something. After that, you'll be able to see better.

If you agree, you can fix some of the problems that these astral dissonances cause this month. How? First of all, don't criticize ideas that are too conservative. Change the way you think instead. Act in a way that considers people's fears, or even better, be reassuring. Now that you've done that, let other people help you because no matter how much energy you have, you can't do everything yourself.

Love

Since Mercury left, you have been getting along better with each other. You are more likely to talk and try to understand. Venus in retrograde, on the other hand, causes trouble. This month, what you find beautiful makes you question your freedom. It urges you to make peace with the good things about commitment.

You and your partner start to grow apart. You can make a reconciliation if you want to. How? By being brave enough to say how you feel in a way that isn't very original but has been shown to work.

Single Aquarius, It's easy to meet and talk about ideas. But when feelings get in the way, things get complicated. You can get an idyll this month, but only if you give yourself something.

Career

Is what you're being provided not what you want? It's the same for your company. The actors in your work world appear to be limited, uninteresting, and cautious. Even though this industry is a downer, it does have the advantage of assuring the necessities of existence. In addition, it provides a measure of safety. Consider the ramifications of your decision before making it on the spur of the moment.

This month is going to be a good one for your career. Despite the increased workload, the expected gains would be yours. On the other hand, work would be enjoyable because the atmosphere would be calm and free of anxiety.

Female coworkers or associates could greatly assist you and your career. Your employment prospects will improve as a result of this. Expect a lot more work-related travel in the near future. The best direction would be to go South. In general, it is a good month.

Finance

Financially, this area is stifling your progress. You must be frugal, set a spending limit, and adhere to it. You may initially feel offended by these restrictions, but they will prove to be quite advantageous in the long run.

According to the stars, this is an unlucky month for your finances. Writers, painters, sculptors, and other creative types should plan for an idle period because that is exactly what will happen.

According to horoscopes, this is a month in which your financial situation will be less than stellar. It is imperative that those in the creative fields, such as writers, painters, sculptors, and others, prepare for the possibility of a long and difficult dry spell.

In spite of the fact that some of the brightest minds surround you in the world, most of you will still struggle to attain your goals and fall short of them. Loan applications or proposals from banks or financial institutions are unlikely to succeed. Plans for growth or a new enterprise should be put on hold for the time being since the current climate does not favor such endeavors.

Health

A good month, when the stars are in your favor, and your health stays good. People prone to long-term conditions like rheumatism and complaints like too much gas in the digestive tract will feel much better. The body will use the food well, and all of the nutrients will be taken in.

You are doing the right things to get healthier. This month is a sign that your desire to be healthy and fit will lead you to an active lifestyle that will pay off. Over time, you'll notice changes in how your body looks and how strong you are. In general, you will see results from your hard work, and in this happy situation, you'll have a lot of chances to live a much fuller and better life. Not only in better shape physically but also in a much happier state of mind and heart.

Travel

The stars are in your favor this month, so you should get to go on a lot of fun trips and also make a lot of money. There is a good chance you will go abroad for work and do a great job of reaching your goals.

In any case, many of you would travel around the country for business. Again, there would be a good chance of success. The best direction would be to go South.

Insight from the stars

Don't run away from your feelings and try to get more involved. This won't make you less independent, but it will improve your relationships with other people. You should be proud of yourself because you have overcome every obstacle in your life.

September 2023

Horoscope

Jupiter and Uranus in Taurus are always in conflict, making it hard for you to move forward. When one problem is fixed, another one appears! Don't get down on yourself! Don't forget the little things. Keep making the changes that need to be made. Things will get better one by one as you do this. Venus in Leo, on the other hand, brings the worst problems.

The beauty of the world continues to stand in the way of your desires. You have a vivacious intellect. Your thoughts have an impact. Unfortunately, not everyone shares your beliefs, and you won't be able to sway those who do not share them by rebelling against them. Mars is in Libra this month, and it will force you to make compromises. You may think it's impossible initially, but you're more than competent.

Love

You are unpredictable, and that's usually what makes you so charming. This good trait has turned into a bad one with Venus in Leo. Mars in Libra will help you make the best of things this month. How? By being brave enough to use traditional methods to stir up emotions.

Criticism comes from how you feel and how you interact with others. You can set things up if you want to. It's time to tone down your love of freedom. Your partner will appreciate it.

For Single Aquarius, Venus complicates your life. On the other hand, Mars can help if you want it to. This month, be willing to give up your freedom. Try to make romantic moves. It may seem old-fashioned, but the results will blow your mind.

Career

This month is anything but easy. People with conservative ideas don't like what you have to say because they think it's too farfetched. People try to beat you because they don't want to lose their spot. Aquarius, you need to be more subtle! Don't make trouble for people who have been there a long time. You'll meet new people this way. It may not happen as quickly as you expect, but it will eventually.

The way the stars are aligned doesn't look good for your job prospects. Even if you worked very hard, you wouldn't get what you were hoping for. There are also signs of short-term travel. But this doesn't help you achieve your goals either, though you might be able to get some of what you want from a trip to the West.

Even so, you may be able to enjoy a pleasant working environment. This would still be a source of happiness. This month, you shouldn't count on your contacts to help you out much. Instead, it would be best if you relied on your skills to handle challenging situations.

Finance

From a financial point of view, this sector is still in a period of limits. When filling in the blanks, you must be careful about how much you spend. Don't be afraid. Everything is going to be fine.

According to the stars, there isn't much good news about your money this month. People who do business between states and other countries would have to deal with challenging situations. In fact, you would have to work very hard to get the results you want, and even then, you might not get very far.

It wouldn't be a good time to invest or start new businesses. These will probably get stuck. Furthermore, pending loan applications with banks or other financial institutions will have little chance of being accepted. This is not a good time for you, so it may be wise to keep a low profile until the bad times are gone.

Health

A good month when the stars are aligned to give you a lot of good health. Your body would get the most out of healthy food, which would give your mind and body a lot of strength and energy.

There are some reasons why you shouldn't push yourself too hard. But a reasonable schedule that doesn't put too much stress on you would be more than enough. You would stay active and full of energy throughout the month and be happy in your mind and heart.

Travel

This is a month in which you can expect to make a lot of money from your travels, as the stars are very good on this front. There is a good chance that some of you will have a successful trip abroad and do much more than meet your goals.

Artists, dancers, actors, and other people like them would travel to fun places, some of which might be completely new. You can even look forward to doing a lot of business travel within the country, which will also go very well. This month, the best direction is West.

Insight from the stars

Your success in love or business depends on your willingness to try new ways to deal with people. Try. You will be glad you did it. Be thankful for the good things in your life and give to those who don't have as much.

October 2023

Horoscope

Venus will leave Leo on the 9th, which is a good sign. But it's not just going to be a walk in the park. The differences between Jupiter and Uranus always stop your growth. But unfortunately, they are made worse by those that come from Scorpio. From the 13th, you'll have to talk to Mars, who will be in this sign by then.

At the end of the month, the Sun and Mercury will join it, and you'll have to deal with them. To be all or nothing is not the best approach. For some, this kind of stance is advantageous, but it also works against you in your case. Instead, take a cue from Mercury in Libra, who says you should always be diplomatic.

Love

Your loves have been made fun of by Venus's dissonances. If you agree, you can help fix what's broken. It's time to talk about how you feel and how you want to have a peaceful relationship. If someone says no, don't take it as an insult. Make your point with style.

Mercury in Libra helps you make things right with your partner. So now is the time to talk about love and the future you both want. You should know that you can make your union official, which will solve your problems.

Single Aquarius, Your loves are returning to normal after the Venusian dissonances threw them off. This month, Mercury puts you in touch with people who do everything they can to make you happy. If things don't improve, you should wait instead of getting angry.

Career

Be practical and Put your best foot forward if you want October to be a great month. Try, if you can, to accept these old-fashioned ideas even if they appear ancient to you. If you do this, you will be able to handle any problems that come your way. On your best days, you'll even outperform yourself! Soon, you'll be racking up the points and getting your hands on what you desire.

Your professional prospects aren't very good with how the stars are aligned this month. To put it another way, if you don't watch your step, you risk falling several rungs down the leadership ladder. Some of you may be inclined to break the law to make a fast buck.

This must not happen, or else your problems will never go away. The amount of work will also go up a lot. You have to be patient and deal with this. Your contacts won't be able to help you much, so you'll have to use all your resources to deal with the things that will happen this month.

Finance

In terms of money, it's not a good idea. Saturn puts you under many strict rules, so you can figure out what's most important.

Your financial future doesn't look very good based on what the stars tell you. Those who trade with other countries would be hurt and may have to go through a rough patch. In fact, you would have to work hard to achieve your goals, and even then, you probably wouldn't be very successful.

Also, it would not be a good time to invest in or start a new business. They might get stuck. And finally, any request for a loan or new money from a bank or other financial institution wouldn't have a good chance of being approved.

Health

A month in which you would have to pay a lot of attention to your health to make up for the lack of help from the heavens. Even if you eat well this month, your body might not be able to use much of it. There's no need to worry because this could be fixed with the right kind of medicine.

This is just a bad influence from the stars that won't last forever. With the right help, this could be fixed pretty quickly. This is a time during which you should be careful and take the proper steps to keep yourself from worrying.

Travel

This is a month in which you can expect a fair amount of pleasant travel that will also be good for you in most ways, as this is what the stars say will happen. Most of you would have to travel a lot for your jobs, which would help you achieve your goals. The best direction would be to go West.

Some of you would also travel abroad for business or official reasons, which would be just as successful. Artists, singers, actors, and others who work in the arts would benefit most from travelling.

Insight from the stars

Make real connections with others and don't move on to something or someone else when things get complicated. Your most important wish will come true if you do this. You should try to cut down on unplanned costs that strain your finances.

November 2023

Horoscope

You start the month with Taurus and Scorpio, which are at odds with each other. These energies stop you from moving forward and making your plans come true. Most likely, you are nervous! From the 9th, you can relax because the planets will have moved into friendly signs. Venus in Libra tells you to use your skills so that you don't have to go through events. Then, Mercury, Mars, and the sun, which all take turns in Sagittarius, give you back that optimism that helps you get past problems.

This month, you are wasting your time trying to change the minds of people who disagree with you. On the other hand, it will be more helpful and move your projects forward if you connect with people who agree with you.

Love

Being radical will make things hard for you. On the other hand, if you spend time and energy on your emotional life, it will change the way things go. So, talking about love and the future will help to mend the broken bonds. All of this might seem like nothing, but it's important to the people who care about you.

This month, you should put some of your projects on hold and spend more time with your partner. It might seem small, but it will give your relationship a boost.

Single Aquarius, You might meet that special someone through your friends, and things could quickly get serious. For this tiny miracle to happen, you need to change some of your ideas about life in a relationship.

Career

There are lots of problems in your work life up until and including the 24th. When you solve one problem, a new one comes up. Your patience will be tested this month. You won't be able to keep a smile on your face. Now is your chance to show what you can do, Aquarius. What? 'Or' How? By having patience, sticking with it, and a plan. Once you've done that, you'll be able to handle anything.

A month with a few good things to look forward to regarding your career. Even with a lot of hard work, it's unlikely that the expected gains will come true. However, work may still be fun because of the great working conditions.

During the month, contacts won't be beneficial. Because of this, it would be best to rely mostly on your own skills to get out of challenging situations. You wouldn't get what you expected from travel, but a trip to the North would be good for you. Overall, it was a month in which you have to be careful and work hard on your own.

Finance

When it comes to money, it's the same fight! So instead of thinking that life is out to get you, cut your spending, make a budget, and stick to it. Once you've done that, you'll be able to fix your accounts and keep them going.

A good month for your finances, during which you could make a lot of money, but not without any problems. The success of your projects, no matter what they are, would be boosted by your friendships with smart, spiritually-minded people. In fact, this would give your whole work life a satisfying level of culture and refinement.

You'd be able to achieve most of your goals and make the most money from them. Still, you'll likely run into problems along the way. There is also a chance of being late. But success is sure to happen. A good time to not only get a lot done but also to feel a lot of satisfaction.

Health

A month in which your health is good and you don't have much to worry about. Your body would get the most out of what you eat, so not only would it be healthy, but it would also look healthy. This would make you very busy and full of energy.

This would make for a pretty full life, with more and better things to enjoy. The only thing that stands out, and there is one, is the chance of an accident or a severe injury, which should be taken care of. But this is a long shot.

Travel

A month when you can expect to make a lot of money from your travels because the stars are aligned in your favor. There are signs that the way things are going will force you to travel a lot for your work. If you did these things, you would be successful. The North would be the best direction to go.

These are more signs that any trip you take abroad in the next month will also help you reach your goals. Those who have been thinking about taking such a trip should go now.

Insight from the stars

Don't do things either all or nothing, because that won't help you. Instead, try to find a middle ground and compromise, even if it seems pointless. Your career will progress because you work hard and don't give up.

December 2023

Horoscope

This month, Jupiter and Uranus are linked to Venus in Scorpio. Despite your best efforts, it feels as if your initiatives are running out of time. Do not be concerned about the obstacles that stand in your way. Instead, go where your heart leads you.

Mars is sending you good and lucky vibes all month long. Between 1st and 22nd, the sun does the same thing. Mercury acts on the first, and he comes back to help you on the 24th. In turn, these energies bring you together with people on the same wavelength as you. They do offer something different, but it is something that can be quickly and readily realized.

Love

Things tend to get stuck in this area. Why? Because Venus is in Scorpio, and this sign's way of seducing is hard for you to follow. Don't light the powder on fire if you don't want your love to turn into a war zone.

You feel like you have good luck. Sadly, this is not true when it comes to love. So, don't make your other half angry by living alone. Make an effort to arrive home on time and invest time and money in your family.

Single Aquarius, The problems with Venus won't make your life easier. A classic seduction is best if you don't want to get caught in anything terrible. The devil will not be tempted if you cross him. Venus enters Sagittarius on the 29th. It'll be easier this way.

Career

If you want to be successful, you can't be chained down. In this situation, you rebel against being stuck and having ideas already made for you. This month, a close friend or family member lets you escape the dreary surroundings for a while. Don't miss out on this fantastic opportunity! As a result, you will be able to do as you choose without fear of being held accountable.

This month, job prospects are not very good. You would have to work very hard for not much in return. Gains that were expected wouldn't happen; despite this, the working environment will likely remain pleasant and stress-free.

Also, travelling wouldn't bring you the benefits you'd hope for, though a trip to the South might give you some benefits. Having contacts wouldn't help, so it would be best to rely mostly on your skills to deal with challenging situations. And, given how things are going this month, this skill will help you in the end.

Finance

On the finance side, it's a happy time. Saturn rules this area, so you must be careful with your money. You will have a good holiday because of divine intervention.

Your money situation looks pretty good. There's a good likelihood that a favor done for you by an elderly friend would get you a considerable sum of money. You may reap additional benefits if you form a business or professional relationship with a woman. This has the potential to bring in a lot of money.

It would be a good time to start new businesses and invest. And those of you who have similar plans should get them moving. Also, there would be a good chance that banks and other financial institutions would approve any loan requests that were already in the works or any new proposals for new loans.

Health

This is a great month for your health. The stars are aligned to help you, so you don't have much to worry about. People who are prone to long-term conditions like rheumatism and digestive tract problems will feel better.

When your body absorbs all the nutrients from the food you eat, you will not only feel good about your health, but you will also look good. The powers of reproduction will also be at their best, making life a good time. Not only will you be very active and full of energy, but your mind will also be in good shape. A nice month that would require you to do very little work.

Travel

The stars don't look suitable for travel this month, so you shouldn't expect to get what you want out of it. People whose jobs or businesses require travel a lot may find themselves in an unenviable situation that doesn't live up to their hopes.

People in sales and marketing would do much worse, and even traveling South, which is the best direction, wouldn't help. Also, there is a good chance that business trips outside the country will not live up to expectations.

Insight from the stars

Don't try to find trouble. Instead, focus on what is going well and wait peacefully until Venus is fully on your side. As the year ends, you need to prepare for all the changes in your life during the Mercury retrograde dates in 2023.

PISCES 2023 HOROSCOPE

Overview Pisces 2023

Jupiter begins the year in the 2nd house of Aries for Pisces inhabitants, then moves to the 3rd house of Taurus in May. This brings you wonderful financial resources and family well-being for the year's first three months. The star in May would then impact your short-term travel plans and your relationship with your siblings. Saturn, the renowned disciplinarian, will transit your 12th house for the first quarter of this year before moving to your Ascendant house.

Your overseas travels and spiritual pursuits will likely be significantly hampered. As you return to your home base, the emphasis will be on your overall well-being and health, and Pisceans will likely experience health issues for the next three months.

Regarding the outer planets, Uranus will transit Taurus' 3rd house in 2023, while Neptune will transit your Ascendant all year. Pluto begins the year in your 11th house of Capricorn and then moves to your 12th house of Aquarius later in May-June.

With such a flurry of activity in the zodiac sky, your life is bound to be exciting in the coming year.

Venus, the planet of love, will ensure that your love and marriage paths are unobstructed in the coming year. Even long-distance partnerships would benefit you these days. There would be no flirting or infidelity on the part of the Pisceans, and you would be continuously linked up with a companion. After several difficult times, you will reclaim your partner's love and confidence. Mars also ensures that your love life or marriage is peaceful and without incident.

Pisces folks are expected to do well in their careers in the coming year. Because Jupiter is Aspecting your 7th house, you will be more compatible at work. This year will bring you success in all of your professional endeavors. Your income flow would improve, and you would have more financial options owing to your side hustles.

2023 is not going to be a fantastic year for Piscean people's health. Simply because the planets are not very well aligned and Jupiter would occasionally bring health problems for Pisces, especially in the second half of the year. Saturn in your Ascendant house beyond the first quarter of the year might exacerbate your health issues. Pisceans are more likely to get regular headaches or migraines, and some of you may contract infectious infections throughout the year. Take precautions and care for your overall health and well-being.

Pisceans' financial situation will improve a bit this year. You would succeed in business and services, bringing in a steady income stream. Despite the inflow, savings would be a significant hurdle, with undesired expenditure coming in from all directions. Rahu, which is the Moon's node in your financial house, will cause you to have a lot of money problems this year.

Your fourth house of Gemini has no major planetary transits this year; thus, family life will be mediocre. Saturn and Jupiter would ensure peace and harmony in your world. Your ideas about family and its evolution are currently taking shape. Your family grows as new members join you through marriage or birth. Throughout the year, you should maintain a balance between your personal and professional standing. Saturn brings stability and maturity to your family life and takes care of the fundamental necessities. And Jupiter will bestow upon you ease and all the conveniences of life.

Pisces people have a lot of long-distance travel planned for them this year. Foreign travel would benefit you by expanding your knowledge and making money. Jupiter promotes some travel beyond the first quarter of the year for enjoyment, adventure, and pleasure. However, Pisceans are advised to use caution when travelling during the period, as health concerns and accidents may emerge. Also, exercise caution while making financial arrangements for your travel plans.

The beginning of the year would be ideal for performing religious acts. You'd be expanding your spiritual knowledge this year with Jupiter in your 9th house. For the time being, you will be more spiritually inclined and dedicated to spiritual work. Participate in social and charitable activities to strengthen your confidence in people. Around the end of the year, certain Pisceans may travel on pilgrimages to seek the blessings of sages or saints.

The coming year may appear tough and tight, but if you just go with the flow, life will be easier and happier. You will be blessed pleasantly. Appreciate the good things, be thankful, and share them with others in need. Do whatever provides you with peace and harmony in various facets of your life. Spread joy, perform one good deed per day, and be safe.

January 2023

Horoscope

You evolve in a relationship setting that makes you feel safe and secure. Capricorn's energies help you avoid nasty surprises and bring you the right people. When problems come out of the blue, they bring you the solution. With the weather being so nice, you have every chance of getting what you want. But in the long run, all this work may seem like a waste of time. You feel like you're spinning your wheels.

Mars forces you to leave your comfort zone when it is in Gemini. You seem adorable in his eyes. He makes you promises, but you can't be sure he'll keep them. Ask for advice from someone you can trust and who is competent before making a decision that could later be embarrassing.

Love

Your love is on hold. You have a hard time putting your feelings into words, which makes it seem like you don't care about your loved ones. This month, you'll know where you are thanks to Venus passing through your zodiac sign on the 28th. It appears that your love life is off to a good start and heading in the right direction.

There isn't much excitement going on this month. You're being compelled to take stock of your sentiments and your identity. What you want and don't want is crystal clear by the end of the month.

Single Pisces, You'll feel like time is going by slowly because your love won't be as bright until the 28th. From this date on, the impossible can happen. Someone you know finally tells you what they care about and want to do.

Career

Everything is going according to plan. The only thing left to do is to do what you're already good at: daily maintenance. In spite of this, don't rest on your laurels. Keep your guard up, and don't put your faith in anyone who promises you anything. This month, Pisces, dare to say no with all your might! You won't become a brutal person, but you will have a keen sense of judgement.

During the month, job prospects are not very good. You would have to work very hard for not much in return. Gains that were expected wouldn't happen, but the work environment might stay good and stress-free.

Also, travelling wouldn't bring you the benefits you'd hope for, though a trip to the South might give you some benefits. Having contacts wouldn't help, so it would be best to rely mostly on your skills to deal with challenging situations. And, given how things are going this month, this skill will help you in the end.

Finance

On the astrological front, Jupiter guards this industry. Even though you don't always get money, your financial situation is improving.

Your financial situation is looking up this month. There is a good probability that an elderly friend could provide a significant benefit to you. A business alliance or professional affiliation with a woman will likely bring you even more success. This has the potential to bring in a lot of money.

It would be an excellent time to start new businesses and invest. It's time for those with such intentions to put them into action. Also, there would be a good chance that banks and other financial institutions would approve any loan requests already in the works or any new proposals for new loans.

Health

This is an excellent month for your health. The stars are aligned in your favor, so you don't have much to worry about. Even people prone to long-term conditions like rheumatism and digestive tract problems will feel better.

When your body absorbs all the nutrients from the food you eat, you will feel good about your health and look good. The powers of reproduction will also be at their best, making life a good time. Not only will you be very active and full of energy, but your mind will also be in good shape. A nice month that would require you to do very little work.

Travel

The stars don't look good for travel this month, so you shouldn't expect to get what you want. People whose jobs or businesses require travel a lot may find themselves in an unenviable situation that doesn't live up to their hopes.

People in sales and marketing would do much worse, and even facing South, which is usually the best direction, wouldn't help. Also, there is a good chance that business trips outside the country will not live up to expectations.

Insight from the stars

Keep your promises and kind words to yourself this month. Don't be fooled by outward appearances. This will keep you from making unrealistic plans that jeopardize your long-term success. Your financial situation will be better this year than the previous year.

February 2023

Horoscope

Pisces, Capricorn, and Taurus sign energies promise you their goodwill protection. In order to help you progress, these pragmatic energies create favorable conditions. This month, you're living in an astrological environment that supports the completion of your goals. The appropriate individuals are drawn to you at the right time because of your personality. In an ideal world, everything works out perfectly.

The New Moon in your zodiac sign on the 20th will reawaken your senses. It gives you brilliant ideas. You'll still have to deal with Mars' dissonances in Gemini, though, because they're taking on a life of their own this month. To keep what you've worked for, you need to be innovative and refuse to give in to temptation.

Love

When Venus is in your sign, your world gets back on track. Resumption of pleasant and productive discussions. Love is restored to your relationship with understanding and generosity. Watch out for promises that come from outside of your comfort zone, though. Nothing about them implies that they'll be trusted or appreciated.

When you're in a relationship, it's hard to know what to expect. The mood is tense and distant at times. Once again, Earthly energies force you to take stock to understand where you are in relation to the larger picture.

Single Pisces, you attract attention with your seductive powers. Your charisma sways hearts. If you want a happy, healthy relationship, give more weight to the person who cares about you and ignore the person who makes promises.

Career

People who know your abilities and have complete faith in you are looking out for this area and its growth. Life has suddenly become a lot easier. You take your work seriously and rely on your gut instincts to make decisions. Unfortunately, the pleasant weather here won't protect you from the tiny inconveniences the outside world offers. When a problem emerges, Pisces, don't worry about it. Everything will be OK if you just speak what's on your mind.

According to the horoscope, your professional prospects look bleak this month. You'd have to put in a lot more effort for a lot less money if you increased your workload. The situation would be somewhat made up for by a pleasant and stress-free place to work. But not any more than that.

You wouldn't get the benefits you were hoping for from travel, but a trip to the West would bring you some benefits. Not enough to make up for everything, it needs to be said. The people you know won't be much help, making a difficult situation even harder. Also, don't do anything illegal because that could worsen your problems.

Finance

On the money side, if you come across a dead end, don't worry. It won't last long. Based on their predictions, the stars don't look good for your money this month. You might have a mean streak and be persuaded to take advantage of your employees, subordinates, or just people lower on the social ladder for your own gain. Your efforts to do these things would be met with strong opposition, which could put you in a terrible situation.

So, use a firm hand to stop these behaviors. Also, people who work in international trade could have a rough time. In fact, most of you would have to work very hard to reach your goals, and even then, you might not get very far. A bad spell for you, during which it wouldn't be a good time to invest or start something new.

Health

This month, the stars are in your favor regarding your health, so you have nothing to worry about. Your body would get the most out of the food you eat, which could show in your glowing health. Your ability to reproduce would also be at its best.

Not only will you be very busy all month, but you'll also be in such good shape that your life will be much richer and fuller in every way. There is a chance that you will work too hard. But you can get around this by making a smart plan that doesn't put too much stress on you. Overall, it's a good month that lets you enjoy life.

Travel

The stars don't look good for you on this score this month, so there is a huge possibility of disappointment coming from your travels. People who work in marketing or sales and travel a lot as part of their job or business would have a hard time. Even trips in the best direction, which is West, might not be enough to fix the situation.

A trip abroad would not be a good idea the way things are going. In fact, a trip like this could sometimes make your losses much worse. Also, travelling this month wouldn't be near as fun as it usually is. You also wouldn't get any new opportunities from travelling.

Insight from the stars

Decision-making could be on the cards for you this month. Don't be swayed by the beautiful promises of others. Pay attention to your gut instincts because they are your most reliable compass. A strong sense of romance permeates the air. Spending time with your lover will be enjoyable for both of you. Knowing that you have a lot of love in your life is the best feeling in the world.

March 2023

Horoscope

Saturn is moving into your zodiac sign this month, which is a significant event. This is it if you're looking for an austere but motivating energy. Capricorn and Taurus energies are associated with this; therefore, you'll gain knowledge, experience, and abilities as a result of it. The depth of your relationships with others will increase. Over time, they will become noticeable.

Saturn will also assist you in your endeavor by ensuring you only keep people who will contribute to your growth. This month, Mercury will be in your sign, and he will advise you to take a step back and evaluate the situation before making a decision. When the Full Moon in Virgo appears on the 7th, it's an excellent time to sit back and watch before taking action.

Love

Planets in friendly signs help you take care of this area in a practical way. You adjust to new situations and people while subtly moving away from what doesn't work for you. From the 17th, Venus brings you together with people who care about the same things you do.

Mars in Gemini is a source of discord, and the Full Moon on the 7th makes it even worse. Your relationship goes through a rough patch that can last for a long time. Encourage your partner to take a break from the things that annoy them to avoid these problems.

Single Pisces, Mars is in Gemini, which makes it hard for you to get along with the people you love. Encounters fade away into the universe. On the 17th, the weather improves, and on the 26th, Mars in Cancer confirms this.

Career

When Saturn moves into your sign, it shows how experienced you are and makes you more mature. The star of wisdom makes you stop and think about what is really important. Your goals change over time. They get right to the point. But this transfer can change the way you feel. So, don't worry too much if you feel a little down this month. Don't push yourself more than you need to because it won't help your career.

The way the stars are aligned in front of you doesn't look good for your career. There would be a lot of short trips that wouldn't bring the expected benefits. On the other hand, a trip to the North would be helpful. During this time, it's not likely that people you know will be able to help you much.

So, it would be a good idea to trust in your ability to solve problems. But there are reasons to think that the working conditions and atmosphere would stay pretty good. This would be a big reason to be happy. Overall, it is a month when you must be careful with several sensitive matters.

Finance

When it comes to money, this area is still driven by Jupiter. Money doesn't always come in. In this situation, you must be very careful with your budget, especially around the 7th.

Even though you'll be hanging out with many bright and spiritually gifted people this month, it won't be good for your finances. There is a good chance that most of you will have to work hard to achieve your goals, and even then, you might not get very far.

The climate would also not be suitable for making investments or starting new businesses. They might get stuck. Also, banks or other financial institutions would unlikely approve any pending loan applications or requests for further advances. Also, people who do business overseas would probably have to deal with adversity.

Health

This month, the stars don't look too good for your health, so you'll have to pay much more attention to your well-being. Even if you eat a healthy diet, it's possible that your body won't be able to do much with it.

In other words, your daily meals would be devoid of nourishment, and you'd show signs of malnutrition similar to starvation. This should not be a reason for concern but rather a wake-up call to focus on corrective actions. These could have a significant impact on your health if properly implemented. You can get through this hard time if you take care of yourself.

Travel

Since the stars are in a good mood to bless you this month, you'll reap many benefits from traveling. Traveling for business or pleasure is an option open to everyone, not just those who are accustomed to frequent travel as part of their job duties. You may also be presented with new possibilities as a result of this.

There are strong indications that most of the travel will be by train or road, with a small amount of air travel. The North would be the best direction to travel in. Those that travel overseas are nearly assured of having a wonderful experience. In fact, this is an excellent time to do so.

Insight from the stars

As time passes, planets in friendly signs help you feel like you belong in your universe again. What's going on with your friends? It's perfectly natural. Keep your distance, and don't try to make up ground. Some of your friends will betray you, so you should be careful about who you let into your circle of friends.

April 2023

Horoscope

As a result of the influences originating from Pisces and Taurus, you feel like you are being thrust into the real world. As they continue to sort out your relationships, they strengthen the ones that had been loose. You'll be surrounded by comforting and soothing energy when you're with folks you can trust. They are the ideal people to help you achieve your goals. You make the appropriate decisions based on their advice and rationale.

As a result, Mars in Cancer helps you to focus on what you enjoy and what is best for your life. Venus in Gemini between the 12th and the 30th is the only issue. This negative impact can be lessened if you accept the idea that you have the choice to decline anything that does not suit your preferences.

Love

Your relationships grow in a calm and stable environment due to the good vibes of Venus and Mars. You find peace that brings out the best in you. Things get worse after the 12th. Use your courage to say no to things that bother you.

Everything about your relationship is fine until the 11th. Then things get tricky! This month, Mercury supports in-depth discussions. It aids you in dealing with a difficult situation and finding a lasting solution.

Single Pisces, planets in friendly signs put you in touch with people who are attracted to your charm. Even a bad genius could try their luck, though. If you talk about important things, they'll reveal their true motives and make the right choice.

Career

As time passes, this area gets to a speed where it can keep going. There is success. You work very hard at what you do. Everything is fine, but you don't seem very motivated. Have you taken a look at what you do? Perhaps. In the meantime, there would be a lot of hard work, but the benefits wouldn't match the work. Also, travel is mentioned, but again, this wouldn't live up to expectations in a meaningful way.

Contacts won't help you much either during this time, though some female coworkers or friends will try to promote your professional achievements. It would be better to rely mostly on your skills and hard work. A month where you'd have to work hard to keep going.

Finance

On the money side of things, things are getting better. There is money coming in. You get many rewards for all your work. Before you spend money without thinking, look at how much you have and the level of comfort it provides.

But even if you worked very hard, the way things are now, you wouldn't get the results you expected or planned for. There are also no promising signs of starting an expansion or a new business.

If you want a loan from a bank or other financial institution, your project is likely to move slowly and get in the way. There is also a risk that people doing business with people outside your country or with a different legal status will encounter difficulties and even lose money.

Health

It will be a good month in which you will be healthy and thrive from the food you eat. This means that you are in good health and your body can use the food you eat. Any sudden, severe illness should be treated right away.

If you treat these symptoms as soon as you notice them, you can be sure that nothing terrible will happen. If you were to test your reproductive ability, you would be pleased to find that it is way above average. A good month that doesn't need much of your attention.

Travel

Since the stars aren't aligned in a good way, this is not a good month for making money from travel. You could get hurt or have some other physical trouble during your travels. Because of this, you should be careful.

Also, your job or business would require you to travel for a certain amount of time this month. This would not work out very well, though. Even trips to the best direction, the West, would not help. Some of you might go on a trip outside the country, which wouldn't help you achieve your goals.

Insight from the stars

Stability is gained when you surround yourself with people who are serious about their work. Frivolous people cause you to fall down a steep hill. You won't get lost if your conversations have substance. You will meet new people and have a beneficial impact on everyone's life.

May 2023

Horoscope

Reconnecting with your loved ones is made possible by Taurus and Cancer's soothing and supportive energies. Some of the people who have been away may return to you. Your relationships are trustworthy because you chose them yourself.

When Jupiter moves into Taurus on the 17th, the ideas driving your conversations for the past few weeks will be more stable. He hopes that you will spend more time studying them. He encourages you to accept them if you're on board. With the help of the lucky star and evolution, you can improve your life by adding more comfort and safety. Venus and the Sun in Gemini cast the only shadows on the board, but only briefly. The only way to permanently eliminate it is to be adamant about it.

Love

Venus in Gemini stirs up trouble until the 7th. The energies of Taurus and Cancer make it easy for you to choose peace and safety. The Sun in Gemini will start to question this choice on the 22nd unless you stop listening to the siren song.

Your relationship finds its way and becomes more real. You manage to get your point across and take charge of the situation again. But until the 7th and after the 22nd, you'll have to be disciplined with yourself if you don't want things to get out of hand.

Single Pisces, You are surrounded by people who want to help you, but a lousy person keeps trying to throw you off. Don't move away from your positions if you want to get rid of them.

Career

If your motivation has been low, a smile should help. This month's discussions are centered on your personal and professional growth.

Some people extol the virtues of your abilities. The others want to know what you can do. If you think things aren't going well, you should wait. As time passes, your partners will be clearer about what they want. If someone makes you an exciting offer, don't look any further, Pisces. Think about it carefully and choose wisely.

There would be a lot of travel, but it wouldn't go as planned, though a trip to the South might be helpful. People you know wouldn't be as beneficial as usual either. Because of this, you should rely mostly on your skills and resources. Persistent caution in dealing with difficult situations is called for throughout this month.

Finance

When it comes to money, this sector is doing exceptionally well, which shows how hard you have worked to get there.

Since the stars are in your favor, you should do very well financially this month. People who do business with other countries or across state lines would do very well and gain a lot. Most of you would be able to get the planned gains from your current operations during this time.

Also, this would be a good situation for people who want to grow their businesses or start new ones. Those with loan requests pending with any bank or financial institution will obtain the required loans. It's important to remember that working with women in business or the workplace would be beneficial.

Health

A month in which you're almost sure to be in good health. People prone to long-term problems like rheumatism and too much gas in the digestive tract will feel much better. They only need to use the usual amount of care to get relief from their illnesses.

The food you eat will feed your body and keep you in great shape. You will have above-average reproductive vitality, giving you a healthy mind and body. There are a few reasons to take a sore throat seriously if you have one. The rest should go well.

Travel

The signs from the stars make it clear that there isn't much chance of making money. People whose jobs or businesses take them around a lot will not get much out of the exercise. Even for the rest of you, your business trips wouldn't bring in much money. Even going in the best direction, which is South, would not change the situation.

You could worsen your problems by going on expensive trips abroad that would not help you achieve your goals. This could make things even worse for you. Under these circumstances, you should keep your plans as simple as possible.

Insight from the stars

The quality of your life is steadily improving, but nasty people refuse to change. You can keep them out of your sphere of influence by acting cold and distant. Everything in your life has a purpose, and you must accept this. Instead of doubting everything, have faith in the process.

June 2023

Horoscope

The lucky placement of Jupiter in Taurus makes it easier for you to achieve your goals, which were previously limited by strict rules. This comfort is shown by living a less austere way of life. The presence of Uranus in your chart means that blessings from the sky will also help your daily life.

This month, you'll get great rewards for all your hard work. Slowly but surely, you find the balance you need. Also, how people act and feel toward you might be a pleasant surprise. Still, the dissonances that come from Gemini can ruin this friendly atmosphere. You can argue to make them happy, but it will work better to stay in your world and wait for it to pass.

Love

During this month, Venus has little effect on your life. She, on the other hand, has an effect on others. All of a sudden, the roles have been switched. Others will use their inventiveness to their advantage to entice or satisfy you. So you don't have to do anything but accept the gifts and words of love that are meant for you.

Even though things are looking better by the day, an overflow is still possible. If you want harmony in your life this month, don't budge from your principles. Everything returns to normal at the end of the month.

Single Pisces, Your admirers use various creative methods to entice you. If you had doubts about your ability to seduce, they would be gone this month. You decide what to do next!

Career

Your work life gets easier and more comfortable, and you may get more responsibilities. At the time, you can tell you won't be able to do it or that the weight is too much for your small shoulders. Pisces now is not the time to talk badly about your skills and strengths. Instead, tell yourself repeatedly that you are where you should be and that everything is fine.

Even if you worked really hard, you're unlikely to get anywhere near the goals you set out to achieve. The way things are going, this just isn't going to happen.

Travel also wouldn't give you what you were hoping for, but a trip to the West might bring you some luck. There are also reasons to think having contacts won't help you much. So, it would be best to rely on your skills and hard work. Not a good time and you should only get through it if you know how to handle difficult situations well.

Finance

On the money side, don't let this part of your life run you. Instead of giving this job to someone else, keep a close eye on it.

The signs from the stars don't give you much reason to be optimistic about your money this month. You might find that you're working hard to achieve your goals, but you're not getting anywhere because of the bad things that keep happening. On top of that, the environment would not be favorable for expanding operations or starting new businesses.

People who work in the arts, like painters, writers, sculptors, and so on, should be prepared for a particularly tough time. It's preferable to keep a low profile for the time being until the bad times are past.

Health

The way the stars are aligned this month is a clear blessing for your health. In this case, you have nothing to worry about. In fact, your body will get the most out of the food you eat, putting you in the best shape possible. This would mean having a healthy body and mind. You'd be able to maintain a high level of physical and mental activity.

And those who like to judge how well they reproduce will be pleased to find that they are much better than average. Any kind of infection in the chest or lungs must be treated immediately. If this is done, there is no danger or reason to worry. If you didn't do this, your problems would get much worse. Those are little things that you should not ignore.

Travel

This month, you should try to travel as little as possible since doing so won't get you what you want and may even worsen things. There are signs that people whose jobs or businesses require them to travel a lot will be disappointed.

Even trips to the best direction, the West, wouldn't help. People who trade with other countries or have any kind of business with other countries may find, much to their dismay, that their trips abroad turn out to be useless.

Insight from the stars

Putting on an air of being distant keeps intruders away and encourages others to show how honest they are. Keep going in this direction. It will help you find the balance you want. You will finally be happy with the results of your investments last year.

July 2023

Horoscope

Your group is like a close guard who cheers you on when you need it. They help you make good decisions by giving you good advice. So, you walk in a planned and organized way toward a comfortable success. Your plans for reaching your goals are clear. Jupiter gives you the opportunity to accomplish your goals. Saturn doesn't really cause too many problems.

However, when Mars moves into Virgo, it can be more challenging to deal with. Be careful of how you act to avoid making trouble for yourself. Starting on the 11th, Mars will test your ability to stick to a plan. Before you start, use your past experience. Take some time to think about what you're being given, even if it seems boring.

Love

You're nice, but you don't move forward. You watch what happens and how people react. This month, the other people in your life will have to work harder than usual to win your heart. Some will go all out in their declarations of love, while others will do everything they can.

There's a lot of interest now that Mars is in Virgo. You may feel pressure from your partner to make a commitment, and your aloof demeanor could be a reason for their mistrust. Your best friend now is resistance.

Single Pisces, It's all because of your efforts! It brings you into contact with people who can entice you in different ways. This month, passion comes to you without you trying.

Career

You've been moving forward without any trouble for a few weeks. You have it easy in every way! If something goes wrong, you know what to do. From the 11th, you should be careful about how you act. Take the time to think about what to do, especially if someone from your past makes you an offer. Think about what you've done and what you've accomplished since this time. If you do this, you'll use the best attitude that won't make anyone unhappy.

Despite your efforts, it does not appear that you will achieve your objectives. There would be risks involved in some of your plans and efforts. Under these conditions, avoiding taking any kind of risk would be best.

There is also a good amount of travel shown. But again, you wouldn't get the gains you were hoping for. Even so, you might be able to get something out of a trip to the North. A month that doesn't look good for your career.

Finance

From a financial point of view, this sector works like a charm because your activities make a lot of money.

This month, businesses and companies that deal with other countries or associations between states will do very well. In fact, most of you could be working on new business deals, proposals, and financial contracts that would benefit you.

Also, the climate would be good for investing and starting new businesses. So, if you have plans like this, you should move them forward. Partnerships and professional groups also tend to cause less trouble.

Health

A great month when the stars are aligned to give you good health. You will not only stay healthy, but you will also look great because your body is getting the most out of what you eat. This is the way things should be in a good month.

Not only will you be active and full of energy throughout the month, but those who are proud of their reproductive abilities will be pleasantly surprised to find that they are, if anything, above average. This could improve your physical, emotional, and mental well-being, putting you in a good mood. The stars want you to be happy throughout this month.

Travel

A month when you won't make much money from travelling because the stars are all against you getting this blessing. Those who travel a lot for business or official work would fall into this category. At the end of the month, these people may not have much to show for their travels.

Even if things were normal, business travel wouldn't be as profitable as it would be in a typical month. Even going in the most helpful direction, which is North, wouldn't have the usual effect. Artists, writers, singers, and people like them would find their travels mostly empty and unproductive.

Insight from the stars

Do not allow anything to derail your progress; instead, maintain your current speed and rhythm. You will be ecstatic when you see the results of your hard work pay off. In everything you do, rely on your intuition. Consider the consequences of your actions before taking action.

August 2023

Horoscope

In a relaxed setting, you can progress at your own pace. Continued support from Uranus and Jupiter will help you to grow and expand while protecting your successes. Opportunities will present themselves, and you should take advantage of them because they will have no consequences. Saturn, on the other hand, provides you with the time you need to accomplish your goals.

On the other hand, Mars and Mercury in Virgo can make you more upset than you should be. Be careful of too much discouragement and running away at the wrong time. Find the right balance for this to work out well for you. Be careful not to overestimate your abilities, as they aren't limitless. Take a break if things get too tense. Also, stay away from the heated discussions that are sure to ensue.

Love

Your attitude seems a little far away, and you're not sure you want to commit. This can make people react in unexpected ways and start heated conversations. But you can stay away from them. How? By focusing on the good things in life instead of the bad, you can help each other.

Criticism comes from everywhere. A contentious subject isn't going to get your attention, sadly. By the end of the month, even the tensest situations will have calmed down considerably. As a result, you'll be in a better position to negotiate and come to an agreement with your spouse.

Single Pisces, You will probably meet people who want to help this month. Before you start, think about whether you also want a serious relationship. This will keep you from making a mistake that will make you look bad.

Career

Helpful influxes keep this sector going. You don't have to worry. On the other side, you need to be cautious about your own reactions and decisions. This month, you may be influenced by situations beyond your control to make unwise decisions. To avoid making a bad decision, you need to step aside from the opinions of others. Trust your intuition and use your experience.

If you put in the time and effort, you won't be able to attain the goals you set out to accomplish. This would have a depressing effect on you.

The stars say that traveling this month is for business or service. But again, the benefits that were hoped for might not happen. In general, having contacts would also be very useful. Although, it would be best to depend mostly on your skills and hard work. Overall, it is a month, which doesn't look good for your job prospects.

Finance

When it comes to money, it's the same fight! The only taste you should follow is your own, not the likes of others. You'll be more likely to purchase items that meet your tastes and preferences if you follow this strategy rather than the opposite.

The stars have nothing outstanding to say about your money situation this month. Almost every dispute or lawsuit you might be involved in would go against you. Try to get a decision put off until a later, better time.

People who do business with the government would have to go through a rough patch, as would those who do business with other countries or between states. In short, you would have to work hard and struggle to achieve the planned goals, and even if you did your best, you wouldn't have much success. There isn't much hope for pending loan applications or steps for new advances from banks and financial institutions.

Health

A month in which you will have to take extra care of your health to make up for the lack of blessings from the heavens. You could get sudden, severe illnesses, which would be scary. Aside from this, there may be times when your body seems to get no benefit from eating healthy food.

This wouldn't be too bad by itself and would only last for a short time. Don't worry; try to find ways to improve things, which is possible. A rough patch, for sure, but one that can be worked through with a bit of extra care and won't have any long-term effects.

Travel

During the month, you won't be able to get the usual benefits from travelling because the stars don't look good. If your job or business requires you to travel a lot, this may not amount to much this month.

Even if you didn't have to work, most travel during this time wouldn't be enjoyable or bring you any significant gains. In some situations, it could even make things worse. This would be true even for trips to the West, which is the best direction. Some of you would lose a lot more money if you went on a business trip overseas.

Insight from the stars

It's possible that your peace of mind could be in jeopardy. You're free to keep it, though. How? By coming up with a compromise that makes everyone happy and keeps your freedom. You'll find yourself apologizing to those you've harmed and pleading for forgiveness. Moving on with your life without remorse is possible if you make atonement.

September 2023

Horoscope

You've been given the opportunity to learn and grow in an environment that is ideal for your development. But you'll have to deal with Mercury and the Sun in Virgo's dissonances.

Don't try to get away when things get hard. Don't base your decisions on what other people say. Don't think that bad things just happen to you. Instead, take the time to figure out what's going on. Think about it until you know what it means. It might seem like a lot of work, but if you do it, you'll find that you're much more capable than you think.

The key to your success this month is articulating your goals and aspirations to people in a straightforward manner.

Love

Commitment gives life to your thoughts and the thoughts of others. Your friends and family may grow impatient while they wait for you. Your gentle words or gestures would be much appreciated! You might think that all of this is unimportant, but it is for the average person.

Don't leave your partner's questions unanswered. This month, grab your courage with both hands and find a way to say what you're feeling. Why? Because it will keep you from being all by yourself.

Single Pisces, You've got someone about to do something under your spell. At the same time, another person you admire is on the lookout for a tranquil getaway. Instead of avoiding these two people, consider what you actually want in life.

Career

Jupiter's presence in Taurus continues to have a positive and calming effect on this area. It's all good. However, Mercury in Virgo, which is also retrograde until the 15th, will wreak havoc on your plans. Pisces, your strategy will be thwarted by finicky brains. On the worst days, there are a lot of critics. If you think about this, especially around the 15th, you will make the wrong choice. Wait until the end of the month instead.

To succeed, you should rely solely on your abilities and efforts. This would be even more important if the course of events did not favor the achievement of your objectives.

.

Finance

If you want to buy something, don't worry about what other people like. According to the stars, this is an unlucky month for your finances. Writers, painters, sculptors, and other creative types should plan for a very slow period because that is what will happen.

Despite being friends with some intelligent, bright individuals, you will struggle to achieve your goals, and even if you do, you won't have much success. Loan applications or proposals from banks or other financial institutions are unlikely to succeed. " Plans for growth or a new enterprise should be put on hold for the time being since the current climate does not favor such endeavors."

Health

A good month, when the stars are in your favor, and your health stays good. People prone to long-term conditions like rheumatism and complaints like too much gas in the digestive tract will feel much better. The body will use the food well, and all of the nutrients will be taken in.

In this happy situation, you'll have a lot of chances to live a much fuller and better life. Not only in better shape physically but also in a much happier state of mind and heart.

Travel

The stars are not aligned in a way that makes this a good month for travel. Artists, actors, poets, and others in the same line of work would find that their trips to do their jobs don't lead anywhere.

People whose jobs or businesses require them to travel a lot may also be disappointed because they may not be able to do as well as they should. People who work in sales and marketing may feel this hurts the most. There are also signs that a trip to another country during this time would be just as useless.

Insight from the stars

You have the option to remove yourself from situations or people. But only if it's to take stock and lead to a positive outcome. Pisces in business, you keep thinking about growing your businesses. It's a fantastic idea to grow your business, but you must be willing to put in the effort.

October 2023

Horoscope

You've been living for a while in a safe world that keeps your knowledge and unique personality safe. But you may feel like your life is being trampled on the spot. You might feel kind of bored as it can creep up on you in various ways.

Mars in Scorpio, which starts on the 13th, allows you to push the limits of what is possible. He tells you to use your skills and do something that will help you grow personally and financially. Due to the dissonances caused by Venus in Virgo, however, you might hesitate or turn down these options.

If you don't want to do anything you'll regret, you should wait until Mercury leaves Scorpio on the 23rd. So be patient if you don't want to make a mistake. In addition to your preferences, it will allow you to make a decision based on the preferences of others.

Love

Your family or spouse isn't sure if they can trust you to stick with something. This month, it's how you make them feel that hurts them. You can only tell them what they want to hear until the 22nd. But then you say something honest that gets things back on track.

You can only keep the peace if you're willing to make some sacrifices. Unfortunately, your partner is still unconvinced about your plans for the future of your relationship. Mercury helps you put all your cards on the table at the end of the month.

Single Pisces, People who want to settle down and people who want to try new things are both drawn to you. So, you stay away and keep hoping to find the right person. This little miracle could happen this month.

Career

The job market in this area is thriving. Sadly, Virgo's dissonances disrupt this pleasant and beneficial atmosphere. Avoid listening to others' comments if you're interested in an offer that's been made to you by someone else. Reconnect with your famous intuition and trust it. Wait until the 23rd if you're not sure. In Scorpio, you'll know exactly what to do and will make your decision without regret or guilt.

It's hard to say that you'll be lucky this month because you'll have to work hard for all the good things that will happen. Relax and enjoy the positive energy. Most of the good things that will happen at work will call for a party. So, if you're interested in your career, this is something you'd love to see. If you receive job offers, promotions, or see a rise in your business income, you may be confident that you will be able to meet your financial responsibilities.

Finance

Make your own decisions when it comes to money, and do not rely on other people's recommendations. You'll make a lot of money, but you'll have to save for the bad days. You aren't in a position to splurge on frivolous or pointless purchases at the moment.

Being thrifty will be a huge asset for you. You should only buy the things you absolutely need, just like a mother would. At this time, your success will not be tied to money. You'll get favors, but they'll be based more on relationships and sentiments than anything else.

Health

The stars are shining brightly on your health this month, so take advantage. Your body and mind would profit significantly from a diet rich in vitamins and minerals, as your system would be able to utilize these nutrients to their maximum potential. In fact, even the finest of your, mental, physical, and creative powers would remain intact.

However, there are some reasons why you shouldn't push yourself too hard. A reasonable schedule that doesn't put too much stress on you would be more than enough. A positive outlook and feeling upbeat would keep you physically active and energized throughout the month.

Travel

During this month, the wisest among you can drastically cut back on your travel plans to avoid the harmful effects of the stars, which will keep you from making big money through travel. People who have to travel a lot for work or business may be the ones who suffer the most.

But it's comforting to know that these things will lead to better times. Artists, singers, dancers, and others like them may not get the usual benefits from their travels, either. Exporters and others who work with countries outside of the U.S. should also try to avoid going abroad as much as possible since they might not get much out of it.

Insight from the stars

Making compromises may alleviate some of your frustration, but it does little to motivate you. If you want to progress, seize the moment while it is still in front of you. You'll finally be able to appreciate all of your hard work. You've waited long enough, and now amazing things are about to come your way.

November 2023

Horoscope

This month, the Scorpion energies will keep pushing you to go even further. With the help of planets in the signs of Taurus and Capricorn, you can pull off this small miracle. Unfortunately, the dissonances caused by the planets' moving through Sagittarius will put up barriers you will have to overcome.

If you agree, your condition may improve this month. To do this, you should not consider the problems you will face as fatalities but as challenges. Don't worry if you have doubts. There is nothing you can't overcome. Take your time and avoid getting caught up in the task at hand. Follow your gut and take things one step at a time.

Love

Commitment is a cause for worry until the 8th. Then you try to find good middle ground. Unfortunately, you probably have some problems. Instead of getting lost by making plans for a perfect world, be direct. Think about yourself instead of always thinking about other people.

It's not easy to be in your relationship. Thanks to compromises, things are getting better between you both. Even if you find an answer that works for everyone, ensure it doesn't hurt you.

Single Pisces, It's easy to woo people who want to settle down. On the other hand, it takes persistence to catch that special someone. You can choose between a perfect life and a lasting relationship this month. If you stay calm, what you want will come true.

Career

This month, you can change the path of your career. You might get a different job or work in a country outside of your country. If your career is changing, Pisces, there's a good reason. So stop putting yourself down or thinking you won't be able to do the job. If you need to, contact someone who will teach you everything. They will try to get you to take this opportunity when it comes up.

This shows that you're in charge of your career and are going at your speed. You want to make your dreams come true, and you want to make sure you do. You're ready for a challenge, and there will be a lot of good opportunities for you. Your drive and ambition will take you places, and you'll have great memories from your business trips.

Finance

On the money side, if you need to make a big purchase, ask other people what they think and then choose based on what you like. This could mean stability in terms of money and work. This month will be clear and give you confidence. It will help your finances because your gut will tell you where to put your money in business.

Don't get into fights about money, as this can greatly affect your financial situation.

Health

A month in which you would have to pay a lot of attention to your health to make up for the absence of any heavenly blessings during this month. During this month, you might see signs of wasting, which is when the body isn't able to use much of what it eats, even if it's healthy food. There's no need to worry because this could be fixed with the right medicine.

Your ability to reproduce may also be down, but again, this is just a bad effect of the stars that will only last for a while. This could be quickly remedied when you are much stronger.

A time during which you should be careful and take the proper steps to keep yourself from worrying and keep your mind at ease throughout this time

Travel

According to the stars, this month is not a good time to travel. Not only would it not be profitable, but it could even cost you extra money. On your trips, you could get hurt or have some other kind of physical trouble. This is especially true for those who like to take risks and try new things.

Even if nothing else went wrong, the trips taken this month would not produce the expected results. Even trips in the best direction toward the West would be the same. The same thing will happen on trips abroad. Because these trips are expensive, they can sometimes make your losses much worse.

Insight from the stars

You can expand your sphere of influence. Do not allow yourself to be swayed by ease if you want to achieve this little miracle. Opt to excel and surpass yourself instead. Weak immunity necessitates extreme caution when it comes to your health.

December 2023

Horoscope

The energies of Taurus and Capricorn always help you rise to the top. Venus, who will be in Scorpio from the 5th to the 29th, has replaced Mars in Scorpio as the planet of support. Despite your lack of willpower, your intuition has been bolstered. Your emotions will serve as your best guide. Your life takes a turn for the better, thanks to the support of your family and friends.

Mars will add to the problems that come from Sagittarius until December 31. If you really want to get what you want, you will have to fight against these energies. To do well at this little trick, be nice to people who have been with you for a long time and distance yourself from people who bring you down.

Love

The energies of Sagittarius can make you lose control of yourself. Venus in Scorpio steps in to help you get back on the right track. Even though it will be hard, try to ignore outside influences this month. Give people with their heads on their shoulders more of your time.

There are still issues in your relationship that could get you in trouble. To avoid this, you must have the wisdom to divide your life into sections. Put yourself and your partner in a safe space. You won't have to be concerned about anything after that.

Single Pisces, Because you live in different worlds, you meet different people. Think about what you really want before making a decision. This will keep you from getting involved in a relationship that could hurt you.

Career

Jupiter still favors this sector. As it retrogrades, you'll have more time to organize your affairs so that you don't have to worry about it more than necessary. However, relying on the advice of others should be avoided because it can lead to poor decisions. Fighting isn't in your blood, Pisces, but you'll do it if the situation calls for it. So, don't be afraid to say no to things that aren't right for you.

An uninspiring month for your professional advancement. Work may be enjoyable, but it is doubtful that promised rewards would materialize after many hours of diligent effort.

This month, contacts won't be very useful. Because of this, it would be best to rely mostly on your skills to get out of challenging situations. You wouldn't get what you expected from travel, but a trip to the North would be good for you. Overall, this is a month in which you must be cautious and rely on your efforts.

Finance

On the money side, if you want to make someone happy, you should do it before December 27th, because the Full Moon will make it hard for you to understand how you feel.

A good month for your finances, during which you could make a lot of money, but not without any problems. The success of your projects, no matter what they are, would be boosted by your friendships with smart, spiritually-minded people. In fact, this would give your whole work life a satisfying level of culture and refinement.

You'd be able to achieve most of your goals and make the most money from them. Still, you'll likely run into problems along the way. But success is sure to happen. A good time to not only get a lot done but also to feel a lot of satisfaction.

Health

A month in which your health is good, and you really don't have much to worry about. Your body would get the most out of what you eat, so not only would it be healthy, but it would also look healthy. This would make you very busy and full of energy.

In fact, those of you who like to test your fitness ability would be pleasantly surprised to find that, if anything, your physical skills are way above average during this time. This would make for a pretty full life, with more and better things to enjoy. The only thing that stands out, and there is one, is the chance of an accident or a severe injury, which should be taken care of. But this is a long shot.

Travel

Since the stars are in your favor, this is a month when you can expect to make a lot of money from your travels. There are signs that the way things are going will force you to travel a lot for work. If you did these things, you would be successful. The North would be the best direction to go.

These are more signs that any trip you take abroad in the month will also help you reach your goals. Those who have been thinking about taking such a trip should go now.

Insight from the stars

Your success will depend on how well you stay on the right path. This month, pay attention to people who share your values. Everything will be fine if you do this. Don't settle for less than what you can do because you can do great things. Always try to do your best. Even during the Mercury retrograde in 2023, you will do great things that will surprise you.

Printed in Great Britain
by Amazon

11774979R00246